Hatching Tier Two and Three Interventions in Your Elementary School Counseling Program

To every student who deserves a quality and effective intervention.

Hatching Tier Two and Three Interventions in Your Elementary School Counseling Program

Trish Hatch, **Ashley Kruger**, Nicole Pablo, and **Whitney Triplett**

Foreword by Carey Dimmitt

FOR INFORMATION:

Corwin

A SAGE Company

2455 Teller Road

Thousand Oaks, California 91320

(800) 233-9936

www.corwin.com

SAGE Publications Ltd.

1 Oliver's Yard

55 City Road

London EC1Y 1SP

United Kingdom

SAGE Publications India Pvt. Ltd.

B 1/I 1 Mohan Cooperative Industrial Area

Mathura Road, New Delhi 110 044

India

SAGE Publications Asia-Pacific Pte. Ltd.

18 Cross Street #10-10/11/12

China Square Central

Singapore 048423

Program Director: Jessica Allan

Content Development Editor: Lucas Schleicher

Senior Editorial Assistant: Mia Rodriguez

Production Editor: Tori Mirsadjadi

Copy Editor: Melinda Masson

Typesetter: C&M Digitals (P) Ltd.

Proofreaders: Dennis W. Webb and Susan Schon

Indexer: Maria Sosnowski

Cover Designer: Candice Harman

Marketing Manager: Deena Meyer

Printed in the United States of America

ISBN 978-1-5443-4528-4

This book is printed on acid-free paper.

SUSTAINABLE FORESTRY INITIATIVE

Certified Chain of Custody

Promoting Sustainable Forestry

www.sfiprogram.org

SFI-01268

SFI label applies to text stock

19 20 21 22 23 10 9 8 7 6 5 4 3 2 1

Contents

Visit the companion website at
http://www.hatchingresults.com/elementary-t2-t3-online-
appendix for an online appendix of additional resources.

Foreword

Trish Hatch is a force of nature. Her excitement and love for the school counseling profession are evident, whether you are engaging in professional development with her, attending a conference session she's leading, or just talking with her casually. She has been working for continuous improvement in our field for decades now, and her passion for supporting students' success and well-being is unparalleled.

In this book, Trish Hatch and her co-authors Ashley Kruger, Nicole Pablo, and Whitney Triplett take on the critical task of integrating school counseling practice with Multi-Tiered System of Supports (MTSS) practices. MTSS is a widely used data-based framework for assessing and providing services for all students in schools (Sugai & Horner, 2009). As increasing numbers of schools and districts adopt MTSS, school counseling is well-positioned to identify how to work within the structures of MTSS and develop school counseling program components that coordinate with the work being done by others in the building using this framework.

Schools are constantly evolving institutions, requiring ongoing systemic changes that respond to the research about educational best practices and about current student needs. Sometimes educational models emerge that seem to be fads, and other times there is widespread adoption of ways of working that completely shift the paradigm. MTSS has evolved over time in ways that demonstrate its utility, and it is clearly here to stay. Multiple scholars in the field are writing about school counseling and MTSS (Goodman-Scott, Betters-Bubon, & Donohue, 2016; Sink & Ockerman, 2016; Ziomek-Daigle, Goodman-Scott, Cavin, & Donohue, 2016, to name a few), providing a valuable range of perspectives and insights about how to do this work. It is critical that school counselors understand the ideas behind MTSS as well as the benefits of collaborating with other school professionals using these ways of working with students.

A strength of the approach taken in this book is its integration with the American School Counselor Association's Comprehensive Model for School Counseling Programs (ASCA National Model) (American School Counselor Association, 2012). Aligning the goals and structures of the ASCA National Model with MTSS ensures that the work done by school counselors is integrated into the schoolwide practices being adopted by all other school professionals in the building. The school counseling focus on ensuring that students' social-emotional and career development needs are met as well as their academic needs is critical for students, for schools, and for our society in general, and is often missing from other books on MTSS. This book articulates a vision for how to do all this, in clear and practical ways that are a hallmark of the work that Trish and her practitioner collaborators are known for. This book has Trish's signature passion and aspirations for effective school counseling programs, along with Ashley's, Nicole's and Whitney's insights and stories from their current school counseling practice—an effective model for learning new ways of working!

Carey Dimmitt, PhD
Director, Fredrickson Center for School Counseling
Outcome Research and Evaluation (CSCORE)
Co-founder and Co-chair, National Evidence-Based
School Counseling Conference (EBSCC)
Professor and Coordinator, School Counselor
Education Program
Furcolo Hall S116
University of Massachusetts, Amherst
Amherst, MA 01003
www.cscor.org
www.ebscc.org
cdimmitt@educ.umass.edu

SOURCES CITED

American School Counselor Association. (2012). *ASCA national model: A framework for school counseling programs* (3rd ed.). Alexandria, VA: Author.

Goodman-Scott, E., Betters-Bubon, J., & Donohue, M. (2016). Aligning comprehensive school counseling programs and positive behavioral interventions and supports to maximize school counselors' efforts. *Professional School Counseling, 19*(1), 57–67.

Sink, C. A., & Ockerman, M. S. (2016). School counselors and a multi-tiered system of supports: Cultivating systemic change and equitable outcomes. *The Professional Counselor, 6*(3).

Sugai, G., & Horner, R. H. (2009). Responsiveness-to-intervention and school-wide positive behavior supports: Integration of multi-tiered system approaches. *Exceptionality, 17*(4), 223–237.

Ziomek-Daigle, J., Goodman-Scott, E., Cavin, J., & Donohue, P. (2016). Integrating a multi-tiered system of supports with comprehensive school counseling programs. *The Professional Counselor, 6*(3), 220–232.

Acknowledgments

As the Multi-Tiered System of Supports (MTSS) movement has garnered momentum nationally, school counselors are increasingly seeking ways to align this new and important tiered systems approach with the ASCA National Model. In 2018, Hatch, Duarte, and De Gregorio released *Hatching Results for Elementary School Counselors: Implementing Core Curriculum and Other Tier 1 Activities.* Now we are so excited to make available *Hatching Tier 2 and 3 Interventions in Your Elementary School Counseling Program* to equip school counselors with the tools and resources needed to thoughtfully implement Tier 2 and 3 interventions at the elementary level.

As current or former elementary school counselors who teach current and future school counselors, we recognize the tremendous need to fill the attitude, skills, and knowledge gaps in designing, implementing, evaluating, and improving school counseling program interventions at the Tier 2 and 3 levels. Based on the varied experiences of the co-authors, this book seeks to close those gaps so that school counselors are better resourced to remove barriers to learning. As we provide professional development to K–8 school counselors and administrators nationwide, we hope the guidebook design of this text with its samples and examples will assist educators to "think through" the data-based problem-solving and decision-making process for supplemental and intensified supports.

First, we want to acknowledge the entire Hatching Results training team! Your implementation and feedback of the processes in this text contributed to its improvement. We are very grateful to our colleagues Dr. Brett Zyromski, Dr. Carey Dimmitt, and Dr. Carolyn Stone for taking the time to provide editorial insights and professional wisdom. Thank you to Danielle Duarte and Whitney Triplett for your expertise and suggestions. Your feedback and consult supported us, challenged us, and helped us to improve this text.

We are grateful for the research assistance from Zoe Leshner and Araminta Koppenheffer. A very special thank you to our staff editor Morgan Hurley, who dedicated countless hours assisting with attention to the details of revising and replacing text and forms over and over again. We couldn't have done it without you!

We are also grateful to the students from San Diego State University (SDSU) who participated in the group counseling class taught by Ashley and Nicole over the last few years and who test-drove ideas and content in this text. We would like to acknowledge the many leaders and scholars who have written about the school counselor's role in MTSS. We thank you for paving the way in the MTSS/RTI/PBIS work. We look forward to your thoughtful consideration of our ideas presented here, to collegial conversations, and to the continuous improvement process that we hope will guide our future conversations. Finally, thank you also to Corwin (Jessica Allan, Lucas Schleicher, Mia Rodriguez, Melinda Masson, and Tori Mirsadjadi) for your support, assistance, incredible patience with last-minute changes and updates, and belief in the importance and value of school counseling texts.

FROM TRISH:

As a new school counselor in 1987, I had no text, no curriculum, and no one to turn to for thoughts on how to design or implement small groups or, for that matter, any activities at my school. My group counseling class had been focused on talk therapy for adults, and therefore providing interventions for social skills, learning strategies, or academic behaviors was uncharted territory. When I attended my first American School Counselor Association (ASCA) conference, I remember spending hundreds of dollars on books to read and curriculum to try out—but none of the curriculum was vetted or aligned with evidence-based practices. And I didn't know if the interventions made a difference unless I hand-counted report card data and discipline referrals. Through my many years since (over 30 now), I am so grateful to have collaborated with fabulous researchers, grant writers, program evaluators, administrators, and practitioners trying to find a way to create a more robust system for determining when and how students receive guaranteed interventions. The systemic nature of thinking through the work has been the most important contribution to this text. Processing the who, what, when, why, how, and "so what" of the work is vital to eliminating random acts of Tier 2 and 3 interventions. No longer can school counselors run emergency room school counseling programs. There is simply not enough time and there are too many students to expect we can see them all. There must be a systems approach to determine which students qualify for interventions and which students may need to be supported through other mechanisms.

As school counseling moves toward full alignment and integration with MTSS statewide in California, we are so very fortunate to collaborate with Jami Parsons and Mayu Iwatani, our partners at the Orange County Department of Education, and with colleagues at the California Department of Education to ensure all school counselors in California are provided the opportunity to be trained in the Multi-Tiered, Multi-Domain System of Supports (MTMDSS) and its alignment with the ASCA National Model. Thanks to the entire Hatching Results team for supporting this project. To my co-authors, Ashley, Nicole, and Whitney: thank you for hanging in there. People don't know how hard a book is to write until they try it themselves. Thank you all for the thousands of hours collaborating on the design and redesign again and again until we got our flow in a way we could "teach" it. Special thanks to Whitney Triplett for joining our team in aligning the 4th edition of the ASCA National Model to the text, and for your eagle-eyed attention to detail!

To the many, many elementary counselors whom I collaborated with on the elementary and secondary school counseling grants, thank you for test-driving these ideas, for trusting the process, for your complete commitment to excellence, for taking the "use of data" concepts and applying them within your respective districts, for sharing your results, and for your dedication to making a difference in the lives of the students you serve.

Finally, to my dear, dear family who continue to support my total addiction to school counseling, thank you for loving me.

FROM ASHLEY:

I am so incredibly honored to have been given the opportunity to co-author this book. Never in my wildest dreams did I think I would be a published author! I would like to begin by thanking my two graduate school professors, Dr. Trish Hatch and Dr. Beverly Booker, for inspiring me to be a change agent, an advocate, and a leader in the field of school counseling. This book was truly a work of passion and love. I am so grateful that I get to wake up each day knowing I have the chance to positively impact a child.

Writing this text was much more difficult than I could have ever imagined, but it has also allowed me to grow immensely both personally and professionally. There are so many individuals in my life who have helped shape who I am today, and I am forever grateful to each of you. First and foremost, thank you to my parents, Michelle and David Kruger, and my sister, Jennifer Kruger, for always being my biggest cheerleaders. Sister, I love you so much and am amazed at how our friendship has blossomed over the years, and I look forward to the incredible memories I know we will continue to make together. Mom and Dad, I would not be the person I am today without your unwavering love, support, and encouragement. I am so grateful for all you have taught me in life and attribute my passion for helping others to you both. Thank you to my best friend and husband, Phil Green, for your patience and understanding throughout this whole process. You make me want to continually be a better person and always challenge me to be "comfortable in the uncomfortable." Thank you to the Murrieta Valley Unified elementary school counseling team and to all of the staff, parents, and students who put your trust in me and support my role as a school counselor. A special shout-out to three amazing mentors and friends, Dr. Tonika Green, my CARES and TLC partner; Dean Lesicko, my former supervisor; and Pam Roden, my current principal. To my dear friends (you know who you are), thank you for always understanding when I had to say "I would love to, but I have to write"; your words of encouragement helped me believe in myself even when I felt like giving up. To my co-authors, Trish, Nicole, and Whitney: this has been quite a journey, and I am so glad we were in this together. Trish, you are a remarkable human being and have truly created a legacy. I am humbled and honored to have worked beside you in developing this book. Nicole, to my "write or die Tier 2/3 partner," we made it, and I could not have done this without you! The many hours we spent writing, rewriting, laughing, almost crying, and eating a ridiculous number of breakfast burritos have all been worth it! Nicash Krublo is one of a kind, and I hope that she can inspire elementary and middle school counselors around the nation! Whitney, you always amaze me with your brilliance and attention to detail. Thank you for all of your support in helping us take the book to the next level! And lastly, to my nephew, Jack, and my niece, Lily, I love you both more than I ever thought possible. I am so excited to see you both grow and know you will both do wonderful things in your life.

FROM NICOLE:

I would like to thank and dedicate this work of heart and the hopeful educational impact it makes to anyone who has supported me along my journey. Thank you to those who inspired, challenged, believed in, invested in, collaborated with, and jumped on board with my "crazy" counseling ideas. Without your support, my knowledge, growth, and opportunities to have the career that I love doing every day would never have been possible. Thank you to my family—most especially, May and Bob Pablo, who taught me patience (by modeling it with me during my youthful Tier 2 days), hard work, and to stand up for what I believe in, which ignited my passion for first-generation low-income student equity and access in education. Thank you to Andrzej Roman for being my rock during this process, for pushing me and keeping me sane. Thank you to my mentors and dear friends Danielle Duarte and Marisol Dyste. Thank you to my CBFF Vanessa Ho, for inspiring me in grad school and continuing to be my sound board, self-care, and balance. Thank you to my extended Tropa family for always being my cheerleaders and understanding that when I was MIA, it was to support kids. Thank you to all my admin, teachers, and colleagues I was blessed to work with and learn from starting from my Libby Elementary roots in Oceanside Unified with the counseling dream team—Monica Loyce, Kathie Ketcham, and Lauren Aponte—from which much of the ground work came from, to my Snap Queen support staff Ariana Vargas, Gabby Ramos, and Eric Solorzano at Mission Middle in Escondido Unified, to my new families in Poway Unified. Thank you to all my students and families who trusted me. Thank you to my nieces and nephews who motivate me to stay relentless for positive systems change and shaking up the status quo. Biggest grateful heart to my team—Trish, Ashley, and Whitney—for their patience, support, and commitment. I appreciate all the memories, hard work, morning burritos, and guidance in birthing this baby. Thank you, Trish, for always seeing the leader in me and creating opportunities of growth; you helped me fly on my own. Thank you both for helping me make this childhood dream come true.

FROM WHITNEY:

It was truly an honor to edit and write alongside this amazing team of authors! Trish—your visionary passion for excellence in the field of school counseling consistently births ideas for applying the work in new and efficient ways. I always learn so much from you, I feel like I'm in the "EdD Program of Trish Hatch," LOL! Ashley and Nicole—you really are experts when it comes to elementary school counseling, especially with regard to Tiers 2 and 3. I'm always in awe of your expertise. Your ingenuity in creating Nicash Krublo to assist the reader in following the process through from beginning to end was brilliant and I appreciate your vulnerability in sharing your successes and "areas of thoughtfulness" throughout the book. To all of the authors: thank you for your many hours of thoughtfulness, brainstorming, planning, and writing, and for welcoming me as a co-author later in the process. I had a blast and learned a great deal reading and editing your pages and, later, aligning your work to the 4th Edition of the ASCA National Model. The groundwork you've laid for a secondary version of this book is invaluable, and I'm so very grateful.

Thank you also to the elementary school counselors of Chicago Public Schools, whose trust, patience, honesty, persistence, and faith provided the conditions for me to learn what it really means to be an elementary school counselor. Finally, thank you to my wonderful family for the immense support and encouragement throughout this process. Love you all. :)

About the Authors

Trish Hatch, PhD, retired in August of 2019 as a Professor at San Diego State University (SDSU), where she was Director of the School Counseling Program from 2004 until 2015 and the Founder and Executive Director of the Center for Excellence in School Counseling and Leadership (CESCaL). She is the best-selling author of *The Use of Data in School Counseling: Hatching Results for Students, Programs, and the Profession* (2014) and co-author of *Evidence-Based School Counseling: Making a Difference With Data-Driven Practices* (Dimmitt, Carey, & Hatch, 2007) and the *ASCA National Model: A Framework for School Counseling Programs* (ASCA, 2003, 2005). Her latest books include *Hatching Results for Elementary School Counseling: Implementing Core Curriculum and Other Tier One Activities* (Hatch, Duarte, & De Gregorio, 2018) and *Hatching Results for Secondary School Counseling: Implementing Core Curriculum, Individual Student Planning, and Other Tier One Activities* (Hatch, Triplett, Duarte, & Gomez, 2019).

Dr. Hatch is President and CEO of Hatching Results, LLC, where she has gathered a diverse team of expert school counselors, school counselor educators, and leaders to provide training and consultation across the nation on evidence-based practices and the use of data to increase outcomes for students.

As a legislative advocate and national leader, Dr. Hatch served as a national expert consultant on school counseling for the Obama administration at the White House and U.S. Department of Education. A former school counselor, site and central office administrator, state association president, and ASCA Vice President, Dr. Hatch has received multiple national awards, including the American School Counselor Association (ASCA) Administrator of the Year award, and its highest honor, the Mary Gehrke Lifetime Achievement award. She was also inducted into the H.B. McDaniel Hall of Fame at Stanford University for lifetime achievement in school counseling. Most recently, she received the Excellence in Education Award for "improving the field of education and service to students" from the National Association for College Admission Counseling (NACAC) and the inaugural California Association of School Counselors (CASC) School Counselor Educator of the Year (2016) award.

Ashley Kruger is currently an elementary school counselor with extensive experience in designing, implementing, and evaluating comprehensive programs that demonstrate improvement in students' academic and behavioral outcomes. Ashley has worked under two federally funded Elementary and Secondary School Counseling (ESSC) grants and has used data as a means of creating sustainability for the school counseling programs. In April 2016, Ashley and her elementary counseling team won the H.B. McDaniel award, which recognized their program for providing leadership and excellence in the field of school counseling. As a leader in the school counseling field, Ashley has trained school counselors nationwide about best practices in creating programs aligned with the American School Counselor Association (ASCA). She frequently presents at national and state conferences about how to use data to drive Tier 2 and Tier 3 interventions. She is also the co-developer and facilitator of the Hatching Results online courses. Ashley is currently Executive Vice President for the California Association of School Counselors (CASC) and has served as an adjunct faculty member at San Diego State University (SDSU) in the school counseling graduate program since 2014. Ashley is passionate about using data to design and improve comprehensive school counseling programs as a means of effectively serving students.

Nicole Pablo is currently a school counselor at two middle schools. Due to her expertise in utilizing data to create and evaluate systemic and site interventions, she was hired specifically to build the foundation for her district's new middle school Response to Intervention (RTI) counselor position. Nicole has trained diverse schools at all grade levels across the nation on implementing a comprehensive ASCA National Model. As a school counseling leader, she has received the Escondido Elementary Educators Association's Educator of the Year Award (2017). Collaboratively, Nicole has partnered with San Diego State University as a practicum site supervisor since 2011 and has supervised SDSU practicum site supervisors and students. As an adjunct lecturer, she has taught courses such as Practicum and Evaluations, and continues to teach Group Counseling. Nicole was formerly an elementary school counselor with experience in facilitating the Elementary and Secondary School Counseling (ESSC) federally funded grant to create a comprehensive, data-driven school counseling program where none previously existed. Her outcomes on the grant led to sustainability after federal funding ended. She presents her Tier 2 outcomes locally for her district and nationally at conferences such as the ASCA Annual Conference, National School Counseling Leadership Conference, and California Association of School Counselors (CASC) Conference.

Whitney Triplett, the Director of Professional Development for Hatching Results and co-author of *Hatching Results for Secondary School Counseling: Implementing Core Curriculum, Individual Student Planning, and Other Tier One Activities* (Hatch, Triplett, Duarte, & Gomez, 2019), trains school counselors and administrators across the nation. Previously at Chicago Public Schools, Whitney supported the district's 850+ school counselors and college and career coaches while serving on the board for the Illinois School Counselor Association and instructing school counseling students at Loyola University Chicago. It was through these roles that she was recognized in 2018 as the School Counseling Advocate of the Year for the state of Illinois. Whitney received RAMP recognition in 2011, and is a former Lead RAMP Reviewer for the American School Counselor Association. As a school counselor, Whitney received a Counselor Leadership Award and an Oppenheimer Recognition Award for her collaborative work in raising the Freshmen-on-Track rate at her school. A former Education Pioneers Visiting Fellow, Whitney is passionate about school reform, closing achievement gaps, and school counseling to promote equity, access, and the success of all students!

Introduction

by Trish Hatch

When serving as an elementary school counselor at both Ramona and Butterfield Elementary Schools, I recall the challenge of servicing 1,300 students in two high-needs schools (one on a traditional schedule and the other year-round). I needed to find a way to work at only one school, as the ratio was not sustainable. I decided to "prove" I was making a difference by collecting discipline data and reporting improvements for students receiving interventions. We didn't have Student Information Systems (SIS) at that time, and everything needed to be counted by hand. I recall asking teachers if I could make a copy of their report cards in order to avoid researching through cumulative folders. The impact of these interventions led to a full-time position at one school, and then an invitation to serve at the district level. I was committed to finding funds to support hiring more school counselors. I worked in a district that supported hiring more elementary counselors, but funding was lacking. So, I wrote my first Federal Elementary School Counseling Demonstration Act Grant. Since that time, I've written over $16 million in federal grants and implemented the programs in dozens of districts. Each of the grants included a strong focus on using data to drive Tier 2 interventions.

Co-authors Ashley and Nicole were my graduate students at San Diego State University (SDSU) and were hired immediately upon graduation as elementary school counselors implementing the federal grants supporting data-driven school counseling programs. As the evaluator for these grants, I had the pleasure of working closely with them as they implemented all components of what has now become this text focusing on Tier 2 and 3 systems of intervention. Each has demonstrated leadership and high impact at multiple schools she has worked in, supporting sustainability and future funding for elementary counselors.

The purpose of *Hatching Tier 2 and 3 Interventions in Your Elementary School Counseling Program* is to provide elementary school counselors, administrators, district-level leaders, and graduate students with a hands-on guide to creating and implementing a high-quality Tier 2 and 3 school counseling system of support. The content within *Hatching Tier 2 and 3 Interventions in Your Elementary School Counseling Program* provides elementary school counselors with a step-by-step tool to create and implement a high-quality school counseling system of support.

Building on the content from *The Use of Data in School Counseling: Hatching Results for Students, Programs, and the Profession* (Hatch, 2013) and aligning with the content in *Hatching Results for Elementary School Counseling: Implementing Core Curriculum and Other Tier One Activities* (Hatch, Duarte, & De Gregorio, 2018) and *Hatching Results for Secondary School Counseling: Implementing Core Curriculum, Individual Learning Planning, and Other Tier One Activities* (Hatch, Triplett, Duarte, & Gomez, 2019), this new text focuses on Tier 2 and Tier 3 activities at the elementary level within a Multi-Tiered, Multi-Domain System of Supports (MTMDSS).

The Tier 2 system of support focuses on implementing targeted, data-driven interventions (small group counseling/instruction, referral to interventions on campus, etc.) and is designed for *students* who are identified by pre-scheduled and pre-determined data screening elements. These include, for example, attendance, behavior, work skills and study habits (report card marks), and/or equity and access issues. Tier 2 activities include *short-term* progress monitoring and collaboration among teachers, parents/guardians, and the school counselor until improvement and/or referral to appropriate services can be found and implemented. Tier 2 activities are designed for students who (1) exhibit barriers to learning; (2) are struggling to achieve academic success; and/or (3) are identified as deserving of instruction and/or supports in addition to Tier 1 curriculum activities (foster youth, dual language learners, etc.).

Tier 3 includes individualized student interventions (e.g., 1:1 crisis counseling) that are designed for students to address emergency and crisis response events. These include short-term, solution-focused counseling to address life-changing events (divorce, death, severe academic needs, etc.) provided on a limited basis and, if unresolved, lead to referrals to outside services. This includes *short-term* consultation and collaboration among teachers, parents/guardians, and the school counselor until the crisis is resolved and/or referral to appropriate responsive services can be identified and implemented.

School counseling graduate students can use this text as they learn about developing their elementary school counseling program, with a particular benefit to students interning at the elementary school level. Pre-service training in school counseling requires that graduate students learn how to use data to identify students in need of interventions. Learning to design group intervention lesson plans is a critical element in creating effective Tier 2 support systems, yet school counselors often receive minimal, if any, education in this area in their pre-service program or professional development.

Another area of focus in this text is ensuring elementary school counselors provide effective small group interventions using progress monitoring, collaboration, and communication with teachers and other educators. School counselors are expected to create small group lesson plans, teach curriculum, deliver engaging content, manage behaviors, and provide assessments. By providing elementary school counselors with strong skills to identify which students will benefit from the appropriate interventions, this text will help accomplish better outcomes for school counselors and students.

There are very few textbooks on the market for elementary school counselors, and there is a lack of vetted, evidence-based materials for implementing effective Tier 2 and Tier 3 interventions. While some texts do address small group counseling, many are not specific to schools and do not include systemic, data-driven supports. In addition, many of these texts have a strong focus on psycho-therapeutic techniques, which is out of the scope of a school counselor.

The need for materials is so great; thousands of elementary school counselors have started Facebook groups to share information. Unfortunately, many of the materials shared in social media spaces are not vetted through an evidence-based approach. As educators, elementary school counselors are held to similar standards and expectations as teachers, in terms of setting measurable goals, objectives, and outcomes when providing structured interventions. In addition, the focus on using data to measure the impact of education includes evaluating the outcomes of a comprehensive school counseling program.

Within implementation of MTMDSS, school counselors, like teachers, provide more intensive support for elementary school students who are still struggling after the delivery of Tier 1 curriculum in the three areas (academic, social/emotional, and college/career). To support this work, the *Hatching Tier 2 and 3 Interventions in Your Elementary School Counseling Program* text provides clear direction for today's elementary school counselor in how to design, implement, evaluate, and improve academic, college/career, and social/emotional or behavioral interventions.

This text includes much-needed content on how to respond to crisis situations, clarifying and differentiating the school counselor's role from that of other student service providers (such as school psychologists and social workers). It includes best practices—from professional trainers and consultants, as well as practicing school counselors throughout the United States—which have proven to be effective through measuring the impact on students' knowledge, attitudes, skills, and behaviors.

When school counselors are competent in using data, they can more accurately measure the impact of their services. As educators, school counselors are held to similar standards and expectations as teachers in terms of setting measurable goals, objectives, and outcomes when providing instruction in the classroom. This text emphasizes using data to measure the impact of school counseling services and evaluate the students' outcomes aligned with the school counseling program.

The federal funding regulations in the Every Student Succeeds Act (ESSA) currently indicate that Title IV funds can be spent on hiring and supporting elementary school counselors. As federal accountability measures shift, many states are supporting local control of funding decisions. In California, for instance, there has been a 30% improvement in student-to-counselor ratios over five years with the release of local control funding formulas (from 1,016:1 in 2010–2011 to 630:1 in 2018–2019). Now, more than ever, school counselors must be held accountable to show how their programs and services positively impact academic achievement, school climate, attendance, parent and student engagement, and so on. This text provides examples of how to measure results in all areas within Tiers 2 and 3. Readers can assess their growth and progress relative to these outcomes by utilizing the multiple tools presented throughout the text, including applied activities, check-for-understanding tools, and reader self-assessments. Finally, readers will learn to use data for program improvement as they share results and recommendations with faculty and other stakeholders.

Hatching Tier 2 and 3 Interventions in Your Elementary School Counseling Program includes a variety of pedagogical formats, including vignettes from practicing school counselors, templates and samples for developing intervention action plans, PowerPoint slides, pre- and post-assessments, and Flashlight Results, along with a variety of graphs and other ways to present school counseling program data.

Although elementary school counselors are the primary, targeted audience for the text, administrators and central office school counseling coordinators will benefit from this book to help them understand the role of elementary school counselors within Tiers 2 and 3, while they support and evaluate school counselors' implementation of these programs and interventions.

The 4th Edition of the ASCA National Model was released just *after* the final draft of this book was submitted to our publisher. In light of this, the writing team decided to postpone the publication date to allow the authors time to align the book's content (where possible) with the 4th edition. Readers may notice that some of the 4th edition changes are reflected, while others are not. The authors felt it was important to balance incorporation of 4th edition updates (where most appropriate and aligned with the text) with maintaining the terminology and content of the 3rd edition for consistency with previous textbooks in our series.

We are grateful to co-author Whitney for joining our team and assisting in this process.

Additional resources are available in the online appendix.

The text will prepare readers in the following areas:

ATTITUDES

- *Believe* all students deserve to receive data-driven school counseling interventions.
- *Believe* in the importance of elementary school counselors taking an active role in designing and implementing Tier 2 and 3 interventions.
- *Believe* in the importance of developing consistent, schoolwide data elements that trigger appropriate interventions.
- *Feel* confident and competent as they deliver school counseling interventions, teach small group lessons, and support students when referring them to outside interventions.
- *Believe* elementary school counselors must assess the impact of their Tier 2 interventions.

KNOWLEDGE

- *Articulate* the elementary school counselor's role in Multi-Tiered, Multi-Domain System of Supports (MTMDSS).
- *Describe* the components of Tier 2 and 3 interventions.
- *Describe* ways to garner staff input on Tier 2 and 3 interventions.
- *Differentiate* between the different types and uses of data, as they pertain to Tier 2 interventions.
- *Compare and contrast* a wide range of small group engagement and management strategies.
- *Explain* their appropriate role in student interventions, as compared to other student service providers.

SKILLS

- *Locate, compare,* and *select* an appropriate small group curriculum.
- *Create* a menu of services for Tier 2 and 3 interventions.
- *Create* a Tier 2 Action Plan for Small Groups.
- *Write* high-quality, small group lesson plans with measurable objectives.
- *Write* high-quality assessments and surveys to determine which small group interventions are most appropriate.
- *Create* pre-/post-tests for assessing students' attitudes, knowledge, and skills.
- *Calendar* intentional interventions.
- *Share* results from the school counseling interventions.

1

Multi-Tiered, Multi-Domain System of Supports

A Framework for Tier 2

This text is designed to guide elementary (K–8) school counselors in developing, implementing, and evaluating Tier 2 and Tier 3 interventions. As we begin, it will be helpful to provide an overall contextual framework regarding the Multi-Tiered System of Supports (MTSS) and introduce the new Multi-Tiered, *Multi-Domain* System of Supports (MTMDSS), which aligns with the role of the school counselor at any grade level and the American School Counselor Association (ASCA) National Model (ASCA, 2012).

AN INTRODUCTION TO MTSS IN EDUCATION

The Multi-Tiered System of Supports (MTSS) is a comprehensive framework that addresses the academic and behavioral needs of all students within the educational system (Cowan, Vaillancourt, Rossen, & Pollitt, 2013; Hawken, Vincent, & Schumann, 2008). Research shows that schools benefit from multiple, evidence-based interventions of varying intensity to meet the range of behavioral, social/emotional, and academic needs of all students (Anderson & Borgmeier, 2010). MTSS is an outgrowth of RTI and encompasses PBIS.

RTI and PBIS

Response to Intervention (RTI) is a framework for a multi-tiered approach to supporting students' learning needs through early identification and intervention. It calls for quality classroom instruction for all students (Tier 1), targeted interventions for some students (Tier 2), and intensive interventions for those students who require additional support (Tier 3) (Positive Behavioral Interventions & Supports, 2019; RTI Action Network, n.d.). Although it emerged after the No Child Left Behind Act (2002) to promote equity in special education referrals and to reduce unnecessary referrals for special education (Fuchs & Fuchs, 2006; Gersten & Dimino, 2006), it quickly became apparent that RTI was an efficient and effective mechanism for ensuring that all students receive supports according to their tiered level of need. Originally designed to support the academic instruction of students, it later expanded to include behavioral instruction and supports for students as well (Stormont, Reinke, & Herman, 2010). Like RTI, MTSS facilitates effective universal implementation, which focuses on core academic and differentiated interventions to support the academic success of all students.

The purpose of PBIS is to improve social, emotional, and academic outcomes for students by implementing effective, equitable, and efficient systems of support in schools (www.pbis.org). PBIS is designed to reinforce appropriate behavior and prevent inappropriate behavior by teaching core principles and providing systematically applied interventions based on identified need. PBIS promotes systems change to ensure consistency, schoolwide activities, and core curriculum instruction for students on behavior expectations. Like PBIS, MTSS is a problem-solving model that employs a continuum of positive, proactive, multi-tiered behavioral interventions (Kennelly & Monrad, 2007). See Figure 1.1 for illustrations of the RTI and PBIS models.

Combining RTI and PBIS, MTSS is a tiered systems approach of increasingly intensive interventions. Within the MTSS framework utilized in general education programs (see Figure 1.2), MTSS Tier 1 is the foundation for both academic and behavioral systems of support. Tier 1 contains universal support and core instruction that *all* students receive from their classroom teacher. For example, all students receive multiplication tables in the third grade. Similarly, all students participate in universal instruction on appropriate playground behavior delivered throughout the school. Preventative in nature, Tier 1 programs and activities are implemented with the entire student population. Typically, general education teachers proactively differentiate (modify or adapt) their instructional practices to support students' specialized needs, providing a more challenging or more supportive learning environment as necessary.

Tier 2 within MTSS is composed of supplemental interventions, in addition to Tier 1 core instruction, for students identified (through the use of data identifiers or indicators) as needing additional supports, such as small group practices and skill building. Teachers and others collaborate to determine the data-driven identifiers that will serve as the mechanism for the students to receive a Tier 2–level intervention (e.g., scoring less than proficient on a benchmark assessment). Tier 3 addresses students with the highest level of need, providing supports of a greater intensity, specifically tailored to meet the needs of individual students (Illinois State Board of Education, 2010).

Figure 1.1   Traditional Tiered Educational Models: RTI and PBIS

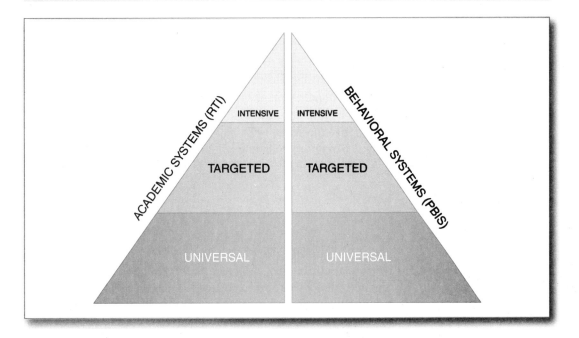

Figure 1.2   Traditional Tiered Educational Models: MTSS

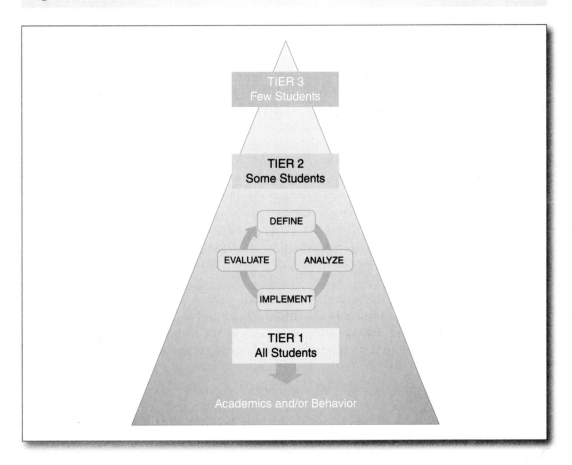

Students who are not responsive to the Tier 1 supports may receive a Tier 2 intervention. These students continue to receive the Tier 1 intervention, but more structure and assistance is provided to assist them in meeting schoolwide expectations. Students receiving Tier 2 supports typically exhibit behavior that is not dangerous to themselves or others, but is disruptive to their learning or the learning of their peers. Tier 2 interventions are implemented similarly across groups of students who exhibit similar behavior problems and are therefore likely to benefit from the same type of intervention. For example, students who exhibit deficits in social competence (e.g., conflict resolution skills) might participate in a skills group, in which all students in the group receive the same level and intensity of instruction, as well as similar feedback on their behavior (Anderson & Borgmeier, 2010).

Introduction to MTSS and School Counseling

In recent years, the field of school counseling has aligned its work with RTI, PBIS, and most recently MTSS. As scholars have noted, school counselors are integral to the RTI process within a school building, participating and collaborating with the RTI team to implement appropriate supports for students at all tiers (Goodman-Scott, Doyle, & Brott, 2014; Ockerman, Mason, & Feiker-Hollenbeck, 2012; Ryan, Kaffenberger, & Carroll, 2011; Ziomek-Daigle, Goodman-Scott, Cavin, & Donohue, 2016). As active members, of the RTI teams, counselors provide interventions through the use of data, progress, monitoring and delivery of services and interventions (Ockerman et al., 2012; Ziomek-Daigle et al., 2016).

Goodman-Scott, Betters-Bubon, and Donohue (2019) aligned the three-tiered model approach to prevention and intervention activities within the PBIS model with school counseling, recommending school counseling activities be organized by listing a variety of delivery components within the counseling program with the three-tiered model approach of PBIS—for example, core curriculum and individual student planning as part of the 80% Tier 1 portion of PBIS ensuring counselors are providing both direct and indirect services (Goodman-Scott et al., 2014; Shepard, Shahidullah, & Carlson, 2013).

Similar to the PBIS approach, school counselors are encouraged to spend 80% of their time with students in Tier 1 providing core curriculum and individual student planning. In Tier 2 (approximately 15%), responsive services are aligned, which includes small group counseling, consultation, and collaboration. In Tier 3, which is reserved for 5% of the population, the authors identify referrals to other providers, consultation, and collaboration. School counselors are unique in the process, serving as leaders, advocates, and change agents collaborating in the school on data-driven frameworks, decision-making models, program evaluation, and progress monitoring.

MTSS and School Counseling

As RTI and PBIS frameworks have combined to comprise the new innovation of MTSS, counselor educators in the school counseling field have collaborated to align comprehensive school counseling program models to MTSS (Sink, 2016). Calling on counselors to be leaders, implementers, facilitators, and supporters of MTSS, in this work, Ziomek-Daigle et al. (2016) describe the overlap between the two frameworks (RTI and PBIS), calling attention to the specific overlaps of data, evidence-based practices, collaboration, advocacy, cultural responsiveness, and systemic change. Most recently, Goodman-Scott et al. (2019) have released a new and comprehensive text titled *A School Counselor's Guide to Multi-Tiered Systems of Support*, in which they provide school counselors with extensive information and practical resources. Written by national experts in the field and providing practical resources for strengthening a comprehensive school counseling program (CSCP) through the alignment with MTSS across three tiers of support, and with a strong research and theoretical base, this text is designed to improve CSCPs, particularly through MTSS alignment.

CONNECTING MTSS TO SCHOOL COUNSELING DOMAINS: MTMDSS

While much has been written discussing the school counselor's role within the MTSS framework, this text describes the new model being proposed, which focuses on a more inclusive framework for *applying* the concept of MTSS to the school counselor's "deliver" component for *all three domains* within the ASCA National Model (2019a). While MTSS is focused on two areas (academic and behavioral), school counselors focus on *three* domains: (1) academic, (2) college/career, and (3) social/emotional development. To align with the work of the school counselor, the Multi-Tiered, *Multi-Domain* System of Supports (MTMDSS) (see Figure 1.3) was designed to align with MTSS as a decision-making framework that utilizes evidence-based practices in core instruction and assessments to address the universal and targeted data-driven intervention needs of *all* students in *all* school counseling domains. (We also include college in the career domain.) Note that for purposes of this text, from this point forward, we refer to the three school counseling domains of academic, college/career, and social/emotional development.

School counseling programs are an integral part of the total educational program for student success. The entire school community is invested in student academic achievement, college and career readiness, and social/emotional well-being. Schoolwide proactive, preventative, and data-driven intervention services and activities belong to the entire school. Therefore, it is recommended that schools *add the third domain* (college and career readiness) to their MTSS program and create a comprehensive, schoolwide *Multi-Tiered, Multi-Domain System of Supports (MTMDSS)*.

MULTI-TIERED, MULTI-DOMAIN SYSTEM OF SUPPORTS (MTMDSS)

The MTMDSS is a framework (see Figure 1.3) designed specifically for school counseling programs to organize a continuum of core activities, instruction, and interventions to meet students' needs with the goals of (1) ensuring that all students receive developmentally appropriate core instruction in all three domains; (2) increasing the academic, college/career, and social/emotional competencies of all students; (3) ensuring guaranteed interventions for students demonstrating a data-driven need; and (4) maximizing student achievement. The MTMDSS model organizes school intervention services into three levels, or tiers.

Figure 1.3   Multi-Tiered, Multi-Domain System of Supports (MTMDSS)

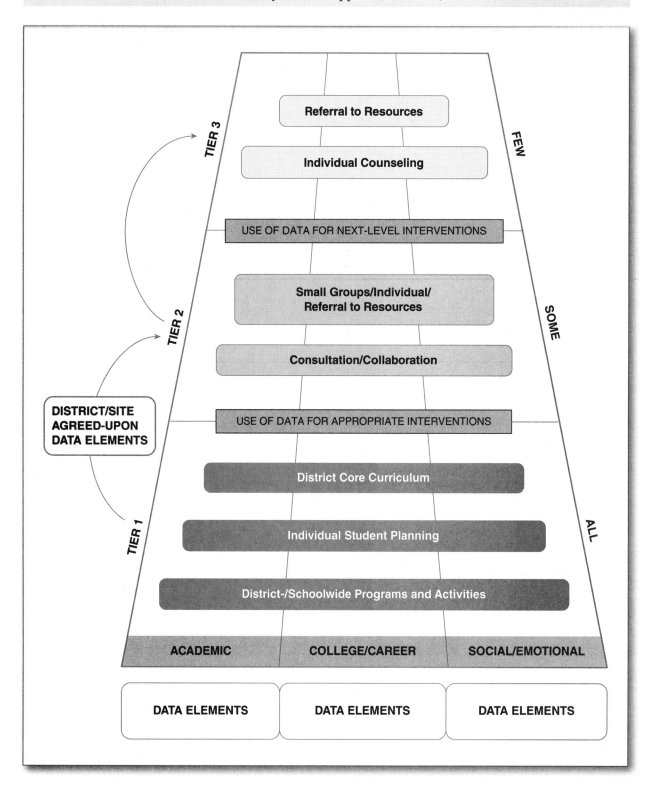

Tier 1: Core Program (Universal Supports) (100%)—For *All* Students

The core program comprises the delivery of services that *all students* receive (curriculum, individual student planning, and schoolwide events). A standards- and competency-based (ASCA Mindsets & Behaviors) school counseling *core curriculum* (formerly called "guidance curriculum" and now called "instruction" in the 4th edition) is developmental in nature, preventative and proactive in design, and comprehensive in scope. *Individual student planning* (aligned with Appraisal and Advisement in the 4th edition), includes 4- and 6-year college/career planning and career readiness (generally for secondary schools). *Schoolwide activities* for all students, such as national awareness weeks and celebrations (e.g., Red Ribbon Week, College Signing Day, FAFSA Challenge, The Great Kindness Challenge), conflict resolution/restorative practice programs, and parent education programs, are provided to all students and/or parents, align with classroom lesson content and standards, and support the core program.

Tier 2: Targeted Interventions (20%)—For *Some* Students

Similar to what general education teachers do when designing Tier 2 interventions, targeted data-driven interventions (small group counseling/instruction, referral to interventions on campus, etc.) are designed for students who are identified by pre-scheduled and pre-determined data-screening elements (Hatch, 2017). At the elementary level, these include, for example, attendance rates, behavior infractions, work habits and social skills, and demographic indicators to address equity and access issues. At the secondary level, these may also include course failures or credit deficiencies. Tier 2 interventions include *short-term* progress monitoring and collaboration among teachers, parents/guardians, and the school counselor, until improvement and/or referral to appropriate services can be identified and implemented. Tier 2 activities are also designed for students who (1) exhibit barriers to learning; (2) are struggling to achieve academic success; and/or (3) are identified as deserving of instruction and/or supports in addition to Tier 1 curriculum activities (foster youth, dual-language learners, etc.).

Tier 3: Intensive Interventions (5–10%)—For a *Few* Students

Individualized student interventions (e.g., one-on-one counseling or advisement) are designed for students to address emergency and crisis-response events. In the social/emotional domain, these include short-term, solution-focused counseling sessions to address life-changing events (divorce, death, imprisonment of a parent, etc.) or unresolved challenges unaffected within Tier 1 and Tier 2. In the academic domain, these include student-centered interventions and meetings (IEP, SST, and 504). Services are provided on a limited basis and, if issues are unresolved, lead to referrals to outside resources (Hatch, 2017). This type of intervention includes *short-term* consultation and collaboration among teachers, parents/guardians, outside agencies or resources, and the school counselor until the crisis is resolved and/or referral to appropriate responsive services can be identified and implemented. Figure 1.4 provides an example of an MTMDSS for the elementary school level.

Figure 1.4   Multi-Tiered Multi-Domain System of Supports (MTMDSS) Elementary Example

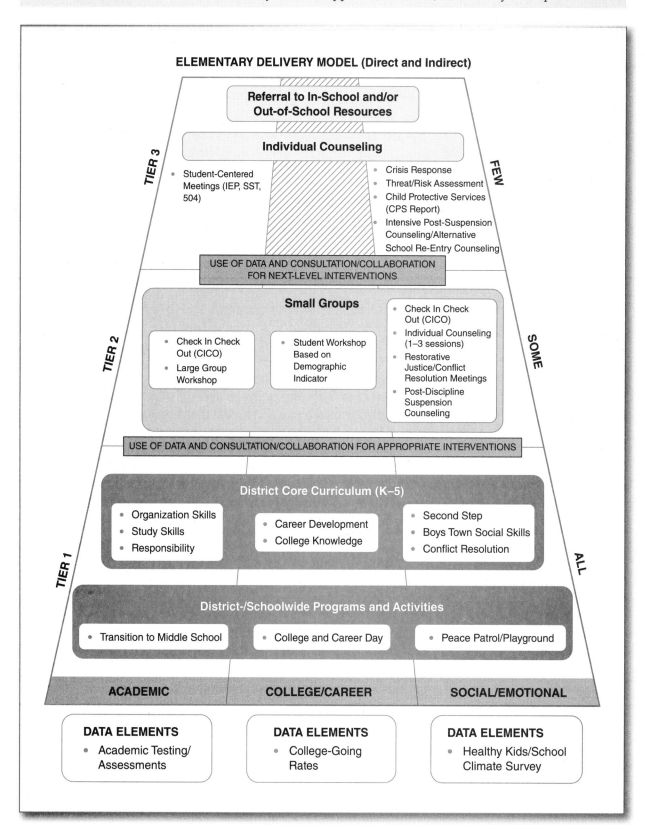

ACTIVITY 1.1

Readers are encouraged to review the three-minute video (located at www.hatching results.com/videos) outlining the tiered approach to MTMDSS and to assess their own program in relationship to the video.

MTMDSS ALIGNMENT TO TEXT

The purpose of this text is to provide thorough instruction on the activities that elementary school counselors provide within Tiers 2 and 3. Throughout this text, we will dive deeply into planning, implementing, and evaluating Tier 2 and 3 activities, those provided to *all* students "because they qualify." These include direct (individual, small and large group interventions, etc.) and indirect (consultation, collaboration, referral, etc.) services focusing on data-driven and developmentally targeted interventions.

Tier 2 and 3 instructional content is data-driven, evidence-based, franchisable, developmentally appropriate, and standards-aligned, similar to the Tier 2 and 3 interventions provided by teachers. Rather than conducting "random acts" of Tier 2 and 3 activities, school counselors assess the developmental and data-driven needs of students and create targeted intervention action plans. School counseling data collection and intervention activities within the three domains (academic, college/career, and social/emotional) are calendared prior to the start of the year (see Chapter 5). Data collection times are calendared, and data collected at various intervals (e.g., monthly, at progress reports, quarter, semester) may be used to identify student needs. The calendar and the intervention action plan are then shared with faculty, families, and other stakeholders.

Aligning MTMDSS With the ASCA National Model

Activities in the MTMDSS fall within several components of the ASCA National Model (4th edition, Figure 1.6), with a recommendation that 80% of time be spent on direct and indirect student services. Previous versions of the ASCA National Model (ASCA, 2003, 2005) suggested that school counselors spend approximately 30–40% of their time in responsive services (see Figure 1.5). In MTMDSS, responsive services occur in Tiers 2 and 3. As mentioned previously, MTSS recommends 15–20% of students receive interventions in the Tier 2 category and 5–10% of students receive services in the Tier 3 category. Given the shift to MTMDSS, the authors encourage school counselors to consider that the implementation of a strong Tier 1 program devoting significant time to teaching classroom lessons and schoolwide activities within the Tier 1 framework will provide a strong foundation of evidence-based prevention education programs and services that students need to succeed, which in turn will reduce the likelihood of students' qualifying for Tier 2 and 3 interventions. Therefore, a time frame of 30% is suggested as a guide for their total time in Tiers 2 and 3 when first beginning to design and implement an entire school counseling program, but this time allotment is not given as a prescription.

Figure 1.5   ASCA National Model Suggested Use of Time

	Delivery System Component	Elementary School % of Time	Middle School % of Time	High School % of Time	ASCA Recommendation
Direct Services	Core Curriculum **(Tier 1)**	35%	30%	20%	
	Individual Student Planning **(Can be Tier 1/2/3)**	5%	15%	25%	
	Responsive Services **(Can be Tier 1/2/3)**	25%	20%	20%	80% or more
Indirect Services	Referrals, Consultation, Collaboration **(Can be Tier 1/2/3)**	20%	20%	20%	
	System Support **(Can support Tiers 1/2/3)**	15%	15%	15%	20% or less

Source: Adapted by Whitney Triplett from Gysbers & Henderson (2000) and American School Counselor Association (ASCA). (2012). *ASCA National Model: A framework for school counseling programs* (3rd ed.). Alexandria, VA: Author.

Figure 1.6   ASCA National Model Diamond

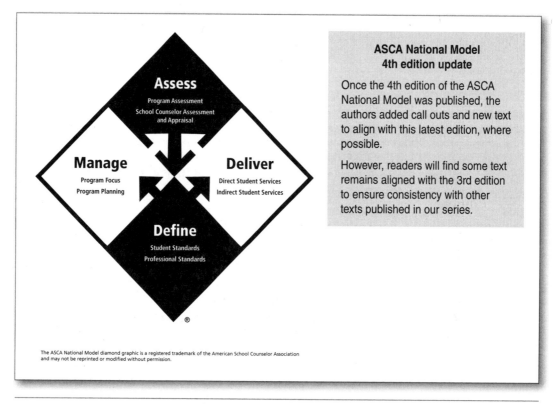

ASCA National Model 4th edition update

Once the 4th edition of the ASCA National Model was published, the authors added call outs and new text to align with this latest edition, where possible.

However, readers will find some text remains aligned with the 3rd edition to ensure consistency with other texts published in our series.

The ASCA National Model diamond graphic is a registered trademark of the American School Counselor Association and may not be reprinted or modified without permission.

Source: Reprinted with permission from the American School Counselor Association.

Aligning MTMDSS With the ASCA Ethical Standards

The purpose of the ASCA Ethical Standards for School Counselors (ASCA, 2016a) is to guide the ethical practices of school counselors who are expected to read and abide by the ethical guidelines thoroughly. Some of the guidelines that align with Tiers 2 and 3 in the MTMDSS model include the following:

A.3. Comprehensive Data-Informed Program

School counselors:

a. Collaborate with administration, teachers, staff and decision makers around school-improvement goals.

b. Provide students with a comprehensive school counseling program that ensures equitable academic, career and social/emotional development opportunities for all students.

c. Review school and student data to assess needs including, but not limited to, data on disparities that may exist related to gender, race, ethnicity, socio-economic status and/or other relevant classifications.

d. Use data to determine needed interventions, which are then delivered to help close the information, attainment, achievement and opportunity gaps.

A.6. Appropriate Referrals and Advocacy

School counselors:

a. Collaborate with all relevant stakeholders, including students, educators and parents/guardians when student assistance is needed, including the identification of early warning signs of student distress.

b. Provide a list of resources for outside agencies and resources in their community to student(s) and parents/guardians when students need or request additional support. School counselors provide multiple referral options or the district's vetted list and are careful not to indicate an endorsement or preference for one counselor or practice. School counselors encourage parents to interview outside professionals to make a personal decision regarding the best source of assistance for their student.

c. Connect students with services provided through the local school district and community agencies and remain aware of state laws and local district policies related to students with special needs, including limits to confidentiality and notification to authorities as appropriate.

A.7. Group Work

School counselors:

a. Facilitate short-term groups to address students' academic, career and/or social/emotional issues.

b. Inform parent/guardian(s) of student participation in a small group.

c. Screen students for group membership.

d. Use data to measure member needs to establish well-defined expectations of group members.

e. Communicate the aspiration of confidentiality as a group norm, while recognizing and working from the protective posture that confidentiality for minors in schools cannot be guaranteed.

f. Select topics for groups with the clear understanding that some topics are not suitable for groups in schools and accordingly take precautions to protect members from harm as a result of interactions with the group.

g. Facilitate groups from the framework of evidence-based or research-based practices.

h. Practice within their competence level and develop professional competence through training and supervision.

i. Measure the outcomes of group participation (process, perception and outcome data).

j. Provide necessary follow up with group members.

Note: The ASCA Ethical Standards for School Counselors can be found on the ASCA website at www.schoolcounselor.org/asca/media/asca/Ethics/EthicalStandards2016.pdf.

Aligning MTMDSS With the ASCA Position Statements

The school counselor and MTSS position statement calls for school counselors to be stakeholders in developing and implementing an MTSS that includes but is not limited to RTI and behavioral interventions and supports such as PBIS (see Figure 1.7). According to the position statement, the school counselor's role is to provide *all* students with a standards-based school counseling core curriculum to address universal academic, college/career, and social/emotional development. As school counselors align their work with MTSS and comprehensive school counseling programs designed to improve student achievement and behavior, the MTMDSS model in this text adds the third domain of college and career readiness to MTSS, which typically addresses only academics and behavior. Ensuring an informed, intentional approach to the student core curriculum in all three domains at the Tier 1 level is important, along with helping students with various challenges by providing Tier 2 and 3 interventions.

Figure 1.7   The School Counselor and Multitiered System of Supports

The School Counselor and Multitiered System of Supports
(Adopted 2008, revised 2014, 2018)

American School Counselor Association (ASCA) Position
School counselors are stakeholders in the development and implementation of a Multitiered System of Supports (MTSS), including but not limited to response to intervention (RTI) and responsive positive behavioral interventions and supports (PBIS). School counselors align their work with MTSS through the implementation of a comprehensive school counseling program designed to affect student development in the academic domain (achievement), the career domain (career exploration and development) and the social/emotional domain (behavior).

The Rationale
MTSS is a culturally responsive, evidence-based framework implemented in K–12 schools using data-based problem solving to integrate academic and behavioral instruction and intervention at tiered intensities to improve the learning and social/emotional functioning of all students (Sink, 2016). Guided by student-centered data, MTSS teams engage in cyclical data-based problem solving; make informed decisions about general, compensatory and special education; and assist in the creation of a well-integrated and seamless system of instruction and intervention (Ehren, Montgomery, Rudebush, & Whitmire, 2006).

Within the framework of a data-driven, comprehensive school counseling program school counselors augment their collaboration, coordination and leadership skills (Shepard et al., 2013) to meet the needs of all students and identify students who are at risk for not meeting academic and behavioral expectations. School counselors collaborate across student service disciplines with teachers, administrators and families to design and implement plans to address student needs and to promote students' academic, career social/emotional success (American School Counselor Association [ASCA], 2012). Data are collected and analyzed to determine the effectiveness of the learning supports for continual improvement efforts over time.

MTSS offers school counselors opportunities to have a lasting impact on student academic success and behavior development while integrating the framework within a comprehensive school counseling program (Ziomek-Daigle, Goodman-Scott & Donohue, 2016). The application of MTSS aligns with the role of school counseling at any grade level and can be used across multiple domains (Hatch, 2018; Hatch, Duarte, & Degregorio, 2017), such as academic, college/career and/or social/emotional development, based on the ASCA National Model.

The School Counselor's Role
The ASCA National Model serves as the foundation that assists school counselors in the academic, career and social/emotional development of students through the implementation of a comprehensive developmental school counseling program by:
  • Providing all students with a standards-based school counseling core curriculum to address universal academic, career and social/emotional development
  • Analyzing academic, career and social/emotional development data to identify struggling students
  • Identifying and collaborating on research-based intervention strategies implemented by school staff
  • Evaluating academic and behavioral progress after interventions
  • Revising interventions as appropriate
  • Referring to school and community services as appropriate
  • Collaborating with administrators, other school professionals, community agencies and families in the design and implementation of MTSS
  • Advocating for equitable education for all students and working to remove systemic barriers

Where MTSS interacts with school counseling programs the school counselor can serve in roles of supporter and/or intervener (Ockerman, Mason, & Feiker-Hollenbeck, 2012). In the supporting role, the school counselor may provide indirect student service by presenting data or serving as a consultant to a student support team. In intervener role, the school counselor may provide direct student service through the delivery component of the ASCA National Model.

(Continued)

Figure 1.7 (Continued)

Summary
School counselors implement a comprehensive school counseling program addressing the needs of all students. Through the review of data, school counselors identify struggling students and collaborate with other student services professionals, educators and families to provide appropriate instruction and learning supports within an MTSS. School counselors work collaboratively with other educators to remove systemic barriers for all students and implement specific learning supports that assist in academic and behavioral success.

References
American School Counselor Association. (2012). *The ASCA National Model: A framework for school counseling programs*. (3rd Ed). Alexandria, VA: Author.

Ehren, B., Montgomery, J., Rudebusch, J., & Whitmire, K. (2006). *New roles in response to intervention: Creating success for schools and children*. Retrieved from https://www.asha.org/uploadedFiles/slp/schools/prof-consult/rtiroledefinitions.pdf

Hatch, T. (2018) Multi-tiered, multi-domain system of supports (MTMDSS) video https://www.hatchingresults.com/videos/

Hatch, T., Duarte, D., & DeGregorio, L. (2017). Hatching results for elementary school counseling: Implementing core Curriculum and Other Tier One Activities. Thousand Oaks, CA: Corwin/Sage.

Ockerman, M.S., Mason, E.C., & Feiker-Hollenbeck, A. (2012) Integrating RTI with school counseling programs: Being a proactive professional school counselor. *Journal of School Counseling 10*(15).

Shepard, J.M., Shahidullah, J.D., & Carlson, J.S. (2013). Counseling Students in Levels 2 and 3: A PBIS/RTI Guide. Thousand Oaks, CA: Corwin/Sage

Sink, C. (2016). Incorporating a multi-tiered system of supports into school counselor preparation. Retrieved from http://tpcjournal.nbcc.org/wp-content/uploads/2016/09/Pages203-219-Sink.pdf

Ziomek-Daigle, J., Goodman-Scott, E., Cavin, J., & Donohue, P. (2016). Integrating a multi-tiered system of supports with comprehensive school counseling program. http://tpcjournal.nbcc.org/integrating-a-multi-tiered-system-of-supports-with-comprehensive-school-counseling-programs/

Resources
Hatch, T. (2018). Multi-tiered, multi-domain system of supports. https://www.hatchingresults.com/blog/2017/3/multi-tiered-multi-domain-system-of-supports-by-trish-hatch-phd

McIntosh,K. & Goodman, S. (2016). Integrated Multi-Tiered Systems of Support: Blending RTI and PBIS. Guilford Press.

WWW.SCHOOLCOUNSELOR.ORG

Source: **ASCA, 2018b.** Reprinted with permission from the American School Counselor Association.

ACTIVITY 1.2

Review the ASCA Position Statement and the ASCA Ethical Standards for School Counselors with your administrator. Discuss how a comprehensive school counseling program provides tiered supports to meet the needs of all students.

Table 1.1   Myths vs. Facts About School Counselors' Role in a Multi-Tiered Multi-Domain System of Supports

Myth	Fact	Learn More
School counselors only provide Tier 2 and 3 supports.	School counselors provide all students with a standards-based school counseling core curriculum to address universal academic, college/career, and social/emotional development.	ASCA position statement about the school counselor in MTSS: http://bit.ly/2n3ouaY
School counselors provide Tier 3 individual counseling to all students.	Tier 3 consists of short-term, highly structured interventions and wraparound services defined as "intensive, individual interventions for students at high risk."	ASCA position statement about the school counselor in MTSS: http://bit.ly/2n3ouaY
School counselors provide supports in only one domain (i.e., college/career or social/emotional).	Today's school counselors are vital members of the education team, helping all students in the areas of academic achievement, college/career development, and social/emotional development.	ASCA National Model executive summary: http://bit.ly/2fZJNqO
Most of the school counselor's time is spent on Tier 2 and 3 supports.	The greatest amount of the school counselor's time should be spent on implementing Tier 1 with a high degree of integrity, which is the most efficient means for serving the greatest number of students.	"Integrating RTI With School Counseling Programs: Being a Proactive Professional School Counselor" (Ockerman et al., 2012). Researchers indicate that around 75–80% of children should be expected to reach successful levels of competency through Tier 1 delivery (Shapiro, n.d.). "Spending 90% of the school counselor's time with 10% of the students is not the philosophy of intentional guidance" (Hatch, 2013, p. 41).

Source: Triplett, W. (2017). *Utilizing a multi-tiered system to implement your school counseling program* [PowerPoint slides]. Created for Chicago Public Schools.

BABIES IN THE RIVER

"Babies in the River" is a wonderful parable often told to illustrate the difference between prevention and intervention. Co-author Trish adapted this version from Pat Martin, a dear friend and colleague.

On a spring afternoon, after the students had left at the end of a minimum day, a group of high school counselors walked to a nearby park area next to a river to eat lunch together for the first time all year. Considering that they rarely even ate lunch at all, this was a treasured event. After a few minutes of talking and eating, Mariana noticed a baby floating down the river. Alarmed, she jumped up to assess the situation. As she did, she noticed several babies floating. She screamed for her colleagues to help, and for the next 20 minutes, they retrieved dozens of babies out of the river, until finally the babies stopped floating by. Exhausted, Mariana returned to her picnic and realized that Bob was missing. Where was Bob? Hadn't he been helping rescue the babies? Pretty soon Bob was heard whistling down the walkway. The rest of the group inquired, "Where were you? We were busy retrieving babies, and you were nowhere to be found!"

"Well," he said, "I decided to go up the river to see how they were getting in! Turns out someone, in his or her wisdom, decided to build a nursery/preschool next to the river! I noticed that the door had a broken lock, so first I fixed that. Then I realized that the babies didn't know how to swim, so I taught them. Then I learned that the teachers had no floaties, so I bought floaties and put them near the exit, so that if any babies fall in again, they can throw a floaty in the water in order for the babies to assist themselves. Finally, I filed a complaint with the city to ensure that no one ever builds a nursery or preschool within a mile of a river again!"

Though the prevention approach is almost always the most appealing, it can be difficult for counselors if they think that shifting to prevention education means turning their back on those students currently in need. It is also not always obvious how to work within the system to redesign how it functions—to build it differently, to partner to train those on the front lines and assist them in understanding how to provide first-level interventions and supports. But this is a requirement if school counselors are going to meet the needs of *all* students, because there is not enough time to rescue every drowning student (hypothetically) and there are far too many in the caseload.

The bottom portion of the MTMDSS pyramid (see Figure 1.3) is the largest section and reflects the importance of prevention education. Just as in the "Babies in the River" story, school counselors can either fill their day with reactive services (i.e., rescuing the babies one after another) or get out in front of things and engage in proactive prevention (i.e., teaching the babies how to swim). When counselors spend 80% of their day mired in Tier 2 and 3 reactive services, they may feel like they are in an emergency room rather than a school, and they won't have time for teaching prevention education and for designing systems of support to catch students early. Without a strong prevention system in place, the need for responsive services will continue to grow. Implementing a strong Tier 1 program, complete with classroom lessons and schoolwide activities, will allow students to gain the attitudes, knowledge, and skills necessary to reduce their need for Tier 2 services, thereby reducing the time spent in this tier. By pre-scheduling Tier 2 data collection, school counselors make sure students receive an early and immediate intervention with the goal of reducing the number of students in need of Tier 3 support.

Shifting the perspective of the counselors' role within MTMDSS from the myths to facts (as highlighted in Table 1.1) is helpful in shifting the school counselor program activities from being primarily responsive to being proactive. It takes commitment, planning, time, and cooperation, from administration and faculty alike. As school counselors begin to shift the pyramid to focus more on Tier 1, consideration should be given to addressing the potential challenges of finding balance between the time spent in classrooms and the number of reactive services they previously provided. School counselors will benefit from scaffolding the transitions at their school site to a proactive approach by adding lessons to their Tier 1 action plans each year, or by beginning with just one grade level and adding a grade level each year. In addition, by collaborating with teachers and administrators to gain support for Tier 1 in-class activities and services and participating on leadership teams to create necessary systemic processes, school counselors will improve efficiency and effectiveness as they determine which students are referred for additional Tier 2 and 3 data-driven interventions.

This text is written to support school counselors as they begin the process of eliminating old patterns of random interventions and creating new ones, setting up systems to support intentional, data-driven interventions that will catch students early. Ideas in this text are written to provide thoughtful, equity-based interventions designed to eliminate barriers to learning and to reduce the number of Tier 3 students requiring immediate response (i.e., rescuing out of the river). When students receive early intervention and are taught the skills they need to improve, they are less likely to be at risk of drowning down the river. Of course, there will always be crisis response as students and families experience tragedies and trauma. The goal is that when counselors provide scaffolded interventions, they save time by reducing the amount of time spent on students in Tier 2 who do not qualify for (or require) intervention and instead focus on those who do.

MTMDSS ASSESSMENT

ACTIVITY 1.3

Please review the Multi-Tiered, Multi-Domain System of Supports (MTMDSS) diagram (Figure 1.3) regarding school counselor activities within an MTMDSS. Next, complete the blank MTMDSS (see Figure 1.8) by listing your current Tier 1, 2, and 3 activities, lessons, and interventions per each domain: academic, college/career, and social/emotional. Look for strengths and potential areas for growth.

(Continued)

(Continued)

Figure 1.8 Blank MTMDSS Diagram

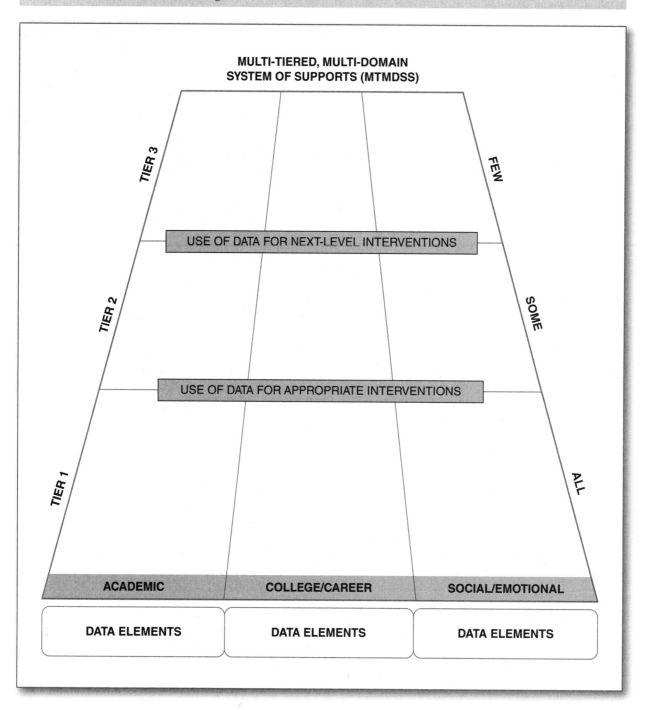

2

Using Data to Drive Tier 2 Interventions

TRISH'S STORY

When I was a new school counselor back in 1987, I taught lessons in the classroom, counseled students in small groups, and provided individual counseling for students in crisis. At the time, I organized my small groups in many different ways:

- *Teachers, parents, or administrators would ask me if I had an intervention for students who needed study skills, and I'd start one when we had six students in need.*
- *I had a stack of referrals with the same issues and put them in a group.*
- *Sometimes I would post a sign in the teachers' lounge or pass out an information sheet at the faculty meeting and ask if teachers had any students who would benefit from the group.*

Although I thought I was using data to put students with similar issues in a similar group, it wasn't the most efficient and effective way to use data to drive focused and intentional interventions. This is because the process was reactive, not proactive, and none of these ways involved the use of student behavior data to determine need.

L ooking at past practices, it was not uncommon for school counselors to create groups by sorting teacher referrals into common areas of concern or to create group topics and ask teachers to sign up their students. Today's school counselors are called upon to align their work with the ASCA National Model and to use data to drive decision making. Rather than wait for teachers to refer students to the school counselor, the school counselor is expected to utilize a more proactive approach (see Figure 2.1). Today's school counselor is intentional. What does *intentional* mean? According to an online dictionary:

- *Intent* suggests "a clearer formulation or greater deliberateness."
- *Intention* is defined as "what one has in mind to do or bring about."
- *Intentional* refers to "an action done deliberately, on purpose, and not by accident."

How often are interventions provided by elementary school counselors done *deliberately, on purpose,* and *not by accident*? Far too many school counselors report they provide "random acts of intervention." They share they feel like they are in an emergency room rather than a professional office. To manage this reactive condition, today's school counselors recognize that best practices for determining Tier 2 interventions

- are driven by data (i.e., attendance, behavior, work/study habits);
- are pre-determined and agreed upon;
- are pre-scheduled and calendared;
- utilize screening elements;
- are conducted on a short-term basis;
- are content specific, aligning with data-driven need;
- include ongoing progress monitoring;
- measure results and impact; and
- empower them to create systemic change.

Figure 2.1   Tier 2 Service: From Then to Now

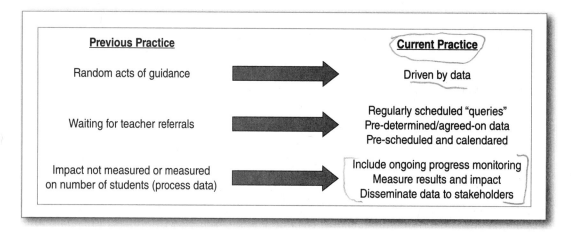

SCHOOL COUNSELORS AND DATA PROFICIENCY

With so much data available at our fingertips, where does a school counselor begin? Let's start with identifying some of the types of data school counselors use in their programs when delivering curriculum or Tier 2 interventions. To do this, we will first identify important terms as they relate to the "Hatching Results Conceptual Diagram" (see Figure 2.2).

Process, Perception, and Outcome Data

Process data is often used to describe in detail the activities school counselors will perform. The 4th edition of the ASCA National Model now calls this "participation data." However, the answers are similar to the question "Who participated in what activities?" (ASCA, 2019a, p. 35). It's a sort of instruction or descriptor of what school counselors do and with whom they do it. The process describes who, what, where, when, and how long. *Who will be served? What will they receive? Where will they receive it? When will activity occur? For what duration?*

Example

- *90 fourth graders will receive student skills lessons using XYZ curriculum in their classroom in October.*
- *12 fifth graders will receive a group counseling intervention in the counseling office utilizing XYZ curriculum for six weeks beginning November 1.*

Perception data measure the extent to which students learn the *standards and competencies* they are intended to learn as a result of the lesson or intervention. The 4th edition of the ASCA National Model now calls this "Mindsets and Behaviors Data" and answers the question, "What did students learn through participation in the school counseling activities?" (ASCA, 2019a, p. 35). Perception data are intended to measure competencies by asking questions about the *attitudes, skills,* and *knowledge* students learn. (Note combining the first letter of these words creates the acronym ASK.) School counselors ASK students what they learn as a way to measure the impact of the lesson or activity.

Example

- *Attitudes:* Students believe using study strategies will help them do better on tests.
- *Skills:* Students can demonstrate utilizing a study strategy on a sample test.
- *Knowledge:* Students can identify three study strategies.

The 4th edition of the ASCA National Model (2019a) has shifted the language from "perception data" to "mindsets and behavior data." Aligning with the Farrington Report, ASCA has divided the standards into mindsets (beliefs and attitudes) and behaviors (skills).

Research supports, and ASCA's 4th edition confirms, that school counselors measure student changes in attitudes, knowledge, and skills from content delivered (ASCA, 2019a, p. 35). The following Conceptual Diagram (Figure 2.2) assists the reader in the thought process of measuring the impact of their instruction by insuring all three types of data (attitudes, skills, and knowledge) are assessed, as together they serve to impact student behaviors and actions, which lead to improved student outcomes.

Outcome data measure behavior change in students as well as student performance. Divided into two categories, *achievement* and *achievement related,* student outcomes data assist the school counselor in determining if more interventions are needed (Dimmitt, Carey, & Hatch, 2007). Outcome data also provide information on whether counseling activities may be contributing to students' improvement. Note in the Conceptual Diagram that when a student's "ASK data" improve, the next step is to check for behavior change. When students change their behavior, it impacts achievement-related outcomes first, and achievement outcomes second.

Achievement-related data elements represent the type of data that research tells us support achievement (ASCA, 2003, 2005; Dimmitt, Carey, & Hatch, 2007; Hatch, 2013). These data elements include (but are not limited to) the following:

- Discipline/referrals/suspensions
- Attendance/truancy/tardies
- Classwork/homework completion
- Work skills and study habits
- Test-taking strategies
- Citizenship marks
- School climate data
- Parental involvement
- Student engagement

Achievement data are the big-ticket data items, which previously in No Child Left Behind (NCLB; U.S. Department of Education, 2002) were the only types of data posted on state websites. While at the secondary level these include graduation rates, Advanced Placement (AP) passing rates, college-going rates, and other

Figure 2.2   Hatching Results Conceptual Diagram: Elementary

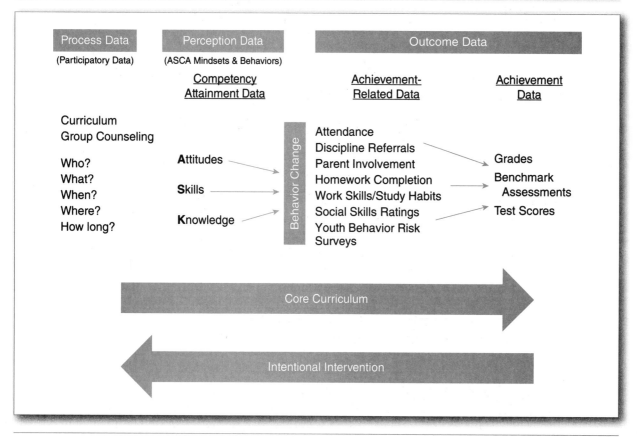

Source: Adapted from Hatch, T. (2006).

outcome data elements, at the elementary level these include benchmark assessments, standardized test scores, and retention rates.

As a result of the release of the Every Student Succeeds Act (ESSA) in 2015, data items previously not measured and shared in a public way are now a part of data sharing. This is great news for school counselors who most often focus on and measure improvement in data elements that support achievement data. Additionally, at the elementary level, the achievement-related data elements are often early warning indicators of students at risk of dropping out. The primary indicators of dropout behavior are students who are struggling with attendance, behavior, and academic mindsets (Balfanz, Herzog, & Mac Iver, 2007).

The 4th edition of the ASCA National Model calls for school counselors to measure three primary outcome data types: attendance, discipline, and achievement.

In many states, data dashboards also include other types of outcome data. For example, the California Dashboard includes student engagement and parent involvement, to which school counselors often contribute. Because of this, we believe it is important to expand this list to include other types of outcome data. Additionally, while the ASCA National Model 3rd (2012) and 4th (2019) editions no longer distinguish between achievement related and achievement data, we believe it is important to differentiate these outcome data points to support counselors as they carefully consider which outcome data to collect and report. Therefore, in the text that follows, we will continue to use the terminologies process, perception, and outcome data, as well as achievement and achievement related data—all of which align with other texts in this series. To assist readers in the thoughtful process of this work, we will reference 4th edition terminologies as helpful and appropriate.

Hatching Results Conceptual Diagram

The Hatching Results Conceptual Diagram visually represents an explanation of how school counseling activities contribute to student-achievement-related behavior data, as well as student achievement. Although this text will focus on Tiers 2 and 3, it's important to review Tier 1 and the Conceptual Diagram first. The Hatching Results Conceptual Diagram: Elementary (see Figure 2.2) provides a practical model for school counselors to guide their use of data by visually laying out the relationship between the "types of data" (standards and competency, achievement related, and achievement) and the "ways to evaluate data" (process, perception, and outcomes). Used for *core curriculum*, Figure 2.2 reads from left to right and represents an action framework connecting what school counselors do (process data) to the attainment of specific student competencies (measured with perception data) and behavior change, leading to an improvement in results (achievement-related data and, subsequently, student achievement data).

When used for *intentional interventions*, however, the Hatching Results Conceptual Diagram (Figure 2.2) reads from right to left. When students (or groups of students) are not performing to expectations on achievement data elements, it is appropriate to inquire about what *achievement-related* data elements are lacking (attendance, behavior, classwork or homework completion, etc.). Once the barrier to learning is identified, the school counselor works to identify what type of intervention the student may need to gain the *attitudes*, *skills*, and *knowledge* needed to improve behavior.

For example (see Figure 2.3), when school counselors teach a *core curriculum* lesson on conflict resolution, they might assess whether students acquire (1) the *attitude* that it is important to solve problems peacefully; (2) the *skill* of role-playing

Figure 2.3   Hatching Results Conceptual Diagram: Elementary Conflict Resolution Example

Source: Hatch, T. (2006–2019).

steps to conflict resolution; and (3) the *knowledge* of where and when to seek help when needed to avoid a conflict. In this scenario, the goal of the lesson would be to support the reduction of discipline referrals and suspensions (achievement related), which can support and lead to improved school climate (achievement related), which in turn supports improved student academic performance (achievement).

Intentional interventions work conversely. Because school climate impacts student achievement (achievement data), school counselors provide interventions for students with multiple discipline referrals (achievement related). They use data to determine which students have the greatest number of referrals. The counselor then meets with the student to determine the barrier to appropriate behavior. Has the student not acquired the *attitude* that it is important to solve problems peacefully; the *skill* of role-playing steps to conflict resolution; or the *knowledge* of where and when to seek help when needed to avoid a conflict? In this scenario, the goal of the intervention would be to support students in gaining the attitudes, skills, and knowledge needed to shift their behavior, leading to a reduction of discipline referrals and suspensions (achievement related), which can support and lead to improved school climate (achievement related), which in turn supports improved student academic performance (achievement).

Fishnet Approach

When determining which students qualify for an intervention, school counselors query data using a "fishnet approach" (see Figure 2.4) to identify and focus on those students who meet certain criteria—for instance, students

- who are not on target academically,
- who are in danger of retention,
- with multiple truancies,
- with multiple suspensions, and
- with incomplete classwork.

Using a fishnet approach, the school counselor disaggregates the data to determine which students need additional intervention. Determining when to "fishnet" students ensures every student who qualifies is referred. The fishnet approach relies not on teacher referral but rather on the timing of the school counselor's query of data.

Perhaps school counselors want to intervene with students who have five or more absences. Will the counselors get new students who qualify day by day? This might prove a bit chaotic. A more efficient way to intervene might be to determine a point in time (e.g., 30 days into the school year) when school counselors will fishnet all those students who have five or more absences. In this way, the counselors schedule time-certain intervention points to gather data. Setting aside a specific time to look at the number of students in need ensures a system is in place to manage the data and put interventions into motion.

Figure 2.4   Fishnet Approach to Data Collection

Once students have been identified, the next inquiry (moving left on the diagram) is to look at the perception data to inquire as to what might be a potential barrier to learning. *Attitudes? Skills? Knowledge? Does the student not believe it's important to be on time? Or not have the skills to set an alarm clock? Or not know what time school starts? Or perhaps a combination of these?* Once determined, moving left again to the process data, an intervention is designed to address the specific need.

It's important to determine the barrier to learning when data indicate a need. By working closely with students and their families, targeted interventions can be provided instead of random ones. For example, perhaps students are placed in a counseling group to improve motivation when the issue is that they need tutoring. Or, perhaps the students do not need tutoring or counseling for motivation but instead have irregular attendance or do not feel safe at or connected to school. All too often, the intervention is decided for students before the specific barrier is identified. Struggling students, who come to school counselors from many diverse backgrounds and experiences, are often provided interventions without time taken to consider the particular needs emerging from each student's unique world.

The Conceptual Diagram for school counselors provides a practical model to drive both *prevention* and *intervention*. School counselors looking for more information on how to use data to design and implement core curriculum are encouraged to look at texts that specialize in this area (e.g., *The Use of Data in School Counseling: Hatching Results for Students, Programs, and the Profession* [Hatch, 2013]; and *Hatching Results for Elementary School Counseling: Implementing Core Curriculum and Other Tier One Activities* [Hatch, Duarte, & De Gregorio, 2018]).

In this text, however, we will focus on how school counselors, using the Conceptual Diagram, can thoughtfully utilize data to

- identify students in need,
- design appropriate interventions,
- progress monitor interventions,
- analyze intervention impact,
- report results, and
- recommend additional or alternative strategies.

TIER 2 INTENTIONAL INTERVENTIONS

The Hatching Results Conceptual Diagram in Figure 2.2 is a visual representation of how data can be used to determine both Tier 1 and Tier 2 supports. When school counselors provide core curriculum in classrooms, they are providing Tier 1 instruction for all students, and the diagram reads from left to right. The Conceptual Diagram for intentional interventions, in contrast, reads from right to left. When students (or groups of students) are not performing to expectations on achievement or achievement-related data elements, it is appropriate to provide the identified students with a Tier 2 intervention.

Consider a school counselor who notices that a large number of fourth-grade students are performing poorly on the benchmark test (achievement data). The school counselor may query the data to determine which students are in need of additional support (based on pre-identified criteria). Once students have been identified, the next inquiry (moving left in the diagram) is to look at the perception data to discover what is needed. Do the students *believe* (*attitude*) that doing well on the benchmark test is important? Are students able to *demonstrate* (*skill*) the use of various test-taking techniques? Do the students *know* (*knowledge*) different test-taking strategies to use? Once this is determined, moving left again to the process data, an intervention could be designed to address the identified need.

When determining which students qualify for Tier 2 interventions (see Figure 2.5), school counselors are encouraged to collect and analyze consistent data elements throughout the year. The third edition of the ASCA National Model includes a data profile tool with recommendations for the types of data counselors may want to consider (ASCA, 2012). *The Use of Data in School Counseling* (Hatch, 2013) also provides extensive information in Chapters 3 and 4. The types of data most commonly used in targeting Tier 2 interventions for elementary students align with

- attendance,
- discipline referrals or demerits,

- suspensions,
- classwork completion, and
- homework completion.

Figure 2.5   Tier 2 Data and MTMDSS

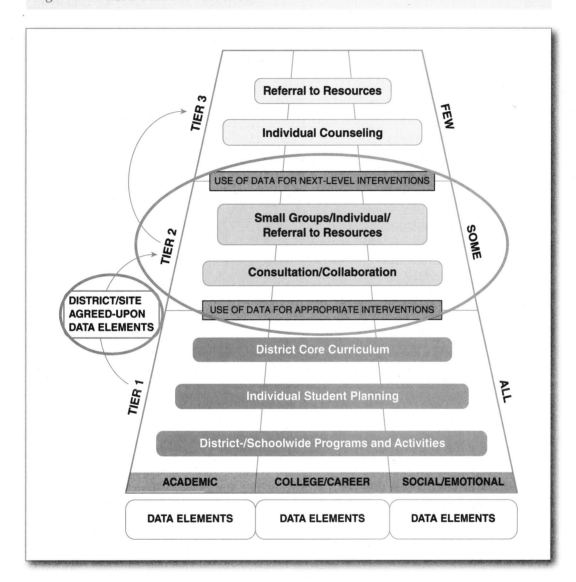

Preventing Dropout Behaviors

Dropping-out-of-school behaviors do not begin in high school. Rather, early warning signs are often evident in the primary grades. Dropout prevention researchers recommend collecting data to track early warning indicators of potential dropouts (e.g., attendance, behavior, grades in reading and math, and benchmark test scores) as early as elementary school (Balfanz et al., 2007). Dr. Robert Balfanz, a pioneer for using early warning indicators, has created multiple evidence-based models for identifying and monitoring at-risk students through early warning systems (Balfanz, Bridgeland, Moore, & Fox, 2010). Recognizing the early warning signs of dropout behavior, and intervening to teach the attitudes, skills, and knowledge students need, can help prevent future student failure. Successful student habits developed in the formative years build the foundation for academic success in later years. Experts and practitioners in schools are now consistently using early warning indicators to address core challenges, like reducing chronic absenteeism and assigning tiered interventions, as well as promoting students' social/emotional learning (SEL) and college/career readiness.

School counselors are encouraged to utilize data to identify those students who receive moderate grades but may lack sufficient study and organizational skills. Intervening early may help the students gain the skills they need to succeed as the academic curriculum increases in its rigor (Hatch, 2013).

The University of Chicago Consortium on School Research literature review proposes a framework for thinking about how these factors interact to affect academic performance, and what the relationship is between non-cognitive factors and classroom/school context, as well as the larger socio-cultural context. *Teaching Adolescents to Become Learners* (Farrington et al., 2012) summarizes the research on five categories of non-cognitive factors related to academic performance (see Figure 2.6):

- Academic behaviors
- Academic perseverance
- Academic mindsets
- Learning strategies
- Social skills

Figure 2.6   Five Non-Cognitive Factors and Academic Performance

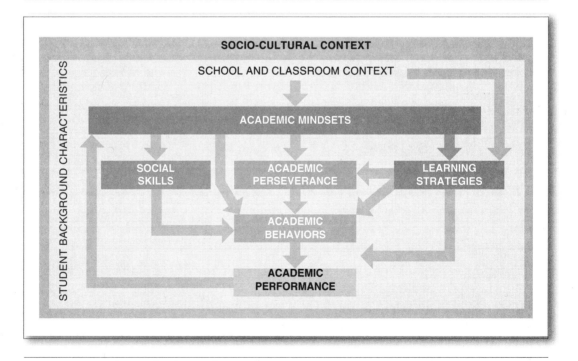

Source: Farrington, C.A., Roderick, M., Allensworth, E., Nagaoka, J., Keyes, T.S., Johnson, D.W., & Beechum, N.O. (2012). Teaching adolescents to become learners. The role of noncognitive factors in shaping school performance: A critical literature review. Chicago: University of Chicago Consortium on Chicago School Research.

The Work Habits/Social Skills data elements on students' report cards align with research on non-cognitive skills and academic mindsets (Dweck, Walton, & Cohen, 2014; Farrington et al., 2012; see Figure 2.7). The learning strategies factor contains study skills, metacognitive strategies, self-regulated learning, and goal setting. These data are often collected in schools on the SEL portion of the work skills/study habits or citizenship areas of the elementary report card. Disengagement in the classroom (which can be measured through engagement scales and behavior marks on report cards) is also considered a precursor to student dropout (Finn 1993, Finn 2006, Bridgeland et al., 2006). This often underutilized data elements provide early insight into which students are struggling in the classroom and serves as an excellent screening tool for small group interventions (Duarte & Hatch, 2014).

Figure 2.7 Non-Cognitive Factors and Academic Mindsets

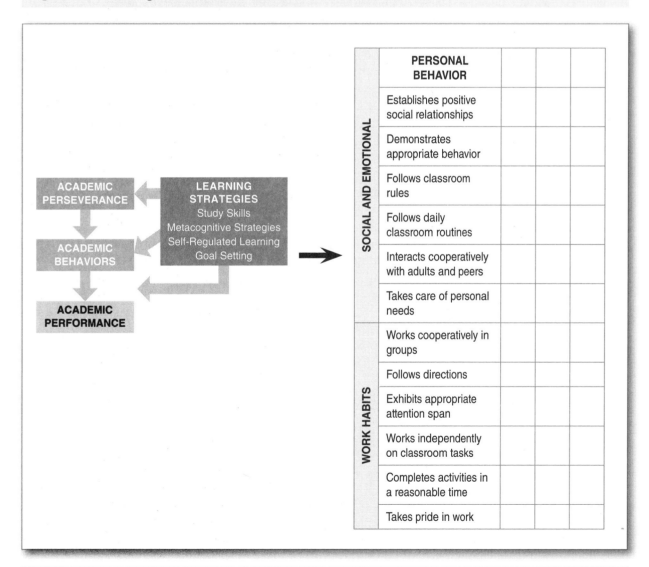

Source: **Farrington, C.A., Roderick, M., Allensworth, E., Nagaoka, J., Keyes, T.S., Johnson, D.W., & Beechum, N.O. (2012).** Teaching adolescents to become learners. The role of noncognitive factors in shaping school performance: A critical literature review. Chicago: University of Chicago Consortium on Chicago School Research.

Researchers agree: the earlier the intervention, the better. Creating consistent, guaranteed interventions as early as possible will contribute to more engaged students and less dropout as students leave elementary and enter secondary schools. Researchers at the University of Montréal have developed a prevention program based on the fundamental elements to decrease the rate of dropout by addressing social skills, problem-solving skills, and social-cognitive skills provided within the school setting (Lehr, Johnson, Bremer, Cosio, & Thompson, 2004). The National High School Center at the American Institutes for Research recommends establishing "a data system that tracks individual student attendance, grades, promotion status, and engagement indicators, such as behavioral marks, as early as fourth grade" (Kennelly & Monrad, 2007, pp. 1–2).

Helpful Tip

Disclaimer

Just as caring professionals don't agree on everything in your school, so too it is when it comes to data collection and perspectives on what constitutes students' "behavior." Not all educators, professors, or state and national organizations agree with the types of data that qualify as achievement related and achievement. Some believe report card marks are "perception data" because they are subjective and come from a teacher perspective. Others argue that if this is true, then discipline, and academic grades for that matter, could also be considered "perception data" because they are also subjective and come from a teacher perspective. Additionally, most schools lack rubrics or norming assessments to ensure marks are actually based on students' behavior. Nonetheless, there are significant data to support the positive relationship between study skills and academic success (Agnew, Slate, Jones, & Agnew, 1993; Elliott, Godshall, Shrout, & Witty, 1990; Jones, Green, Mahan, & Slate, 1993; Jones, Slate, & Marini, 1995). Research supports the perspective that study skills are as important as academic skills in the development of children and youth because they are observable and reliably measured, function as academic enablers, and can be directly taught in or outside of any classroom (DiPerna & Elliott, 2002). Study skills can be improved using common cognitive-behavioral intervention strategies many educators possess in their teaching repertoires.

Nearly 20 years ago, it was empirically established that interpersonal (self-management) skills play a key role in facilitating students' achievement in reading and mathematics by directly influencing their motivation, which in turn influences engagement and study skills. Students who are socially skilled spend more time on task and more time helping others. As a result, learning time goes up, classroom problem behavior goes down, and achievement increases (DiPerna & Elliott, 2002).

When asked to comment on this discussion, Brett Zyromski, PhD, assistant professor of counselor education at The Ohio State University, shared the following: "In this time of discussion around what constitutes process, perception, and outcome data, it may be that we are creating a system for defining outcome data that is too rigid in its definition and based off opinion rather than research. It may be that changes in student behaviors can be captured in significant ways that are beyond the current definition proposed by ASCA" (personal communication, January 22, 2019).

All of this is to say school counselors who are planning to apply for national awards like the Recognized ASCA Model Program (RAMP) are encouraged to inquire with the American School Counselor Association (ASCA) as to whether the committee will allow work habits, study skills, classwork or homework, or any other data element to "count" as "behavior change."

Tier 2 Data-Driven Intervention Tool (What Data Should We Collect?)

When school counselors are determining data-driven interventions, tools can be useful, such as the one provided in Figure 2.8. This planning tool is designed to be used as a thoughtful brainstorming worksheet rather than a prescription.

Selecting the At-Risk Indicator

The Tier 2 data-driven interventions planning tool (see Figure 2.8) is designed to list all of the possible data elements that school counselors may want to consider at the elementary level. School counselors collaborate with other site leaders (e.g., data-based decision-making team, school leadership team, MTSS team, PBIS team) to determine which data elements they want to measure. Ideally, school counselors with programs in place already collect and analyze these data elements regularly. However, as counselors are beginning to use this approach, it is recommended that they select a few elements that best support the school and district specific, measurable, achievable, relevant, and time-bound (SMART) goals.

It is also important that everyone agrees on the definition of the data element. How will you define *attendance*? Will you include tardies? Some districts utilize terms like *habitual truant*. Be certain to investigate the details of what each data element means before selecting.

Readers will notice that course failure is not listed. At the primary level, course failure is not typically the most appropriate school counseling intervention to address for students. Often, other professionals in the schools can assist with core subject interventions (e.g., reading intervention). At the secondary level, focusing on grades may be more appropriate, and therefore could be added to the list. Having said that, K–8 counselors may want to add course failures for upper grades, 5–8.

Targeted Data Indicator (Data Element)

Do you want to select students based on the number or percentage of incidents? Perhaps you want to ensure each student with three or more office referrals receives an intervention. If this data element is selected, the next step is to create a query or way to be alerted when students reach the third office referral threshold. Another way is to consider interventions with students who possess the most referrals (although caution is suggested; if these are so frequent, they are actually Tier 3 students). Some counselors query after the first month of school to see which students have been marked as truant or committed multiple behavior infractions. Others wait

Figure 2.8 Determining Data-Driven Tier 2 Intentional Interventions

DETERMINING DATA-DRIVEN TIER 2 INTENTIONAL INTERVENTIONS

How do you determine which intentional interventions to deliver? To answer this question, it can be helpful to engage in data-based decision making to determine the targeted data indicator, data element for targeted-intervention, grade level or student group, and time frame/frequency that data will be collected and reviewed to determine which students receive the appropriate intervention.

Tier 2 Intentional Intervention Planning Tool

<u>Directions</u>: *For each targeted data indicator, mark the checkbox (where applicable) if it will be a factor at your school/district. Then consider which specific data, according to the student population or grade level identified, will prompt a Tier 2 intentional intervention. Next, consider the frequency or time frame to review the data element. Enter additional indicators in the blank spaces provided if necessary.*

Select	Targeted Data Indicator	Data Element for Targeted Intervention	Students/ Grade Level	Time Frame/ Frequency
☐	**Attendance/ Tardiness**	☐ ___ # full day absences ☐ ___ # partial day/specific period absences (_____) ☐ ___ % of the school year missed ☐ Lowest ___ % attendance ☐ ___ or more tardies ☐ ___ % instructional time missed	☐ All students ☐ Grade level(s): ____ ☐ Student groups: _____	☐ First 20? or 30? days ☐ Progress report(s) ☐ Q1; Q2; Q3; Q4 ☐ T1; T2; T3 ☐ S1; S2 ☐ End of the year
☐	**Behavior**	☐ ___ # of discipline referrals ☐ ___ # of level _____ infractions ☐ ___ # of suspensions ☐ ___ % discipline (e.g., top 10%) ☐ Specific type(s) of infraction(s): _____	☐ All students ☐ Grade level(s): ____ ☐ Student groups: _____	☐ First 20? or 30? days ☐ Progress report(s) ☐ Q1; Q2; Q3; Q4 ☐ T1; T2; T3 ☐ S1; S2 ☐ End of the year
☐	**Study Habits Marks on the Report Card**	☐ ___ # *N*s and/or ___ # *U*s ☐ Local criteria: _____	☐ All students ☐ Grade level(s): ____ ☐ Student groups: _____	☐ Progress report(s) ☐ Q1; Q2; Q3; Q4 ☐ T1; T2; T3 ☐ S1; S2 ☐ End of the year
☐	**Citizenship Marks on the Report Card**	☐ ___ # *N*s and/or ___ # *U*s ☐ Local criteria: _____	☐ All students ☐ Grade level(s): ____ ☐ Student groups: _____	☐ Progress report(s) ☐ Q1; Q2; Q3; Q4 ☐ T1; T2; T3 ☐ S1; S2 ☐ End of the year
☐	**Homework/ Classwork Completion**	☐ ___ # "0"s ☐ ___ % < 50% ☐ Local criteria: _____	☐ All Students ☐ Grade level(s): ____ ☐ Student groups: _____	☐ Progress report(s) ☐ Q1; Q2; Q3; Q4 ☐ T1; T2; T3 ☐ S1; S2 ☐ End of the year
☐	**Promotion/ Retention**	☐ Local criteria: _____	☐ All students ☐ Grade level(s): ____ ☐ Student groups: _____	☐ Progress report(s) ☐ Q1; Q2; Q3; Q4 ☐ T1; T2; T3 ☐ S1; S2 ☐ End of the year
☐	**Other:**			

until students meet a threshold. Either way, it is consistency and a thoughtful, well-organized plan that matters most. This is important because in this process, teachers will be asked to withhold referrals since school counselors are already querying the data. Therefore, once the data criteria have been agreed to and counselors begin to query the Tier 2 criteria, the process for ensuring an intervention takes place becomes a priority.

Students/Grade Level

The third column in Figure 2.8 is provided to help school counselors be thoughtful regarding the grade levels that will be selected. Experienced counselors will want to review all data on a regular basis. When beginning, however, we often encourage counselors to select one or two grade levels and look at multiple data, or to select one element and look at all grades. The goal is to not become overwhelmed as the process begins and to pay attention to ratios and time, to ensure a balance of interventions with other activities.

Time Frame/Frequency

How often will data be collected? Every day? Week? Month? Quarter? Whatever the decision, the idea is that data will be consistently utilized to drive group counseling or other Tier 2 interventions. For instance, if the counselor is reviewing data on attendance, it might be helpful to collect data by month, whereas report card data are released quarterly for some and on a trimester basis for other schools. The goal is to agree upon what data will be *pre-scheduled and pre-determined*. Once this is done, the next task is to consider how the data will be gathered.

Thinking through how often to "query" data helps school counselors to be proactive. Some might want to set up a weekly review system of vital data elements. Depending on the different types of data, school counselors might decide to collect certain data at different times in the year. Some data can be collected at intervals, and some can be collected when students reach a certain threshold.

TRISH'S STORY

Where Do We Find the Data?

When I first started teaching school counseling graduate students in San Diego, I made an assumption. I asked the students to bring to class the number of referrals for three grade levels (3–5) so that we could discuss using real data from the schools they were placed in. I remember when several students told me they spent six hours in the individual student records (cumulative) files. I was surprised to learn that many students hand-counted the referrals. I was even more shocked that the local schools had no mechanism for record keeping of office referrals. It turns out that many elementary schools still struggle with archaic (or non-existent) data-based collection systems. Hopefully, if you are reading this text, you can use this story and this chapter to help counselors and others advocate for state-of-the-art data-based systems. Without them, random acts of intervention continue to prevail.

Utilizing Data Systems as Screening Elements

It is not a good use of school counselor expertise to hand-count office referrals. Instead, if no mechanism exists, counselors are called on to think creatively about how to get the best data in the least amount of time and to advocate for ways to improve the process through purchasing student database systems. Student database systems are the most efficient and effective way to query which students meet the identified need. Regardless of the student database system a school uses, school counselors should establish systems and procedures to ensure that data are collected at regular, pre-determined intervals. For instance, attendance and discipline rates may be queried on a monthly basis. Rather than having a teacher refer a student for discipline or study skills interventions, the school counselor proactively queries students at the end of the month or quarter, or sets up a system to be notified when the students receive the identified number of discipline referrals.

Another example might be a school counselor queries the progress report data, which include coursework completion, and intentionally recruits students missing a specific number/percentage of assignments, and then assesses the students' appropriateness for group or other interventions. Where student database systems are inaccessible or non-existent, school counselors are encouraged to advocate for access to or the purchase of such a system, or to utilize forms (such as the sample report card documents provided in this chapter) to identify need, monitor progress, and measure impact.

If you are fortunate to have a student database system, take the time to learn its ins and outs. Schedule a time to talk to the individuals in charge and ask them to query the data or, better yet, ask them to teach you *how* to query the data.

When completed, the data elements selected can be listed in a way similar to Table 2.1.

> ### TRISH'S STORY
>
> *When I was a counselor, I recall the teachers copying off report cards for the principal to sign. In most places, this all happens electronically now, but if your district is not online, this may also be an option. One of my creative graduate students asked the teachers to make a copy of any report card that had Ns (Needs Improvement) and Us (Unacceptable) in the work skills/study habits portion (this way it's not the whole class, hopefully) and to place it in her box. This ensured the counselor had the real data (teacher marks) to use as she created a spreadsheet of report card data.*

Report Card Data

Many report cards in elementary school include a Work Skills/Study Habits section. They vary from site to site. Throughout this text, we may refer to these sections in varying ways (Work Skills/Study Habits; Work Habits/Study Skills; Citizenship and Study Habits; Social Skills/Study Skills; etc.), and there is no consistent norming on these topic areas. If your district has a report card like this,

Table 2.1   Example of Data Selected by One District

At-Risk Indicator	Data Element Criteria	Grade Level	Time Frame (How often will these data be collected?)	Source Used to Gather Data
Attendance	5 Days	K–5	Monthly	Student Database System
Tardies	5 Tardies	K–5	Monthly	Student Database System
Behavior	3 Office Referrals	Grades 3–5	Monthly	Student Database System
Behavior	Suspension	Grades K–5	At Time of Suspension	Admin Notifies
Report Card Study Habits	2 or More Ns/Us	Grades 3–5	Q1, Q2, Q3, Q4	Online Report Card System
Report Card Citizenship	2 or More Ns/Us	Grades 3–5	Q1, Q2, Q3, Q4	Online Report Card System
Homework Completion	Missing More Than 30%	Grades 4 and 5	Q1, Q2, Q3, Q4	Online Teacher Grading Tool
Classwork Completion	Missing More Than 30%	Grades 3–5	Q1, Q2, Q3, Q4	Online Teacher Grading Tool

this is a great place to begin (see Figure 2.9). Notice the report card shown in Figure 2.9 offers *E, G, S, N,* and *U* (*Excellent, Good, Satisfactory, Needs Improvement,* and *Unacceptable*) as choices. Your district may instead use checks, minuses, pluses, or numbers such as 1, 2, and 3. Regardless of the rating system used, school counselors can gather the data to determine which students are in need of Tier 2 services. If your district does not yet have a report card that includes these measurements for work skills/study habits and social skills, school counselors are encouraged to consider being a part of the next report card revision and to recommend one (a great example of advocacy!).

In the meantime, school counselors can take the samples provided in Figure 2.10 to create and utilize a screening tool for teachers to determine which students have the greatest need and in which area. When all teachers are asked to fill out an intervention survey, the counselor ensures fewer random acts of intervention referrals. Instead, the teachers refer students through a consistent, fair, timely, and equitable process. For example, teachers can complete the survey after the first month or marking/progress period. Examples of surveys are provided in Chapter 5.

Figure 2.9 Sample Learner Responsibilities on Report Card

Learner Responsibilities

E = Excellent   **S** = Satisfactory
G = Good   **N** = Needs Improvement
   U = Unacceptable

	1st	2nd	3rd
Follows school and playground rules	N	S	N
Follows class rules	N	S	S
Follows directions/listens effectively	N	S	S
Demonstrates self-control	N	S	N
Works independently	N	S	S
Treats others with courtesy and respect	S	S	S
Demonstrates organizational skills	S	S	S
Starts and completes classwork on time	N	S	G
Completes homework on time	N	S	S

Figure 2.10 Samples of Work Skills and Study Habits Section of Report Card

a)

	PERSONAL BEHAVIOR	T1	T2	T3
SOCIAL AND EMOTIONAL	Establishes positive social relationships			
	Demonstrates appropriate behavior			
	Follows classroom rules			
	Follows daily classroom routines			
	Interacts cooperatively with adults and peers			
	Takes care of personal needs			
WORK HABITS	Works cooperatively in groups			
	Follows directions			
	Exhibits appropriate attention span			
	Works independently on classroom tasks			
	Completes activities in a reasonable time frame			
	Takes pride in work			

b)

INDIVIDUAL GROWTH AND WORK HABITS	Q1	Q2	Q3	Q4
Respects rights and property of others				
Asks for help if needed				
Shows self-control				
Takes care of school and personal materials				
Listens attentively				
Follows oral directions in the classroom and outside the classroom				
Begins and completes work on time				
Works well independently				
Works cooperatively in groups				
Communicates ideas and information in a group setting				

c)

CHARACTER DEVELOPMENT/LEARNING BEHAVIORS	☐ Satisfactory ✓ Area of Concern I Improving			
CHARACTER DEVELOPMENT	Q1	Q2	Q3	Q4
Demonstrates trustworthiness				
Demonstrates respect				
Demonstrates responsibility				
Demonstrates fairness				
Demonstrates caring behavior				
Demonstrates citizenship				
LEARNING BEHAVIORS				
Follows directions on assignments				
Completes assignments on time				
Completes homework on time				
Uses time wisely				
Cooperates in group activities				
Works independently				
Demonstrates organizational skills				
Comments:				

Rubrics and Norming

To gather and utilize meaningful data, teachers must be consistent when marking report cards in the areas of citizenship and work skills/study habits to ensure what they are measuring and what they represent. For example, without thoughtful rubrics to help facilitate the use of qualitative report card marks, one teacher may give many students an *N*, citing that every student needs improvement, while another teacher may give an *N* for a certain percentage of missing assignments. Consistency is important, and counselors will benefit from partnering with teachers to create rubrics to clarify what each of the ratings signifies.

School counselor Ashley knew the importance of using data to determine which students were in need of small groups from her graduate program training. Ashley decided to use report card data to identify the students who needed extra support in the social skills and work study habits areas. She concluded that all students with an *N* (*Needs Improvement*) mark on their report card would automatically qualify for a small group. To her surprise, after reviewing all of the report cards, Ashley counted *147 students* who qualified for her small group intervention using the criteria she had selected. Ashley knew that it would not be feasible to run enough small groups for that many students; however, she was stuck and unsure of how to choose which students were most in need of this Tier 2 intervention.

At the time, an *N* was the lowest-possible mark students could earn for Social Skills and Work Habits. Ashley wondered why such a large percentage (28%) of students were receiving *N*s in this area. Following the Response to Intervention (RTI) model, Ashley knew that approximately 15% of students should qualify for these extra supports. Ashley thought it would be helpful to disaggregate the data further. What she found was surprising and very interesting (see Figure 2.11).

Ashley's data, as represented in Figure 2.11, were helpful in many ways. First, she noticed there were outliers. As the reader may have already noticed, students with Teachers 18–22 received many more *N*s than students with the other teachers. In particular, one-third of the students with Teacher 18 received *N*s in every area: *Be Respectful, Be Responsible,* and *Be Safe.*

Figure 2.11   Number of *N*s per Teacher

Teacher	Be Respectful	Be Responsible	Be Safe
Teacher 1	0	0	0
Teacher 2	0	0	0
Teacher 3	0	0	1
Teacher 4	0	0	0
Teacher 5	2	0	3
Teacher 6	0	0	0
Teacher 7	1	3	0

Teacher	Be Respectful	Be Responsible	Be Safe
Teacher 8	0	0	0
Teacher 9	1	3	1
Teacher 10	1	4	0
Teacher 11	2	2	2
Teacher 12	0	3	0
Teacher 13	2	2	2
Teacher 14	3	7	3
Teacher 15	1	7	1
Teacher 16	1	2	0
Teacher 17	4	3	2
Teacher 18	9	9	12
Teacher 19	1	13	0
Teacher 20	2	8	0
Teacher 21	2	10	2
Teacher 22	3	8	0

What do you see when looking at the data? What stands out to you?

When data like these are presented, thoughtful inquiry is recommended. *Is this a student issue, a teacher issue, or a school issue?* Ashley shared the skewed data with her principal, and they agreed that it would be helpful to show the data at a staff meeting. Ashley presented the data spreadsheet to her staff and led a candid discussion about the discrepancies. Since Ashley did not use teacher names while showing staff the data, the teachers were able to objectively look at the data without feeling defensive, because no one in particular was being "called out." Teachers were asked to share what they saw from the data and what possible explanations they may have for the disproportionality in the marks. The teachers all agreed that one of the contributing factors to the variance was that each of them had a different definition of what constitutes an *N* on the report card. *Bingo!* Ashley and her administrator agreed with this theory, and since the idea came from the teachers, Ashley received far more buy-in to create a "norming process."

While collecting data is important, it is crucial that school counselors gather quality data. Just as teachers have rubrics for determining the academic grade a student will receive, so too should they have an objective way of measuring how behavior grades will be distributed. Ashley brought this dilemma to her elementary school counseling team, and together they developed a rubric to clearly outline the criteria needed to earn each of the grades on the Social Skills/Work Habits section of the report card.

(Continued)

(Continued)

School counselors must always collaborate with their school site before implementing something new. Therefore, after a draft of the rubric was created, Ashley sought feedback from her school site leadership team. This allowed administration and at least one teacher from each grade level to provide input and contribute to the rubric that they would be using. See Table 2.2 for the final product.

Table 2.2   Rubric for Norming Behavior Grades on Report Card

	Needs Improvement	Approaching Expectations	Meets Expectations	Outstanding
	Frequent assistance required, rarely, minimal, lacking (below 7/10)	Occasional assistance required, inconsistently (7/10)	Minimal assistance, sufficient, typically, usually (8/10)	No assistance required, extraordinary, mastery, independently, consistently (9/10+)
Growth Mindset				
Demonstrates effort, commitment, and perseverance	Rarely	Inconsistently	Usually	Consistently
Be Respectful				
Cooperates with others	Frequent assistance required (2 or more ODRs)	Occasional assistance required (1 ODR)	Minimal assistance required (no ODR)	No assistance required (no ODR)
Respects others' rights, feelings, and property	Frequent assistance required (2 or more ODRs)	Occasional assistance required (1 ODR)	Minimal assistance required (no ODR)	No assistance required (no ODR)
Solves problems appropriately	Frequent assistance required (2 or more ODRs)	Occasional assistance required (1 ODR)	Minimal assistance required (no ODR)	No assistance required (no ODR)
Shows concern for others	Frequent assistance required (2 or more ODRs)	Occasional assistance required (1 ODR)	Minimal assistance required (no ODR)	No assistance required (no ODR)
Fosters peer relationships	Frequent assistance required (2 or more ODRs)	Occasional assistance required (1 ODR)	Minimal assistance required (no ODR)	No assistance required (no ODR)

	Needs Improvement	Approaching Expectations	Meets Expectations	Outstanding
Be Responsible				
Organizes self and materials for learning	Frequent assistance required	Occasional assistance required	Minimal assistance required	No assistance required
Listens and follows directions	Frequent assistance required	Occasional assistance required	Minimal assistance required	No assistance required
Completes classwork consistently	Rarely (less than 70%)	Inconsistently (70–80%)	Usually (80–90%)	Consistently (90–100%)
Completes homework consistently	Rarely (less than 70%)	Inconsistently (70–80%)	Usually (80–90%)	Consistently (90–100%)
Be Safe				
Keeps all hands, feet, and other objects to oneself	Frequent assistance required (2 or more ODRs)	Occasional assistance required (1 ODR)	Minimal assistance required (no ODR)	No assistance required (no ODR)
Follows school and classroom rules	Frequent assistance required (2 or more ODRs)	Occasional assistance required (1 ODR)	Minimal assistance required (no ODR)	No assistance required (no ODR)
Uses materials appropriately	Frequent assistance required (2 or more ODRs)	Occasional assistance required (1 ODR)	Minimal assistance required (no ODR)	No assistance required (no ODR)

Note: 4 low-level referrals = 1 office discipline referral (ODR)

With any new procedure, other challenges can arise. After introducing this new document to staff, both Ashley and her principal began to notice an increase in office discipline referrals (ODRs). Any thoughts as to why that might have occurred? Upon discussing this trend with teachers, Ashley realized that many teachers gave more ODRs in order to justify why an *N* was being given. Ashley knew she had more work ahead of her!

Once again, Ashley brought this dilemma to her principal and then to the leadership team. Together, they decided that it may be helpful to also norm the criteria that should be met for a student to earn an ODR. After repeating the same process of gathering feedback from staff, a behavior flow chart was created to ensure that all teachers were following the same protocol when giving a student an ODR (see Figure 2.12).

(Continued)

(Continued)

Figure 2.12   Protocol for Office Discipline Referrals (ODRs)

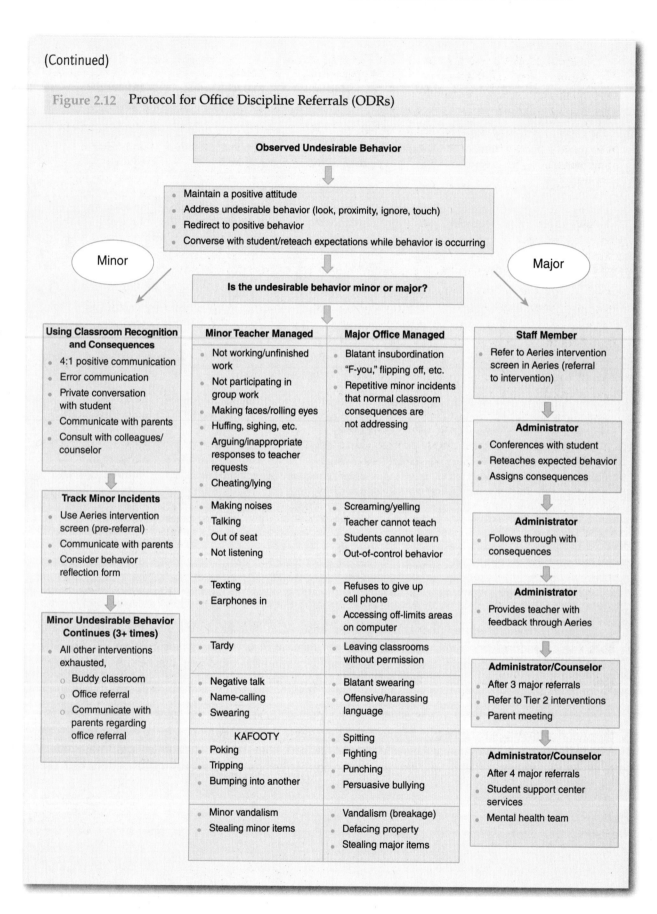

Observed Undesirable Behavior

- Maintain a positive attitude
- Address undesirable behavior (look, proximity, ignore, touch)
- Redirect to positive behavior
- Converse with student/reteach expectations while behavior is occurring

Minor

Major

Is the undesirable behavior minor or major?

Using Classroom Recognition and Consequences

- 4:1 positive communication
- Error communication
- Private conversation with student
- Communicate with parents
- Consult with colleagues/counselor

Track Minor Incidents

- Use Aeries intervention screen (pre-referral)
- Communicate with parents
- Consider behavior reflection form

Minor Undesirable Behavior Continues (3+ times)

- All other interventions exhausted,
  - Buddy classroom
  - Office referral
  - Communicate with parents regarding office referral

Minor Teacher Managed	Major Office Managed
Not working/unfinished work / Not participating in group work / Making faces/rolling eyes / Huffing, sighing, etc. / Arguing/inappropriate responses to teacher requests / Cheating/lying	Blatant insubordination / "F-you," flipping off, etc. / Repetitive minor incidents that normal classroom consequences are not addressing
Making noises / Talking / Out of seat / Not listening	Screaming/yelling / Teacher cannot teach / Students cannot learn / Out-of-control behavior
Texting / Earphones in	Refuses to give up cell phone / Accessing off-limits areas on computer
Tardy	Leaving classrooms without permission
Negative talk / Name-calling / Swearing	Blatant swearing / Offensive/harassing language
KAFOOTY / Poking / Tripping / Bumping into another	Spitting / Fighting / Punching / Persuasive bullying
Minor vandalism / Stealing minor items	Vandalism (breakage) / Defacing property / Stealing major items

Staff Member

- Refer to Aeries intervention screen in Aeries (referral to intervention)

Administrator

- Conferences with student
- Reteaches expected behavior
- Assigns consequences

Administrator

- Follows through with consequences

Administrator

- Provides teacher with feedback through Aeries

Administrator/Counselor

- After 3 major referrals
- Refer to Tier 2 interventions
- Parent meeting

Administrator/Counselor

- After 4 major referrals
- Student support center services
- Mental health team

Since putting these systems into place, Ashley has noticed a dramatic change in the number of *N*s given to students. In fact, about a year after implementing the rubric, Ashley found that the percentage of students qualifying for Tier 2 services was almost exactly the 15% recommended number of students receiving discipline referrals. Ashley is now able to provide support to the students who are most in need.

As Ashley learned, creating systems in a school is often very challenging and time-consuming; however, once systems are in place, school counselors will be able to collect quality data that truly reflect the needs of students.

Final Thoughts

Before a school counselor rushes into creating groups with the data, it is important to look at the big picture. Strategic thinking allows school counselors to look for trends and anomalies when analyzing data to determine which interventions are most needed or would result in the most improvement. They also seek to consult with others to determine if the data and interventions recommended are suitable for or align with the school's goals and objectives. Further, they are thoughtful about trends in the data and disaggregate it, looking for gaps. For example, when looking at study skills, the school counselor noticed a predominance of *organization referrals* in the fourth grade, which led her to believe that students may benefit more from a classroom lesson or two on organizational skills, rather than pulling more than half the class out into small groups. Using data for interventions can validate or call for a revision of core curriculum lessons.

3

Determining the Appropriate Tier 2 Interventions

Once data have been collected to identify students in need of Tier 2 services (see Chapter 2), it is time to dive into the process of selecting the most appropriate Tier 2 interventions based on student need. Although this text focuses heavily on how to design, implement, and evaluate small groups, it is important to note that there are many Tier 2 interventions school counselors can utilize. While small groups are impactful for certain students, at times, other interventions may be more efficient and effective.

This chapter outlines a variety of Tier 2 services that can be implemented for students who qualify based on pre-identified criteria. The interventions are broken down by direct services and indirect services. Both direct and indirect Tier 2 services are often used to ensure the interventions provided meet the students' needs. Throughout this chapter, the authors describe common interventions and then discuss the benefits and challenges of each. Examples of how to successfully incorporate interventions into a comprehensive school counseling program are also provided.

DIRECT TIER 2 SERVICES

According to the American School Counselor Association (ASCA, 2019a), *direct services* are "in-person interactions between school counselors and students" (p. 77). Although the ASCA National Model does not classify direct services by tiers, this chapter covers some of the more commonly practiced direct Tier 2 services such as

- individual counseling,
- small group counseling,

- large group workshops,
- post-discipline/-suspension counseling,
- restorative justice meetings/conflict mediations, and
- Check In Check Out (CICO).

Individual Counseling

Individual counseling as a Tier 2 support is *short term* and *solution focused*. In Tier 2, individual counseling is designed for students experiencing difficulty with academics, social/emotional issues, or personal relationships. School counselors meet with identified students individually a *few* times (from one to three times or so) to support them in identifying and resolving social/emotional problems and/or providing instruction on skills to remove barriers to academic success. For many students, a few individual solution-focused meetings may be enough to help resolve the issue. For example, a school counselor identifies a student struggling with attendance. By meeting individually with the student once or twice, the school counselor may be able to determine that the barrier the student is facing in not getting to school on time is something that can be easily solved (waking up late each morning because the student does not have an alarm clock; the school counselor can support the student in getting an alarm clock to quickly resolve the issue). If the issue is not solved immediately, the individual meetings can assist the school counselor in determining the most appropriate Tier 2 intervention for the student going forward (small group, large group, conflict mediation, referral to resources in or outside the school building, etc.). If it is determined that a student is not an appropriate fit for small group counseling due to behaviors or other extenuating circumstances, then individual counseling for a longer period (6 to 8 weeks) may be considered as a Tier 3 support (see Chapter 9, "Tier 3 Intensive Interventions"). In keeping with the ASCA Ethical Standards (2016a), counselors are reminded that individual counseling lessons should be short term and non-therapeutic.

Small Group Counseling

Small group counseling is a Tier 2 intervention school counselors utilize when several students are experiencing challenges that call for a similar type of intervention. Rather than meeting with each student individually, school counselors can meet with students in small groups, typically four to eight students (depending on developmental level), to provide instruction and support with academic, social/emotional, and/or attendance issues. Using a small group format allows school counselors to use their time more efficiently by seeing multiple students at once. Small groups target an *identified need* as determined by data, and curriculum is either selected (pre-packaged or evidence based) or developed (school counselor generated) to address that particular need. With a structured small group curriculum, school counselors can create meaningful assessments (i.e., progress monitoring, pre-/post-assessments) to evaluate the effectiveness of the intervention. Because implementing small groups often requires students to miss instructional time, every effort must be made to ensure teacher and administrator support. As an intentional intervention, curriculum selection and development may initially be time-consuming for the school counselor. However, once the curriculum is delivered and deemed effective, it can be utilized over and over. We will discuss several evidence-based resources in Chapter 6, "Selecting and Developing Small Group Curriculum," that can help school counselors in creating a meaningful and effective small group curriculum.

Large Group Workshops

When school counselors notice a large number of students experiencing a similar issue, a large group instructional workshop intervention may be more appropriate. This Tier 2 service can meet the needs of many students (approximately 8–20) at one time. These workshops are typically presented to upper-grade students for 30–45 minutes over a period of one or two days. Students are invited to learn about a specific topic (similar to core curriculum) with the intent that the knowledge and skills gained will support them to overcome a particular barrier.

After reviewing her data, Danielle, a K–8 school counselor, noticed a consistent trend. At each grading period, she found that about 100 of her school's eighth-grade students were on track to earn below the expected 2.0 grade point average (GPA). Wanting to be more proactive and fine-tune her group counseling invitation process, she decided to facilitate an intervention, prior to the end of the grading period. The goal was to reach out to the students before the end of the grading period to decrease the number who earned below a 2.0 GPA, which would in turn decrease the number of students who would require a Tier 2 intervention, such as small group. With the feedback of a diverse handful of her eighth-grade students, Danielle carefully planned and implemented the short-term large group workshop, which she called "Tiger Talk," based on the school mascot. Below is a list of steps that Danielle followed to implement Tiger Talk:

- Query all the eighth graders' GPAs prior to the end of the grading period.
- Coordinate the use of a computer lab workshop space.
- Create schoolwide signage and distribute flyers to invite students seeking to improve their GPA to include
  - using the flyer as a front-of-the-line lunch pass incentive to attend;
  - the ability to invite a friend;
  - the ability to earn a reinforcement for simply attending the information session; and
  - advertisement of the benefits of attending the workshop (e.g., earn a pizza party and an improved GPA).
- Design the lunch workshop lesson plan to include
  - reminder of the role of a school counselor;
  - discussion of the importance of grades and helpful study skills;
  - explanation of the two-week GPA competition that would be based on a group effort and number of times the students reported practicing a study skill for the time prior to the end of the grading period;
  - practice of reviewing grades, missing assignments, and test retakes;
  - reinforcement of the students immediately practicing the study skill of reviewing grades online by allowing them to add a point to their competition chart at the workshop;
  - distribution of parent letter of student involvement; and
  - explanation of counselor–teacher communication for reinforcement of student involvement.
- Follow up on any GPA improvements of participants at the end of the grading period.
- Coordinate and implement the celebration party for the group winners to include evaluation and feedback to improve the large group workshop intervention.

While a large group workshop intervention is time efficient and can be quite effective, some school counselors may find the outcomes less robust than a more focused and structured small group format. It is crucial that school counselors incorporate a follow-up plan to assess which students showed improvement and which students may need additional, more intensive support (such as a small group).

Post-Discipline/-Suspension Counseling

Post-discipline/-suspension counseling describes a meeting that is held between a school counselor and a student upon a student's return to school from a discipline/suspension incident. This meeting allows such students to express their feelings and to feel heard while debriefing the problem situation, and provides time for brainstorming ideas on how to make more positive decisions in the future. This is also an opportunity for school counselors to re-teach expected behaviors and build a stronger relationship with students. Post-discipline/-suspension counseling aligns with restorative practices (described in the next section) and allows for a solution-focused approach. By waiting to meet with students until after they return to school, the school counselor has the opportunity to support them when they are most likely less emotional and more rational. Post-discipline/-suspension counseling requires strong communication between the school counselor and the administrator, and it is recommended that a system be put into place where the school counselor is always notified when a student receives a suspension so that consistent follow-up can occur. Post-discipline/-suspension meetings can be held during the school counselor's "protected meeting time," explained in the "Helpful Tip" box (see page 54). In this way, school counselors already have time in their schedule to meet with the student, and they will not have to interrupt pre-planned activities. Figure 3.1 provides an example of what a post-discipline/-suspension meeting might look like. Since the goal of the post-suspension meeting is to re-engage students back into the school upon return, a more positive way to describe it is as a "re-engagement meeting."

Restorative Justice Meetings/Conflict Mediation

Restorative justice practices are used as an alternative to exclusionary discipline practices (i.e., suspension and expulsion) and focus on positive relationships and *restoring* those relationships when harm occurs (González, 2012; Gregory, Clawson, Davis, & Gerewitz, 2016). Restorative justice meetings and conflict mediations allow both the person who was harmed and the person who harmed to discuss their perspective of the problem situation and express their feelings associated with the harm that was done. Ultimately, the goal is to find a solution as to how the person who caused the harm can *restore* the relationship with the person who was harmed. These meetings allow for an immediate intervention and can provide students with the ability to utilize proactive, problem-solving skills. Restorative justice meetings can be very beneficial in improving school climate, and school counselors who have a very busy schedule can utilize the "protected meeting time" (see "Helpful Tip" on p. 54) to proactively utilize this intervention.

Figure 3.1   Re-Engagement Meeting (Post-Suspension)

Re-Engagement Meeting

Student Name: _____

Meeting Date: _____

The overall goal of this meeting is to develop a plan to support you in being successful academically and socially after returning to school from a suspension.

Goals of the meeting:

- Promote school safety (yours and others).
- Ensure the student's behavior is not repeated.
- Assist the student in feeling supported.
- Rebuild the connection between the student and those who may have been harmed.
- Develop an action plan for making positive choices.

Questions to ask:

1. What happened, and how do you feel?
2. What is the school's (or person's) perspective on what happened?
3. Looking back, what could you have done differently?
4. What can you do now to help make amends (correct any damage caused)?
5. How can I assist you as you return to campus today?
6. Is there something that I or the school staff can do to support your academic and social success?
7. What steps are you committed to as you leave this meeting to ensure this doesn't happen again?

Student commitment:

_____

School counselor commitment:

_____

Student Signature: _____ Date: _____

School Counselor Signature: _____ Date: _____

> **Helpful Tip**
>
> **Scheduling "Protected Meeting Time"**
>
> School counselors have very busy schedules, and it is important that time be carved out each day to respond to Tier 2 services (targeted parent meetings, conflict resolutions, post-suspension/-discipline meetings, targeted parent workshops, etc.). Rather than rearranging pre-planned activities to address incidents as they arise, scheduling a 30-minute to one-hour chunk of time each morning may be beneficial.

ACTIVITY 3.1

Do you currently have "protected meeting time" for responding to Tier 2 needs? If not, discuss it with your administrator. How might this system benefit students? What, if any, potential challenges will need to be addressed in order to effectively implement such a system?

Check In Check Out (CICO)

Check In Check Out (CICO; Crone et al., 2010) is a Tier 2, evidence-based program designed for students who exhibit problem behaviors and have not been responsive to Tier 1 supports. Research has shown CICO to be most effective for "students whose behavior is maintained by adult attention rather than students whose behavior is maintained by peer attention or avoidance of academic tasks" (Campbell & Anderson, 2011, p. 316). CICO was initially created to serve as a group intervention, but is often implemented by school counselors and other school staff in many different ways. Some school counselors group students together based on behavioral data, which may indicate a student in need of more frequent and positive feedback by adults (as shown by office discipline referrals and/or report card citizenship data). Once students are selected, they are given a brief overview of the CICO program. Each student receives an individual "point card" that outlines the schoolwide expectations, such as *Be Safe, Be Responsible*, and *Be Respectful*. All students in the group check in with a trusted adult for 5 to 10 minutes (this may be the school counselor or another trusted adult) either daily (at the beginning of the day and at the end of the day) or weekly (at the beginning of the week and at the end of the week).

CICO is a comprehensive program that encompasses many components. Figure 3.2 is an example of a CICO tracking form that lists the schoolwide expectations. This form would be most appropriate to use with multiple students in a group setting who are all working toward meeting schoolwide expectations.

Figure 3.2   General Check In Check Out (CICO)

Student: _____

Teacher: _____

Check In Adult: _____

Today's Date: _____/_____/_____

Check In Check Out

Parent Signature:

_____

Points Possible: _____

Points Received: _____

% of Points: _____

Goal Met (Y/N): _____

Schoolwide Expectations	CHECK IN	English Language Arts	Math	Recess	Computer Lab	Math Rotations	STEM	CHECK OUT	Total
Be Respectful	2 1 0	2 1 0	2 1 0	2 1 0	2 1 0	2 1 0	2 1 0	2 1 0	
Be Responsible	2 1 0	2 1 0	2 1 0	2 1 0	2 1 0	2 1 0	2 1 0	2 1 0	
Be Safe	2 1 0	2 1 0	2 1 0	2 1 0	2 1 0	2 1 0	2 1 0	2 1 0	

2 = Usually demonstrated skill   1 = Sometimes demonstrated skill   0 = Rarely demonstrated skill

Daily:

- When your child meets targeted goals, acknowledge your child's efforts for doing well in school.
- When your child does not meet targeted goals, refrain from further punishment. Your child will have another opportunity tomorrow to meet these goals.

Weekly:

- When possible, set up a special treat, a special activity, or extra privileges when your child has used the CICO home report to keep you informed on progress.

If I earn my goal of _____ points, my reward will be:

_____

One thing I did well was:

_____

One thing I am going to work on is:

_____

Source: Created by Felipe Zañartu, 2019.

Figure 3.3 Skill-Based Check In Check Out (CICO)

Student: _____

Teacher: _____

Check In Adult: _____

Today's Date: _____/_____/_____

Check In Check Out

Parent Signature:

_____

Points Possible: _____

Points Received: _____

% of Points: _____

Goal Met (Y/N): _____

Skill-Based Expectations	CHECK IN	English Language Arts	Math	Recess	Computer Lab	Math Rotations	STEM	CHECK OUT	Total
Raise hand when I have something to say	2 1 0	2 1 0	2 1 0	2 1 0	2 1 0	2 1 0	2 1 0	2 1 0	
Wait until my teacher calls on me to speak	2 1 0	2 1 0	2 1 0	2 1 0	2 1 0	2 1 0	2 1 0	2 1 0	
Stay in my seat	2 1 0	2 1 0	2 1 0	2 1 0	2 1 0	2 1 0	2 1 0	2 1 0	

2 = Usually demonstrated skill   1 = Sometimes demonstrated skill   0 = Rarely demonstrated skill

Daily:

- When your child meets targeted goals, acknowledge your child's efforts for doing well in school.

- When your child does not meet targeted goals, refrain from further punishment. Your child will have another opportunity tomorrow to meet these goals.

Weekly:

- When possible, set up a special treat, a special activity, or extra privileges when your child has used the CICO home report to keep you informed on progress.

If I earn my goal of _____ points, my reward will be:

_____

One thing I did well was:

_____

One thing I am going to work on is:

_____

Source: Created by Felipe Zañartu, 2019.

In addition to supporting students in a group setting, CICO can serve as a more individualized intervention in which students receive a point card based on their specific/identified challenges. A point card for a student who has individualized goals is shown in Figure 3.3. Notice the goals on the left-hand side are created based on specific challenges the student may be facing.

Regardless of the manner in which the intervention is implemented, students participating in a CICO program have the opportunity to earn various reinforcements at the end of the day or week if their goals are met. According to Everett, Sugai, Fallon, Simonsen, and O'Keefe (2010), there are several benefits to the CICO program, which include

- increased positive adult contact,
- embedded social skills training,
- direct link to schoolwide behavioral goals and expectations,
- frequent feedback,
- daily home–school communication, and
- positive reinforcement contingent on meeting behavioral goals.

It is important to note that school counselors are not the only school staff who can implement CICO. Teachers, deans, librarians, security staff, and in fact any staff member can support students in this Tier 2 intervention. Indeed, the intervention may be most effective when implemented by an adult with which the student already has a relationship.

Table 3.1 provides a chart describing the benefits and challenges of common Tier 2 direct interventions.

INDIRECT TIER 2 SERVICES

Indirect services are those provided on behalf of students. School counselors can utilize indirect Tier 2 services either in conjunction with direct Tier 2 services (as previously described) or as a primary Tier 2 intervention, if it is deemed to be appropriate. The next section describes a variety of indirect Tier 2 services such as

- consultation/collaboration,
- teacher and student support in the classroom,
- teacher education,
- targeted family support and education,
- referral to in-school resources, and
- referral to outside resources.

Table 3.2 provides a chart describing the benefits and challenges of indirect Tier 2 services. The authors acknowledge that some of these are subsets of consultation and collaboration; however, they are important enough to discuss separately.

Table 3.1 Direct Tier 2 Interventions

DIRECT Tier 2 Intervention	Description	Benefits	Challenges/Considerations	Example
Individual Counseling	• Short-term, solution-focused counseling • 1–3 sessions	• A few individual meetings may make a difference; efficient • Good for student who does not work well in a group • Helpful in determining which of the following interventions would be most appropriate	• Keeping it short term and non-therapeutic	• Student is having a problem with attendance, and school counselor can check in and provide a solution • Student experiences a crisis and needs minimal individual support (1–3 sessions)
Small Group	• 6–8 group counseling lessons with 4–8 students needing support in a similar area	• Time efficient • Curriculum can be designed to directly address the data-driven need • Structure allows for more meaningful evaluation • Students can learn from one another	• More time out of class • Scheduling • Curriculum development • Progress monitoring • Assessment development	• School counselor meets with several students to address common topics (e.g., emotion management study skills, organization, self-regulation, social skills)
Large Group (workshop)	• Grouping of many students (8–20) having a similar issue to receive short-term intervention	• Time efficient • Services many students at once • Less time out of class	• May not meet individual student needs • May not have as robust of an impact as a smaller, more structured group	• < 2.0 GPA workshop (see example on page 51)

DIRECT Tier 2 Intervention	Description	Benefits	Challenges/Considerations	Example
Post-Discipline/-Suspension Counseling	• Meeting with students after returning to school due to discipline/suspension	• Opportunity to debrief and develop a future plan • Solution focused • Aligns with restorative practices	• Scheduling • Communication with administrator	• Student is suspended by principal, and school counselor meets with student upon return to school to discuss how student can handle a similar situation in the future (see "Post-Discipline/-Suspension" section of this chapter for an example)
Restorative Justice Meetings/Conflict Mediations	• Meeting with one or more students involved in a conflict	• Immediate intervention • Restorative • Solution focused	• Reactive • May interrupt counselors' calendar • Requires scheduling	• Student fills out "request to see the counselor" form and indicates that she has tried to solve a problem with another student, but needs support • Student meets with another student or staff member to discuss how the student has been hurt and how the hurt can be mended
Check In Check Out (CICO)	• Checking in on a regular basis with a student or group of students to monitor their progress	• Individualized support to meet students' needs • Collaborative	• Time out of class • Sometimes long term • Time-consuming if not shared by school staff	• Counselor or other school staff member meets with student individually or in a group on a daily or weekly basis to review expectations, set goals, and monitor progress

Table 3.2 Indirect Tier 2 Interventions

INDIRECT Tier 2 Intervention	Description	Benefits	Challenges/Considerations	Example
Consultation/ Collaboration	• Consultation: Meeting to seek or give information or advice on student needs • Collaborating, working with parents, teachers, and other staff to achieve a common goal	• 1–3 consultation meetings may resolve the problem • Gather information and deliver appropriate intervention and appropriate service provider	• Coordinating and scheduling meetings • Following up in a timely manner	• Providing teachers/parents with strategies for addressing problematic behaviors in the classroom
Teacher and Student Support in the Classroom	• Providing teachers with tools to address problematic behaviors for a particular student in the classroom	• Student is not removed from classroom • Teacher feels supported and gains skills through successful intervention	• Requires strong relationship with teachers • Time • Administrative support is needed	• A student is exhibiting concerning behaviors in the classroom, and rather than pulling the student out of class to teach the student skills, the school counselor meets with the student and teacher to develop tools that can be incorporated within the classroom
Teacher Education	• Providing teacher instruction	• In classrooms where the data are skewed (e.g., a teacher who has 3 times the amount of Ns as compared to other teachers or a teacher who has a skewed number of classroom management issues)	• Requires after-hours commitment	• School counselor meets with teachers to provide them with information to improve their understanding of support in the classroom (e.g., function of behavior, classroom management strategies, conflict resolution)

INDIRECT Tier 2 Intervention	Description	Benefits	Challenges/Considerations	Example
Targeted Parent/ Guardian Support and Education	• Meeting (individual or small group), workshop, or parent classes	• Developmentally appropriate for younger students • Home–school engagement • Provides parental education in areas of need (e.g., study skills and attendance)	• Time • Often requires after-hours commitment • Parental attendance • Adult curriculum and engagement strategies	• School counselor provides workshops/classes on topics to support parents/ guardians in working with their students (e.g., behavior management at home, how to help your child study, state test preparation, college and career readiness)
Referral to In-School Resources	• Ensuring student is receiving appropriate intervention from appropriate student service provider (e.g., social worker, psychologist)	• Targeted identified need is addressed to appropriate service provider	• Requires student resources on campus	• School counselor collaborates with other stakeholders to determine which professionals in the school can best support student's need (e.g., referral to social worker, academic interventionist, or school psychologist)
Referral to Outside Resources	• Connects student with appropriate resources outside of the school	• Targeted identified need is addressed by appropriate service provider	• Requires parent commitment and resources	• If a student is experiencing issues such as homelessness, for example, the school counselor can connect the family with community resources

Consultation/Collaboration

According to the ASCA Ethical Standards (2016a) glossary, *consultation* is "a professional relationship in which individuals meet to seek advice, information and/or deliberation to address a student's need." School counselors are acting proactively and ethically when they consult with many stakeholders both within and outside the school building to provide optimum services to students. Key stakeholders include, but are not limited to

- teachers,
- administrators,
- parents/guardians,
- school psychologists,
- school social workers,
- special education case carriers,
- nursing staff,
- classified employees (attendance clerk, librarian, custodian, etc.),
- program coordinator(s) (Advancement Via Individual Determination [AVID], after-school programs, etc.),
- community agencies,
- university interns,
- academic coaches,
- therapists and other mental health providers, and
- doctors or physician assistants.

Consultation allows school counselors to gain multiple perspectives when determining the appropriate intervention and service provider to best meet the student's needs. Some stakeholders require a memorandum of understanding (MOU) and/or a release of information (ROI). An MOU is an agreement between two or more parties to establish a formal partnership. It may be documented and shared with both/all stakeholders. Although not a legal document, it is an agreement upheld with mutual understanding regarding the work being completed and oftentimes the approval of communication by the parent/guardian of the student (Rouse, 2018). There may also be instances where an ROI document signed by the collaborating parties will be helpful communication to benefit the student. The ROI is also a formal document provided to the collaborating parties allowing information to be shared. It is advised that school counselors check with an administrator or district office personnel, as an established form may already be in place for use. It may be challenging to coordinate and schedule times to meet with both on-site and off-site stakeholders. The use of MOUs/ROIs is highly recommended to help with these scheduling barriers. For example, holding a regularly scheduled support service meeting (which may include the school psychologist, the administrator(s), the occupational therapist, the speech therapist, the resource/intervention teacher, the school social worker, and other on-site stakeholders) once a month provides a forum for both on- and off-site providers to discuss student concerns and ensure decisions are made in a collaborative manner.

Teacher and Student Support in the Classroom

Teachers often look to school counselors for support in addressing student behavior problems in the classroom. While some counselors may have extensive experience as teachers or specialized training in behavior and classroom management, others may have very little. An important component of a school counselor's job is consultation and collaboration with school staff as a means of improving student outcomes. Therefore, it is recommended that school counselors become well versed in classroom and behavior management. Once they have the knowledge and skills necessary to support teachers with behavioral challenges in the classroom, school counselors can provide assistance to both the teacher and the student(s) inside of a classroom.

While small group and individual interventions are often beneficial, working within the classroom environment can also support both the teacher and the students in many ways:

1. The student does not lose instructional time.

2. The student can practice pro-social skills within the problem environment (where the negative behavior is occurring). This is extremely important, as students may often experience difficulty applying skills taught outside of the classroom (in the school counselor's office during small groups) to the problem environment.

3. The teacher feels supported and can gain skills through the school counselor's modeling of appropriate behavior management/modification.

School counselor Kate was excited to begin her new round of small group counseling lessons for the 2017 school year. Kate had collected behavior data by analyzing office discipline referrals and querying students who had received two or more *Ns* (*Needs Improvement*) in the Work Habits/Social Skills section of the report card. She then met with her grade-level teams to discuss students who met the minimum criteria to qualify for Tier 2 services. The team collaborated to determine which students would be an appropriate fit for small group counseling services. Kate screened group members, carefully developed appropriate curriculum, and created meaningful assessment tools. At the end of the small group lessons, Kate looked at the outcome data for all students who had received a small group counseling intervention. Kate noticed a pattern—students in third through fifth grades showed significant improvement in their behaviors in the classroom (as indicated by a decrease in office discipline referrals and a decrease in *Ns* on the quarterly report card); however, students in kindergarten, first grade, and second grade showed minimal progress.

When Kate met with the grade-level teams to discuss these results, she learned that the teachers believed students were having a difficult time applying the knowledge and skills they learned during the small group counseling lessons held in Kate's office to the

(Continued)

(Continued)

classroom. In order to determine if there was merit to this hypothesis, Kate shifted the Tier 2 services for students in kindergarten, first grade, and second grade during the next quarter and adopted a push-in model instead. Each week, instead of pulling students out of class for Tier 2 support, Kate would schedule a time with the teacher (based on when the problem behaviors were most likely to occur) and would support the students *inside* of the classroom as the behaviors appeared. In this way, students gained a better understanding of how to *apply* the skills they had previously learned in the appropriate environment. Throughout the intervention, Kate monitored the students' progress informally by checking in with teachers. After the eight-week intervention was complete, Kate reviewed office discipline referrals and the quarterly report and noticed a greater improvement with this intervention as compared to the previous small group counseling intervention. Teachers also self-reported that observing Kate integrate skill development in the midst of the problem behavior allowed them to gain new skills they could incorporate in the classroom on a regular basis.

The Tier 2 approach of supporting teachers in the classroom requires the school counselor to have strong, positive relationships and high levels of credibility with teachers and administrators. It is vital teachers feel confident that the school counselor providing support is well trained and has a strong understanding of behavior and classroom management. School counselors who feel less confident in this area are encouraged to seek professional development to improve their classroom support skills.

Teacher Education

School counselor John had the opportunity to attend the national Positive Behavioral Interventions and Supports (PBIS) conference with his principal in 2016. The theme of the conference was "PBIS in the Classroom." During the conference, the keynote speaker discussed the notion that the majority of teachers receive little or no training on classroom management, behavior modification, trauma, or child development (Barbetta, Norona, & Bicard, 2005). This was the first time John had heard this information, and he was quite surprised. In fact, John had always assumed that teachers receive extensive training in these areas, as they are crucial components to a teacher's work with students. With this new knowledge, John decided to research best practices in supporting students with behavioral challenges in the classroom. John read books like *Positive Discipline in the Classroom* (Nelsen, Lott, & Glenn, 2013), *Preventing Challenging Behavior in Your Classroom* (Tincani, 2011), and *The Trauma-Informed School* (Sporleder & Forbes, 2016). John also attended several professional development conferences to learn more about the use of PBIS in the classroom. With a better understanding of how to implement best practices in the classroom to improve behaviors, John felt more equipped to support the teachers at his school when challenges in the classroom arose.

The ultimate goal of a school counseling program is to remove individual and systemic barriers to learning in order to improve student outcomes. School counselors often provide students with direct service to accomplish this task; however, indirect services, such as teacher education, help to create a positive school culture and increase student engagement. Section B.2 of the ASCA Ethical Standards (2016a) states that "school counselors: . . .

1. Provide leadership to create systemic change to enhance the school.

2. Collaborate with appropriate officials to remove barriers that may impede the effectiveness of the school or the school counseling program.

3. Provide support, consultation and mentoring to professionals in need of assistance when in the scope of the school counselor's role."

School counselors may witness inequities in the school, which may occur due to a lack of staff training. While teachers often receive opportunities for in-service in curriculum development and implementation, they may not be trained in areas such as creating a safe and supportive school climate. As leaders within the school, counselors can provide teachers and classified staff with professional development in areas such as PBIS, trauma-informed practice, behavior modification, classroom management, and student engagement strategies. Again, school counselors must have strong knowledge of these topics before offering professional development opportunities.

Ideally, teacher education is scheduled on a regular basis as part of the regular workday. For example, school counselor Kathie provides 20 minutes of teacher education at monthly staff meetings. Kathie also offers more thorough trainings during teacher professional development days (when students are not present). Unfortunately, not all school counselors state confidence in collaborating with their administrator to incorporate teacher education trainings into regularly scheduled school hours/days. Therefore, school counselors are encouraged to offer after-school or lunchtime workshops to teachers. The challenge with workshops outside of the teacher's daily schedule is that it will be voluntary, not mandatory. Therefore, incentives may be helpful in increasing teacher attendance. Strong, well-received presentations will lead to improved interest.

While it is recommended that school counselors provide *all* teachers with trainings to support school climate and student engagement, inviting individual teachers to participate in training based off of data may be more appropriate in some cases. For example, in Chapter 2, Ashley shared the following data collected from the spring 2017 report card. Figure 3.4 represents the *number* of Ns (*Needs Improvement*) given to students for each category: *Be Respectful*, *Be Responsible*, and *Be Safe*.

Figure 3.4 Sample Report Card: Number of *N*s per Teacher

Teacher	Be Respectful	Be Responsible	Be Safe
Teacher 1	0	0	0
Teacher 2	0	0	0
Teacher 3	0	0	1
Teacher 4	0	0	0
Teacher 5	2	0	3
Teacher 6	0	0	0
Teacher 7	1	3	0
Teacher 8	0	0	0
Teacher 9	1	3	1
Teacher 10	1	4	0
Teacher 11	2	2	2
Teacher 12	0	3	0
Teacher 13	2	2	2
Teacher 14	3	7	3
Teacher 15	1	7	1
Teacher 16	1	2	0
Teacher 17	4	3	2
Teacher 18	9	9	12
Teacher 19	1	13	0
Teacher 20	2	8	0
Teacher 21	2	10	2
Teacher 22	3	8	0

While analyzing data, school counselors may notice outliers. As indicated in the Multi-Tiered, Multi-Domain System of Supports (MTMDSS) model, approximately 15–20% of students qualify for Tier 2 services. Consider Teacher 18 in Figure 3.4. Notice that 12 out of 30 students received an *N* in the *Be Safe* expectation. This indicates that 40% of Teacher 18's students are being unsafe in the classroom and could benefit from a Tier 2 intervention. In a case like this, it is important for the school counselor to consider whether counseling is needed for the individual students or if it may be more beneficial to support the teacher in developing more consistent and structured expectations in the class.

The data in Figure 3.4 also suggest that students in the classes of Teachers 18–22 are struggling in the area of *Be Responsible*. Rather than grouping all of the students who received an *N* together and providing them with a small group intervention focused on being responsible, it may be helpful to provide a targeted classroom lesson to the whole class. School counselors must be critical consumers of data. In other words, while data can help school counselors identify individual students in need of support, data can also assist school counselors in identifying specific teachers and/or classrooms who may benefit from additional assistance.

Targeted Parent/Guardian Support and Education

School counselors can support students indirectly by providing parent/guardian education. While Tier 1 parent/guardian education includes providing parent workshops/classes to *all* parents/guardians, Tier 2 parent education is targeted for parents of students who have been identified as needing additional support. Parent support and education allows school counselors to create a link between the home and the school. In this way, skills and knowledge taught at school can be practiced and reinforced in the home environment.

At the elementary level, attendance is one piece of data that suggests that family intervention may be beneficial. Students with poor attendance may be missing school for reasons outside of their control. Therefore, providing an attendance intervention for these students may not be effective, especially for students in primary grades. Facilitating family education for the parents/guardians of students who are chronically absent may have a greater impact on students attending school regularly. In addition to providing parent education, school counselors can collaborate with families to remove any barriers that may be making it difficult to get their child to school every day.

Parent support and education can be beneficial to families in many ways. Sometimes, parent attendance and finding a convenient time for families can be challenging. School counselors can consider offering child care, food, and/or prizes as an incentive to increase attendance. Also, as a reminder that these are adult learners, counselors are encouraged to create trainings that are developmentally appropriate for adults and that include a variety of engagement strategies. It may be helpful for school counselors to collaborate with other support staff as they develop meaningful and engaging content.

Referral to In-School Resources

School counselors have extensive training in improving student outcomes and can offer meaningful support for students; however, it is critical that school counselors also work *within* the educational system and utilize the expertise of other student service providers. When school counselors take on roles beyond their legal or ethical scope, they take personal and professional risks. It also impacts the time to focus on their role in *counseling* students. When determining the most appropriate Tier 2 intervention for a student, school counselors identify service providers and other in-school resources that will best meet the student's needs.

> After querying the quarterly report card, school counselor Ricardo recognized that a fourth-grade student, Maya, received two *N*s in the citizenship section of her report card. After meeting with the grade-level team and holding an individual conference with Maya, Ricardo determined that Maya was truly struggling with understanding the math curriculum, which was why she was not completing classwork or homework. While Ricardo felt confident in his math abilities and was certain that he could support Maya in understanding these concepts, Ricardo knew that this would not be the best use of his time or expertise. Ricardo consulted with his administrator and the intervention teacher to learn more about possible math supports on campus that could help Maya. The team decided that holding a student intervention meeting and offering an intensive math program, provided by the intervention teacher, would be in Maya's best interest.

Utilizing a team approach to determine the most appropriate service provider for a particular student need is necessary to ensure that school counselors are spending their time efficiently. Collaborating and consulting on a regular basis with the various service providers at a site will allow the school counselor to gain a better understanding of how to appropriately triage different interventions based on student need. Other providers may include, but are not limited to, school social workers, school psychologists, and academic intervention teachers. The challenge arises when limited resources/service providers are available and the school counselor is one of the only student support providers. In these cases, school counselors may need to utilize outside resources more frequently.

Referral to Outside Resources

Referrals to outside resources as a Tier 2 intervention will look very different from state to state, district to district, and even site to site based on the available resources on campus and within the community. When the need of the student and/or family is outside of the school counselor or other school staff's expertise, it is the school counselor's ethical responsibility, as outlined in A.6 of the ASCA Ethical Standards (2016a), to connect the student and/or family with a list of possible community/local resources to address the student's need. For example, parents may meet with the school counselor and disclose that they are homeless and unable to meet the student's basic needs (food, clothing, shelter, etc.). Empathically supporting homeless families is within the role of the school counselor; however, a targeted intervention in this area is best provided by making a referral to an outside agency specializing in supporting homeless families. Alternatively, consider a student who is demonstrating a significant change in behavior. More specifically, this student begins exhibiting attention-seeking behavior from all of the adults in the school. After an individual meeting with the student and a conversation with the student's father, the school counselor becomes aware that the father is recently a single parent, working several jobs, and the student is often home alone. The school counselor in this situation may want to consider connecting this student with a community program such as Big Brothers Big Sisters, which connects children with an adult role model. By providing this community resource to the student, the school counselor may find that the behaviors subside. Chapter 10 will discuss how referrals to outside resources are used as a Tier 3 intervention as well.

TIER 2 SERVICES BASED ON A DEMOGRAPHIC INDICATOR

In recent years, there has been a great deal of discussion about the difference between two very important terms: *equity* and *equality*. *Merriam-Webster* defines *equality* as "the quality or state of being *equal*," which is defined as "of the same measure, quantity, amount, or number as another" (Equality, 2019). In education, students are considered to be treated "equally" if they are all provided with the same resources and tools (Coleman, 1966). Conversely, equity recognizes that students come from different backgrounds and have been given varying levels of resources and opportunities from birth, which impacts the place in which they begin their education. Equity focuses on giving students what they need to be successful, which may not always be equal for all students.

Research indicates certain student groups perform at lower rates and are traditionally more marginalized than others.

The "achievement gap" in education refers to the disparity in academic performance between groups of students. It is most often used to describe the troubling performance gaps between African-American and Hispanic students, at the lower end of the performance scale, and their non-Hispanic white peers, and the similar academic disparity between students from low-income families and those who are better off. In the past decade, though, scholars and policymakers have begun to focus increasing attention on other achievement gaps, such as those based on sex, English-language proficiency and learning disabilities. The achievement gap shows up in student grades, standardized-test scores, course selection, dropout rates, high school graduation rates and college enrollment/completion rates, among other success measures. (Musu-Gillette et al., 2017)

When an achievement gap exists, it is crucial that students are given what they need to "level the playing field." Consider the following data (see Figure 3.5), which show the percentage of English learner (EL) students, compared to that of non-ELs, meeting or exceeding standards on the math section of the California Assessment of Student Performance and Progress (CAASPP). Figure 3.6 highlights the achievement gap between ELs and non-ELs for English language arts (ELA) on the CAASPP. While these data are specific to EL students in the state of California, nationwide data indicate that this is a common phenomenon. *Child Trends* (Murphey, 2014) suggests that the achievement gap between EL and non-EL students remained unchanged from 2000 to 2013, with EL students performing 40 percentage points below in both fourth-grade reading and eighth-grade math. Research also suggests that low-income and foster youth consistently perform at a lower rate on standardized tests and graduate high school at a significantly lower rate than other student populations (Frerer, Sosenko, & Henke, 2013).

Figure 3.5   California ELs and Non-ELs Meeting or Exceeding Standards in Mathematics (%), by Grade, SY 2016–17

	Grade 3 (%)	Grade 4 (%)	Grade 5 (%)	Grade 6 (%)	Grade 7 (%)	Grade 8 (%)	Grade 11 (%)
Share of ELs who met or exceeded standard	24.9	14.5	8.4	7.0	6.8	6.4	5.7
Share of non-ELs who met or exceeded standard	55.2	48.8	40.7	42.7	42.2	40.5	35.0

EL = English learner; SY = school year.

Note: Data on non-ELs include both the fluent-English proficient and English-only categories.

Source: California Department of Education, "Smarter Balanced Assessment Test Results for: State of California." Retrieved from https://caaspp.cde.ca.gov/sb2017/ViewReport?ps=true&lstTestYear=2017&lstTestType=B&lstGroup=4&lstCountry=00&lstDistrict=00000&lstSchool=0000000.

Figure 3.6   California ELs and Non-ELs Meeting or Exceeding Standards in English Language Arts (%), by Grade, SY 2016–17

	Grade 3 (%)	Grade 4 (%)	Grade 5 (%)	Grade 6 (%)	Grade 7 (%)	Grade 8 (%)	Grade 11 (%)
Share of ELs who met or exceeded standard	18.0	14.2	11.7	9.0	8.0	6.2	10.3
Share of non-ELs who met or exceeded standard	53.5	54.8	55.7	54.8	56.3	54.3	65.0

EL = English learner; SY = school year.

Note: Data on non-ELs include both the fluent-English proficient and English-only categories.

Source: California Department of Education, "Smarter Balanced Assessment Test Results for: State of California." Retrieved from https://caaspp.cde.ca.gov/sb2017/ViewReport?ps=true&lstTestYear=2017&lstTestType=B&lstGroup=4&lstCountry=00&lstDistrict=00000&lstSchool=0000000.

A new funding system was created in 2013 in California, called the Local Control Funding Formula (LCFF), which includes a focus on these and other achievement gaps. Under LCFF, school districts are provided with funding for all students, but are also allotted additional funding for students who fall within three targeted student populations: *English language learners, foster youth,* and *low-income students.* The additional funding allows school districts to implement intentional interventions for these student groups with the goal of closing the achievement gap.

Regardless of the state you're in, when school counselors provide additional supports for students who have been traditionally marginalized, they are acting as social justice agents of change. Providing a Tier 2 service based on a demographic indicator does not use specific/individual data to identify students in need of support. Rather, school counselors use global data/research to drive the selected intervention. School counselors are leaders, advocates, and change agents. Therefore, when research demonstrates significant gaps in academic achievement based on factors such as race/ethnicity, school counselors have the opportunity and responsibility to assist in closing those gaps.

School counselor Teresse served as an elementary school counselor in a district with a high population of American Indian/Alaska Native students. Teresse and her school counseling team recognized the existing data that indicated poor educational outcomes for this population, and several interventions were implemented to support these students and their families. All of the interventions selected were based on research indicating that high levels of student/parent engagement and one-on-one mentoring support improvement in American Indian/Alaska Native students' academic success.

One important component of Teresse's work focused on educating staff and faculty to dispel myths and assumptions that they may have held about American Indian/Alaska Native families (Fleming, 2006).

Teresse and her school counseling team began by visiting the tribal communities where her students lived. She took a proactive approach to connect with the students and families outside of school to develop a better understanding of their culture, values, and lifestyle. American Indian/Alaska Native students were provided tutoring support and frequent check-ins by school staff (students were assigned to meet once a week for five minutes with the school counselor, school psychologist, principal, or Title I teacher). In addition, while Teresse provided parent workshops for all parents, she also held workshops specifically for parents of American Indian/Alaska Native students, due to a difference in need/focus. By providing parent workshops to this targeted population, Teresse was focused on earning the trust of the families while learning about the parents' perceptions and attitudes toward college, which helped her to understand how she could support them. Many of the parents reported that they did not feel college was necessary, as it had not been important in their own families, and that they never felt like they "belonged" in college. In addition, some parents reported that they would not be able to afford college for their child; therefore, discussing post-secondary options was not a priority for them. Dispelling some of their fears and myths allowed the parents to see a different perspective. The meetings also allowed parents to develop a stronger relationship with school personnel (the school counselor, the principal, and several teachers) and feel more connected to the school. In turn, students began to feel more engaged and supported.

While working with the American Indian/Alaska Native student population is one example of creating a proactive intervention based on a demographic characteristic, several other student groups may also benefit from targeted support based on research:

- Lesbian, gay, bisexual, and transgender (LGBT) students
- Foster youth
- English language learners
- African American and Latino students
- Students receiving special education services
- Students who are socio-economically disadvantaged
- Students who are new to the country and/or do not speak English
- And many more!

ACTIVITY 3.2

Which of the previously listed student groups (or others not listed) are performing disproportionately with regard to grades, test scores, and other measures in your school? Which, if any, interventions might you implement to address the gap?

Another way to support students based on a demographic indicator is to do a quick Tier 2 "check-in." In other words, students who are part of a student group that has been traditionally marginalized (students in categories previously mentioned) can meet with the school counselor each year for a brief check-in. This check-in will allow the school counselor to know if additional Tier 2 support is needed for the students. It is important to remember that not all students belonging to a specific student group will need support. Imagine a school counselor who is informed that a new student—one who is in the foster care system—will be coming to the school. The school counselor may draw upon past experiences and decide that this student will need Tier 2 services. However, the new student may in fact be very well adjusted emotionally and perform well in all subject areas. Therefore, this student may not need a Tier 2 intervention and could actually benefit from a brief check-in meeting with the school counselor, who would quickly assess whether or not more support is needed.

DISAGGREGATING SCHOOL DATA AND CLOSING THE GAP

Closing the Gap is a term used by ASCA to describe when school counselors "address academic or behavioral discrepancies that exist between student groups" (Sabella, 2017). School counselors can identify achievement gaps within the school by disaggregating school data in the areas of achievement, attendance, and behavior. School counselors can look for an overrepresentation or an underrepresentation within specific student groups for an identified area. For example, when looking at statewide testing data, school counselor Monique noticed that students identified as English language learners performed significantly lower on the math and ELA portion of the test each year. Since there was a consistent overrepresentation of one student group (English language learners) performing below the majority of students on the statewide test, Monique decided to investigate why this gap was occurring.

Sabella (2017) explains that when school counselors address an achievement gap identified by using school data, it is important to consider four questions:

1. **What is the underlying reason or concern?** In the example above, the reason for the Closing the Gap project would be that there is a disproportionate number of English language learners performing poorly on the statewide test.

2. **Are the same students in multiple student groups?** For example, if school counselor Monique noticed that English language learners *and* students who are socio-economically disadvantaged were performing similarly below average on the statewide tests, are some of the students who are English language learners also identified as socio-economically disadvantaged?

3. **Is there more information before the issue can really be understood?** School counselor Monique may discover other factors that may be contributing to the low performance of these students. Perhaps the identified students are struggling to understand English and, therefore, are unable to answer the questions on the test. If this is the case, the school counselor may not be the most appropriate person to support the students in this area.

4. **Is this an area (academic, college/career, or social/emotional) the school counselor is uniquely qualified to address through an activity or intervention?** If school counselor Monique interviews the identified students and determines that the students are performing poorly as a result of low motivation and low levels of school connectedness, the school counselor would be an appropriate individual to implement an intervention.

Student Issue or Systems Issue?

Sometimes the data point to a systems issue, rather than a student issue. In Chapter 2, Ashley recognized that the number of Ns on students' report cards varied greatly from teacher to teacher. In addition, Ashley noticed that certain teachers consistently gave a large proportion of their class an N every year (when comparing year-over-year data). With this pattern, Ashley recognized that several system issues needed to be addressed and that she would provide education and support to the teachers, rather than to the students.

Matt is a brand-new school counselor, and a month into his position, the principal comes to him and says, "There are hundreds of playground referrals for kids touching each other. Can you please look to see which students have the most referrals, put them in a group, and talk to them about keeping their hands to themselves?" While looking through the referrals, Matt notices a pattern; the majority of them were written while students were lining up after recess to go back to their classrooms. The school procedure had always been the same: When the

(Continued)

(Continued)

bell rings after recess, students line up in a pre-identified area and wait for the teachers to come get them to bring them back to the classroom. Matt noticed that over 60 kids had two or more referrals for touching other students while waiting in these lines. Running a group for this many kids would not be an efficient use of time. Matt also wondered if there was a specific protocol for the "line-up procedure" and decided to speak with the principal about it. The principal responded and said, "I'm not sure why they line up first. That is how they did it before I got here, so we just continued doing it." Matt suggested that it might be beneficial to change the procedure and allow students to walk directly to class after the bell rings, which could eliminate the time students are waiting in line (where the problem is most frequently occurring). Matt's principal agreed, and within one month, playground referrals decreased by 63%.

According to the ASCA Ethical Standards (2016a), school counselors

- advocate for equitable school counseling program policies and practices for all students and stakeholders,
- promote cultural competence to help create a safer, more inclusive school environment, and
- provide leadership to create systemic change to enhance the school.

As leaders and change agents, school counselors are charged with examining and improving policies and systems. As shared above, not all issues that arise are student issues, and as such, not all interventions need to be student interventions. Sometimes the most efficient and effective solution is to consider policy and practice changes utilizing the school counselor leadership, advocacy, and systemic change process. The goal is to work within the system to change the system and ensure equity and access for all students. Some examples of ways school counselors can advocate systemic change is to promote that

- agreed-upon data elements are being used to identify students in need of more support;
- a consistent data collection process is in place;
- a student information system is being used to assist with data collection;
- a schoolwide discipline plan is created and followed;
- consistent rules, expectations, and procedures are developed and implemented in every classroom; and
- policies and procedures are reviewed and evaluated on a regular basis (Hatch, 2013).

This chapter outlined the many *direct* and *indirect* Tier 2 services that can be provided for students in need of additional support. School counselors are encouraged to use data to determine which students need support beyond Tier 1. It is important that school counselors work within their scope of practice and utilize the resources available both within and outside of the school/district to ensure that students are provided with the most appropriate intervention. In addition to providing interventions for students, school counselors are responsible for examining systems to ensure that practices are equitable and beneficial for all students.

4

Franchising Tier 2 Interventions

NICASH'S STORY BEGINS

Nicash was ready to begin her first year as a school counselor in a new school district. She had felt frustrated in her previous school district. While all of the school counselors in the district delivered the same core curriculum, there was a lack of consistency in terms of identifying and providing support to students in need of Tier 2 services. Some school counselors were placing sign-up sheets in the teacher's lounge to determine which students were in need of Tier 2 supports, others used data to identify students, and a few were too busy responding to crises at their school and did not have time to provide Tier 2 interventions. Nicash knew that developing a common set of criteria to identify students who may benefit from a Tier 2 intervention would ensure that students in need of the most support would actually receive it. Nicash was excited for a new opportunity and was ready to be a leader in helping the K–8 school counselors to develop a system by which Tier 2 interventions were provided for students.

Who is Nicash? *Throughout this text, Trish, Ashley, and Nicole provided samples and examples from their own experiences as well as those of school counselor colleagues. To support the readers in understanding the process and steps taken when implementing Tier 2, we are introducing "Nicash," a school counselor whose name symbolizes a blending of Ashley and Nicole's names and multiple experiences across several schools and districts. Some readers might wonder why other combinations weren't used, but if you consider what those might have sounded like, you may have a chuckle!*

The recently released text *Hatching Results for Elementary School Counseling* (Hatch, Duarte, & De Gregorio, 2018) introduces the concept of franchising. In that text, Tier 1 activities (core curriculum and schoolwide programs and activities) are franchised, meaning that curriculum is agreed upon and provided each year by all counselors in the district. Franchising is a concept most often used in the business world, but metaphorically applicable when creating a comprehensive school counseling program. School counselors are encouraged to create standardized, developmental, scaffolded, and consistently implemented curriculum, both counselor-to-counselor and school-to-school. Just as teachers have common core curriculum and textbooks with scope, sequence, and pacing charts, in Tier 1, counselors are called on to provide consistent prevention curriculum. Similarly, in Tier 2, teachers create data-driven mechanisms that provide a common set of interventions. For example, teachers use benchmark assessments, and if students score below a particular threshold, they are automatically referred for a Tier 2 intervention. In the same way, school counselors are called to determine and create their list of Tier 2 interventions by collaborating with their colleagues and agreeing on which intervention individual students will receive because they qualify (data element).

As professional development specialists, the Hatching Results team travels around the country training in different districts and counties. While in various cities, the professional development specialists select their hotel. Danielle, our previous director of professional development, loves to stay at Hampton Inn because she knows it will always have tea available and she really, really, really loves tea. She also knows it will have a free breakfast in the morning so she can eat as little or as much as she would like. Wi-Fi is also always included—isn't that grand? Finally, Danielle knows she will always have a good sleep because the sheets are soft and the bed is comfortable. It is comforting for Danielle to stay at Hampton Inn because she knows exactly what to expect and she knows she will not be disappointed. Now, imagine if each time Danielle traveled, she stayed in a "mom and pop" hotel, or a non-franchised hotel. While some of these hotels may certainly be cute and quaint, they may each have very different accommodations and amenities. Imagine Danielle's recent surprise when she learned that the only hotel in town charged for internet, did not include breakfast, and, even worse, did not have tea when she arrived! All the nice sheets in the world couldn't make up for the lack of tea. The point is that happy customers appreciate it when they know what to expect, and they are more likely to come back! This is the beauty of franchises!

What do your Tier 2 services within your school counseling program look like? Are student interventions in your school more like the family-owned hotel, which may be cute and quaint but random, unpredictable, and inconsistent? Or is your school counseling program more similar to a consistent, franchised hotel where people know exactly what to expect?

Franchising your school counseling program is especially important in districts where families talk to each other and compare programs and services ("Why did your student get an intervention and mine didn't?"). It is also important with high-transiency populations so that students moving between schools still receive similar services. As students move from site to site, consistency in programs is important so that families, students, and administrators know what to expect and what they can *count on.* How many times have you had new administrators who want you to do what their other school counselor did at their previous school? Having a consistent, franchised school counseling program districtwide allows for a seamless transition when a new administrator starts at your school, as the programs and services will stay virtually the same.

School counselors are encouraged to work as a team to decide what, at a minimum, faculty and families can count on from the school counseling program and what the program might provide that is unique to the school's demographic. For instance, when Danielle stayed at the Hampton Inn in the South, it had sweet tea— but it still had tea!

To drive it home just a bit more, no longer are elementary school counselors seen as Mary Poppins with a bag of tricks and a blanket spread out on the lawn, providing random acts of intervention they found online. Today's school counselor is expected to be a part of the educational system that uses data and runs systemically, intentionally, consistently, efficiently, and effectively. In *Hatching Results for Elementary School Counseling* (Hatch et al., 2018), the authors describe school counseling as being both an *art* and a *science.* The *science* of our work is creating the systemic structures (data collection systems, providing evidence-based interventions, scheduling time for counseling activities, etc.) within which counseling occurs. The *art* of the work is what happens during the counseling lessons (building rapport, utilizing counseling strategies, etc.). The art of the work is also happening when the counselor uses the data and thoughtfully applies the appropriate intervention to the data-driven need.

The process of developing agreed-upon data elements and minimum guaranteed interventions is most effective when utilizing a collaborative approach. Some school counselors meet as a district to determine these criteria (elementary, middle, and high school counselors), some school counselors meet with their same-level colleagues (all elementary counselors, all middle school counselors, and all high school counselors), and some school counselors work with their site administrator and other stakeholders. Table 4.1 demonstrates school counselor Nicash working with her elementary and middle school counseling team to develop a plan for franchising their Tier 2 curriculum.

Helpful Tip

"Mouse Trap Approach"

Have you ever played "mouse trap"? In this game, players construct a trap for a mouse. Once the structure is developed, a marble is dropped. The mechanisms built on the board function in such a way that when the mouse crosses a certain area, the trap drops over the mouse. The point is that a system was created that ensures that when the marble drops, the mouse gets trapped. If it is not built correctly, the marble will fall, and the mouse will run free. Of course, we all know that children are not mice, but creating a functional system of appropriate interventions ensures that students don't fall between the cracks.

Some might ask, how is this different from the fishnet approach, referenced in Chapter 2? The difference is that the fishnet approach is a metaphor for filtering those who qualify for an intervention from the entire student population. In contrast, the mouse trap approach is a metaphor for the *engineering of building* a system that functions seamlessly and efficiently to ensure interventions are provided for students in need. In this way, the fishnet approach and the mouse trap approach work hand in hand.

NO MORE RANDOM ACTS OF INTERVENTION

While many Tier 2 interventions can be utilized to support students' needs, a team approach is recommended to develop an agreed-upon list of minimum interventions that will be implemented by all school counselors in a district or on a team, to ensure consistency and equity throughout the school counseling program. When school counselors implement random acts of intervention, it becomes difficult to gather impact data on students, show the difference a school counselor can make, and advocate for additional resources. It can also be difficult for administrators to know what exactly they are advocating for—the person (school counselor) or the program. The school counseling program should guarantee interventions regardless of who the school counselor is.

The idea behind creating an agreed-upon list of data elements that guarantee interventions is to create a mouse trap approach, such that every student who qualifies based on pre-determined criteria receives at least a minimum level of intervention. The intervention may vary, depending on resources and student needs, but ideally, a few minimum data elements are agreed to at every school and/or within a district so that stakeholders know what services are consistent.

NICASH'S STORY CONTINUES

Nicash and her elementary and middle school counseling team decided it would be helpful to create a list of data elements that could be used throughout the district to ensure consistency in how students "qualified" for Tier 2 services. The first step in this process was determining which data elements would be used to qualify a student for a Tier 2 service based on attendance, behavior, and/or academic data, utilizing the tool introduced in Chapter 2 (see Figure 2.8, page 36). Next, the school counseling team brainstormed various interventions that could be provided for students meeting the indicated criteria.

While the school district already had a process in place for responding to students with excessive unexcused absences, the school counselors wanted to clarify their role in supporting students and families who met pre-determined criteria. As a team, the school counselors believed it would be most beneficial to meet with families after the second attendance letter was sent out by the school. By attending the School Attendance Review Team (SART) meeting, the school counselors could provide families with information regarding the importance of school attendance, as well as offer services/resources that might assist the families in getting their child to school on time. For example, during one SART meeting, it came to school counselor Nicash's attention that a parent was having difficulty finding someone to take her daughter to school at 8:15 a.m., because she began work at 7:30 a.m. Nicash was able to offer a before-school service to the parent, which allowed her to bring her daughter in before work. The parent had not been aware of this resource, and by attending the SART meeting, Nicash was able to problem-solve with the parent and ensure that the student was attending school daily.

The elementary school counseling team also created a uniform system to respond to discipline referrals. Once a student received three office discipline referrals, the school counselor was to be notified by an administrator. At some schools, the principal notified the school counselor after each discipline referral; however, Nicash and her team did not feel that this would be a realistic expectation for all school sites. Therefore, they decided to create a minimum criteria notification in all schools (franchising). Once the school counselors learned which students received three discipline referrals, they provided a pre-intervention survey (see the "Pre-Intervention Survey" section of Chapter 5, page 111) to determine if a small group intervention would be an appropriate fit for the student or another Tier 2 service should be offered.

The school counseling team also agreed on the importance of meeting with every student who received a suspension. Post-suspension conferences became a guaranteed intervention. Imagine a student who has been suspended for two days. After the two days, the student returns to class, having missed instruction and possibly feeling embarrassed, angry, and/or disappointed. A meeting with such students after they have had time to decompress and consider their actions and feelings allows for reconnection and problem solving between the student and the school counselor. As noted in Chapter 3, the goal of a post-suspension meeting is to discuss the problem behavior, re-teach the expected behavior, identify necessary supports and resources, and create a plan for making more positive choices in the future.

Finally, the school counseling team agreed on which criteria would qualify a student to receive a Tier 2 intervention based on the Work Habits/Social Skills section of the report card. The elementary school counseling team determined students would qualify for a Tier 2 intervention if they had two or more Ns (Needs Improvement), out of a possible four Ns, in that section. If a student met the criteria, the school counselor would consult with grade-level teams and use a pre-intervention survey to determine the most appropriate Tier 2 intervention.

The sixth-grade school counselors knew that course failure was a serious concern and decided that any student receiving two or more Fs in a core class (math, English, science, or social studies) would also receive a Tier 2 intervention. The Tier 2 interventions available would depend on the student's need and the reasoning for the student's struggle.

A summary of the concerns, data elements selected, and possible interventions developed by Nicash's K–8 school counseling team is presented in Table 4.1.

Table 4.1 Districtwide Interventions for Identified Data Elements

Tier 2 (K–8)	Data Element	Intervention
Attendance: Unexcused Absences (K–8)	• 3 unexcused absences • 7 unexcused absences • 10 unexcused absences	• School sends letter 1 • School sends letter 2 • School counselor attends School Attendance Review Team (SART) meeting for purposes of consultation and problem solving • School counselor provides intervention(s) with students and/or families, as identified in SART meeting • School sends letter 3 • Principal holds SART meeting (school counselor may or may not attend, depending on need)

(Continued)

(Continued)

Tier 2 (K–8)	Data Element	Intervention
Behavior (K–8)	• 3 or more office discipline referrals • In- or out-of-school suspension	• School counselor collaborates with administrator and provides pre-intervention survey to determine the appropriate intervention • School counselor meets with grade-level teams to strategize and select appropriate interventions • School counselor provides small group for students who are an appropriate fit • School counselor holds a post-suspension (re-engagement) meeting with student individually • School counselor provides Tier 2 service(s) for students who are not receiving small group support
Report Card: Work Habits (K–5)	• 2 or more *N*s (out of a total of 4) each quarter	• School counselor meets with grade-level teams to strategize and identify appropriate interventions • School counselor provides small group for students who are an appropriate fit
Report Card: Social Skills (K–5)	• 2 or more *N*s (out of a total of 4) each quarter	• School counselor meets with grade-level teams to strategize and identify appropriate interventions • School counselor provides small group for students who are an appropriate fit
Course Failures (6–8)	• 2 or more *F*s in a core class (end of each grading period)	• School counselor facilitates large group intervention workshop, during which students create an academic plan (e.g., Tiger Talk, described in Chapter 3, page 51) • School counselor reviews academic plan with student • Student completes progress monitoring with teacher • School counselor sends parent letter home • School counselor facilitates a small group for students who still have 2 or more *F*s at the next grading period after the workshop (who are an appropriate fit) • School counselor provides a referral to other in- or out-of-school resources, as appropriate

ACTIVITY 4.1

Visit the online appendix for a template of Table 4.1. With your school district and/ or counseling team(s), fill in the empty boxes indicating the data elements that will be used and agreed-upon interventions that will be provided to students as a result.

Utilizing the agreement document allows Nicash and the K–8 counseling team to ensure that a student attending any of the schools in the district will be guaranteed at least one of the interventions listed. Stakeholders will know which interventions will be provided for individual students once they qualify for a Tier 2 service after meeting specified criteria. By franchising the Tier 2 services, Nicash's school counseling team has created legitimacy, consistency, and predictability within the school counseling program.

Shifting Paradigms

Historically, "guidance counselors" often planned the activities for their day based on the needs of teachers, parents, administrator(s), and other stakeholders. Well-meaning counselors were called on and often responded by being everything to everyone, feeling like they were running around putting out fires all the time, and their counseling offices felt more like emergency rooms. It seemed everyone wanted the counselor to fix everything! Previously, it may not have been unusual for a counselor to respond to a request from

- a parent who wants the counselor to talk to her student because he is fighting with his brother at home,
- a teacher who wants the counselor to talk to his student who did not bring in her homework from the previous night, or
- an administrator who wants the counselor to see a student immediately following a low-level playground referral.

Figure 4.1 outlines the most important differences between the role of a "guidance counselor" and the responsibilities of a school counselor.

Today's school counselors, however, are called on to be intentional and strategic in their work and focus on providing students with preventative services. As described in *The Use of Data in School Counseling: Hatching Results for Students, Programs, and the Profession* (Hatch, 2013), "School counselors who are always available to see families or students are actually NOT performing the role of a professional school counselor" (p. 199). For some educators, these ideas may require a shift in mindset.

Figure 4.1   The Role of a Guidance Counselor vs. School Counselor

Guidance Counselor ➡	School Counselor
• Reactive counseling	• Proactive, preventative counseling
• Serves some students	• Serves all students
• Focuses mostly on mental health	• Focuses on providing support within three domains (academic, social/emotional, and post-secondary) to impact student achievement
• Utilizes a clinical model focused on student deficits	• Utilizes an educational model, focused on student strengths
• Ancillary support	• Integral member of the school leadership team
• Loosely defined role	• Clearly defined role
• Focuses mostly on counseling services provided	• Focuses on outcomes from services provided
• Works in isolation or only with other counselors to serve students	• Collaborates with all stakeholders
• Guards the status quo	• Acts as a change agent, especially for educational equity for all students
• Gatekeeper of rigorous courses	• Advocates for all students to have access to rigorous courses
• Little or no accountability	• Full accountability for student success
• Helps mostly the college-track students plan for college	• Advises all students on multiple post-secondary pathways
• Depends on system's resources for helping students and families	• Brokers services from community agencies, as well as the school system's resources
• Spends most time in Tiers 2 and 3	• Spends most time in Tier 1

Source: Adapted by Whitney Triplett (2015) from Erford (2014, p. 55) and Stone & Dahir (2015, p. 16).

ACTIVITY 4.2

How well are you shifting roles and responsibilities from a guidance counselor to a school counselor? Figure 4.2 is a self-assessment that school counselors can use to track their progress. Give it a try!

Figure 4.2   School Counselor vs. Guidance Counselor: A Self-Assessment

For each description, reflect on your duties and responsibilities currently. Circle the number that best reflects your role on a continuum of 1 being most in line with Guidance Counselor and 5 being School Counselor. Then add up your points from page 1 and page 2 and write your total at the bottom of the self-assessment.

GUIDANCE COUNSELOR				SCHOOL COUNSELOR
Reactive counseling				**Proactive, preventative counseling**
①	②	③	④	⑤
Serves some students				**Serves *all* students**
①	②	③	④	⑤
Focuses mostly on mental health				**Focuses on providing supports within three domains (academic, social/emotional, post-secondary) to impact student achievement**
①	②	③	④	⑤
Utilizes a clinical model focused on student *deficits*				**Utilizes an educational model focused on student *strengths***
①	②	③	④	⑤
Ancillary support				**Integral member of the school leadership team**
①	②	③	④	⑤
Loosely defined role				**Clearly defined role**
①	②	③	④	⑤
Focuses mostly on counseling services provided				**Focuses on outcomes from services provided**
①	②	③	④	⑤

Page 1 Points: _____

Hatching Results® 2907 Shelter Island Drive #150-287, San Diego, CA 92106 | www.hatchingresults.com

(Continued)

Figure 4.2   School Counselor Self-Assessment (Continued)

GUIDANCE COUNSELOR				SCHOOL COUNSELOR
Works in isolation or only with other counselors to serve students				**Collaborates with all stakeholders**
①	②	③	④	⑤
Guards the status quo				**Acts as a change agent, especially for educational equity for all students**
①	②	③	④	⑤
Gatekeeper of rigorous courses				**Advocates for all students to have access to rigorous courses**
①	②	③	④	⑤
Little or no accountability				**Full accountability for student success**
①	②	③	④	⑤
Helps mostly the college-track students plan for college				**Advises *all* students on multiple post-secondary pathways**
①	②	③	④	⑤
Depends on system's resources for helping students and families				**Brokers services from community agencies, as well as the school system's resources**
①	②	③	④	⑤
Spends most time in Tiers 2 and 3				**Spends most time in Tier 1**
①	②	③	④	⑤

Page 2 Points: _____

TOTAL Points: _____ / 70

Hatching Results®   2907 Shelter Island Drive #150-287, San Diego, CA 92106 | **www.hatchingresults.com**

Just as teachers implement a tiered level of support within the classroom, so too do school counselors implement a tiered level of support outside of the classroom. Consider a student who traditionally performs well in math, but then receives a failing grade on a math test. It would be unusual for the teacher to immediately send the student to the principal. Rather, the teacher would begin by meeting with the student to determine the cause of the problem (Does the student understand the content? Did the student choose not to study?). If in fact the student did not understand the content being tested, the teacher may decide to provide the student with additional support in the classroom.

Conversely, if during the conversation the student reveals to the teacher that he could not focus because he had not been sleeping due to violence or abuse in the home, the support provided by the teacher will be very different. In this case, it is important for the teacher to follow the proper procedures and consult with the school counselor and administrator(s) and submit a child abuse report. The level of support the student receives and the individual who delivers the service will be determined based on the student's need. It is crucial that teachers and other staff understand the process by which a student is referred to the school counselor, the school psychologist, the school social worker, and/or the administrator(s). A clearly defined and agreed-upon system must be developed, written down, shared with all stakeholders, and implemented with fidelity.

For example, a school counseling department in Indiana created an acrostic to teach and help school staff remember what constitutes a "crisis"—in the moment or now—as opposed to a historical issue:

Cps referral needed (now)

Relative passing (now)

Imminent harm (now)

Suicidal ideation (now)

Involvement of law enforcement (now)

Self-harm (now)

At a recent Hatching Results training, professional development specialist and co-author Ashley was asked a question by one of the school counselors: "I am trying my best to focus my time providing Tier 1 and Tier 2 services, but I am inundated with referrals from teachers who consider their student to be Tier 3 'urgent.' How do I stop teachers from constantly submitting referrals but still help them feel supported?"

This was not the first time Ashley had heard school counselors report their frustration with having to "put out fires." Some schools have a long line of students waiting to see the principal or even the school counselor. Ashley shared that at her school, she and her principal agreed it was imperative that there be a system in place to ensure that students are properly triaged based on their specific needs. Ashley, her principal, and other stakeholders worked together to develop well-thought-out systems.

In order to create a clear system for staff, Ashley knew that developing an effective and clear school counselor referral form was imperative.

REFERRAL FORMS

School Counselor Referral Forms

While Chapter 2 focused on using data to determine students in need of Tier 2 support, it is recommended that school counselors also provide staff with a referral form for incidents that may need attention but may not be evident when using the systematic data collection process as described. It is important that school counselors make it clear to staff that students in need of Tier 2 interventions will, for the most part, be identified by using data; however, a small number of students may experience a crisis or show a sudden change in behavior, academic progress, and/or affect, and require immediate assistance.

For example, consider a student who consistently turns in her homework, completes classwork in a timely manner, and is extremely organized. Suddenly, this student shows a drastic change in attitude toward school. When the student misses some homework assignments and the teacher asks about them, the student replies, "Who cares? It's not important anyway." The teacher may not feel comfortable waiting until the next report card to provide this student with support. Rather, this may be an appropriate time for the teacher to fill out a school counselor referral form, such as the one demonstrated in Figure 4.3. By meeting with the student, the school counselor can gather more detailed information on what may be causing the student's change of behavior, what type of support the student may benefit from, whether the school counselor can offer the support, or if there are other supports, either on-site or off-site, that the student may benefit from. Educating the staff on the counseling referral process is an important step in reinforcing the data-driven process that coincides with the school counselor referral forms.

Because some teachers are more inclined to refer students for assistance than others, one of the problems with referral forms is that some teachers refer many students, while others refer few or none. Having a systemic data-driven intervention program in place, with a guaranteed, data-driven fishnet approach to identifying students in need of interventions, will cut down on frivolous referrals and ensure those who have needs receive the support they require.

The referral form in Figure 4.3 has unique characteristics that have proven helpful to school counselors. First, the teacher is required to contact the parent before referring the student to school counseling (unless the issue is abuse-related, or of a sensitive or personal nature to the student). This will ensure that the teacher and parent have already had an opportunity to resolve the problem prior to a counseling referral, or if the problem is not resolvable, then at least the parent is alerted that the student may receive services from the school counselor. Every effort should be made to refrain from seeing students whose families have not been notified of a concern by the teacher. A form serves as an accountability tool everyone will appreciate having if or when an incident occurs.

The referral form provides a reminder to teachers that students who have chronic difficulties with attendance, behavior, or achievement will be identified using the systematic data collection process and that the form should *only* be used for students who have shown a significant change in these areas. The form also asks the teacher to indicate the level of severity of the problem. Just as an emergency room intake worker must decide which patients need immediate attention and which must wait longer to be seen, school counselors must "triage" their referrals to determine which students require immediate intervention. Figure 4.3 is a sample referral form that teachers can use to refer students to see the school counselor if a *change* has occurred.

Figure 4.3 Elementary Counselor Referral Form

Please complete as many details as possible and return to your counselor's box.

STUDENT'S NAME: _____ GRADE: _____ TEACHER: _____

REFERRED BY:_____ Date: _____

**Reminder: Students who have ongoing/habitual issues will be targeted through data collected. This form is for concerns regarding *CHANGES* in student behavior.

☐ Change in Attendance ☐ Change in Behavior ☐ Change in Academics ☐ Change in behavior/demeanor/social interaction

Please describe your reason(s) for this referral and any additional concerns or information:

_____

_____

Steps taken to address concern:

What interventions are in place? ☐ Breakthrough ☐ Parent Conference ☐ Outside Counseling ☐ Individualized Education Program (IEP)

☐ Student Study Team (SST) ☐ Behavior Support Plan ☐ Principal ☐ Behavior Contract

☐ Other: _____

How long have you had this concern? ___ Today ____ A few days ___ One week ____ Two weeks ____ Other

Has this issue been discussed with the student's parent/guardian? ___Y ___N Last date of contact: _____
(Required unless this is a personal nature or related to possible abuse/violence)

Parent/guardian response:

_____

Please rate this referral.

On a scale of 1–10, please circle how serious (immediate) this problem is:

Less Serious		Moderately Serious				Very Serious	
1 2	3	4	5	6	7 8	9	10

Please note: This referral will be screened and responded to based on the level of severity

----

For School Counselor Use Only

Parent/Guardian Contact: ___Yes ___ No Date: _____ Time: _____

1st Intake: ___ _____Date _____Time Ongoing counseling services needed: ___Yes ___ No

Type of Services: ___Individual __Group ___ Monitoring ___ Other (___Weekly ___Biweekly ___Monthly)

Referred to community agency: ___Yes ___No Which provider:_____Date: _____

Comments:_____

School Counselor's Signature: _____

The referral form in Figure 4.3 was adapted by Nicash in collaboration with the leadership team. Once the referral form was developed, it was time for Nicash to provide a staff training to clearly describe the process in which this form was to be used. By explaining the school counselor's role in using data to identify students in need of Tier 2 support, a school counselor referral form was now only necessary in extreme situations in which a *change* or *crisis* has occurred. Students who experienced an ongoing problem with their behaviors or academics would be identified automatically using the pre-determined criteria.

Discipline Referral Forms

While school counselors are not responsible for administering discipline, they work closely with administrators to develop procedures so that discipline referrals can be systematic and triaged to the appropriate professional for follow-up. A distinction must be made between the "discipline" referral and the "school counseling" referral. These are different forms, used for fundamentally different purposes. If a student is misbehaving and a teacher is concerned and wants help finding out what might be going on personally for the student that may be contributing to the behavior, then it is appropriate to refer the student for school counseling. If, however, the teacher has exhausted the classroom discipline plan and is now referring the student to receive a consequence, a discipline referral is appropriate, but it should be sent to an administrator. Simply stated, does the teacher want the student to receive assistance or a consequence? There may be times when a follow-up conversation with the student is appropriate after the consequence is delivered (e.g., a post-suspension conference). School counselors are encouraged to work with their administrators to put systems in place to ensure post-suspension conferences occur in a timely manner.

NICASH'S STORY CONTINUES

At Nicash's school, staff were directed to utilize the discipline referral form for instances in which a student was breaking a rule or not following expectations. Similar to Ashley's story introduced near the end of Chapter 2, Nicash and her principal noticed that a large number of discipline referrals were being submitted and many of the referrals were for minor incidents that could be better addressed in the classroom by the teacher. In addition, Nicash and her principal noticed that there was a discrepancy in the number of discipline referrals submitted by different teachers. Some teachers were writing multiple referrals on a daily basis, while others did not write any for the whole semester. Nicash and her principal felt it would be helpful to create a systemic process that clearly outlined the expectation for submitting a discipline referral and to determine whether the referral was considered "minor" or "major."

First, Nicash and her principal developed a document outlining the differences between a "major referral" and a "minor referral" and discussed it with teachers for feedback. Major referrals were categorized based on a violation of the California Education Code and were to be dealt with by administration immediately. Minor offenses were incidents that were to be addressed inside the classroom by the teacher. Figure 4.4 is what staff received as a clear outline of the differences between major and minor referrals for Nicash's school site.

Figure 4.4 Major vs. Minor Offenses

Making Distinctions Between Minor Offenses and Office Referrals/Major Infractions

Minor Offenses: Minor offenses are misbehaviors corrected "on the spot" (classroom, common areas, etc.). If misbehavior continues after correction attempts and is repeated, the behavior must be documented. Documentation used to address minor offenses is the *Pre-Referral to Intervention on Aeries.* **Parent must be contacted.**

Major Offenses: Major infractions are violations of the Education Code that require the immediate attention of administrative staff. This will be documented by administration on *Aeries Assertive Discipline,* and **admin will contact parent.**

Minor Offense Pre-Referral to Intervention (Aeries)	Major Offenses Immediate Phone Call to Office
• Disruption • Defiance • Non-Compliance • Property Misuse • Dress Code • Mild Physical Contact • Inappropriate Language • Tardy • Lying • Cheating • Out of Bounds • Trash/Littering	Safety Education Codes 48900 & 48915 • A1, A2, A3 – Fight; Assault (EC48915) • B – Weapon; Explosives • C – Alcohol or Drugs; under influence or possession (EC48915) • D – Look Alike Drug • E – Robbery/Extortion • M – Imitation Firearm • N – Sexual Harassment • O – Witness Harassment • P – Drug SOMA • Q – Hazing • R – Bullying • S – Terrorist Threat • T – Hate Violence (harass/intimidate/threats) • V – Inappropriate Item • W – Spreading Rumors Non-Safety Education Code 48900: Referral to Intervention (Aeries) • Repeated Minor Offense • F – Damaged Property; Graffiti • G – Theft • H – Tobacco • I – Profanity/Obscenity • J – Drug Paraphernalia • K – Repeated Disruption/Defiance; Dress Code; Inappropriate Use of Social Media • L – Received Stolen Property • U – Attendance Review/Bus Referral/Class Cuts

Note: Aeries is a Student Information System (SIS).

(Continued)

(Continued)

Figure 4.5 Minor vs. Major Behavior Flow Chart (PBIS aligned)

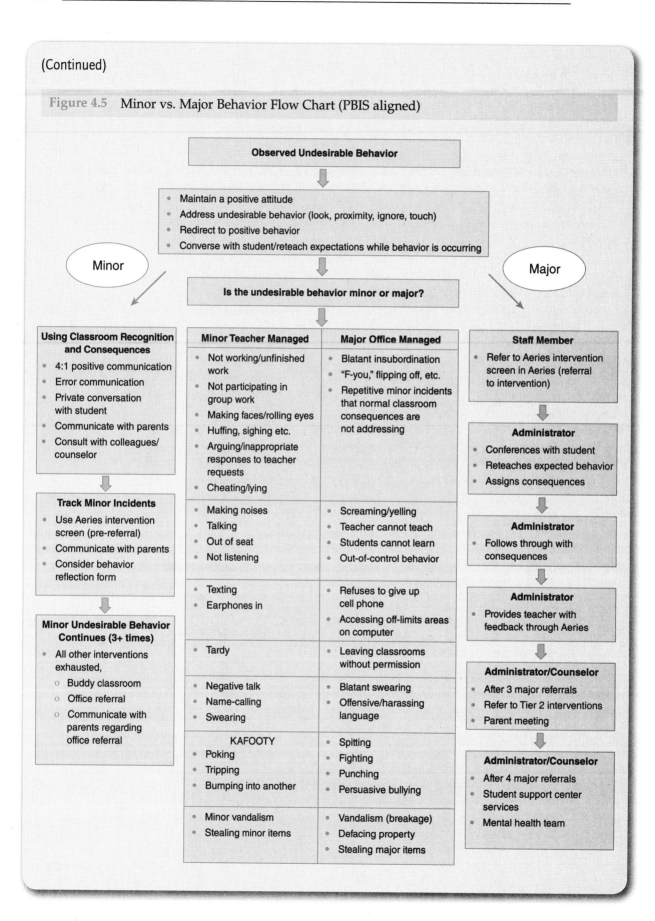

Nicash also provided a flow chart, seen in Figure 4.5, which is a visual example of the referral process and the distinction between major and minor referrals. Notice that behaviors are clearly defined and guidance is provided on whether the problem should be managed within the classroom or requires the support of an administrator.

Once staff understood the distinction between levels of referral, the process to submit a referral was presented during a staff meeting, and a visual presentation was sent to every staff member for reference. As part of a Positive Behavioral Interventions and Supports (PBIS) school, both Nicash and her principal believed that just as students come to school to learn about math and English, they also come to school to learn how to get along with others, how to make positive choices, and how to cope with strong emotions. Therefore, if a student exhibited a behavioral challenge categorized as a minor offense, rather than sending the student up to the office immediately, it was the teacher's responsibility to re-teach the expected behavior. Once the expectation had been re-taught, the teacher was then expected to document any further incidences of that behavior in the Student Information System (SIS) as a minor offense. The documentation also required that the teacher indicate which interventions were implemented to address the behavior, as well as provide confirmation of parent contact. After a teacher documented three minor incidents in the SIS, the teacher could then submit a major referral (also known as an office discipline referral), which was then automatically forwarded to the principal.

Teachers were also educated about when to submit an office discipline referral immediately (for a major offense). With this clear procedure in place, the number of students sent to the office to meet with the principal dramatically decreased.

In order to ensure they understood this process, staff members participated in an activity (shown in Figure 4.6) where they were given a scenario and were responsible for determining the appropriate steps to take. With the given information, teachers needed to choose whether they would

- *meet with the student to re-teach the expected behavior,*
- *document a major or minor offense in the SIS,*
- *send the student up to the office/principal immediately (major referral/office discipline referral),*
- *submit a school counselor referral form,*
- *send the student to the school counselor immediately, or*
- *contact another service provider (school psychologist, school social worker, nurse, etc.).*

With these tools, Nicash was hopeful that the staff would now know the appropriate steps to take in a given situation. After staff individually went through each scenario and indicated their response, Nicash reviewed the appropriate responses with the whole group.

(Continued)

(Continued)

Figure 4.6   What Would You Do? Activity

What Would You Do?

Please read the following scenarios and select the *first* step you would take to address the situation:

- Meet with the student to re-teach the expected behavior
- Document a major or minor offense in the SIS
- Send the student up to the office/principal immediately
- Submit a school counselor referral form
- Send the student to the school counselor immediately
- Contact another service provider (school psychologist, school social worker, nurse, etc.)
- Other:

Scenario 1

A fourth-grade student brought a knife to school and showed it to his friends. His friends reported this to you.

Scenario 2

When asked to do her work, a second-grade student rolled her eyes at you and said, "I am not doing this. It's boring!"

Scenario 3

During silent reading time, you notice your third-grade student with his head down on the desk. When you go to speak to him, you notice he has been crying. When you ask him what is wrong, he shares that his mother died the previous evening.

Scenario 4

Your fifth-grade student has really poor hygiene. Other students have begun to complain about having to be around her.

Scenario 5

Adam, one of your strongest math students, has failed his last four math tests. In addition, he has been eating alone for the past two weeks during lunch. You are very worried and have tried to talk to him, but he has indicated that he is "fine."

Once staff understood the distinction between a major referral and a minor referral, Nicash connected the procedure for giving Ns on the report card and writing referrals. More specifically, Nicash indicated that students who receive an N on their report card have most likely received at least two office discipline referrals (major referrals). To ensure consistency in reporting, teachers were expected to have documentation of the referrals given prior to giving a student an N on the report card.

Although it took a lot of time and work in the beginning to create the system, Nicash and her principal have saved countless hours since, by only meeting with students based on their level of need. In addition, Nicash and her principal now have time to follow through with all regularly scheduled activities and are not interrupted throughout the day.

It is important to remember that setting up systems and processes such as the one described can take a great deal of time and requires administrative support. In order for this system to work, it is crucial that the process be followed on a consistent basis. When staff do not follow the outlined system, it is important for the school counselor and administrator to re-teach the expected actions. Of course, there are extenuating circumstances in which a teacher referral is not appropriate and immediate contact of the school counselor is necessary (suicidal ideation, sudden death in the family, etc.). These situations should be clearly identified and discussed with staff.

In addition to providing training to teachers on systems and processes, families can be educated on this topic, as well. School counselors can educate families on the role of a school counselor and the systems in place to triage students based on their needs by designing monthly newsletters or holding parent meetings.

MENU OF SERVICES

As discussed throughout the text, it is highly recommended that school counselors utilize a collaborative approach when identifying the Tier 2 intervention that will be provided to a student. A schoolwide menu of services is a list of all interventions available at the school site. A menu of services can include, for example, (a) assessment services, (b) intervention processes, (c) disciplinary options, (d) educational skills training available, (e) integrated support services, and (f) positive activity options. It is recommended that this menu of services be developed by a team of individuals and may include, but is not limited to, the school counselor, the school psychologist, administration, resource teachers, speech therapists, occupational therapists, and behavior specialists. For this collaborative team, the menu of services can include *all* interventions available to students and allows for an efficient selection of the most appropriate service.

It is helpful for a menu of services to be available to all stakeholders so there is a clear understanding of the Tier 1, Tier 2, and Tier 3 supports available within a given school/district. While school counselors provide support in each tier, it is important to remember that other on-site professionals can also provide Tier 2 and Tier 3 services for students. In some situations, services provided by another school professional may benefit the student more than the services a school counselor would provide.

Some school counselors may want to create an additional school counseling program menu of services, which would list or highlight all of the services the school counselor provides in the school/district. In this way, if the team decides counseling services are the best intervention for a student, the school counselor can easily share with the rest of the team which specific counseling services are offered. A sample of a schoolwide menu of services is provided in Figure 4.7.

Figure 4.7   Schoolwide Menu of Services Sample

Assessment Services	Intervention Process	Integrated Support Services

• Individualized Education Program (IEP) Assessments:
  ○ Cognitive
  ○ Academic
  ○ Social/Emotional
  ○ Speech Therapy
  ○ Occupational Therapy
• Health Screenings
  ○ Vision
  ○ Hearing
• English Language Proficiency Assessments for California (ELPAC)
• Outside Referrals
• Student Success Team (SST) Referrals
	• School Attendance Review Team (SART)
	• School Attendance Review Board (SARB)
	• Conflict Resolution/Restorative Justice Meetings
	• Mental Health Referrals
	• Academic Tutoring
	• Outside Referrals
	• Risk Assessments
	• Foster Youth and Homeless Support
	• Individualized Education Program (IEP)
	• Section 504 Plan
		• Individual
		• Small Groups
		  ○ Organization and Study Skills
		  ○ Time Management
		  ○ Self-Regulation
		  ○ Emotion Management
		  ○ Mindfulness
		  ○ Social Skills Groups (District Led)
		• Mentoring
		• Conflict Resolution/Restorative Justice Meetings
		• Parent Education

Education (Skills) Component	**Behavior Support**	**Positive Activity Options**
• Classroom Lessons (Instruction) • New Student Orientation • Transition to Kindergarten • Transition to Middle School • STEM Camp	• Behavior Support Plan • Behavior Contracts • Classroom Behavior Support • No-Contact Contracts • Loss of Privilege • Suspension • Post-Suspension Conference	• School Clubs • Student Valet • Kindness Crew • Student Technology Leaders • Community Sponsored Events • Peer Mentoring Program • Schoolwide Positive Behavior Interventions and Supports (PBIS) • Incentives • Attendance Incentives • Field Trips • After-School Discovery Classes • Recognition and Awards Assemblies

Role Clarification

Many elementary schools are fortunate to have multiple student service providers, while others may have limited access to student support professionals. A review of the professional models within each discipline, as well as their ethical guidelines, reveals many commonalities among school counselors, school psychologists, and school social workers. Each discipline uses evidence-based practices, collaborates with families and other stakeholders, and addresses systems issues, and because these professionals work in a school, the goal of their prevention and intervention is to improve achievement for all students by removing barriers to learning.

In order to ensure that all student support professionals are focusing on their particular area of expertise, it may be useful for school districts to develop a document that outlines the roles and responsibilities of each service provider. Figure 4.8 is one example of a breakdown of the roles of each service provider in a school; however, it is not intended to be a prescription. This allows for all stakeholders to have a clear understanding of the differences between support staff positions and offers the service providers the ability to "stay in their lane."

Figure 4.8   Example of Student Support Service Providers

Service Provided	School Psychologist	School Social Worker	School Counselor
Core Curriculum (Academic)			X
Core Curriculum (Social/Emotional)		X	X
Core Curriculum (College/Career)			X
Individual Counseling	X	X	X
Small Group (Academic/Study Skills)	X		X
Small Group (Attendance)		X	X
Small Group (Behavior)	X	X	X
Family Counseling		X	
Family Therapy			
Coordination/Leadership Schoolwide Intervention/ Curriculum (Red Ribbon/Bully Prevention, etc.)			X
Support/Participation Schoolwide Intervention/ Curriculum (Red Ribbon/Bully Prevention, etc.)	X	X	
Participant on MTMDSS/Behavioral Teams	X	X	X

(Continued)

Figure 4.8   (Continued)

Service Provided	School Psychologist	School Social Worker	School Counselor
Participant on PBIS Team	X	X	X
Chronic Absenteeism Supports		X	X
Dropout Prevention		X	X
Teacher Consultation	X	X	X
Staff In-Service/Professional Learning	X	X	X
Fostering Family Partnerships	X	X	X
Deliver Behavior Therapy per IEP	X	X	
Assessment of Students for Possible Special Education Services	X		
Develop FBA/BIP for Students With Disabilities	X		
Wrap-Around Services	X	X	X

Note: MTMDSS = Multi-Tiered, Multi-Domain System of Supports; PBIS = Positive Behavioral Interventions and Supports; IEP = Individualized Education Program; FBA/BIP = Functional Behavior Assessment/Behavior Intervention Plan.

In a recent Hatching Results training, school counselors, school psychologists, and school social workers were asked to list the activities that they provide within the Multi-Tiered, Multi-Domain System of Supports (MTMDSS) model on sticky notes. The school counselors wrote their answers in one color, school social workers in another color, and school psychologists in yet another. As is evident in the picture, there is an overabundance of social/ emotional interventions being provided by all three professions, and there is a lack of college/career readiness (i.e., Tier 2 for marginalized groups; see the "Tier 2 Services Based on a Demographic Indicator" section of Chapter 3, page 69). It is also important to note that when student support service providers deliver random acts of Tier 2 intervention, they often, perhaps without intent, "veer into each other's lanes."

Multi-Tiered, Multi-Domain System of Supports (MTMDSS)

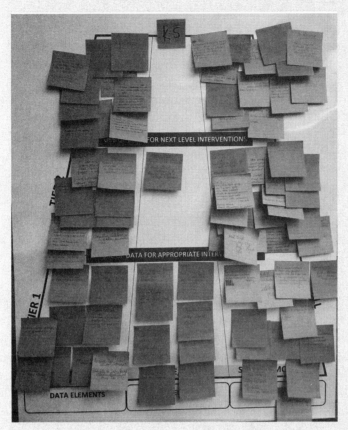

The next step of the activity was to have all participants consider whether they are "staying in their lane." It is important that all student support providers understand their role and not veer outside of that role (or "lane"). We ask participants to imagine that we are all driving in the same direction and have the same objectives and goals of moving student outcomes forward. Sometimes, as student service professionals, our services are collaborative (similar to carpooling, where we are all working together toward the same goal), and other times there is overlap and we can appear to be veering into someone else's lane (or role). When considering how you work with other student service professionals, consider the following questions:

- Am I staying in my lane?
- Am I veering into someone else's lane?
- Do I put on my blinker first, or do I merge without signaling?
- Are we carpooling?
- How can we avoid duplication of services, while ensuring that all students receive the supports they need to be successful?
- Are protocols or flow charts needed?

While every school district and school site has specific needs, it can be helpful for school counselors to franchise their Tier 2 and Tier 3 interventions to ensure consistency from site to site. When families, students, and other stakeholders know what to expect, legitimacy is created in the school counseling program. Rather than providing random acts of intervention, it is clear that when students meet certain criteria, they will receive a minimum level of intervention, regardless of the school they attend. While deciding on the criteria is important, it is also recommended that school counselors begin by developing systems and processes (norming report card data, creating a clear school counselor and discipline referral process, etc.) to ensure that the data used to "qualify" a student for a Tier 2 or Tier 3 intervention is accurate and objective. This allows school counselors to feel confident that they are providing meaningful interventions for the students with the most needs.

NICASH'S STORY CONTINUES

Nicash was feeling very confident about franchising Tier 2 supports across the district. All of the school counselors had determined a minimum level of criteria they would use to identify students in need of Tier 2 supports, and a clear, consistent, and systematic process was developed for discipline referrals as well as for school counselor referrals. Nicash understood that it would take some time for all staff to follow the process as outlined, but with consistency and review, the process would allow Nicash to address the needs of the students who were most in need of additional support.

5

Planning for Small Groups

NICASH'S STORY CONTINUES

At the beginning of the school year, Nicash sat down with her principal and other members of the data-based decision-making team to systematically schedule the time periods in which small groups would be held for the whole school year. The team decided which data elements would be used to identify students in need of Tier 2 services and when to query the data. As previously planned and indicated on her calendar and Annual Agreement, Nicash ran a query at the end of the quarter to identify students who had received two or more Ns (Needs Improvement) in the Work Habits/Social Skills section of their report card. She was pleased to see that after working with her staff on "norming" the report card marks (see Chapter 2), there was more consistency among teachers' assignment of Work Habits/Social Skills marks. Furthermore, the data were closely aligned to the Multi-Tiered, Multi-Domain System of Supports (MTMDSS) recommendation that 15% of students receive Tier 2 supports.

Nicash then met with grade-level teams to discuss the students identified through the data. The team selected the most appropriate Tier 2 intervention for each qualifying student and determined which students would receive small group counseling interventions. Nicash now knew which students would participate in her small groups, but needed to select group topics, determine the small group composition, schedule when the small groups would occur, and develop a Tier 2 Action Plan.

Chapter 3 described several Tier 2 interventions that could be implemented to support students in need of targeted or additional supports. Because small group counseling is one of the most commonly used Tier 2 interventions, the chapters that follow are dedicated to discussing (a) planning small groups, (b) selecting and implementing small groups, (c) facilitating small groups, (d) developing effective small group curriculum, and (e) evaluating the small group.

Before school counselors begin facilitating a small group counseling intervention, several logistical and planning steps must occur. As Nicash's story demonstrates, school counselors must address many important components prior to facilitating a small group, which include

- determining the type of small group,
- selecting lesson topics,
- selecting composition of the group,
- scheduling group lessons, and
- completing an action plan.

TYPES OF COUNSELING GROUPS

School counseling groups can contribute to student outcomes by teaching the attitudes, skills, and knowledge (ASK) necessary to change behavior. Small groups at the elementary level create a supportive network of individuals who may be experiencing a similar academic or social/emotional challenge. Counseling groups can be facilitated differently based on where the group occurs (in a clinical setting vs. a school setting), the training of the facilitator, and the intended outcome.

In today's schools, school counselors most often facilitate psycho-educational groups (Bore, Hendricks, & Womack, 2013), which focus on the students' present situation and teach skills to improve their current challenges. In contrast, psycho-therapeutic counseling groups are generally long term and explore how past experiences impact individuals' emotional and psychological well-being (see Table 5.1). Psycho-therapeutic groups are outside the scope of a school counselor's role and not recommended in a school setting.

Psycho-educational small group counseling is *short term* (6 to 8 weeks), *skill based*, and *highly structured*. Small groups in schools promote skill building in the areas of social/emotional, academic, and/or college/career development. When planning to facilitate a psycho-educational small group, school counselors select topics based on students' needs. For example, if the identified students struggle with study skills, the school counselor can directly align the counseling topics to the specific study skills needed. It is common for group topics to inadvertently

Table 5.1 Psycho-Educational vs. Psycho-Therapeutic Groups

	Psycho-Educational Groups	**Psycho-Therapeutic Groups**
Time Frame	6–8 weeks	Long term
Focus	Focus on present situation	Focus on exploring past experiences
Purpose	Teach students skills intended to improve current challenges	Teach individuals coping strategies to improve their mental health

deviate from the students' actual needs if this component is not monitored with a critical and thoughtful eye. Best practice suggests the same data used to select small group counseling members be utilized to determine the lesson topics for the small group.

Aligning Small Group Counseling to ASCA

The American School Counselor Association advocates that school counselors "select topics for groups with the clear understanding that some topics are not suitable for groups in schools" (ASCA, 2016a, A.7f). See Figure 5.1 for the ASCA Ethical Standards aligning to small group work.

The American School Counselor Association Position Statement on Student Mental Health (ASCA, 2015b; see Figure 5.2) states that when school counselors are implementing a comprehensive school counseling program, they should "direct students and parents to school and/or community resources for additional referrals that treat mental health issues (suicidal ideation, violence, abuse and depression)." While these serious topics are important, processing these types of Tier 3 experiences in a group setting (unless it is done during crisis response) is outside the scope of a school counselor's role. School counselors support students experiencing difficulties in these areas by referring them to outside counseling resources with a trained mental health professional. See Figure 5.2 for the full details of the position statement.

Figure 5.1   ASCA Ethical Standards: Group Work

School counselors:

a.   Facilitate short-term groups to address students' academic, career, and/or social/emotional issues.

b.   Inform parent/guardian(s) of student participation in a small group.

c.   Screen students for group membership.

d.   Use data to measure member needs to establish well-defined expectations of group members.

e.   Communicate the aspiration of confidentiality as a group norm, while recognizing and working from the protective posture that confidentiality for minors in schools cannot be guaranteed.

f.   Select topics for groups with the clear understanding that some topics are not suitable for groups in schools and accordingly take precautions to protect members from harm as a result of interactions with the group.

g.   Facilitate groups from the framework of evidence-based or research-based practices.

h.   Practice within their competence level and develop professional competence through training and supervision.

i.   Measure the outcomes of group participation (process, perception and outcome data).

j.   Provide necessary follow-up with group members.

Source: Reprinted with permission from the American School Counselor Association.

Figure 5.2   ASCA Position Statement on Student Mental Health

The School Counselor and Student Mental Health
(Adopted 2009, Revised 2015)

The American School Counselor Association (ASCA) Position
School counselors recognize and respond to the need for mental health and behavioral prevention, early intervention and crisis services that promote psychosocial wellness and development for all students. School counselors are prepared to address barriers and to assess ways to maximize students' success in schools, communities and their family structure by offering education, prevention, and crisis and short-term intervention until the student is connected with available community resources.

The Rationale
Students' unmet mental health needs can be a significant obstacle to student academic, career and social/emotional development and even compromise school safety. Schools are often one of the first places where mental health crises and needs of students are recognized and initially addressed (Froeschle & Meyers, 2004). Most students in need do not receive adequate mental health supports (Centers for Disease Control and Prevention [CDC], 2013). Research indicates 20 percent of students are in need of mental health services, yet only one out of five of these students receive the necessary services (Kaffenberger & Seligman, 2007).

Furthermore, students of color and those from families with low income are at greater risk for mental health needs but are even less likely to receive the appropriate services (Panigua, 2005; Vera, Buhin, & Shin, 2006) despite increased national attention to these inequities (Alegria, Vallas, & Pumariega, 2010). Of school-age children who receive any behavioral and mental health services, 70 percent–80 percent receive them at school (Atkins et al., 2010). Preventive school-based mental health and behavioral services are essential. Without planned intervention for students exhibiting early-warning signs setbacks in educational, social and career development during later school years and adulthood can result. The ASCA Mindsets & Behaviors (ASCA 2014) identify and prioritize the specific attitudes, knowledge and skills students should be able to demonstrate as a result of a school counseling program. School counselors use the standards to assess student growth and development, guide the development of strategies and activities and create a program that helps students achieve their highest potential. This includes offering education, prevention and short-term intervention services designed to promote positive mental health and to remove any barriers.

The School Counselor's Role
School counselors focus their efforts on designing and implementing comprehensive programs that promote academic, career and social/emotional success for all students. School counselors acknowledge they may be the only counseling professional available to students and their families. While implementing a comprehensive program school counselors:
- Deliver the school counseling core curriculum that proactively enhances awareness of mental health; promotes positive, healthy behaviors; and seeks to remove the stigma associated with mental health issues
- Provide responsive services including internal and external referral procedures, short-term counseling or crisis intervention focused on mental health or situational (e.g. grief, difficult transitions) concerns with the intent of helping the student return to the classroom and removing barriers to learning
- Recognize warning signs: changes in school performance (changes in grades, attendance), mood changes, complaining of illness before school, increased disciplinary problems at school, experiencing problems at home or family situation (stress, trauma, divorce, substance abuse, exposure to poverty conditions domestic violence), communication from teachers about problems at school, and dealing with existing mental health concerns
- Provide school-based prevention and universal interventions and targeted interventions for students with mental health and behavioral health concerns
- Provide students with individual planning addressing their academic, career and social/emotional (including mental health) needs

- Educate teachers, administrators, parents/guardians, and community stakeholders about the mental health concerns of students, including recognition of the role environmental factors have in causing or exacerbating mental health issues and provide resources and information
- Advocate, collaborate and coordinate with school and community stakeholders to ensure that students and their families have access to mental health services
- Recognize and address barriers to access mental health services and the associated stigma, including cultural and linguistic impediments
- Adhere to appropriate guidelines regarding confidentiality, the distinction between public and private information and consultation
- Direct students and parents to school and/or community resources for additional assistance through referrals that treat mental health issues (suicidal ideation, violence, abuse and depression)
- Help identify and address students' mental health issues while working within the ASCA's Ethical Standards; Competencies for School Counselors; and national, state and local legislation (Family Educational Rights and Privacy Act and Health Insurance Portability and Accountability Act), which guide school counselors' informed decision-making and standardize professional practice to protect both the student and school counselor
- Seek to continually update their professional knowledge regarding the students' social/emotional needs

Summary
Students' unmet mental health needs pose barriers to learning and development. Because of school counselors' training and position, they are uniquely qualified to provide education, prevention, intervention and referral services to students and their families. Although school counselors do not provide long-term mental health therapy in schools, they provide a comprehensive school counseling program designed to meet the developmental needs of all students. As a component of this program, school counselors collaborate with other educational professionals and community service providers.

References
Allegria, M., Vallas, M., & Pumariega, A. J. (2010). Racial and ethnic disparities in pediatric mental health. *Child and Adolescent Psychiatric Clinics of North America, 19*(4), 759–774. doi:10.1016/j.chc.2010.07.001

American School Counselor Association. (2012). *The ASCA National Model: A framework for school counseling programs* (3rd ed.). Alexandria, VA: Author.

American School Counselor Association. (2014). *Mindsets & behaviors for student success: K-12 college- and career-readiness standards for every student.* Alexandria, VA: Author.

Atkins, M., Hoagwood, K. E., Kutash, K., & Seidman, E. (2010). Toward the integration of education and mental health in schools. *Administration and Policy in Mental Health, 37,* 40–47.

Centers for Disease Control and Prevention (2010). Mental health surveillance among children – United States, 2005-2011. Retrieved from http://www.cdc.gov/features/childrensmentalhealth

Erford, B. T., Newsome, D. W., & Rock, E. (2007). Counseling youth at risk. In B. T. Erford (ed.) *Transforming the school counseling profession* (2nd ed.) (pp. 279-303). Upper Saddle River, NJ: Pearson.

Erickson, A., & Abel, N. R. (2013). A high school counselor's leadership in providing school-wide screenings for depression and enhancing suicide awareness. *Professional School Counseling, 16*(5), 283-289. doi: 10.5330/psc.n.2013-16.283

Froeschle, J., & Moyer, M. (2004). Just cut it out: Legal and ethical challenges in counseling students who self-mutilate. *Professional School Counseling, 7,* 231-235.

Kaffenberger, C., & Seligman, L. (2007). Helping students with mental and emotional disorders. In B. T. Erford (ed.) *Transforming the school counseling profession* (2nd ed.) (pp. 351-383). Upper Saddle River, NJ: Pearson.

(Continued)

Figure 5.2 (Continued)

Panigua, F. A. (2005). *Assessing and treating culturally diverse clients: A practical guide* (3rd ed.). Thousand Oaks, CA: Sage.

Vera, E. M., Buhin, L., & Shin, R. Q. (2006). The pursuit of social justice and the elimination of racism. In M. G. Constantine and D. W. Sue (Eds.) *Addressing racism: Facilitating cultural competence in mental health and educational settings* (pp. 271-287). Hoboken: Wiley.

Reback, R. (2010). Schools' mental health services and young children's emotions, behavior, and learning. *Journal of Policy Analysis and Management, 29*(4), 698-727. doi: 10.1002/pam

Source: ASCA, 2015b. Reprinted with permission from the American School Counselor Association.

The "Appropriate Activities for School Counselors" section of the ASCA National Model Executive Summary (ASCA, n.d.) is clear: It is inappropriate for school counselors to provide "long-term counseling in schools to address psychological disorders" (see Figure 5.3).

Figure 5.3   Appropriate vs. Inappropriate Duties

Appropriate and Inappropriate Activities for School Counselors

Appropriate Activities for School Counselors	Inappropriate Activities for School Counselors
▪ advisement and appraisal for academic planning	▪ building the master schedule
▪ orientation, coordination and academic advising for new students	▪ coordinating paperwork and data entry of all new students
▪ interpreting cognitive, aptitude and achievement tests	▪ coordinating cognitive, aptitude and achievement testing programs
▪ providing counseling to students who are tardy or absent	▪ signing excuses for students who are tardy or absent
▪ providing counseling to students who have disciplinary problems	▪ performing disciplinary actions or assigning discipline consequences
▪ providing short-term individual and small-group counseling services to students	▪ providing long-term counseling in schools to address psychological disorders
▪ consulting with teachers to schedule and present school counseling curriculum lessons based on developmental needs and needs identified through data	▪ covering classes when teachers are absent or to create teacher planning time
▪ interpreting student records	▪ maintaining student records
▪ analyzing grade-point averages in relationship to achievement	▪ computing grade-point averages
▪ consulting with teachers about building classroom connections, effective classroom management and the role of noncognitive factors in student success	▪ supervising classrooms or common areas
▪ protecting student records and information per state and federal regulations	▪ keeping clerical records
▪ consulting with the school principal to identify and resolve student issues, needs and problems	▪ assisting with duties in the principal's office
▪ advocating for students at individual education plan meetings, student study teams and school attendance review boards, as necessary	▪ coordinating schoolwide individual education plans, student study teams, response to intervention plans, MTSS and school attendance review boards
▪ analyzing disaggregated schoolwide and school counseling program data	▪ serving as a data entry clerk

AMERICAN
SCHOOL
COUNSELOR
ASSOCIATION

Source: Reprinted with permission from the American School Counselor Association.

USING DATA TO DETERMINE SMALL GROUP COUNSELING TOPICS

Historically, school counselors may have selected the members of a small group and the group topics using feedback from teachers or students regarding what they felt would be helpful. For example, a school counselor might have put up a flyer around the school that says, "Do you have trouble controlling your anger? Would you like to learn strategies to help cope with these emotions?" Another school counselor may have posted a document in the staff room: "Friendship Crew, do you have a student who you think could benefit from learning skills to be a better friend? If so, please write the student's name on the sign-up sheet."

As the school counseling profession evolves, the work of the school counselor is becoming increasingly *strategic* and *intentional*. Rather than relying on random acts of situational experiences of students to determine the topic of a group, best practice calls for counselors to *identify data* to determine the needs of students. This ensures that the *actual* needs of the students, rather than their *perceived* needs, are being met. Office discipline referrals, report card data, and pre-intervention surveys are tools that can be used to decide on meaningful small group counseling lesson topics at the elementary school level.

> "School counselors have the necessary training to determine which interventions are needed and appropriate and with whom they should be conducted. Teachers, parents, and students do not. Surveys asking teachers, parents, or students to identify which small groups are needed or which students belong in a specific group are inappropriate" (ASCA National Model, 4th ed., 2019a).

Office Discipline Referrals

As discussed in detail in Chapter 4, in Nicash's school, when a student does not follow school or classroom expectations (a minor offense), the teacher re-teaches the student the expected behavior. After three incidents of re-teaching, or for a major offense, the teacher submits an office discipline referral (ODR). ODRs serve as a valuable source of data when school counselors are determining which students need Tier 2 interventions. In Nicash's school, if students receive three or more ODRs, they automatically qualify for a Tier 2 intervention, which often includes a small group. When examining the ODRs, school counselors look for patterns in behaviors to determine if specific skills need to be addressed during group topics. For example, if students selected for small group counseling have all received ODRs for disrespect, it may be helpful to include a focus on the importance of respect and how to demonstrate respect.

Report Card Data

Progress reports and report cards provide rich data for school counselors to review when determining small group counseling topics. As discussed in Chapter 2, students' work habits and social skills contribute to their achievement at school. Analyzing the academic and social/emotional (i.e., Work Habits/Social Skills/Citizenship) progress areas on the report card focuses the school counselor on specific areas of need for students who qualify for Tier 2.

NICASH'S STORY CONTINUES

Nicash joined the district's report card committee to ensure that the Work Habits/Social Skills section of the report card assessed areas that could then be used to develop small group topics. Once the report card was created to include relevant information, Nicash was able to utilize the data to target students' specific areas of need. Figure 5.4 provides an example of the district's updated report card, which Nicash uses to determine students' needs.

Figure 5.4 Sample Report Card

Work Habits and Social Skills		
Growth Mindset	A	
Demonstrates effort	*	
Has a positive attitude toward learning		
Perseveres through challenges	*	
Be Respectful	N	
Cooperates with others	*	
Respects others' rights, feelings, and property	*	
Solves problems appropriately	*	
Shows concern for others		**O** = Outstanding
Fosters peer relationships		
Be Responsible	N	**M** = Meets Expectations
Organizes self and materials for learning	*	**A** = Approaching Expectations
Listens and follows directions	*	**N** = Needs Improvement
Completes classwork consistently	*	
Completes homework consistently	*	
Be Safe	M	
Keeps all hands, feet, and other objects to self		
Follows school and classroom rules		
Uses materials appropriately		

During staff training, teachers were instructed to mark an O for Outstanding, M for Meets Expectations, A for Approaching Expectations, and N for Needs Improvement, in the categories identified as Growth Mindset, Be Respectful, Be Responsible, and Be Safe. Subcategories, such as "Cooperates with others" and "Completes classwork consistently" were to be marked with an asterisk to indicate any concerns in that specified area. In order for a student to receive an N in

(Continued)

(Continued)

any main category (Growth Mindset, Be Respectful, Be Responsible, or Be Safe), teachers needed to mark at least two asterisks within the subcategories. Providing clear boundaries and structure about report card markings ensured the data obtained were less subjective and more accurate.

Figure 5.4 is a sample report card from a third-grade student, Lillian. When analyzing the report card, consider what stands out. Which of the main categories is Lillian struggling with the most (Growth Mindset, Be Respectful, Be Responsible, or Be Safe)? What information can you gather from looking at the subcategories?

After reviewing Lillian's report card, Nicash met with her administrator and grade-level team to discuss her recommendation for a Tier 2 intervention that would most appropriately meet Lillian's needs. Lillian was at grade level in both reading and math, but still struggled in the areas of Be Responsible and Be Respectful.

Based on the data presented, the grade-level team concluded that some of Lillian's behaviors (as indicated by the Be Respectful category) were a result of her frustrations with being disorganized in class. Therefore, the team agreed that Lillian would benefit most from participating in an Academic Success Skills small group to address the areas of need in the Be Responsible category.

Once the overarching group topic was chosen, it was time to determine the weekly topics for each small group lesson. Nicash pulled language directly from Lillian's report card to deduce which skills would be taught during the group. Nicash noticed four asterisks in the area of Be Responsible: (a) Organizes self and materials for learning, (b) Listens and follows directions, (c) Completes classwork consistently, and (d) Completes homework consistently. These specified areas of need were used to create the group lesson topics. Nicash repeated the process, identifying other students who were experiencing difficulty in the same areas, allowing for a group to be formed and lesson topics to be easily implemented.

By aligning group curriculum directly with the report card categories, Nicash was able to focus on data-driven needs and analyze the next progress report/report card marks to assess for change. If the topics are not aligned with the report card titles, it may be difficult to accurately assess whether or not improvement is made. For example, if Nicash teaches students in her group strategies regarding how to turn homework in regularly, but that task is not measured on the report card, Nicash would need to develop another tool to assess the change in this area. Additionally, if students' challenge is to "Be Responsible" and they are placed in a group learning to "Be Safe," improvements may never be seen.

Non-Cognitive Needs Assessment Survey

The Non-Cognitive Needs Assessment Survey (NCNAS) is a screening tool for at-risk students. It can assist school counselors in identifying students in need of a Tier 2 intervention (see Figure 5.5). The NCNAS can also be used to help school counselors who may not have access to a Work Habits/Social Skills section of a report card to select appropriate topics for their small group counseling lessons.

The aforementioned story describes a scenario that may seem unfamiliar to many school counselors. Not every school counselor is in a district where the report card measures these relevant areas or has consistency in reporting among teachers. In order to gather meaningful and objective data, specific systems must be put into place, and this can only be done with the support of the district, staff, and administration. If systems such as these have not yet been set up in a particular school district, there are still tools school counselors can use to gather meaningful data.

Figure 5.5 Hatching Results Non-Cognitive Needs Assessment Survey (Tier 2)

HATCHING RESULTS, LLC

NON-COGNITIVE NEEDS ASSESSMENT SURVEY
A Screening Tool for At-Risk Students

STUDENT NAME: _____ STUDENT ID#: _____ GRADE: _____

TEACHER/COUNSELOR/PARENT NAME *(Circle)*: _____ DATE: _____

<u>INSTRUCTIONS</u>: To the best of your knowledge and based on your *own* observations and experience during the current school year only, please rate the students frequency in or ability to perform the following behaviors:

ACADEMIC BEHAVIORS

1. Rate the student on frequency of demonstrating:	5 Almost Always	4 Frequently	3 Average	2 Seldom	1 Almost Never
a.) Attendance—regularly attends class on time	☐	☐	☐	☐	☐
b.) Student work completion—homework, projects, class	☐	☐	☐	☐	☐
c.) Organization of materials	☐	☐	☐	☐	☐
d.) Participation—engaged, contributes to discussion	☐	☐	☐	☐	☐
e.) Study skills—use of in school and/or at home	☐	☐	☐	☐	☐

COMMENTS:

ACADEMIC PERSEVERANCE

2. Rate the student on frequency of demonstrating:	5 Almost Always	4 Frequently	3 Sometimes	2 Seldom	1 Almost Never
a.) Grit—staying focused on task despite obstacles	☐	☐	☐	☐	☐
b.) Tenacity—determination and resolve	☐	☐	☐	☐	☐
c.) Delayed gratification	☐	☐	☐	☐	☐
d.) Self-discipline	☐	☐	☐	☐	☐
e.) Self-control—forgoing short-term needs for long-term goals	☐	☐	☐	☐	☐

COMMENTS:

ACADEMIC MINDSETS

3. Rate the student on frequency of demonstrating:	5 Almost Always	4 Frequently	3 Sometimes	2 Seldom	1 Almost Never
a.) Belonging to the academic community	☐	☐	☐	☐	☐
b.) Effort to grow in ability and competence	☐	☐	☐	☐	☐
c.) Success (as important to the student)	☐	☐	☐	☐	☐
d.) Value of his/her work	☐	☐	☐	☐	☐

COMMENTS:

Hatching Results®, LLC
Based on the *Teaching Adolescents to Become Learners: The Role of Noncognitive Factors in Shaping School Performance (2012)* by the University of Chicago

(Continued)

Figure 5.5   (Continued)

LEARNING STRATEGIES

4. Please rate your student's frequency of demonstrating:	5 Almost Always	4 Frequently	3 Sometimes	2 Seldom	1 Almost Never
a.) Study Skills	☐	☐	☐	☐	☐
b.) Metacognitive Strategies	☐	☐	☐	☐	☐
c.) Self-regulated Learning	☐	☐	☐	☐	☐
d.) Goal-Setting	☐	☐	☐	☐	☐

COMMENTS:

SOCIAL SKILLS

5. Please rate your student's ability to demonstrating:	5 Almost Always	4 Frequently	3 Sometimes	2 Seldom	1 Almost Never
a.) Interpersonal Skills	☐	☐	☐	☐	☐
b.) Empathy	☐	☐	☐	☐	☐
c.) Cooperation	☐	☐	☐	☐	☐
d.) Assertion	☐	☐	☐	☐	☐
e.) Responsibility	☐	☐	☐	☐	☐

COMMENTS:

Hatching Results®, LLC
Based on the *Teaching Adolescents to Become Learners: The Role of Noncognitive Factors in Shaping School Performance (2012)* by the University of Chicago

Source: Based on *Teaching Adolescents to Become Learners: The Role of Noncognitive Factors in Shaping School Performance* (2012) by the University of Chicago.

Figure 5.5 is an example of a Hatching Results NCNAS (Tier 2) that a school counselor can give to staff members in order to assess relevant areas of need. It is still recommended that work be done with staff to ensure consistency and an agreed-upon understanding of what each rating signifies in order to maintain objectivity in the data.

Pre-Intervention Survey

Whether the school counselor has determined the students in need of intervention from ODRs, the report card, the NCNAS, or another data source used by the school, it is still important for the school counselor to meet with the students to ensure that participating in the small group is the appropriate intervention. As mentioned in Chapter 4, using a pre-intervention survey, another type of data available to school counselors, assists the school counselor in determining the over-arching themes of lesson topics in small groups. In *The Use of Data in School Counseling* (Hatch, 2013), the author discusses the idea of using this method prior to meeting with students who are not achieving academically and may be at risk. For example, students who have poor attendance or high numbers of discipline referrals may be given a pre-intervention survey during an individual meeting. This survey allows the school counselor to understand students' perspective as to *why* they may be struggling in a particular area. The survey data can also help the school counselor determine whether the student is a good fit for the group or an alternative Tier 2 support. For the purposes of this text, the survey will be referred to as a "pre-intervention survey."

Gathering students' perspectives (when developmentally appropriate) is impor-tant to ensure that each student receives the most effective/relevant intervention. Pre-intervention surveys allow school counselors to

- understand students' perspective on their personal challenges,
- determine if a student is an appropriate fit for a small group,
- narrow lesson topics,
- introduce students to the purpose of a small group,
- assess students' level of readiness for a group setting, and
- determine appropriate group membership.

Pre-intervention surveys may also be given to teachers and/or families as a means of gathering more comprehensive data to determine the appropriate Tier 2 services for the student. Teachers and families observe students in different settings and may offer a different perspective, which may assist the school counselor in determining underlying challenges and appropriate small group membership.

Not every student who surfaces through data will be best served by small group counseling. Consider the following: The results of a pre-intervention survey admin-istered to a fourth-grade student, Mary, revealed that her difficulty with completing classwork and homework was not at all related to a lack of study skills. On the pre-intervention survey, Mary indicated that she was having trouble focusing due to recently being removed from her home due to sexual abuse. Mary would not be an appropriate fit for a small group intervention and may need to be referred to an outside therapist to address her specific needs.

In order to confirm that a small group intervention in the area of "Be Responsible" would be the most beneficial for Lillian, Nicash administers a pre-intervention survey with her, shown in Figure 5.6.

Figure 5.6 Pre-Intervention Survey Academic

Pre-Intervention Survey

Student Name: _____   Grade: _____ Date: _____

Circle the face that shows best how you feel about coming to school and learning

----

Directions: Rate yourself on **how often** you do the following items below:

Questions			
Follow directions	Rarely	Sometimes	Often
Set goals for myself	Rarely	Sometimes	Often
Manage my time	Rarely	Sometimes	Often
Stay organized	Rarely	Sometimes	Often
Give up when I don't understand something	Rarely	Sometimes	Often
Complete classwork on time	Rarely	Sometimes	Often
Complete homework on time	Rarely	Sometimes	Often
Have what I need to do my homework (quiet space, computer, books, paper, pencils)	Rarely	Sometimes	Often
Have somebody at home that can help me with my homework	Rarely	Sometimes	Often

What is something in school that is hard for you in school?
Staying organized with all of my stuff

What is something you would like to improve in at school?
Turning in more homework

Please share if there are any other concerns either in school or outside of school that you think may be impacting your schoolwork?
Sometimes I just get distracted and can't focus on what I'm supposed to be doing. But it's also hard for me to keep things together and I lose a lot of stuff.

After reviewing the survey, Nicash learned that Lillian is in need of support in the areas of organization, following directions, and completing classwork and homework (also indicated by the report card data). Students may sometimes indicate on the survey that the reason they do not complete their homework is that they don't have an appropriate space at home to do it, or that they don't have the proper materials. In this case, Nicash may seek out a more appropriate resource for the student. However, with the information she had, Nicash determined that a small group intervention would benefit Lillian.

Creating Pre-Intervention Surveys

With the use of report card/progress report data and the pre-intervention survey, school counselors can better understand students' needs. When determining the overarching group topics, school counselors ask themselves, "What would I like students to learn as a result of this intervention? Do the students need support in study skills and organization? Do they struggle with making and keeping friends, which is impacting their ability to be academically successful? Do they have low self-esteem, and could they benefit from developing a growth mindset?"

When creating a pre-intervention survey, a school counselor may want to consider several factors (Sink, Edwards, & Eppler, 2011, p. 67):

1. **Length:** In general, surveys should not take longer than 10–15 minutes to complete. Typically, a pre-intervention survey should include between 5 and 10 questions/statements.

2. **Clarity:** Questions/statements should be clear and concise. Avoid using double negatives (e.g., "I am not irresponsible").

3. **Student Perspective:** Provide a space for the students to write a response to indicate what they perceive as their need (if developmentally appropriate).

4. **Developmental Level:** It is important that students understand the questions/statements they are responding to. For students in grades K–2, consider including pictures, or simply asking the questions and having a conversation with them.

5. **Types of Responses:**
    o   **Scaling statements**—these allow you to gain a better perspective of the intensity to which a student agrees or disagrees with a statement.

    o   **Questions**—ask open-ended questions that will allow the student to provide you with more information on the topic.

Once the pre-intervention surveys have been administered and completed by students, the school counselor can discuss the purpose of small groups and assess students' interest level in participating. School counselors can also use this time to give students consent forms.

Helpful Tip

Pre-Intervention Survey for K–2 Students

In addition to the pre-intervention survey shown in Figure 5.6, school counselors working with students in grades K–2, English language learners, and/or students with disabilities may consider using emoticons, rather than words, to better assess a student's agreement/disagreement with a particular statement (see Figure 5.7). We also recommend that school counselors working with students at this grade level read the statements to the students throughout the survey.

Figure 5.7   Pre-Intervention Survey (K–2)

Pre-Intervention Survey (K-2)

Student Name: _____   Grade:_____   Date: _____

I like coming to school

People are nice to me at school

I understand what I'm learning

I ask for help at school

I like being at home

Parent/Guardian Notification

Once students have been invited to participate in small group counseling, the next step is to notify parents/guardians of their child's participation. School counselors provide a service to students based on their need. When a student is struggling academically and the data-based decision-making team decides that a reading intervention is necessary, a parent/guardian is notified. Similarly, if a student is struggling behaviorally and meets pre-identified criteria, and it is determined that a small group is an appropriate intervention, a parent/guardian is notified. To ensure parents/guardians are adequately notified far enough in advance, it may be helpful for school counselors to advertise and publicize the fact that students could be selected to participate in small group counseling interventions at various points throughout the year. If marketed early and consistently, most parents/guardians will have already been made aware that school professionals will work together to determine which academic and social/emotional programs are best suited for each student.

School counselors may also send parents/guardians of identified students a letter explaining the small group counseling intervention. This letter can include, but is not limited to, the following:

- The purpose of the small group (academic/social/emotional)
- How their child was selected (based on data)
- Length of the small group (6–8 weeks)
- Time per lesson (30–45 minutes) on a weekly basis
- Summary of the content delivered
- Contact information for questions

Informed Consent

An informed consent form explains the school counselor's role in providing small group services and notifies/requests permission from parents/guardians to allow their child to participate in the small group. Depending on district policy, school counselors may be required to use either *active consent* or *passive consent.*

Active consent requires that parents/guardians return the form to the school counselor and indicate whether or not they are in agreement with their child participating in the small group. If the consent form has not been returned and the school counselor plans to begin the group, it can be helpful to make personal contact with the parents/guardians to help clarify the intervention and answer any further questions. It is advisable to plan enough time prior to the expected start date of the group for the parents/guardians to receive and return the consent form. This will also ensure a maximum amount of students are participating and benefiting from the group counseling service.

Passive consent is used to notify parents/guardians that their student will be participating in a small group. If the school counselor does not receive a form back from a parent/guardian, it is indicated on the consent form that the school counselor can assume that the parent/guardian is in agreement with the child's participation. If parents/guardians *do not* want their child to participate, however, it is their responsibility to send the form back to notify the school that they decline the service.

Be sure to check the school/district policy as it pertains to informed consent. Depending on the state, students have the right to confidentiality at different ages (e.g., in California, the age is 12). As a reminder, school counselors perform regular educational functions, and as such, permission, while recommended, is not required by ethical standards. That said, every effort should always be made to include parents/guardians in their child's education (ASCA, 2016a, B.1).

Figure 5.8 is an example of an active consent form. In this situation, the school counselor needs to wait to receive permission from the parent/guardian before including the student in small group counseling lessons. Figure 5.9 is an example of a passive consent form, in which the school counselor can assume the student will participate in the small group counseling lessons unless the form is returned, indicating the parent/guardian is against the student participating.

Figure 5.8   Active Consent Form Sample

Dear Parent/Guardian:
ABC School District's Counseling Program emphasizes the importance of academic, social/emotional and college and career development for every student. Your child has been given the opportunity to participate in a small group to improve academic skills. Students have been chosen to participate in this group based on progress report card data, which indicated that they received at least two "Needs Improvement" in the Work Habits/Social Skills area of the report card.

The topics that will be included in the small group are:

- Following directions
- SMART goal setting
- Time management
- Organizing self and material
- Completing classwork
- Completing homework

The group will meet once a week for eight weeks for approximately 30 minutes each session. The counselor will lead the students in lessons and reinforcing activities.

Please understand that participation in the small group is completely voluntary and student confidentiality is addressed and respected. Please contact me at <u>000-000-0000</u> or by email at firstlastname@schooldistrict.org if you have questions or desire further information.

Please return no later than [DATE]

Sincerely,
[NAME]

____ **I give consent** for my child to participate in the small group. I understand that participation is completely voluntary and that classroom requirements take precedence over participation.

____ **I do not give consent** for my child to participate in the small group.

Date: _____   Student Name: _____   Teacher: _____

Parent Email: _____   Parent/Guardian Signature: _____

Figure 5.9 Passive Consent Form Sample

Dear Parent/Guardian,

Your child has been invited to participate in small group counseling at Example School with the school counselor and school counseling interns. Group counseling sessions may occur once a week for about 30 minutes and aim to help students improve their social skills and academic success. Lessons during these sessions may include activities such as discussions, games, and worksheets. Topics addressed may include time management, problem-solving, managing emotions, or goal-setting.

In an effort to develop trust and respect among our students, any information shared by the student will remain confidential, with the exception of the following circumstances:

- The student reveals intent to harm him or herself
- The student reveals intent to harm another person
- The student reveals that he or she is being harmed

*If for any reason you **do not want** your child participating in the small group described above, **please return this form by October 21, 2019**. In the case that this form is not returned, your child will begin participating in the small group beginning October 28, 2019.*

Parent/Guardian _____   Date_____

Thank you,

Group Composition

Once the group counseling topics have been selected, school counselors can thoughtfully select which students will be assigned to each group. It is beneficial to group students based on similar needs to ensure most efficient use of time and to offer a more targeted intervention. However, in order to ensure that the group is effective, it is important that school counselors be strategic in determining which students will be grouped together. Table 5.2 outlines the different factors to consider that may impact the composition of the group and questions you may want to ask before selecting which members to assign to each small group.

Table 5.2   Factors to Consider for Student Group Composition

Factors	Questions to Ask
Behaviors	**Skill Level** • What skills does this student have or need? • Will this student's strengths complement the other students' needs? **Temperament** • Which types of personalities will mesh well? (*e.g., extroverted vs. introverted*) • Should I group all students with the same behavior needs together? (*e.g., impulse control*) • Will this student's behaviors negatively impact group effectiveness? **Peer Relationships** • What experiences do the members have with each other prior to group? (*e.g., positive vs. negative*) • How well do the students know each other already?
Developmental Appropriateness	**Grade Level** • Will it be beneficial to have all group members in the same grade? • Should I mix grade levels? **Maturity Level** • Is the student socially capable of connecting with other group members? • Will the student's level of maturity benefit or slow down the pace of the group? **Academic Level** • Will the student be able to understand the content? • Is the student's skill level appropriate for the group?
Size	**Number of Students in the Group** • How many students can be placed in this group? • Is the group focused on improving behavior and targeted for students in grades K–2? If so, fewer students would be more appropriate. • Is the group focused on improving academic success skills and targeted for students in fourth and fifth grade? If so, it may be possible to have a larger group.

> **ASHLEY'S GRAD STUDENT SIDEBAR CONVO**
>
> *Grad Student:*   *Do you consider all these factors and analyze each area every time you run a group?*
>
> *Ashley:*   *Well, I used to, but now I just do it in my head.*
>
> *Grad Student:*   *So, it's like driving with a clutch—the first time you do it, you really have to pay attention, and then it becomes automatic?*
>
> *Ashley:*   *Yes! Like the first time you cook, you slowly and deliberately measure everything perfectly, but as you get more experienced, you improve in efficiency and expediency.*

Gender-Specific Groups vs. Mixed-Gender Groups

While it may be common practice for some school counselors to hold "girl groups" or "boy groups," particularly in elementary and middle schools, school counselors must be thoughtful in how they constitute these groups. Random acts of girl and boy groups may send a message that some genders need a group while others don't. It may also undermine gender equity efforts in schools. How does one decide which girls need a group and which boys need a group? To be clear, random acts of gender groups are discouraged. When organizing all groups, including gender-specific groups, a data-driven process is a more equitable practice. In the following two examples, which group do you think will be more effective?

- **Scenario 1:** Jenny, a school counselor, noticed a lot of "girl drama" in the fifth-grade class. She sends out an email to teachers: "Hello. I am hoping to start a small group for girls to talk about being a good friend and the dangers of gossiping. I have noticed some of the girls in your class have been involved in some of these issues. Please let me know if there are students from your class who may benefit from a small group."
- **Scenario 2:** After querying and analyzing the student discipline data, several girls have received discipline referrals for bullying, gossiping, and spreading rumors. When report cards came out, school counselor Megan noticed a trend. Several of these same students also received an *N* in the Be Respectful category. In fact, six girls in fifth grade were given an asterisk in all of the subcategories (cooperates with others; respects others' rights, feelings, and property; solves problems appropriately; shows concern for others; and fosters peer relationships). After administering the pre-intervention survey to eliminate other factors that might be contributing to these behaviors, Megan invites those students who would benefit from group counseling to participate in a girls' group focused on positive peer relations.

In the second scenario above, Megan determined the need for a girls' peer relations group based on discipline and report card data and utilized the pre-intervention survey to confirm that a small group was the appropriate intervention.

Helpful Tip

Group Dynamics

As you look at the dynamics within the group utilizing the questions listed in Table 5.2, please be thoughtful to consider any special cultural circumstances that may not have been mentioned. Other cultural factors to consider are discussed in more detail in Chapter 6.

SCHEDULING GROUPS

As an integral part of the total educational program for students' success, school counselors provide small group and other Tier 2 interventions. While some small groups may be focused on behavior or social/emotional issues, when driven by data and implemented consistently as part of the schoolwide Tier 2 intervention options, small groups contribute to removing barriers to learning and support academic achievement. Students must be stable socially and emotionally in order to be academically successful (Cristóvão, Candeias, & Verdasca, 2017). Small group counseling lessons targeted to improve identified students' academic and social/emotional behaviors are equally as important as any other academic intervention. School counselors who collaborate and work with school staff at the beginning of the year to pre-calendar blocks of time to hold small group interventions will find far more supportive teacher partners when groups start.

Pre-Calendaring Small Group Interventions

With so many important activities occurring throughout the day, school counselors may wonder, *when is the best time to schedule small groups*? There are a variety of ways to help determine the best group counseling time.

While the process of deciding which students will receive small group counseling happens after the data are collected, pre-scheduling a block of time when small group counseling interventions will be held is best decided and calendared prior to the beginning of the school year. Collaborating with the administrator(s) and other stakeholders ensures a team approach.

Some elementary school counselors may decide to provide intervention following a monthly query of attendance and/or discipline referrals. Other counselors may decide that a group may begin as soon as a certain amount of students meet the threshold of agreed-upon criteria (three major discipline referrals, five truancies, etc., as discussed in Chapter 2). When running groups based on report cards/progress reports, strong consideration should be given to scheduling blocks of time immediately following the release of report cards/progress reports. This pre-blocked time would initially be used to analyze data, get permission slips ready, and plan for the group counseling lessons. Aligning the small group counseling schedule for the year with the report card allows school counselors to

- identify which students qualify for small groups using report card/progress report data,

- assess which students have shown progress and can be exited from the group, and
- determine which students have not shown progress and need to be provided with more intensive Tier 3 interventions.

Pre-scheduled times for small group counseling legitimize the intervention, as organizationally, the small group counseling lessons exist on the master calendar and stakeholders are aware that students who qualify are guaranteed an intervention. Figure 5.10 is a sample of a school counselor activity calendar and includes pre-scheduled dates both for querying data and for beginning small groups.

Figure 5.10   Sample Calendar With Small Group Intervention Dates Included

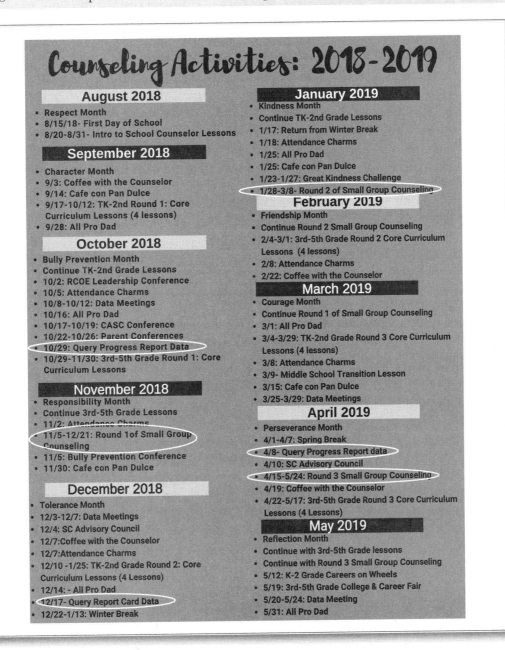

Felipe Zañartu, an elementary school counselor in Murrieta, schedules his counseling program by providing pro-active Tier 1 core curriculum and coordinated schoolwide events during the beginning of the school year in the following way. At the end of the first quarter, he gathers and analyzes the report card data to identify students for the appropriate interventions, which he then provides during the second quarter. Following the MTMDSS model, Felipe provides Tier 1 supports before providing Tier 2, and this method allows teachers the opportunity to use the first quarter to provide support for the students. At the elementary level, teacher conferences tend to occur at the end of the first quarter, after the first 10 weeks. In this way, the teachers and counselors work together to collaborate, allowing teachers to confer with parents and inform them that their student will participate in the small group intervention.

Where and When to Hold Group Counseling Lessons

As previously discussed, small groups are short term, typically lasting 6 to 8 weeks. Many school counselors hold their group counseling lessons once a week for 30 to 45 minutes in their office or another private space. Traditionally, professionals providing an intervention service (school counselors, intervention teachers, etc.) pull students who qualify out of the classroom to teach them the attitudes, skills, and knowledge necessary to improve in an identified area. In recent years, educators have shifted the way in which intervention services are provided, and it is becoming more common for educators to *push in* to the classrooms to provide these services. While it is less common for school counselors to provide Tier 2 support in the classrooms, it is an approach that can be considered.

Some school counselors may notice that their students seem to have the attitudes, skills, and knowledge necessary to demonstrate a desired outcome; however, students often have a difficult time generalizing what they believe, can do, and know in the natural environment.

Some children have difficulty generalizing skills they learn in an outside setting (such as the school counselor's room) into the natural environment (the classroom) where the skills need to be demonstrated.

School counselor Phil had been running small groups using a pull-out model for five weeks. One of his first-grade students, Jonathan, had been showing a lot of progress in learning skills to regulate his emotions (as identified by an assessment provided to students during week 4 of the small group). Jonathan was able to identify several strategies for calming down when he was feeling angry (deep belly breathing, counting, and positive self-talk). He was also able to demonstrate all three of these strategies, and he indicated that he believed regulating his emotions was very important to him. During week 5, immediately following one of the small group counseling lessons, Jonathan's teacher emailed Phil and reported that Jonathan had an intense anger outburst in class and threw a water ball at the teacher. Phil was feeling confused and frustrated! If Jonathan possessed the attitudes, skills, and knowledge necessary to regulate his emotions, why was he still having anger outbursts in class?

In situations where students appear to have difficulty generalizing their attitudes, skills, and knowledge to various environments, it may be helpful for school counselors to consider adjusting their approach to their Tier 2 small group interventions and consider pushing in to the classroom to provide students with support. This may still be considered a small group counseling approach, especially if several students in one class require the support.

The push-in approach allows school counselors to assist students with applying the new skills in situations as they would naturally occur in the environment. Consider a school counselor who has scheduled 40 minutes each week to spend time in a classroom where three first-grade students require a Tier 2 intervention. While in the classroom, if a situation arises where a student becomes emotionally agitated, the school counselor can help the student work through the situation in real time, utilizing identified strategies/skills. This allows the student to *feel* what it is like to implement the strategy in a real-life situation (as opposed to a role-play scenario). Practicing these skills in the natural environment will also allow students to build muscle memory, and the implementation of the identified skills will become more automatic.

It may also be helpful to consider a combination of pull-out and push-in support for students. For example, school counselors can consider pulling out students for one week to teach them and practice a particular skill, such as "belly breathing" as a means of calming down. The next week, the school counselor could push in to the classroom to ensure that the student is transferring and utilizing the previously taught skill appropriately.

Scheduling Group Times

Once the school counselor has identified which students will be a part of the group counseling intervention, how do you know when the best time is to provide the intervention? Collaborating with the teachers to determine the best dates and times to facilitate small group counseling creates buy-in and ensures that the scheduled time will be least disruptive to the students' learning. Sometimes, students who qualify for small group counseling services are also receiving other intervention services, such as speech therapy, reading interventions, and occupational therapy. School counselors collaborate with all school staff to minimize scheduling conflicts and ensure students receive all the supports they need.

Considering both the time of day and the type of group that will be facilitated requires strategic planning. For example, if the students are participating in a small group for social skills, scheduling the group *prior to* recess or lunch, where they have the opportunity to immediately practice the skills learned, may be beneficial. Many teachers also prefer scheduling a small group *after* a transition time during the day (e.g., after lunch or recess, at end of the day) so that there are fewer classroom disruptions.

Some school counselors wonder if it is acceptable to hold small groups during lunch and recess. Holding small groups during students' break times has both benefits and drawbacks. School counselors are encouraged to speak with their administrators to ensure that small groups are valued and implemented as a regular educational service, provided throughout the regular school day. Table 5.3 outlines the benefits and drawbacks of holding small groups during class time versus during student break times.

Table 5.3 Benefits and Drawbacks of Groups During Instructional Time vs. Break Time

	Benefits	Drawbacks
During class time	• Students may be more engaged • More opportunities to hold small group	• Students miss out on academic instruction • Teachers may withhold students' participation from group if an important activity is occurring in class
During break times (i.e., recess or lunch)	• Students do not miss out on academic instruction • Can be a positive/safe environment for students with behavioral challenges	• Group counseling lesson time may be limited • Students may not be as engaged because they prefer their break time • Students may need to serve a consequence with their teacher/administration during their break and be unable to attend group • Students may view small groups as a consequence rather than a learning opportunity • Students in group often need the scheduled break and may not receive as much time to be physically active

Ideally, when school counselors attend teacher department meetings, they collaborate about times that would work best for the identified students to participate in small group counseling lessons. If attending these meetings is not possible, school counselors can send out a survey to gather this information using Doodle, SignUpGenius, or another such system. Whether meeting in person or sending out a survey, providing teachers with several time slots that fit within the school counselor's schedule allows the teachers flexibility to select the best option. In this way, the message sent is not "Can I run a small group?" but "As you know, I am running small groups, and here are some potential dates and times. Please indicate the ones that work best for you."

Helpful Tip

Why Not Use the Data From Last Year?

Some school counselors like to begin their small groups at the beginning of the year, based on data from the previous year. Although these school counselors may be using data from the previous year to determine which students to put in a group, this strategy is not recommended.

The data collected from the previous year may not accurately represent the students' needs for the new school year. Factors that may not be considered when using prior data include developmental growth over time, teacher-student relationships, and situational stressors.

Utilizing data from the previous year may also send the message to stakeholders (students, parents, and staff) that the student has a problem before it has been observed, and that implies the student does not have the ability for positive change.

This does not mean that school counselors shouldn't do a check-in with students who were struggling the previous year; it just means these students should not automatically be put into a small group if the current year's data do not support that. Students deserve the benefit of the doubt before they are removed from valuable classroom instruction.

PREPARING FOR SMALL GROUP FACILITATION

Action Plans

Since the introduction of the ASCA National Model in 2003, school counselors have used action plans to guide their planning and decision-making process for curriculum (Tier 1) and interventions (Tier 2). Action plans support student success as they delinate the curriculum and interventions aligning with students' developmental and data-driven needs. They provide stakeholders with a tangible document, which can be used as a communication and marketing tool for the counseling program. It also helps legitimize the school counselor's well-thought-out plan, encourages collaboration, increases credibility, and ensures accountability that what is planned is implemented. Like Tier 1 action plans for core curriculum, Tier 2 action plans can be shared with all stakeholders, including parents, to help them understand the nature and purpose of the action planning experience. Furthermore, action plans align with, and serve as, a preparation tool for completing results reports.

The latest edition of the ASCA National Model (2019) merged the previous School Counseling Core Curriculum Action Plan, the Small Group Action Plan, and the Mindsets & Behaviors Planning Tool, into one document to be used for both classroom (Tier 1) and small group (Tier 2) instruction, focused on utilizing *standards* to drive interventions. The authors of this text assert that school counselors will continue to benefit from the thoughtful process of developing Tier 2 action plans (see Figure 5.11), for the following reasons:

- Not all Tier 2 interventions are small groups;
- This text focuses on *data-driven* as opposed to *standards-driven* decision-making processes at the Tier 2 level;
- All texts in the Hatching Results series published by Corwin continue to use intervention action plans that align with the Hatching Results Conceptual Diagram;
- Action plans serve as a supportive document when creating the results report; and
- Action plans serve as a concise and effective tool for informing stakeholders of school counseling activities.

Please note, however, that school counselors interested in applying to RAMP are required to use ASCA's 4th edition templates within the application.

How to Complete a Tier 2 Action Plan for Small Groups

Figure 5.11 is the start of the action plan developed by Nicash for her Academic Success Skills small group. Note how the action plan aligns with the thoughtful conceptual diagrams in Figures 5.12 and 5.13. Figure 5.12 provides a conceptual diagram for determining how Nicash will address the students' needs and measure the impact of the small group. Note the questions that are asked and the thought process in determining the type of intervention the students will receive, as well as the data that will be measured. Then Figure 5.13 provides the thinking behind *implementing* the intervention. Both Figures 5.12 and 5.13 contribute to the language that appears in the final action plan in Figure 5.11. Note the signature lines at the bottom of the action plan to ensure the school counselor and administrator are in agreement. Following offers assistance regarding each of the elements found on the action plan.

Target Group

Focus on an overarching topic for a target group of students who are identified because of a data-driven need. Who will you intervene with? What is the principle concern: poor attendance, discipline referrals, lack of homework completion? State the grade level and data element selected here. Be sure to indicate the specific data element or reason these particular students are being targeted for intervention. As a reminder, indicating "all students referred to group by teachers" would *not* be appropriate for this action plan. This plan is for data-driven, *not* referral-driven interventions. If the intervention is related to a SMART goal, it might be appropriate to indicate that here, to align between this action plan and the program goals (Hatch, 2013).

Title/Type of Tier 2 Activity & Content (Process Data)

In this column, school counselors will list the selected Tier 2 intervention and main topics/items to be covered. Please note that while designed primarily for small group interventions, this action plan can also be used as a plan for implementing and evaluating other Tier 2 interventions (e.g., large group workshops, post-suspension counseling, Check In Check Out).

In our example (Figure 5.11), the intervention is a small group. Note the action plan includes the session topics for the small group and that these align closely with both student needs and the evaluation methods.

Materials and Resources Needed (Process Data)

What resources will be required to ensure the intervention occurs? Will the intervention require funds to purchase curriculum or time for school counselors to develop their own curriculum? Will it require a larger space to hold a group meeting? Will it require collaboration from additional staff to assist in implementing the intervention? Are there any technology needs? Identify the resources needed here.

Figure 5.11 Nicash's Small Group Action Plan

🐣 Hatching Results®   **SCHOOL COUNSELING TIER 2 ACTION PLAN—NICASH'S SAMPLE**

School Name: Nicash's Elementary School   **School Year: 2019–2020**

Target Group: 4th graders with 2 or more Ns (Needs Improvement) in the Work Skills/Study Habits of their report card, who were pre-screened and identified as appropriate for a small group intervention

SMART Goal: The number of 4th graders with 2 or more Ns on their report card will decrease by 10% from trimester 1 to trimester 3.

Process Data				Perception Data		Outcome Data
Title/Type of Tier 2 Activity & Content	Materials and Resources Needed	When and for How Long?	Number of Students	ASCA Mindsets & Behaviors *(or other standards)*	Attitudes (A), Knowledge (K), & Skills (S) to be Measured	Achievement-Related Data (AR) Achievement Data (A)
Small Group on Academic Skills (work skills and study habits) • Following directions • SMART goal setting • Time management • Organizing self and materials • Completing classwork • Completing homework	School counselor-generated 8-week curriculum Group space Writing tools Projector Computer Internet access Audio speakers Incentives Pre/post assessment	Oct. 2019–Dec. 2019 6–8 sessions	12-16 students (2 groups of 6–8 4th grade students)	B-LS 3. Use time-management, organizational and study skills B-LS 4. Apply self-motivation and self direction to learning B-LS 7. Identify long- and short-term academic, career and social/emotional goals	*By the end of the activity, students will:* (A) Believe setting SMART goals will help them do better in school (K) Know the definition of prioritizing (S) Accurately organize their student planners (S) Prioritize their daily "need to do" activities	(AR) Decrease in Ns (needs improvement) on report cards (AR) Increase in classwork completion (AR) Increase in homework completion (A) Grades (A) Benchmark assessment

School Counselor: *Nicash's Signature*   Administrator: *Administrator's Signature*   Date: October 1, 2019

Source: Hatching Results (2019)

127

When and For How Long? (Process Data)

Knowing when an activity will occur and when it will be completed is essential to team planning. Be as specific as possible. For example, small groups are generally held for 30 to 45 minutes each week for 6 to 8 weeks at a time. It is ideal to hold all small group lessons consecutively to maintain consistency and ensure content retention. Other Tier 2 interventions may run for varying lengths of time. When scheduling Tier 2 interventions at the beginning of the year, be sure to consider school breaks, testing schedules, and other school activities.

Number of Students (Process Data)

Indicate the number of students (or participants) intended to be impacted by the Tier 2 intervention.

ASCA Mindsets and Behaviors (Perception Data)

School counselors can select standards from the ASCA Mindsets & Behaviors (ASCA, 2014) that most closely align with the focus of the Tier 2 intervention. It is recommended that counselors list no more than two or three of the most important standards, even though it is common for many of the standards to apply. School counselors may determine that use of state or other standards are appropriate as well.

Attitudes (A), Knowledge (K), & Skills (S) to be Measured (Perception Data)

Which attitudes, knowledge, and skills will be measured through pre-/post-tests, worksheets, activity completion, or other means? School counselors may find it useful to write these statements as measurable objectives (e.g., "By the end of the activity, students will be able to . . ."), which allows for easier pre-/post-test development.

Achievement-Related (AR) & Achievement (A) (Perception Data)

In this column, school counselors list the achievement-related and achievement data they intend to impact through this Tier 2 activity. School counselors provide Tier 2 interventions to students to remove barriers to learning. In some cases, the focus of the intervention may not be directly academic, but rather achievement-related, such as to build peer relationships. The goal in this case is to provide students with skills that will help them get along with others, in order to be more successful academically. Therefore, achievement-related data—such as a reduction in discipline referrals or an increase in work skills/study habits scores on the report card—are measured to determine the effectiveness of the intervention. For more details on the differences between achievement-related and achievement data, readers can refer to Chapter 10.

Putting It All Together

Now that Nicash has determined which students will be served in the small group intervention, the group topics have been chosen, the group composition has been carefully planned, and specific times have been scheduled, Nicash can begin her Tier 2 Action Plan. She creates a SMART (specific, measurable, achievable, relevant, and time-bound) goal for the Academic Success Skills small group: The number of 4th graders with 2 or more Ns on their report card will decrease by 10% from trimester 1 to trimester 3. Although Nicash has not yet chosen the curriculum she will be using, she can begin creating her action plan, brainstorm portions yet undeveloped, and add to it as the curriculum is chosen/developed. Items such as perception data, which typically refer to attitudes, skills, and knowledge, are brainstormed here and then created during the lesson planning process when the curriculum is selected/developed (discussed in detail in Chapter 6 but brainstormed here). Once the curriculum has been chosen and the pre-/post-questions have been developed, Nicash can finalize the action plan. Figure 5.11 is the start of the action plan developed by Nicash for her Academic Success Skills small group. Note again how the action plan aligns with the thoughtful conceptual diagrams in Figures 5.12 and 5.13.

Figure 5.12   Conceptual Diagram for Determining Intentional Interventions

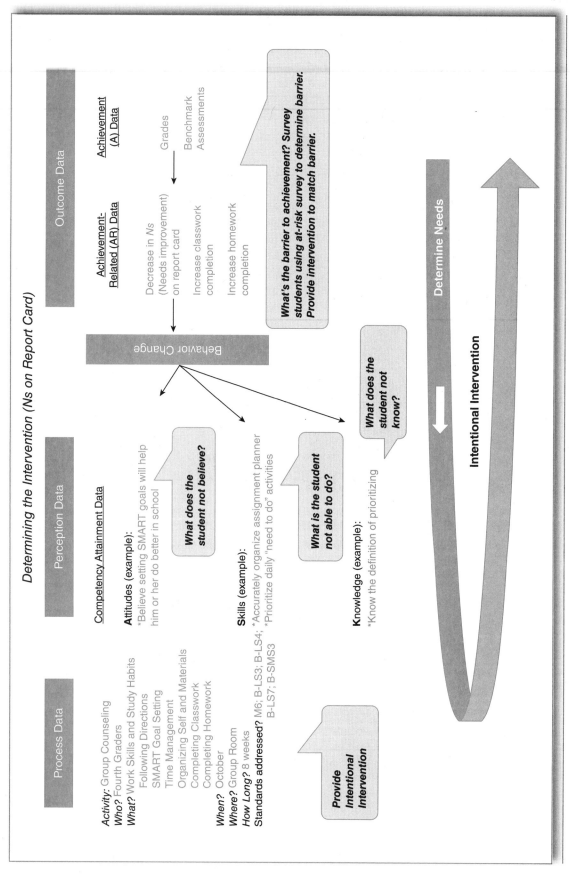

Source: Hatch, T. (2019).

Figure 5.13 Conceptual Diagram Aligning With Nicash's Tier 2 Action Plan for Small Groups

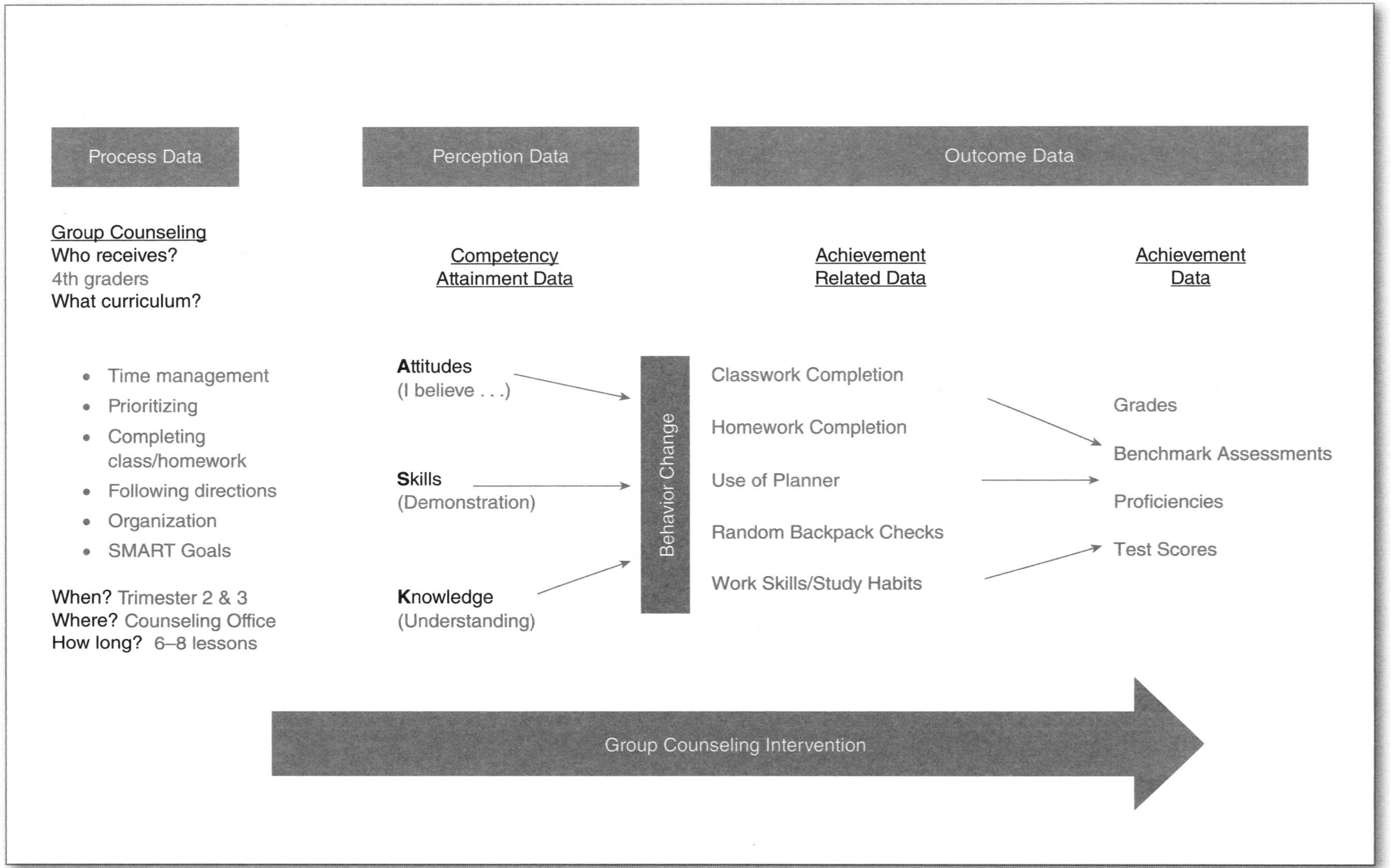

Process Data

Group Counseling
Who receives?
4th graders
What curriculum?

- Time management
- Prioritizing
- Completing class/homework
- Following directions
- Organization
- SMART Goals

When? Trimester 2 & 3
Where? Counseling Office
How long? 6–8 lessons

Perception Data

Competency Attainment Data

Attitudes
(I believe . . .)

Skills
(Demonstration)

Knowledge
(Understanding)

Behavior Change

Outcome Data

Achievement Related Data

Classwork Completion
Homework Completion
Use of Planner
Random Backpack Checks
Work Skills/Study Habits

Achievement Data

Grades
Benchmark Assessments
Proficiencies
Test Scores

Group Counseling Intervention

Source: Hatch, T. (2006–2019).

ACTIVITY 5.1

Using the blank template available on our website, practice creating your own Tier 2 action plan for small groups!

School counselors provide short-term (6-to-8 week), skill-based, and highly structured psycho-educational small groups as one of the most important components of Tier 2. Various data are utilized to determine which type of group is appropriate for each student (emotion management, organization and study skills, etc.). Using information directly from the report card, discipline referrals, and/or pre-intervention assessments, the school counselor selects topics to align directly with the students' needs. School counselors determine the student composition of the small group by taking multiple factors into consideration (behaviors, developmental appropriateness, size, etc.) to create a well-balanced group. In collaboration with teachers, small groups are scheduled with a consideration of the most appropriate time for the teacher, student, and school counselor. As always, parent notification and/or request for consent is central to successful student outcomes.

NICASH'S STORY CONTINUES

Nicash had completed her next steps of planning for her small group by selecting small group counseling topics, using students' report cards and office discipline referrals, choosing the makeup of each small group she would run, sending parents notification of their student's participation, and scheduling specific times for each group to be held. She was finally ready to select her small group counseling curriculum and move on to facilitating her small group counseling lessons for the identified students.

6

Selecting and Developing Small Group Curriculum

NICASH'S STORY CONTINUES

As elementary counselors in the same district, Nicash, Monica, Kathie, and Lauren felt confident about their agreement to use the data element "Work Habits/Social Skills" on report cards when identifying students to consider for group counseling. The report card marks consisted of O (Outstanding), M (Meets Expectations), A (Approaching Expectations), and N (Needs Improvement). The team agreed that students in grades 3–5 who had two or more Ns on their report card would be screened for possible group counseling. However, when it came to choosing the curriculum, the counselors were less confident. Despite their cumulative efforts to find curriculum on study skills, they could not find one they all liked that was also aligned with the areas in which students were struggling (i.e., organizational skills, following directions, time management, and completing classwork).

Previous chapters covered the decision-making process for determining the types of Tier 2 interventions students receive and provided school counselors with instruction on how to utilize data to determine which supports or interventions best address student need. This chapter supports the school counselor to select and/or create the appropriate small group curriculum. We share several types of small group counseling curriculum, along with helpful considerations for choosing or developing group counseling curriculum.

THE ART AND SCIENCE OF SMALL GROUP COUNSELING CURRICULUM

Selecting curriculum for small group counseling is just as important as its successful implementation. Effective school counselors think strategically about the lessons; consider which attitudes, skills, and knowledge (ASK) will be taught to the students; and determine how the curriculum aligns with the desired outcomes. A school counselor's touch of creativity is also important to ensure the curriculum is engaging and comes to life for the students. Group counseling is most impactful when there is a balance between the "art and science" of selecting, developing, and implementing a group curriculum.

Figure 6.1   Science Art Wonder

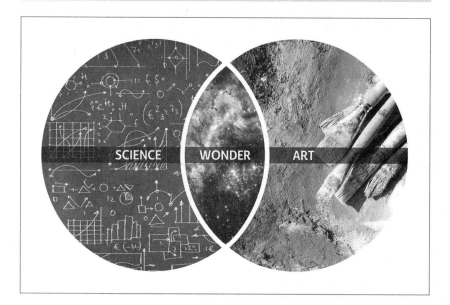

The *science* within small group counseling work is the curriculum and data alignment and evaluation of the intervention; the *art* within the work is the creativity in design and implementation. The combination of *art and science* is present when these concepts work together to ensure thoughtful content is balanced with the school counselor's creativity and delivery and results in the desired student outcomes.

The art component of small group counseling consists of

- an understanding of the students' individual and group personalities when designing lessons;
- creativity to foster engaging and effective lesson plans;
- conscientious, thoughtful collaboration with teachers regarding scheduling of small groups;
- strong facilitation using counseling skills, such as active listening, teaching, managing, empowering, and relationship building; and
- management of challenging behaviors.

The science component is the clinical formation of the small counseling group, which includes

- utilization of data to select students and curriculum topics;
- alignment of an evidence-based, needs-focused curriculum;
- the systematic process of collecting and utilizing data to identify specific student needs;

- evaluation of the change in attitudes, skills, and knowledge as a result of the small group;
- progress monitoring; and
- implementation of upgrades to the curriculum.

The art and science of selecting, developing, and implementing small group counseling requires an important and ongoing combination for an effective small group. One without the other may lead to an unsuccessful experience. For example, a school counselor may select the appropriate curriculum but provide students with ineffective facilitation. On the other hand, the school counselor may effectively facilitate the group but use a curriculum that does not meet the needs of the students. In this chapter, we cover both the art and the science of selecting and/or developing an effective small group curriculum (see Figure 6.1).

Selecting a Small Group Counseling Curriculum

There are many factors to take into consideration when selecting which small group counseling curriculum will work best to fit the students' needs:

- Is curriculum available in my district or online?
- Is the curriculum evidence based?
- If using a pre-packaged curriculum, does it align with my students' needs?
- Has a statewide curriculum currently in use been shown to be effective?
- Would a school counselor–generated curriculum better align with student need?
- Can existing curriculum be revised to better align with student need?

Random Acts of Small Group Curriculum and Evidence-Based Approaches

While a variety of curriculum choices are available for small group counseling, it is important that school counselors proceed with caution when selecting a small group curriculum, as many of these options are simply *random acts* of small group curriculum and not data driven or evidence based. School counselors are encouraged to be *critical consumers* of all curriculum they find in their research to ensure it meets their students' needs and can be evaluated for effectiveness.

Random acts of small group curriculum occur when school counselors

- select lesson topics based on perceived needs instead of data;
- utilize online, shared, educator-created curriculum without tailoring to student needs;
- use a storybook as the sole curriculum;
- mix a variety of unrelated lesson topics;
- experiment with curriculum based on novelty; and/or
- use a free resource without alignment to student need.

It is common practice for school counselors to create a patchwork-quilt style of small group counseling curriculum, made from a variety of lessons they find or pick up at conferences. While school counselors are generally discouraged from combining random curricula, in reality, little research-based curriculum exists for small group interventions, and it may be necessary to compile creatively from the materials available. In these cases, school counselors are reminded to take the time to determine if the content of the lessons actually aligns with the data that brought the students to the group.

DATA-DRIVEN CURRICULUM DECISIONS

Selecting and/or creating small group counseling curriculum is an important component of a successful Tier 2 intervention process. Tier 2 services are *intentional*; thus, it is essential to provide intervention support through targeted curriculum that aligns directly to the students' data-driven needs. If the curriculum does not address these data-driven needs, the desired outcome will not be achieved. An important question to thoughtfully consider when selecting curriculum is, *Are we matching the students to the curriculum or matching the curriculum to the students?*

Using Data to Select Topics/Content

We recommend a systematic, data-driven approach when selecting and/or designing small group topics and curriculum content. For example, consider the report card data in Figure 6.2. Note that learner responsibilities can be disaggregated into two specific topic areas (study skills and social skills). In this example, an elementary school counselor designed two different small groups: Academic Success Skills (Study Skills Group) and Positive Decision-Making Skills (Social Skills Group). Next, the counselor designed the group counseling curriculum by aligning the weekly topics to the specific report card learner responsibility marks. On these report cards, *E* meant the student received an "Excellent" mark on that Work Habits/Social Skills area, *S* represented "Satisfactory," *N* represented "Needs Improvement," and *U* represented an "Unsatisfactory" mark. In this example, the next step for the counselor would be to disaggregate the learner responsibility data and assign students to the appropriate small group aligning with their data-driven need.

EVIDENCE-BASED PRACTICE (EBP) AND SMALL GROUP COUNSELING

Effective small group counseling curriculum is well researched, data driven, and aligned with evidence-based practice (EBP). Originating in the medical field, EBP is defined as "the integration of [the] best research evidence with clinical expertise and patient values" (Sackett, Straus, Richardson, Rosenberg, & Haynes, 2000, p. 1). The EBP approach combines the medical practitioner's integration of knowledge and clinical skills with the best available research. EBP has been applied to nursing, to counseling in psychology, and, most recently, to school counseling (Dimmitt, Carey, & Hatch, 2007). We propose a model of evidence-based school counseling practice that encourages school counselors' use of data to determine (1) the needs that will be addressed (the problem description), (2) which practices or interventions should be implemented (using outcome research), and (3) whether the interventions or practices utilized were effective (the evaluation of the curriculum or intervention).

Figure 6.2 Using Report Card Data to Design Small Group Content

Group Counseling Curriculum at a Glance

Academic Success Skills (Study Skills Group)

Week 1: 1/24 Introduction to Group

Week 2: 1/31 Listening and Following Directions

Week 3: 2/7 Organizational Skills/Time Management

Week 4: 2/21 Completing Classwork/Transitions

Week 5: 2/28 Completing Homework

Week 6: 3/7 Studying/Test-Taking Strategies

Week 7: 3/14 Working Independently/Wrap-Up

Week 8: 3/21 Closure

Positive Decision-Making Skills (Social Skills Group)

Week 1: 1/24 Introduction to Group

Week 2: 1/31 Listening and Following Directions and Rules

Week 3: 2/7 Respecting Others/"Give and Expect Respect"

Week 4: 2/21 Responsibility/Actions and Consequences/ Self-Control

Week 5: 2/28 Taking Charge of Your Academic Success

Week 6: 3/7 Bullying

Week 7: 3/14 Anger Management and Conflict Resolution

Week 8: 3/21 Closure

Learner Responsibilities

E = Excellent

N = Needs Improvement

S = Satisfactory

U = Unsatisfactory

	1st	2nd	3rd
Follows school and playground rules	N	S	
Follows class rules	N	S	
Follows directions/listens effectively	N	S	
Demonstrates self-control	N	S	
Works independently	N	S	
Treats others with courtesy and respect	S	S	
Demonstrates organizational skills	S	S	
Starts and completes classwork on time	N	S	
Completes homework on time	N	S	

Evidence-based approaches (Dimmitt et al., 2007) ask the following questions (see Figure 6.3):

1. Problem Description: *What needs to be addressed?*

2. Outcome Research Use: *What is likely to work based on research?*

3. Intervention Evaluation: *Did the intervention make a difference?*

Utilizing an evidence-based approach, thoughtful group counseling curriculum selection, creation, compilation, and use is best accomplished by (1) aligning content to student need, (2) considering what is likely to work based on research, and (3) evaluating the impact of the group on student attitudes, skills, knowledge, and behaviors.

EBP and Research-Based Curriculum/Programs

Applying EBP to delivering group counseling content refers to selecting a curriculum previously found to be effective, implementing the curriculum, and measuring its impact with the school population. While several evidence-based, school-based programs and curricula are available for Tier 1, very few prepackaged, research-based programs and curricula exist for Tier 2. The additional challenge is that many of the evidence-based Tier 2 programs are not designed specifically for elementary school students and do not meet the guidelines of being short term, brief, and solution focused. For instance, *Coping Power* is an evidence-based curriculum; however, it is 34-week-long program for students identified as severely high risk or severely emotionally disturbed (Institute of Education Sciences [IES], 2011). Clearly, this curriculum, while shown to be effective, is not appropriate for use by a school counselor due to its long-term nature. Counselors are encouraged to research programs prior to investing in them to determine if they meet student and program needs.

Figure 6.3   A Model of Evidence-Based School Counseling Practice

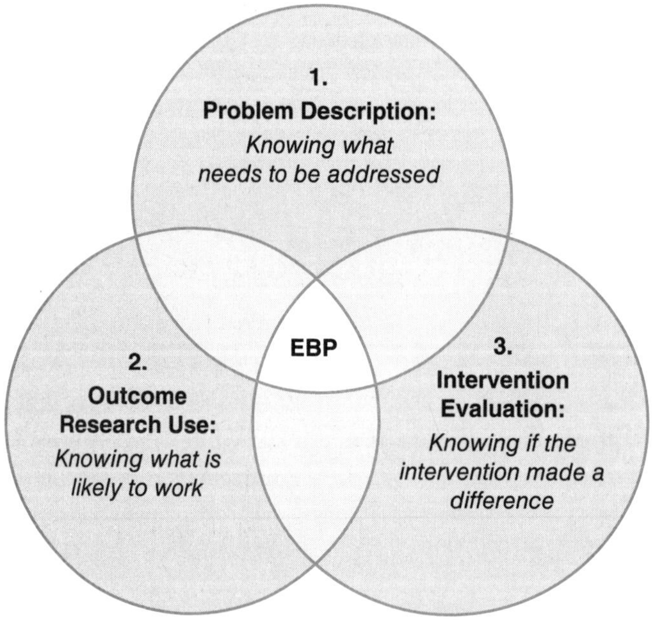

As an alternative, school counselors may consider utilizing portions of programs for small group counseling lessons, such as the Committee for Children's *Second Step* program, found to enhance student outcomes, including improvements in social skills, increased empathy, and less adult intervention in minor student conflicts (Frey, Nolen, Edstrom, & Hirschstein, 2005; Low, Cook, Smolkowski, & Buntain-Ricklefs, 2015). Utilizing an EBP approach allows school counselors to identify lessons for group counseling that meet the data-driven need and to implement the research-based curriculum while evaluating the lesson with perception data and monitoring results to ensure positive outcomes for their particular students' needs.

Dr. Carey Dimmitt, a leading scholar in evidence-based interventions, has compiled a helpful list of evidence-based Tier 1 and Tier 2 (Tables 6.1a and 6.1b) school-based programs and interventions. (Although not all are for small groups, they are included here for reference.) When determining which curriculum is best for the needs of their students, school counselors are encouraged to compare and contrast the different options.

Table 6.1a Tier 1 School-Based Programs

Elementary	Middle School
PeaceBuilders	Steps to Respect
Olweus Bullying Prevention Program	Olweus Bullying Prevention Program
Student Success Skills	Student Success Skills
Promoting Alternative Thinking Strategies (PATHS)	Promoting Alternative Thinking Strategies (PATHS)
Second Step	Second Step
Positive Behavioral Interventions and Supports (PBIS)	Project ALERT
I Can Problem Solve	I Can Problem Solve
Guiding Good Choices	Guiding Good Choices
Caring School Community	Coping Power
Too Good for Violence	Too Good for Violence
Positive Action	Positive Action
Zones of Regulation	Life Skills Training

Source: Compiled by Carey Dimmitt (2017), Ronald H. Fredrickson Center for School Counseling Outcome and Research Evaluation (CSCORE).

Table 6.1b Tier 2 Intervention School-Based Programs

Title	Description
Check and Connect http://checkandconnect.umn.edu/	Dropout prevention intervention • Monitoring of school performance • Case management • Individualized attention and connection in school • Community and family supports
Peer Tutoring	Variety of models • May also use elders, college students, parent volunteers as tutors
Student Success Skills: Small Groups www.studentsuccess skills.com	Booster for at-risk students • Structured groups • Teaches cognitive skills, metacognitive skills, self-management of motivation, optimism • Outcome research: improved FCAT scores for lower-quartile students
Check In Check Out	Focuses on improving classroom behaviors • The teacher provides clear behavioral expectations and incentives • The teacher checks in with the student to set behavioral goals at the start of the period, then checks out with the student at the close of the period to rate that student's conduct and award points or other incentives earned for attaining behavioral goal(s)
Coping Power www.copingpower.com	Meets IES What Works Clearinghouse evidence standards for EBP • Designed for students with aggressive behaviors (at risk or diagnosed with ODD or CD) in grades 4 and 5 and their parents • Emphasizes SEL skills needed during transition to middle school Lessons on goal setting, organizational and study skills, improving emotional awareness, coping with peer pressure, social problem solving, anger management, and peer relationships for students • 34 fifty-minute small group (4–6 students) sessions • 30-minute monthly individual sessions (6–8) for targeted student behavioral change

Skills for Academic & Social Success (SASS)
 	
Currently free (Contact Carrie Masia Warner, PhD, at masiac@wpunj.edu)
	Group sessions—participants learn about social anxiety and connection between thoughts, feelings, and behaviors
	
	• 12 weekly in-school group sessions, 40 minutes, 3–6 students per group
	• 2 follow-up group sessions to address relapse
	• 2 individual student meetings to set goals
	• 4 weekend social events (90 minutes)
	• 2 group meetings for parents
	• Receive social skills training on
	   ○ Starting and maintaining conversations
	   ○ Listening and remembering
	   ○ Assertiveness

Source: Compiled by Carey Dimmitt (2017), Ronald H. Fredrickson Center for School Counseling Outcome and Research Evaluation (CSCORE).

The IES website features the What Works Clearinghouse (https://ies.ed.gov/ncee/wwc/), including resources such as intervention reports and a comprehensive evaluation of different populations and programs. This helpful tool was created to share evidence of effectiveness for different interventions and the specific grade levels examined.

The program guide developed by the Collaborative for Academic, Social, and Emotional Learning (CASEL, 2013; 2015) provides a global review of elementary-based curriculum and programs. The guide identifies, reviews, and offers suggestions for different evidence-based social/emotional learning programs. The programs have not been reviewed in terms of whether or not they are appropriate for group counseling, but they do provide curriculum that can be utilized in a group setting (see Figure 6.4).

ACTIVITY: COMPARE TIER 2 SCHOOL-BASED PROGRAMS

Go online and research the programs in Table 6.1b, then take notes on the pros and cons of each.

Figure 6.4   CASEL Program Guide Review of Elementary-Based Curriculum

TABLE 3   Elementary School Program Design and Implementation Support Ratings

Program Name	Grade Range Covered	Grade-by-Grade Sequence	Average Number of Sessions Per Year	Classroom Approaches to Teaching SEL			Opportunities to Practice Social and Emotional Skills	Contexts that Promote and Reinforce SEL				Assessment Tools for Monitoring Implementation and Student Behavior		
				Explicit Skills Instruction	Integration with Academic Curriculum Areas	Teacher Instructional Practices		Classroom-wide	School-wide	Family	Community	Monitoring Implementation		Measuring Student Behavior
												Self-report	Observation	
4Rs	PreK-8	✓	35 period-long class sessions	✓	✓ English/language arts		●	●	●	●	○	✓		✓
Caring School Community	K-6	✓	Year-long, with 30-35 class meetings		Academic integration strategies provided	✓	●	●	●	●	●	✓	✓	✓
Competent Kids, Caring Communities	K-5	✓	35 lessons	✓	Academic integration strategies provided		●	●	●	●	◑	✓	✓	✓
I Can Problem Solve	PreK-5	✓	59-83 lessons	✓	Academic integration strategies provided		●	●	○	●	○	✓	✓	✓
The Incredible Years Series	PreK-2	✓	64 lessons	✓	Academic integration strategies provided for English/language arts		●	●	○	●	○			
Michigan Model for Health	K-12	✓	8-14 lessons	✓	Academic integration strategies provided		●	●	◑	○	○	✓	✓	✓
MindUP	PreK-8		15 lessons	✓	Academic integration strategies provided		●	●	○	○	○	✓	✓	✓
Open Circle	K-5	✓	34 lessons plus supplementary lessons	✓	Academic integration strategies provided for English/language arts		●	●	●	●	○	✓	✓	✓

KEY   ○ Minimal   ◑ Adequate   ● Extensive

continued on next page

Preschool and Elementary School Edition (9/12)

26   2013 CASEL GUIDE: EFFECTIVE SOCIAL AND EMOTIONAL LEARNING PROGRAMS

Source: CASEL Guide, 2013. www.casel.org

The effectiveness of evidence-based programs and the reported impact on students often depends on the curriculum being implemented in the way that it is presented and proposed to be delivered. If it is not delivered as prescribed, its fidelity and effectiveness may be compromised. Oftentimes, school counselors may need to adjust some of the lessons due to topic alignment, length of group, or other changes that need to be made in a small group. Although some changes to the fidelity of curriculum are inevitable, it is important for school counselors to be aware that these changes can affect the reported outcomes.

Pre-Packaged, Research-Based Curriculum

Pre-packaged, research-based curriculum generally offers pre-tested, structured lesson plans that are well laid out and easy to facilitate, although they may come with a more costly price for the convenience. Typically, these curricula have already been aligned with specific standards and competencies and offer other helpful reproducibles, such as parent letters, staff collaboration documents, and evaluation tools.

WhyTry is an example of a pre-packaged program that focuses on social/ emotional learning and resiliency and is designed for elementary and secondary students (www.whytry.org). In addition to organized units that scaffold students' skills, this pre-packaged program includes structured lessons that provide clear directions and scripts of what is to be said and taught to the students. The WhyTry program also includes colorful lesson posters, videos, and music resources. For some school counselors, having pre-packaged small group counseling curriculum is crucial, especially when time needed to research or create curriculum is limited.

Similar to WhyTry, *Second Step* is a pre-packaged, and highly structured social/ emotional curriculum aimed to transform schools into successful and supportive learning environments (www.secondstep.org). Although intended for classroom lessons, Second Step may be just as effective with students in a small group setting. Students participating in small groups will have the practice to reinforce the skills to allow for mastery.

EBP and School Counselor–Generated Curriculum

When no research-based product exists in the group counseling topic area, school counselors are encouraged to use their professional wisdom as a guide to designing their own lessons that align with research-based best practices. Figure 6.5 provides a sample of no-cost web resources for self-generating curriculum (the entire resource is available online). With this approach, school counselors use their knowledge of and experience with the students they serve to generate a curriculum that meets the developmental and data-driven needs of their students. When developing small group curriculum, school counselors

- research content and resources;
- create lesson plans and actively teach the lessons using a variety of engagement strategies;
- measure students' gains in attitudes, skills, and knowledge;
- assess achievement-related and achievement data aligning with the lesson content; and
- diligently evaluate their materials and lessons to make modifications as needed.

Figure 6.5   No-Cost Web Resources for Self-Generated Elementary School Counseling Curriculum

Hatching Results ®

NO COST WEB RESOURCES FOR SELF-GENERATED ELEMENTARY SCHOOL COUNSELING CURRICULUM

NOTE: This list is not all inclusive of online core curriculum resources for lesson plans and activities—contact us at admin@hatchingresults.com to make additional suggestions of free curriculum sources. Inclusion here is not an endorsement by Hatching Results® or *Hatching Results for Elementary School Counseling: Implementing Core Curriculum and Other Tier 1 Activities* co-authors: Dr. Trish Hatch, Danielle Duarte, or Lisa K. De Gregorio.

GENERAL CORE CURRICULUM RESOURCES

WEBSITE	DESCRIPTION	WHAT YOU'LL FIND
American Foundation for Suicide Prevention https://afsp.org/our-work/education/model-school-policy-suicide-prevention/	Model school policy on suicide prevention.	Lesson Plans [ ] Activities/Worksheets [ ] Tool Kits/Manuals [ ] Brochures/Fact Sheets [ ] Videos [ ] Games [ ] Webinars/PD [ ] Other: Downloadable Guide [✓]
American Hospice Foundation https://americanhospice.org/grief-at-school/	American Hospice Foundation created a model Grief at School training curriculum to train school staff to address the needs of grieving students and discuss grief and loss in the classroom.	Lesson Plans [ ] Activities/Worksheets [ ] Tool Kits/Manuals [✓] Brochures/Fact Sheets [ ] Videos [✓] Games [ ] Webinars/PD [ ] Other: Downloadable Guide [✓]
American School Counselor Association (ASCA) https://www.schoolcounselor.org/	The American School Counselor Association (ASCA) supports school counselors' efforts to help students focus on academic, career, and social development. Provides resources ranging from professional development to lesson plans.	Lesson Plans [✓] Activities/Worksheets [ ] Tool Kits/Manuals [✓] Brochures/Fact Sheets [ ] Videos [ ] Games [ ] Webinars/PD [ ] Other: Handouts [✓]
Attendance Works http://www.attendanceworks.org/	Tools for addressing chronic absenteeism.	Lesson Plans [✓] Activities/Worksheets [ ] Tool Kits/Manuals [✓] Brochures/Fact Sheets [ ] Videos [✓] Games [ ] Webinars/PD [✓] Other: Presentations [✓]
Better Attitudes and Skills in Children http://teamtn.tnvoices.org/sites/teamtn/files/Project%20BASIC%20Anger%20Management%201.pdf	Anger management lessons for PK-3rd.	Lesson Plans [✓] Activities/Worksheets [ ] Tool Kits/Manuals [ ] Brochures/Fact Sheets [ ] Videos [ ] Games [ ] Webinars/PD [ ]

Hatching Results for Elementary School Counseling: Implementing Core Curriculum and Other Tier 1 Activities (2018)

Within this approach, school counselors evaluate perception data (ASK) to determine that the learning objectives for the lessons have been met, and they use the results to make decisions regarding any changes to curriculum they deliver and/or the school counseling program overall. School counselors who generate group counseling curriculum employ a systematic procedure for gathering good-quality data from routine practice and align the work of the school counselor within the evidence-based model approach.

Helpful Tip

Using Chapters 6–10 to Create Evidence-Based Small Group Curriculum

Note that in this chapter, through Chapter 10 ("Other Tier 2 and 3 Evaluations and Sharing Results"), the text goes into depth with respect to each specific step in the process of creating evidence-based, school counselor–generated small group curriculum. Subsequently, this entire textbook serves as a detailed resource and guide on how to generate, facilitate, and evaluate EBP small group curriculum.

So, which is best: a pre-packaged, research-based curriculum, or a school counselor–generated curriculum? It depends. School counselor–generated curriculum may be more closely aligned with the data-driven need, but may lack sophistication and ties to research-based theories. Research-based curriculum may have been proven effective with some populations, but not all. Additionally, the curriculum may only address a portion of the topics intended for the small group based on needs identified.

In other words, trying to determine whether a pre-packaged or counselor-generated small group counseling curriculum is best is like trying to decide between a ready-made can of soup and a home-cooked pot of soup. The answer is, "It depends." A ready-made can of soup offers convenience with its time efficiency, its predictable dependability, and its readily available access. A home-cooked pot of soup may require more time to gather ingredients or the consumer's needs *and* take more time to create, but the chef has more control over the flavor to meet the consumer's specific needs. Oftentimes, what happens for school counselors is a mix of both—utilizing a ready-made can to start, then adding a few other ingredients to meet the needs of the consumer. Considering the consumer and other factors for the chef can help the school counselor decide between a pre-packaged curriculum and a counselor-generated curriculum.

Teachers Pay Teachers (www.teacherspayteachers.com) is a well-known website that allows users to sell and purchase teaching resources and lesson plans. Some of the lesson plans are aligned with or targeted for school counselors. Although these resources can be helpful, it is important for school counselors to be aware that no requirements, restraints, or credentials are needed for the creators and sellers of the material. For example, a quick search for "group counseling curriculum" finds a package for a 10-week group counseling curriculum that can be purchased for $58. This package includes lessons on self-esteem, growth mindset, and friendship skills.

Finding such a pre-packaged group curriculum may save the counselor a lot of time; however, some of the topics included may work for the focus of a counselor's group, while others may not. Should the entire curriculum be used? Is it appropriate to pick and choose which topics align with the focus of the group? Do they connect or build upon the previous ones? Is the pre-packaged curriculum developmentally appropriate for the grade level, or does it need to be modified? Additionally, the fact that the curriculum can be found on the internet does not validate that it is research based or even effective. While utilizing web-shared resources for lessons may be helpful and save time, school counselors are encouraged to be intelligent consumers. A growth mindset lesson may align with the identified need, for example, but a lesson on friendship skills may not. In order to avoid random acts of small group curriculum, it is crucial that the school counselor thoroughly examine the content of the selected lesson with a critical eye, ensuring the activities within the lesson directly align with the needs of the students in the data-driven small group.

School counselors must decide if it is in their students' best interest to match the pre-packaged curriculum to the students' needs or for the student's needs to determine the curriculum, and then to match the selected curriculum to the students' identified needs (see Table 6.2).

Table 6.2   Research-Based Curriculum vs. School Counselor–Generated Curriculum

Table 6.2 offers a resource for helping school counselors to evaluate the benefits and challenges of both types of discussed curriculum: research based and school counselor generated. Utilizing Table 6.2 may help school counselors decide which type of curriculum is best for them to select and implement.

Research-Based Curriculum		School Counselor–Generated Curriculum (self-generated or located online—may also apply to some state curricula)	
Benefits	Challenges	Benefits	Challenges
Evidence supporting effectiveness	EBP still requires school counselors to create local measures to assess impact	Allows counselors to be creative and add the "art" of school counseling	School counselors must create their own lessons through trial and error, and must evaluate and improve lessons regularly
Pre-packaged	Costly and may become outdated	Free	It takes time to make/revise/locate lessons—so it is not "free" if you add up the costs of the extra duties of creating/modifying the curriculum

Research-Based Curriculum		School Counselor–Generated Curriculum (self-generated or located online—may also apply to some state curricula)	
Benefits	Challenges	Benefits	Challenges
Ready made—typically easy to pick up and teach with little prep	May not culturally align with the needs of local students and may be outdated	Can create/revise curriculum to meet cultural or other needs of the student population	Requires prep time to create lessons
Proven impact through research	Many lessons are needed to implement/teach with fidelity	Counselors can collaborate to divide up lessons to create/revise	Lessons may be haphazard and not scaffolded as in pre-packaged programs
Many lessons	Too many lessons for the school counselor to teach alone (requires consolidation or selecting a few)	Online lessons are easy to locate and are often well vetted by many counselors	May lend itself to personal preferences and be overly heavy in one domain, versus balancing the three domains
Packaged in sequential/scaffolded lessons	Not as impactful if randomly taught	Can take local developmental needs into account	Often is created in a vacuum
When teachers buy in, the whole school supports delivery	Requires teacher buy-in	Can be very tech-savvy, cutting-edge, and engaging for students with a skilled school counselor	May be less sophisticated if a school counselor lacks tech training/tools
May have some assessment tools (typically self-reported behaviors)	May not include perception assessments (counselors may have to create their own)	Self-generated content allows pre-/post-tests to align better with attitudes, skills, and knowledge	May require assessment tools and rubrics to be created
May be scripted—easy to pick up and go	Scripted—may not be in line with the counselor's voice or may hinder creativity	May be helpful for first-year counselors who are just starting to learn by creating their own material	Risk of random acts of curriculum

Statewide Curriculum

Some states have collaborated to provide school counselors with statewide counseling core curriculum that may also be utilized as a resource for small group counseling (see Figure 6.6). This statewide curriculum is likely aligned to the state's academic standards, and this option can assist school counselors in efficiently selecting an already vetted curriculum for their small group intervention. Although state-provided curriculum can be beneficial, it is vital for school counselors to continue to critically examine the curriculum's relativity to the attitudes, skills, or knowledge being taught, as well as the effectiveness and fit for the needs of their particular groups.

Two examples of statewide/group curriculum include the following:

1. *Missouri* (www.missouricareereducation.org/project/smallgroup) has lessons on anger management, self-control, study skills, and more.

2. *West Virginia* (http://wvde.state.wv.us/counselors/group-lessons.html) has lessons on listening, following directions, time management, studying, and more.

Figure 6.6 Statewide Core Curriculum Web Resources

Resource	URL	Description
Connecticut's Comprehensive School Counseling Curriculum	https://portal.ct.gov/SDE	Guide to comprehensive school counseling program development
Hinsdale (New Hampshire) School District's Curriculum	www.hnhsd.org/curriculum/all/guidance.pdf	School counseling curriculum including RTI resources, ASCA competencies, student services organizational chart, referral forms, and career development framework
Iowa Department of Education: School Counseling	www.educateiowa.gov/school-counseling	Resources relating to SMART goals, managing and delivering a school counseling program, action plans, and use of data
Missouri Department of Elementary and Secondary Education: Guidance and Counseling Support Materials	https://dese.mo.gov/college-career-readiness/school-counseling/curriculum/guidance-supplemental-materials	Sample guidance units and lessons represent a complete set of units for each element of the guidance and counseling K–12 grade-level expectations
Public Schools of North Carolina: Guidance Curriculum for the Comprehensive School Counseling Program	www.dpi.state.nc.us/docs/curriculum/guidance/resources/programs-study.pdf	Guide to comprehensive school counseling program development for K–12

Resource	URL	Description
State of Washington: K–12 Education	http://k12.wa.us/ OSSI/K12Supports/ CareerCollegeReadiness/	Secondary education and K–12 supports including resources, templates, and curriculum development for schoolwide program
Tucson (Arizona) Unified School District: Guidance and Counseling	http://tusd1.org/Departments/ Counseling/CounselorResources/ ElementaryGuidanceCurriculum/ tabid/79283/Default.aspx	Curriculum geared toward the elementary setting
West Virginia Department of Education	http://wvde.state.wv.us/counselors/ links/advisors/lesson-plans.html	Lesson plans and handouts on a variety of topics

Using Tier 1 Curriculum for Small Groups

Elementary school counselors deliver lessons on social skills, work skills, and study habits to all students through regularly scheduled core curriculum. Core curriculum lessons often encompass content that has already been created, facilitated, and, ideally, evaluated. Re-delivering the classroom content in a small group environment may be exactly what the struggling student needs.

Consider the typical teacher's classroom. If students who have received core subject matter instruction continue to struggle with expected academic progress, they are often supported through small group intervention, with a focus on teaching the same (or similar) material for their specific areas of need. Teachers analyze the concepts that such students did or did not master, and the students may receive a Tier 2 intervention consisting of similar instruction in a one-on-one or small group setting. During the small group academic intervention, teachers may use creative strategies to re-teach the concepts previously taught, but not yet mastered. Teachers often incorporate different learning styles, accommodations, and engaging activities and use data to monitor progress in a smaller setting (Cassidy, 2004).

Similar to teachers, if students have been identified by data as needing more intentional supports, perhaps it is because they lack mastery of the core curriculum taught or the attitudes, skills, and knowledge delivered. One helpful and time-efficient idea is to utilize the same core curriculum lesson taught on the specific topic (study skills, friendship skills, etc.) for delivery in a small group setting and to re-teach the students the content. In this way, when students qualify for Tier 2 counseling interventions, counselors can simply do what teachers do—re-teach the core content in a smaller group. Rather than creating all-new small group curriculum, consider revisiting core curriculum, re-teaching it in a small group utilizing various creative strategies, and monitoring progress through use of data in the same Tier 2 process approach as teachers. Table 6.3 provides a parallel alignment of the teacher's process with the recommended school counselor's Tier 2 intervention process.

Table 6.3   We Are Teachers, Too! Teacher Tier 2 Process vs. School Counselor Tier 2 Process

		Teacher	School Counselor
Tier 1	*What is taught to all students?*	Core curriculum (language arts)	Core curriculum (study skills)
	How is learning assessed?	• Benchmarks • Assessments	• Report card data • Pre-/post-assessments
	What happens when most students don't learn the content?	Re-teach core curriculum to whole class	Re-teach core curriculum to whole class
	What data determine which students receive a Tier 2 intervention?	When students don't meet the benchmark (scoring *below basic* on a reading assessment)	When students don't meet the benchmark (receiving two or more Ns on the Work Habits section of the report card)
Tier 2	*What interventions are provided when some students don't meet the benchmarks?*	Core curriculum is re-taught in small groups (language arts), adjusting for additional student engagement and needs	Core curriculum is re-taught in small groups (study skills), adjusting for additional student engagement and needs
	How do we know if the student is progressing in the identified area?	• Progress monitoring • Benchmarks • Formative evaluations • Summative evaluations	• Progress monitoring • Intermittent teacher feedback • Pre-/post-tests • Outcome data
	What data determine which students receive a Tier 3 intervention?	If students continue to show lack of progress or have a severe need	If students continue to show lack of progress or have a severe need

Collaboration to Create Group Counseling Curriculum (Districtwide Group Curriculum)

When school counselors collaborate districtwide to create their comprehensive counseling programs and services, all stakeholders benefit. As small group counseling curriculum is developed districtwide and delivered consistently as an intervention for Tier 2 students across all schools within the district, equity and access to quality and consistent educational supports are ensured. If students need additional Tier 2 supports, it does not matter which school they attend or who their school counselor is; all students are guaranteed to receive the same supports and interventions.

As a result, regardless of which school students attend within the district, they will be familiar with and have access to the small group counseling curriculum that will teach them the attitudes, skills, and knowledge they may have previously learned and are evaluated upon.

Collaborating to create curriculum saves time for school counselors, which then allows for more time for students. If the same report card data criteria are identified across the different schools and each school counselor is teaching similar standards aligned with the report card marks, the school counselors may be able to work together in a more efficient way.

Helpful Tip

Utilizing Technology

School counselor curriculum collaboration has become more accessible thanks to technology. Today's workplaces utilize technology to access online sharing and learning communities around the world, such as focused groups on social media or content-sharing websites, such as Google Drive and Dropbox. Engaging in these online communities can have many advantages, such as connecting with more experienced professionals, fast access to necessary and effective curriculum and resources, and instant feedback for improvement. Curriculum can also be shared and worked on simultaneously, within a school, district, or state; nationwide; or even globally. The use of online curriculum collaboration supports school counselors by ensuring they do not have to "reinvent the wheel" and allows more time for direct services to students.

NICASH'S STORY CONTINUES

After Nicash and her three elementary counselor colleagues collaborated on the report card data criteria used to identify the small group counseling students, they met to analyze the information and prioritize the different lesson topics that would be addressed in the small group counseling curriculum. To work more efficiently, they split up the work of researching and developing the eight lesson plans and pre-/post-assessment tools. They agreed to begin by each taking on two lessons. They also recognized that the lower grades (first and second) would require a different developmental level than the upper grades (third through fifth). Rather than taking on eight lessons each for two different grade-level settings (16 lessons altogether), each school counselor was only responsible for developing four lessons total (two for the lower grades and two for the upper grades). The counselors' collaboration on the curriculum and pre-/post-assessment evaluation tools not only saved Nicash and her team a large amount of time, but they were also able to franchise their small group counseling intervention to ensure equity of group counseling services across the entire district!

LESSON PLANS

Similar to teachers, effective school counselors design and utilize engaging lesson plans to facilitate their small group counseling lessons. Creating visual aids to present the lessons, such as PowerPoint presentations, that directly align with the lesson plans may be very beneficial for both the students' engagement and the school counselor's organization. As outlined in more detail in Chapter 8 (p. 211), we encourage school counselors to follow the "backward design" approach to developing lesson plans. This ensures that the lesson content is strongly aligned to what is being assessed through the pre-/post-tests. Whether the school counselor utilizes a pre-packaged or school counselor–generated curriculum, consistent use of the ASCA National Model lesson plan template can be beneficial for all stakeholders involved. Some pre-packaged lesson plans may lack one or more of the components of the ASCA lesson plan template and may need to be tailored to add vital information. School counselors are encouraged to use the lesson plan template that works for them, or the one that may be required by their district.

Among the advantages of utilizing the ASCA National Model lesson plan are that it

- creates structure for the group's facilitation;
- establishes a routine that helps students understand what to expect;
- organizes school counselors' group time to help them stay on track;
- identifies ASCA Mindsets & Behaviors that will be attained in the lesson;
- outlines a list of materials needed;
- documents the procedural steps and activities for the lesson;
- allows for the ability to revisit previous lesson plans for upgrades;
- standardizes a group counseling practice for other school counselors;
- enables other professionals (e.g., other school counselors, a co-facilitator, a substitute counselor) to facilitate the lesson in the absence of the school counselor; and
- serves as a quick reference as well as a marketing tool.

The lesson plan template Nicash selected to use for her small groups (see Figures 6.8 and 6.11) was from the ASCA National Model (3rd edition) and aligns with the Tier 2 Action Plan (Figure 6.7). What follows are instructions for completing that lesson plan. School counselors who consider applying to RAMP after 2021 will be required to use the ASCA lesson template provided in the 4th edition.

School Counselor

Identify the school counselor(s) who is responsible for facilitating the lesson. This may include any other personnel who may collaborate and support co-facilitation (school counseling intern, school social worker, etc.).

Date

Identify the specific anticipated date for the lesson facilitation. The date helps the school counselor to recognize the chronological order of different topics/skills in relation to the scope and sequence of the skill-building and scaffolding, and holds the school counselor accountable.

Activity Title

Identify the specific topic focus of the lesson. This may be an objective and direct description of the content, but may also allow for a creative and catchy topic title. It could also help the school counselor quickly identify the content focus of the lesson.

Figure 6.7   Nicash's ASCA Small Group Action Plan

🐣Hatching Results®   SCHOOL COUNSELING TIER 2 ACTION PLAN—NICASH'S SAMPLE

School Name: Nicash's Elementary School   **School Year:** 2019–2020

Target Group: 4th graders with 2 or more Ns (Needs Improvement) in the Work Skills/Study Habits of their report card, who were pre-screened and identified as appropriate for a small group intervention

SMART Goal: The number of 4th graders with 2 or more Ns on their report card will decrease by 10% from trimester 1 to trimester 3.

Process Data				Perception Data		Outcome Data
Title/Type of Tier 2 Activity & Content	Materials and Resources Needed	When and for How Long?	Number of Students	ASCA Mindsets & Behaviors (or other standards)	Attitudes (A), Knowledge (K), & Skills (S) to be Measured	Achievement-Related Data (AR) Achievement Data (A)
Small Group on Academic Skills (work skills and study habits) • Following directions • SMART goal setting • Time management • Organizing self and materials • Completing classwork • Completing homework	School counselor-generated 8-week curriculum Group space Writing tools Projector Computer Internet access Audio speakers Incentives Pre/post assessment	Oct. 2019–Dec. 2019 6–8 sessions	12-16 students (2 groups of 6–8 4th grade students)	B-LS 3. Use time-management, organizational and study skills B-LS 4. Apply self- motivation and self direction to learning B-LS 7. Identify long- and short-term academic, career and social/emotional goals	*By the end of the activity, students will:* (A) Believe setting SMART goals will help them do better in school (K) Know the definition of prioritizing (S) Accurately organize their student planners (S) Prioritize their daily "need to do" activities	(AR) Decrease in Ns (needs improvement) on report cards (AR) Increase in classwork completion (AR) Increase in homework completion (A) Grades (A) Benchmark assessment

School Counselor: *Nicash's Signature*   Administrator: *Administrator's Signature*   Date: October 1, 2019

Source: Hatching Results (2019)

Helpful Tip

Scope and Sequence to Prioritize Lesson Topics

The American School Counselor Association recommends that small group counseling lessons be provided over a 6 to 8 week period (ASCA, 2012). Once small group curriculum topics have been selected, school counselors must prioritize the scope and sequence of the lessons in a thoughtful way. Creating a scope and sequence of lessons is a practice that strategically organizes the lessons to build upon one another. There are different factors to consider when prioritizing topics, such as students' needs and the scaffolding of different knowledge and skills the students will need in order to ensure the next lesson's knowledge and skills are attainable. For example, in Figure 6.2 (page 137), as highlighted by the sequence of the lessons, in order for students to successfully complete classwork and homework consistently (weeks 4 and 5), certain academic success skills, such as organizing themselves and materials for learning (week 3), must prelude the skill of completing homework. Considering the different scaffolding factors and prioritizing the lesson topics accordingly will benefit the efficacy of the curriculum.

Grades

Identify the grade level(s) of the targeted group of students who will be participating, to ensure developmental appropriateness. Students may be grouped together by their grade level or combined in mixed-grade groups; however, it is ideal to consider the developmental appropriateness of the group topics and curriculum being used.

Learning Objectives

Identify the goals of the attitudes, skills, and knowledge to be attained by the end of the small group lesson. Discussing learning objectives at the beginning of the lesson with the students can be beneficial so they understand what to expect. Revisiting the learning objectives at the end of the lesson can also be a way to verify if objectives were met or need to be re-taught. Typically, an average of one to three learning objectives is a reasonable goal for a lesson; however, this may vary depending on the lesson and activities.

ASCA Mindsets & Behaviors

Target two to three competencies to be mastered from within the lesson. Although a variety of Mindsets & Behaviors standards may be practiced in the lesson, we suggest selecting three to five of the most relevant ones. It is beneficial to compare the ASCA Mindsets & Behaviors from lesson to lesson to ensure a wide array of standards and competencies are being met cumulatively and adjust accordingly. It is also a way to reflect upon and ensure what is intended to be taught, in each lesson and as an entire group curriculum, is actually what is being taught.

Figure 6.8 Blank ASCA Small Group Lesson Plan Template (3rd edition)

Lesson Plan #: Title of Lesson

School Counselor:

Date:

Topic & Time:

Grade:

Learning Objective:

1. Students will be able to:

-

ASCA Mindsets & Behaviors:

-

Materials:

-

Procedure/Lesson Outline:

1. Introduction:
2. Lesson Purpose
3. Icebreaker
4. Content
5. Activity
6. Closure

Plan for Evaluation:

Process Data:

Perception Data:

Outcome Data:

Follow Up:

Reference:

Source: Reprinted with permission from the American School Counselor Association.

Helpful Tip

Similar to teachers, it is best practice for school counselors to consider using not only basic recall of facts in pre-/post-assessments and learning objectives, but also higher levels of complexity and critical thinking such as Bloom's "Taxonomy of Educational Objectives." Bloom's framework suggests that there are six levels of knowledge (i.e., remember, understand, apply, analyze, evaluate, create) that build upon each other (see Figure 6.9). Alignment of lesson objectives with the higher levels of cognitive processes challenges students to not simply remember the content, but also practice the ability to truly *apply* the content as a skill—a higher level of creative and critical thinking.

Figure 6.9   Bloom's Taxonomy

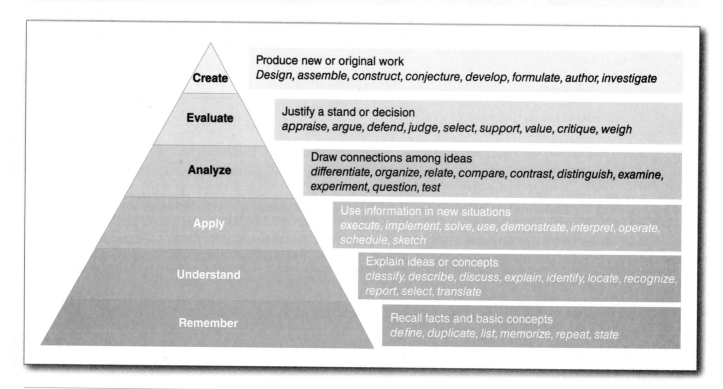

Materials

Explicitly list all the materials necessary for all activities of the facilitation. Consider listing the counseling space to be utilized, technology needs, writing tools, and any behavioral reinforcements or management tools. Listing materials can help school counselors become better organized and able to advocate for group counseling needs.

Procedure

Outline the content and activities step-by-step. The procedure should be written clearly and outlined in detail to show anyone how to facilitate the teaching of the content, activities, and discussions and the evaluation check for comprehension. This is especially helpful in case the lesson needs to be implemented in an absence or, in the future, by another school counselor. While there is flexibility in how or what order school counselors facilitate the procedure process, a typical outline of a group counseling procedure may include

- a check-in, icebreaker, or team builder;
- a revisit of the last topic;
- an introduction to a new topic;
- instruction of knowledge and skills;
- an engaging activity reinforcing the new knowledge and skills;
- a check for comprehension; and
- closure.

Figure 6.10 is a helpful reference tool created by Danielle Duarte that offers a variety of easy-to-use student engagement strategies utilized for core curriculum school counseling lessons, which can be modified and used for small group lessons.

Plan for Evaluation

The plan for evaluation includes the action plan for how the lesson's effectiveness will be assessed. Consider explaining how the lesson may be measured and which types of data may be evaluated to ensure effectiveness.

Nicash's lesson plan on time management (see Figure 6.11) highlights the use of the ASCA small group lesson plan, its alignment of lessons with report card data (see Figure 6.2, p. 137), and the use of multiple learning styles within the lesson.

Figure 6.10   Student Engagement Strategies

Think -Pair-Share

1. Identify point of discussion.
2. Allow students time to think individually.
3. Have students face partner to share ideas.
4. Pair/student contributes to whole group.

"Sole" Mates

1. Pose a question to students and allow time to think and/or write down their answers.
2. Ask students to get up and find their "sole" mate – someone with similar shoes on – to discuss their answer.

Thumbs Up, Thumbs Down

1. School counselor asks a whole class question.
2. Allow students think time.
3. Randomly choose a student to respond to question.
4. Tell students to agree or disagree with response using thumbs up or thumbs down gesture.

Can also be used as school counselor poses a series of statements to the whole group and students respond thumbs up thumbs down, and school counselor calls on individual students to ask rationale.

Pull Cards

1. Give each student a 3x5 index card as they come into the classroom and ask them to write their name on the card.
2. You can also ask them to write other information that aligns with the lesson topic (like how often they write in their planner every week before a lesson on organization) or answer questions (such as a pre-test question).
3. Collect cards and use to randomly choose students to participate during the lesson.

Choral Reading

1. Have a passage or phrase for all students to read together.
2. Once ready, give signal for group to read together chorally.

Appropriate for school counselors to use in whole group and/or small group.

Lines of Communication

1. Have students form two lines facing each other.
2. Provide students with a talking prompt.
3. Decide which side of the line begins the conversation.
4. Give about 1-2 minutes for students to communicate.
5. Have one end person from one line go to end of the line and have students from same line slide down.
6. Give same prompt or different talking point.

Fist to Five

1. Ask students to rate, on a scale of fist to five, with a fist meaning they don't know at all and a five meaning they could teach someone else, the answer to the following question, or whether or not they agree with a statement.
2. Pose the question to the students.
3. Observe the range (or lack of range) within the room and randomly call on students to explain their number.

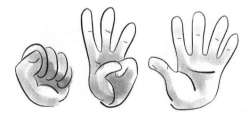

Give One, Get One

1. Using a structured template, have students write a list of facts or ideas learned.
2. Have students begin with a partner assigned by you.
3. Instruct them to collect one new and different fact or idea from their partner.
4. Then they are to give one new and different fact or idea.
5. If neither has a new and different idea, tell them to brainstorm and try to create one.
6. Have students go from person to person until they generate several ideas on the subject.
7. Compile a group list of ideas generated.

(Continued)

Figure 6.10 (Continued)

Echo/Repeat Responses

1. Students "echo" the word, phrase, etc. school counselor states.

- Appropriate for school counselor to use with whole group, and/or with individual students.
- A useful way of ensuring that students practice the target vocabulary being taught.

Think-Ink-Pair-Share

1. Identify point of discussion.
2. Allow students time to think individually.
3. Allow students time to ink/write ideas down.
4. Have students face partner to share ideas.
5. Pair/student contributes to whole group.

Partner Jigsaw

1. Each student receives a portion of the materials to be introduced.
2. Students leave their "home" groups and meet in "expert" groups.
3. Expert groups discuss the material and brainstorm ways in which to present their understandings to the other members of their "home" group.
4. The experts return to their "home" groups to teach their portion of the materials and to learn from other members of their "home" group.
5. Students can use a graphic organizer to write down notes as experts talk.

Code Your Reading

1. Give each student a reading passage related to the lesson topic.
2. Model how students are to code their reading as follows:
   * an aha
   ? question or clarification
   ! validates their learning.
3. After set time, call on students to share their findings.

Guided Notes

1. Create a set of notes with fill in the blank information about the lesson you are teaching (ex: A-G requirements are ____; A growth mindset is ____).
2. Provide guided notes handout to students to fill in as you are presenting the lesson content and allow time to fill in the blanks.

Ticket Out the Door

1. At the end of the lesson, give an index card or piece of blank paper to each student.
2. Pose a question or sentence starter that relates to lesson objective.
3. Have each student write their answer and as they exit they are to turn in their index card or slip of paper containing their answer.
4. School counselor can use student responses to gauge student learning (and even as a brief post-assessment).

Sentence Frames

1. Pose a question to students and provide them with a prompt to respond that aligns with the question.
2. Allow time for students to respond.

- The framework allows students time to structure their thoughts.
- It is helpful to reframe the answer with "because" or "when."
- Example: What makes you angry?
    I feel angry when _____.

Four Corners

1. Read a statement to the class related to lesson topic and allow them to think if they strongly agree/agree/disagree/strongly disagree.
2. Hang signs in the four corners of the classroom with the four choices and ask students to move to the corner that applies to them.
3. When at their corner, give them 1-2 minutes to discuss the reason for their choice with other members of the group and be prepared to share with the entire class.
4. Discuss as a group.

Figure 6.11 Nicash's Time Management Lesson Plan 4 Example

Lesson Plan 4: Time Management

School Counselor: Ms. Nicash Krublo

Date: 11/14/17

Topic & Title: Time Management: Prioritizing My Time

Note the lesson topic alignment with the report card data

Grade: 4th grade

Learning Objective:

Students will be able to:

- Define time management and prioritizing
- Summarize the idea behind "big rocks," "small rocks," "pebbles," and "sand."
- Differentiate between a "Need to Do," "Important to Do," and "Want to Do"
- Identify a plan on how their time can be used more effectively

ASCA Mindsets & Behavior:

- B-LS3: Use time-management, organizational and study skills
- B-LS1: Use critical thinking skills to make informed decisions
- B-SMS8: Demonstrate the ability to balance school, home and other activities.

Materials:

- Priorities chart (Appendix A)
- Youtube video- https://www.youtube.com/watch?time_continue=29&v=F5Jl_6nsgaM
- Copies of student's previous week (Lesson #3) personal SMART goal
- Copies of lesson pre-/post-surveys
- Highlighters (pink, yellow, green)

Procedure/Lesson Outline:

1. Welcome & Check-in:

a. Welcome students back to group (1 minute)

b. Quickly review group norms from Lesson 1 (2 minutes)

c. Group check-in (8 mins):

- Ask students how they are feeling by holding up a finger with the number 1-5 (1 = "I am having a horrible day" to 5 = "today is amazing!")

- Let students know that they are able to share more about their number if they would like.

- Be sure to check in privately with students after group who report lower than a 3 in this activity

- Administer and collect lesson pre-survey

d. Previous lesson review:

- Give students' their personal SMART goal (that students set for themselves during week #3) and allow students to turn to a partner to share any updates (are they taking steps to reach their goals?). Explain to students that in order to meet our goals, it is important to use our time well. (1 minute)

2. _Lesson_

e. Purpose:

- Ask students: ***"Does anyone know the meaning of the word time-management?"*** Provide students time to respond. If students cannot answer, explain that **"time-management means the way we manage our time."** (2 minutes)

- Ask students: ***"How about prioritizing? Does anyone know what this word means?"*** Provide students time to respond. If students cannot answer, explain ***"prioritizing means we put our activities in order from most important to least important."*** (2 minutes)

- Explain that the purpose of the lesson is for students to:
  - identify their priorities in life
  - explore how they are currently using their time

Examples- Playing with my friends (Want to Do), taking a shower (Need to Do), studying for my math test (Important to Do).

• Ask students if they are spending more time doing things they "Want to Do" than doing things they "Need to Do" or are "Important to Do". If the answer is yes, discuss with students why it is important to complete the "Need to Do" and "Important to Do" activities before the "Want to Do" activities.

c. "How I Spend My Time" worksheet (see below, appendix A): 10 minutes
- Hand out one worksheet per student and ask them to take out a writing tool.
- Read the examples with the students and ask them to list any other activities that they do in a typical day.
- Ask the students to highlight:
  • "Need to Do" activities from the list in pink
  • "Important to Do" activities from the list in yellow
  • "Want to Do" activities from the list in green
- Ask the students to turn to their partner and discuss if they:
  • Have more pink and yellow activities highlighted than green
  • Have more green than pink and yellow activities highlighted
- If they are not, ask them if the green areas are helping them to reach their S.M.A.R.T. goal (reviewed during the check-in).

d. Closure: (5 minutes)
- Closure (5 minutes)
- Inform the students that at this time, they can sign the back of their PBIS tickets for a chance to enter the raffle for the three winners who will get the opportunity to pick from the prize box.
- Reinforce with the students that since they completed all the group session tasks successfully, as mentioned, they earned "free play time." Put the alloted amount of time on the projector.

• discuss ways that their priorities may relate to their current use of time how to manage their time more effectively. (3 minutes)

3. Lesson Process:
a. Video and Recap Discussion: *Note the use of the engagement strategy of utilizing multiple learning styles*
- Begin by showing video link to demonstrate the idea of prioritizing by using big rocks, small rocks, pebbles and sand. (4 minutes)

https://www.youtube.com/watch?time_continue=29&v=F5Jl_6nsgaM

- After showing the video, recap with students about their thoughts and main points below: (2 minutes)
• If you don't put the big rocks in first, you'll never get them all in
• If you fill your jar up first with the sand or pebbles, there won't be any room for the rocks
• We need to figure out what our priorities are first (big rocks) and work on those first because those are the things that move you toward your goals.
• Once your goal-related activities are scheduled, then you can fill the rest of your schedule with activities that are less important, but still need to get done

b. "Need to Do, Important to Do, Want to Do" Discussion: 5 minutes
- Ask students if there is a difference between activities that they "Need to Do," "Important to Do," and "Want to Do'.
• Explain "a 'Need to Do' activity is something that you must do for survival (such as eating, sleeping, and hygiene etc)."
• Explain that " an 'Important to Do' activity is something that is a priority for you and your values (ie: chores, homework, family obligations, etc). These are things that help you to reach your goals."
• Explain that "a 'Want to Do' activity is something that you would like to do (such as video games, tv, playing, etc). These activities do not necessarily help you meet your goals."
• Give the students an example of each and ask them to raise their hand to answer which category ("Need to, Important to, Want to Do") the example is from.

(Continued)

Figure 6.11 (Continued)

Lesson #4: Time Management & Prioritizing Pre-/Post-Survey

Please circle the best answer.

1. I believe it's important to manage my time.

   a. Strongly Agree

   b. Agree

   c. Disagree

   d. Strongly Disagree

2. If you had a jar and wanted to fit in the following items, which would you put in first, to make sure everything will fit?

   a. Sand

   b. Little rocks

   c. Big rocks

   d. Water

3. When should your "Want to Do" activities be scheduled?

   a. Last

   b. Second

   c. First

   d. Not at all

4. Putting our activities in order from the most important to the least important is called

   a. Goal Setting

   b. Decision Making

   c. Homework

   d. Prioritizing

   e. None of These

5. Help Johnny prioritize the following activities:

   a. Do homework, go outside to play, eat, talk to a friend

   b. Go outside to play, eat, do homework, talk to a friend

   c. Talk to a friend, eat, do homework, go outside to play

   d. Eat, do homework, go outside to play, talk to a friend

- Give a warning minute for the students to clean up and come back to the circle.

- Once the time is up and students are back in the circle, thank the students for attending the first group and express excitement for the rest of the future sessions.

- Use the bottom portion of "How I Spend My Time" worksheet as a ticket out the door. Have students circle one "Important to Do" activity that they commit to doing more throughout the next week. Ask students to also select a "Want to Do" activity that they can commit to doing less over the next week.

- Thank students for coming and participating.

- Reinforce to students that time management and prioritizing will also be addressed in the next lesson. (2 minutes)

- Remind the students that as they are dropped off to their classrooms, they need to mirror the same positive behavioral expectations they did as they left for group, as they return from group.

- Walk students back to class.

Plan for Evaluation:

Process Data:

Who: Two groups of 6 to 8 4th grade students

What: Lesson on time management and prioritizing time

When: 11/14/17 at 1:30pm

Perception Data: Pre-/Post Survey

Outcome Data: Improvement in Work Habits section of the report card

Follow Up: School counselor will review time-management lesson during check-in and ask how they utilized throughout the week.

Reference: Video

Appendix A: Name: _____

How I Spend My Time Worksheet

Activity	Hours Spent

Ticket out the door:

In order to better prioritize my time, this week I will:

- Increase time _____ ("Important to Do" activity)
- Decrease time _____ ("Want to Do" activity)

165

LESSON POWERPOINT

Nicash created a PowerPoint presentation for each weekly lesson that aligned with the ASCA National Model lesson plan (see Figure 6.12). Presentation tools such as PowerPoint, Google Slides, Prezi, and Pear Deck can be helpful for both the school counselor and for students participating in small groups.

Figure 6.12 Nicash's Lesson Plan PowerPoint Presentation

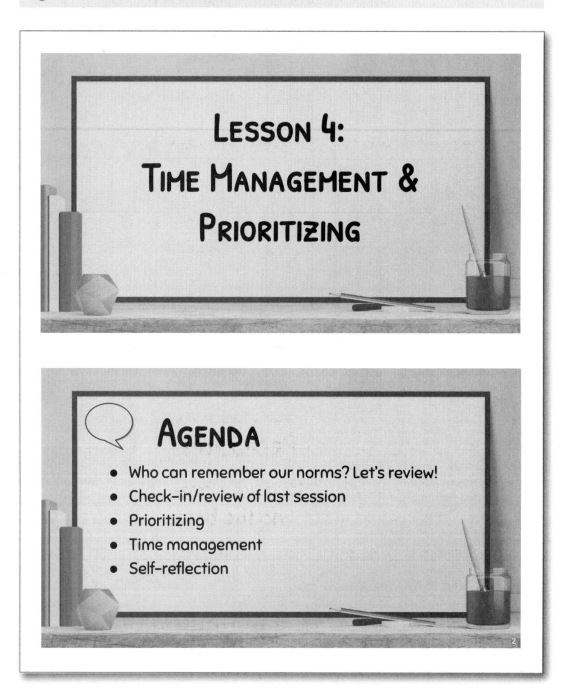

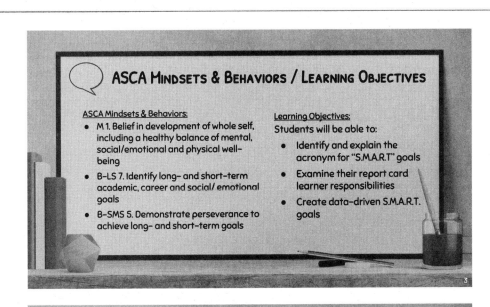

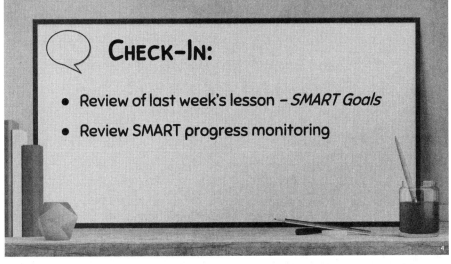

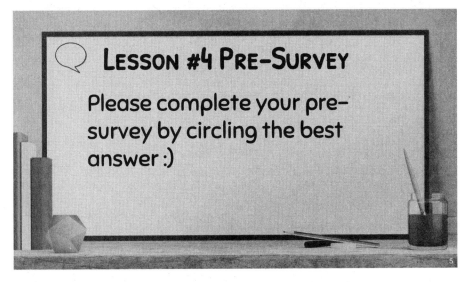

(Continued)

Figure 6.12 (Continued)

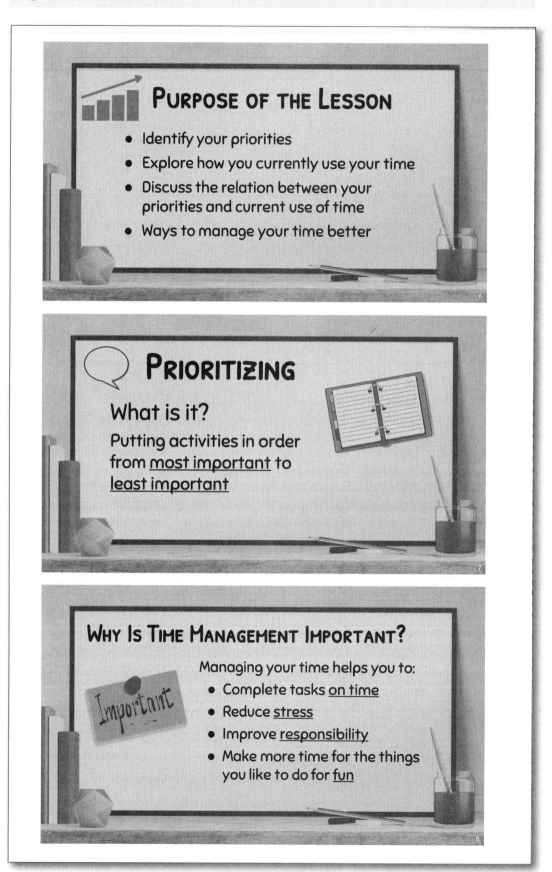

VIDEO RECAP

- What are your <u>priorities</u> (big rocks)? Work on these first because they move you toward your goals
- Once your priorities are scheduled, then you can <u>fill the rest of your schedule</u> with activities that are less important, but still need to get done

(Continued)

Figure 6.12   (Continued)

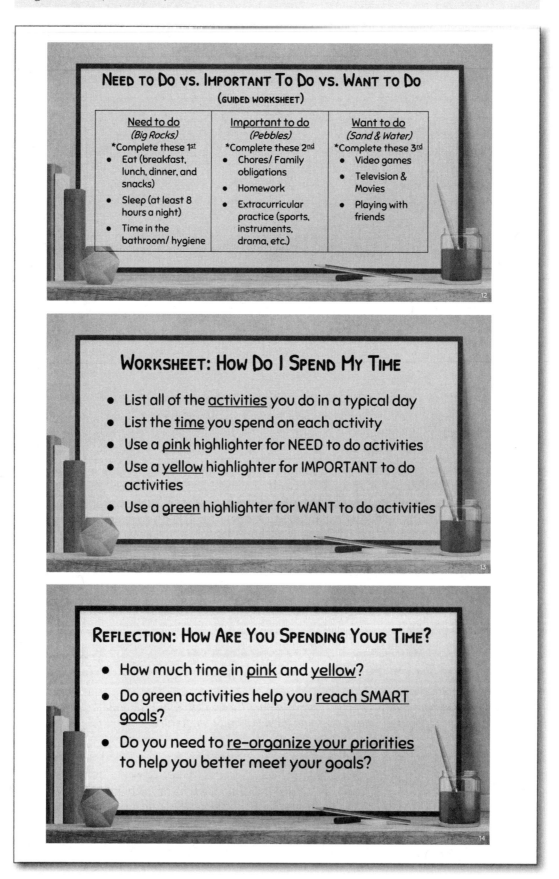

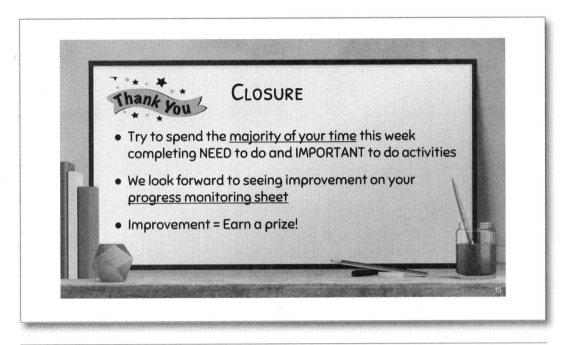

Source: Template by Seyton, retrieved from https://www.slidescarnival.com/

While many options are available when it comes to the selection and development of small group counseling curriculum, the most crucial step is utilizing *data* to drive the selection of the curriculum, as well as the learning objectives and attitudes, skills, and knowledge. When data are used as the guiding light in the selection of curriculum, school counselors ensure alignment of identified student needs with the content being taught, just as teachers do. If any lack of alignment exists between the curriculum and students' needs, school counselors may unintentionally sidetrack from the goals, objectives, and expected outcomes for the group. The ultimate goal of small group counseling is to address students' demonstrated needs through the teaching of focused, relevant content that will lead to behavior change and, ultimately, academic achievement.

NICASH'S STORY CONTINUES

After much research and deliberation in choosing their small group counseling curriculum, Nicash and her district's elementary school counseling team decided it would be in the students' best interest if they collaboratively created their own 6 to 8 week curriculum as a district team (rather than purchasing a pre-packaged curriculum) and aligned it with students' specific needs as identified on their report cards. They also considered evaluating the curriculum for its effectiveness. By doing this, they directly aligned their curriculum with the data-driven criteria that led to the intervention and taught the students the attitudes, skills, and knowledge they needed to improve outcomes (Work Habits marks).

Additional Resources

- Brigman, G., & Goodman, B. E. (2008). *Group counseling for school counselors: A practical guide* (3rd ed.). Portland, ME: Walch Education.

- Jacobs, E. E., Masson, R. L., Harvill, R. L., & Schimmel, C. J. (2011). *Group counseling: Strategies and skills.* Boston: Cengage Learning.

- Springer, S. I., Moss, L. J., Cinotti, D., & Land, C. W. (2018). Examining pre-service school counselors' site supervisory experiences specific to group work. *The Journal for Specialists in Group Work, 43*(3), 250–273.

7

Facilitating Small Groups

What Works and What Doesn't

NICASH'S STORY CONTINUES

Nicash was so excited to start running her small groups. She had collaborated with her district counseling team to select systemized, franchised criteria to identify which students needed more support. She was thrilled that they used report card data, rather than random referrals, to select the students who would be invited. Teachers were happy that she had partnered with them to find a time that worked for them, the students, and her schedule. She coordinated the process to ensure all the students invited were in an appropriate group and the small group curriculum was targeted to meet the identified needs of those students. She worked with parents to explain the group counseling process and had them on board. All that was left was facilitating the groups.

Although her study skills group was going well, Nicash became overwhelmed as she started running her first few behavior groups. She did not know the students very well yet, and they were exhibiting very challenging behaviors. While the students were having fun, they also constantly made jokes, bounced off the walls, and often tried to deviate from the lesson plan. One student's behaviors would feed off the others, and Nicash struggled to get through an entire lesson as planned, leaving her falling behind on timing each week.

Nicash is not alone as a school counselor challenged with effectively facilitating small group counseling. The successful facilitation of small group counseling is just as important as the planning. This chapter discusses the school counselor's small group toolbox, filled with the counseling skills, engagement techniques, and management strategies of an effective small group counseling facilitator.

SCHOOL COUNSELOR TOOLBOX

Experienced school counselors are equipped with a "toolbox" of core knowledge and skills that they utilize to effectively facilitate small group counseling. This toolbox includes

- knowledge of developmental phases of group,
- basic counseling skills,
- cultural considerations,
- creating structure,
- engagement strategies, and
- management strategies.

Knowledge of Developmental Phases of Group

Awareness of the different developmental phases of group counseling assists the counselor to effectively meet the needs of the students in each phase. In *School Based Group Counseling*, Sink, Edwards, and Eppler (2011) describe four main phases of small group counseling development:

1. Formation
2. Group implementation
3. Evaluation
4. Follow-up

Formation

Formation is the first phase of group counseling and begins early on, even before facilitation begins, during the planning stages discussed in depth in Chapter 5. In this phase, logistical details are decided upon, such as who will receive the intervention, what the intervention will consist of, where and when the small group counseling lessons will take place, and why the particular intervention has been selected (process data).

Group Implementation

Group implementation is the phase in which the majority of group facilitation takes place. In this phase, students are oriented to the group counseling process and work with the curriculum content. Within the developmental phases of group, the implementation stage is where the majority of the group counseling time is spent. The core of this chapter on facilitation and implementation mainly focuses in on the group implementation phase.

Evaluation

The evaluation phase of the group counseling process occurs through assessments and progress monitoring, discussed further in Chapter 8 ("Assessments and Progress Monitoring"), and final evaluation of group results and effectiveness, discussed in Chapter 10 ("Other Tier 2 and 3 Evaluations and Sharing Results").

Follow-Up

Follow-up is the closure phase in which reinforcement of the attitudes, skills, and knowledge (ASK) learned occurs. This stage also includes post-group progress monitoring, checking in with the students once group has ended, and evaluation of the group counseling process as a whole, for improvements for the next cycle.

Having knowledge of the different developmental phases of the group counseling process in the school counselor's toolbox helps ensure no critical components of group facilitation are missed. In addition to knowledge of the developmental phases, the school counselor toolbox encompasses group facilitation skills, such as basic counseling skills, the ability to plan and create structure, engagement techniques, and management strategies. Utilizing the knowledge and skills in their toolbox supports school counselors' confidence in promoting their leadership role in the facilitation of the group process.

The different developmental phases of group may be seen within some of the small group tools explored in earlier chapters, such as the Hatching Results Conceptual Diagram (see Chapter 2, Figure 2.2, page 26). This tool helps give a more macro-level perspective of the developmental phases of the group process and the plan in which to achieve it.

Figure 7.1 shows how the developmental phases of group can be seen within the Conceptual Diagram. The formation and implementation phases of group can be highlighted within the process and perception data, as they note who you are planning to serve and the attitudes, skills, and knowledge those served are hoping to attain. The evaluation and follow-up phases of group may also be highlighted within the perception data, which reveals the desired student perception outcome, as well as the outcome data, the ultimate goal of the group.

Figure 7.1   The Development Phases of Group Aligned to the Hatching Results Conceptual Diagram

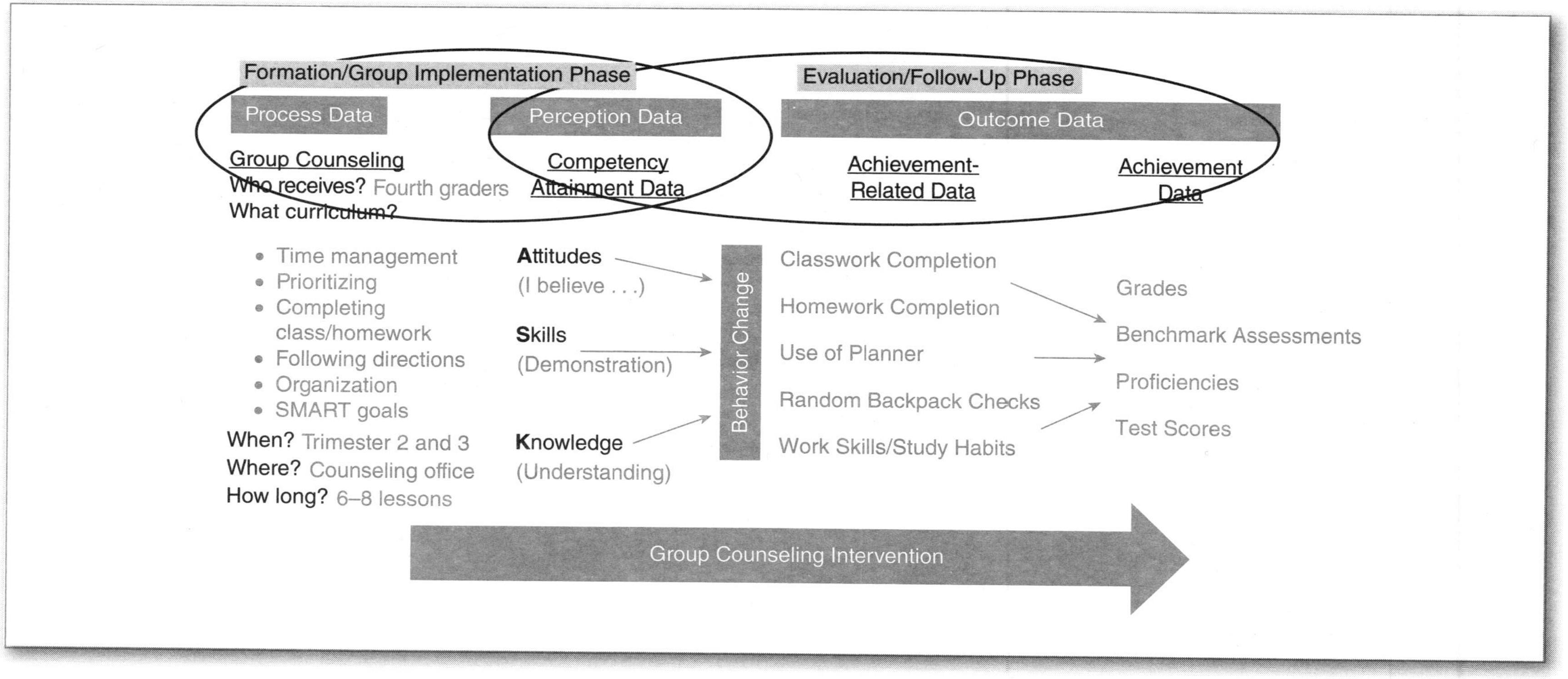

Formation/Group Implementation Phase

Evaluation/Follow-Up Phase

Process Data

Perception Data

Outcome Data

Group Counseling
Who receives? Fourth graders
What curriculum?

Competency
Attainment Data

Achievement-
Related Data

Achievement
Data

- Time management
- Prioritizing
- Completing
  class/homework
- Following directions
- Organization
- SMART goals

Attitudes
(I believe . . .)

Skills
(Demonstration)

Knowledge
(Understanding)

Behavior Change

Classwork Completion

Homework Completion

Use of Planner

Random Backpack Checks

Work Skills/Study Habits

Grades

Benchmark Assessments

Proficiencies

Test Scores

When? Trimester 2 and 3
Where? Counseling office
How long? 6–8 lessons

Group Counseling Intervention

Source: Hatch, T. (2006–2019).

School Counselors Are Teachers, Too!

School counselors are positioned as teachers of the small group counseling process. Similar to teachers, school counselors become instructional leaders and are responsible for teaching students the appropriate attitudes, skills, and knowledge in their small groups. As called for in *Teach Like a Champion* (Lemov, 2010), school counselors, much like teachers, are also charged with maintaining high behavioral expectations, engaging students in the lessons, structuring and delivering quality lessons, and ensuring academic achievement. Therefore, in addition to utilizing effective curriculum, school counselors must have strong group facilitation skills to be effective instructional leaders.

Basic Counseling Skills

The basic counseling skills that school counselors regularly practice in different settings, such as individual counseling or consultation situations, are similar to those used within the small group counseling setting. The skills are implemented in the same way, but with the objective of bringing members of the counseling group closer together, toward accomplishing group goals. Practicing basic counseling skills within each lesson builds group cohesion, facilitates content, and supportively challenges members. Although many counseling skills are used in small group facilitation, some of the more common skills for an effective group facilitation are included in Table 7.1.

Table 7.1   Basic Counseling Skills Used in the Individual Counseling Setting vs. the Group Counseling Setting

	Individual Counseling Setting	Group Counseling Setting
Active Listening	Listening to what the student is saying (e.g., "So it sounds like you are having trouble paying attention in your reading class.")	Listening to what each student is saying, ensuring all students who want to participate have the opportunity, and teaching the students to actively listen to each other (e.g., "So it sounds like many of you agree that you're having a difficult time in your reading classes. Yzabella expressed she was doing well in reading, but was having trouble in another subject. Can someone share what subject Yzabella was having trouble with?")
Clarifying	Confirming what the other student may be saying (e.g., "It sounds like you were pretty upset with a friend at recess. Is that right?")	Confirming what the student or a number of students may be saying (e.g., "It sounds like many of you did something over the weekend that you enjoyed. Is that right?")

(Continued)

Table 7.1 (Continued)

	Individual Counseling Setting	Group Counseling Setting
Reflecting/ Paraphrasing	Summarizing what the other student has expressed (e.g., "You felt stressed after you took your test.")	Summarizing what a student has expressed or students have expressed as a group (e.g., "It sounds like many of you felt stressed in some way or another, after the recent tests that you all took.")
Linking	Highlighting connections between the student and the school counselor with information the student stated (e.g., "You mentioned that you have a hard time raising your hand. Do you remember when I said that I get too excited and impulsive in discussions? I also have a hard time and am working on waiting my turn to speak within groups.")	Highlighting connections between what was said by one student and what was said by another student(s) (e.g., "Michelle, you mentioned that you have a hard time raising your hand. Do you remember when I said that I get too excited and impulsive in discussions? I also have a hard time and am working on waiting my turn to speak within groups. I think I also saw Nivette nodding her head and saying, 'Me too!' Wow—it looks like raising our hand and waiting to speak is something many of us struggle with.")
Self-Disclosure	Sharing personal information to build rapport and make connections with the other student (e.g., "You said that it is hard to stay organized because your parents are divorced and you have to bring your homework to both homes. When I was your age, my parents were also divorced, so I understand what you mean with the challenge of keeping all your things organized.")	Sharing personal information to build rapport with one or more of the members in the group to encourage other group members to share (e.g., "Bobbie, May, Ernest, and Dennis, you all mentioned that it is hard to stay organized. When I was in your grade, I was disorganized too. I lost many of my papers, could not keep track of important dates, could never find my pencil, and always got in trouble for it in class. Let's talk about ways I've learned to be more organized.")
Confronting	Pointing out an observation to the other student that he/she/they may not recognize or align with what the student has previously said (e.g., "Kris, you mentioned that you don't understand why you feel like the teacher always picks on you, but you also said that you sometimes goof off and don't do your work. Do you think the teacher would still 'pick' on you as often if you focused on your work instead of playing?")	Pointing out an observation to the student/ students/group that they may not recognize or align with what they have previously said (e.g., "Kris, both you and Norie shared that you don't understand why you feel like the teacher always picks on you, but you also said that sometimes you goof off with each other and don't get to finish your work. Do you think the teacher would still 'pick' on you as often if you both focused on your work instead of playing, or do you think she would leave you alone more?")
Blocking/Cutting Off	Appropriately interrupting the other student who may be off-topic or monopolizing the conversation (e.g., "Jase, since we are discussing the issue you've had with your friend Torilynn, let's stay focused on that instead of talking about a different issue with a different friend. We can get back to that after, but I really want us to try to solve one issue at a time.")	Appropriately interrupting a student or number of students who may be off-topic, monopolizing the conversation, or increasingly becoming more elevated or aggressive in a dialogue with one another (e.g., "Okay, group, since this topic is so exciting and everyone is starting to have side conversations, I want to stop the different conversations and bring it back so that we can help solve Jase's initial issue.")

Skills of a Strong Group Facilitator

In addition to basic counseling skills, strong group facilitators need to weave additional skills into their practice, since the group setting can add other dynamics (Sink et al., 2011). These include

- assisting groups in working together;
- refraining from interjecting their own opinions;
- remaining alert and observant to group dynamics;
- empowering the group members to lead themselves;
- relinquishing control;
- promoting open, democratic dialogues;
- modeling openness, ownership, and risk taking;
- staying present and patient;
- allowing for flexibility;
- continuously building rapport; and
- encouraging cultural sensitivity.

Cultural Considerations

The American School Counselor Association Position Statement on the School Counselor and Cultural Diversity states that "[s]chool counselors demonstrate cultural responsiveness by collaborating with stakeholders to create a school and community climate that embraces cultural diversity and helps to promote the academic, career and social/emotional success for all students" (ASCA, 2015a).

In the small group setting, school counselors need to be mindful of cultural considerations. This can relate to the school counselors' interactions with the students, as well as the group dynamics among students. When facilitating a group lesson, it is important to consistently consider factors such as the beliefs and behaviors that may be influenced by one's culture. The more aware and culturally sensitive school counselors can be while facilitating group, the more effective the collaboration and cohesion of the group can be.

Some cultural factors to consider during interactions include

- developmental appropriateness,
- ability,
- gender roles,
- gender identity and expression,
- temperament,
- energy level,
- amount of eye contact,

- social class/poverty,
- amount of participation,
- religious beliefs,
- family dynamics,
- race,
- ethnicity,
- nationality, and
- language proficiency.

CULTURAL RESPONSIVENESS AND CONSIDERATIONS WHEN PLANNING FOR SMALL GROUPS AND OTHER INTERVENTIONS

By Danielle Duarte

Being mindful of students' diverse cultures and including multiculturalism when planning curriculum for small group lessons is important to ensure that students' backgrounds are both respected and celebrated during the lesson, which helps students feel connected to the topics they are learning. Culturally responsive teaching aims to improve both engagement and motivation of diverse populations, especially students of color, infusing their culture into lessons to make meaningful connections and improve student outcomes (Brophy, 2017; Gay, 2010; Vavrus, 2008). It is also described as "a process that often requires educators to step out of their comfort zones and change their ways of thinking about students and how best to teach them" (Boyko, 2016, p. xxi). Learning about the diverse backgrounds of students within their school is important to help them address their varying needs, and incorporating this knowledge into planning for small groups and other intentional interventions helps students feel both respected by and connected to their counselor. In some cases, the school counselors may become the students as they learn about the school population and come to understand the needs, challenges, and support that their students require socially and academically.

Gay (2010) outlines essential elements of culturally responsive teaching, including developing a cultural diversity knowledge base. Through deepening their understanding that culture not only is about ethnicity but also encompasses values, contributions, traditions, relational patterns, and communication styles, counselors can better integrate multiculturalism into small group lessons (and their practices in general). Learning about and honoring the unique contributions of different ethnic groups helps all students feel seen. Cross-cultural communication is another essential element; when school counselors understand characteristics of different ethnic communication styles, they will have a better context through which to communicate with diverse students "without violating the cultural value of a student's cultural communication style" (Boyko, 2016, p. xxxiii). Understanding differences in cross-cultural communication among their students can also provide an opportunity for counselors to teach students about code switching to help them successfully navigate different settings and audiences. As school counselors integrate and value the diverse backgrounds of their student populations into small group lessons and other intentional interventions, students will likely feel more connected to the content and the counselor.

When planning for intentional interventions, school counselors can incorporate cultural responsiveness in the following ways:

- Creating a welcoming and inclusive environment that embraces diverse sharing—school counselors can explain and remind students what this looks like as they make group agreements during their first meeting. Additionally, continually referring to these norms during each meeting and praising students for their openness to new perspectives is encouraged.
- Incorporating students' personal and cultural perceptions into the lesson—when school counselors activate prior knowledge by asking students to share their perspectives on a topic, the counselor is both integrating and honoring students' diverse experiences. Additionally, counselors can be mindful in seeking out diverse ideas from the group.
- Embedding diverse student backgrounds and voices into small group lessons—for example, including examples and photos that represent diverse cultures, especially those that directly apply to students in the school community.
- Mindful groupings—school counselors can consider how to incorporate diversity as they assign students to small groups or other interventions. This practice allows for diverse students to collaborate with and learn from one another.

What cultural considerations do you need to make when planning for small groups and intentional interventions? What additional professional development might you need?

Creating Structure

Laying the foundation for group structure begins during screening and continues throughout the different phases of the group counseling process. Creating structure for successful group counseling facilitation includes

- effective screening,
- setting the tone/expectations,
- understanding the purpose of group,
- establishing group norms,
- creating and following procedures/routines, and
- using ASCA National Model lesson plans.

Effective Screening

As mentioned in Chapter 5 ("Planning for Small Groups"), the screening occurs prior to facilitating the small group. Screening again at the beginning of the group process not only helps ensure students are aware they will be meeting as a group to work toward a common goal of improvement, but it also helps support effective group dynamics.

This screening process may include the pre-intervention assessment, but also observations and progress monitoring within the first few meetings as group facilitation begins and continues. Continuous screening or monitoring of the participants at the initial phases of group facilitation helps ensure continued success while implementing the group. During the initial screening phase, students may agree to join a group, but once the group begins, they may have a different understanding of the group process, goals, or expectations. Initially and continuously working with the students to determine their needs, their level of participation, and whether they are the right fit for the group is essential. Sharing the expected results of group may encourage continued participation. If students are not well screened, the school counselor may end up with students who do not want to be in group or are not personally invested in the group's goals. In this case, other Tier 2 intervention options, explored in Chapter 3 ("Determining the Appropriate Tier 2 Interventions"), may be more suitable.

As an elementary school counselor, Danielle used pre-group screening to help build rapport with students and help them create goals, which she then used each week during a success skills group. During her pre-group screening meeting, she brought the students' report cards and explained the citizenship section to the group. Students read each of the section descriptions (works cooperatively with others, maintains self-control, etc.), and Danielle asked them to explain what it meant. She also explained the way they were being rated, such as what Needs Improvement (N) and Satisfactory (S) meant. Danielle made sure to praise the areas in which they were doing well, and then asked them to consider how they could work to improve the areas where they received an N or U (Unsatisfactory). Based on their ideas, Danielle and her students would write a goal together, which they used each week in group to help consider what they were doing to improve. With the students' permission, Danielle shared the goals with their teachers, some of whom put a sticky note of the goal on their desk as a reminder. Danielle found this pre-group screening technique extremely effective, as she was able to spend personal time with each student, help students understand the purpose of group based on their report card, and set a goal with them (which was much easier one-on-one than in the first small group session).

Setting the Tone/Expectations

Setting the tone and expectations for a small group is essential at the very beginning of the process—from initial screening through the first few counseling lessons —and ensures a safe and productive learning environment for all group participants. Some aspects to consider when setting the tone and expectations are outlined in Table 7.2.

School counselors are encouraged to be thoughtful and purposeful in their pre-planning of these different aspects, which can greatly impact group dynamics and effective group implementation.

A student reward board is an engagement strategy that sets group expectations and offers students a visual reinforcement of the school's positive behavioral standards (see Figure 7.2). Each week, students will have a chance to practice those standards during group. If a student successfully demonstrates an expected standard, they earn a "box" on the reward board. If they earn all of the available boxes, they may choose a prize.

Table 7.2 Group Tone/Expectation Factors to Consider

Group Tone/ Expectation Factors	Preparation	Questions to Consider
Confidentiality	Explaining confidentiality and ensuring all students respect the confidentiality of all members and to keep what is said in group confidential, as well as addressing the limitations of confidentiality and reasons for breaching confidentiality	*How would confidentiality be explained in a developmentally appropriate way?* *Do the students understand that some things cannot be kept in confidence?* *Are the students clear on reasons for a breach in confidentiality?* *Do the students understand that confidentiality includes the school counselor as well as all the students in group?*
Level of Participation	Identifying how much and how often participation in the group discussions and activities will be expected for each lesson	*Will the students have a right to pass? If they do not share, but are listening, will that be acceptable?* *Will the counselor be teaching the students to share the talking time? Will there be a management tool for equitable chances to participate?*
Attendance Requirements	Identifying level of attendance that will be expected for the entirety of the group counseling intervention	*Are the students required to attend each lesson?* *Is there a goal or celebration at the end or when a certain amount of attendance is reached?* *Is it okay for students to not attend group? If so, how many lessons are okay to miss?* *Should students inform the school counselor if they were/will be gone? Is there an incentive for attending group?*
Level of Flexibility	Identifying the level of flexibility that the school counselor/ facilitator is comfortable with, but changing it in relation to the curriculum, lesson content, activities, or group lesson structure	*How much of the activities will be counselor or student led? How willing is the counselor with extending lesson time? How flexible are the lessons if the students are or are not engaged in the current one? How willing is the counselor to change topics if another important topic arises from the week before?*
Level of Engagement Among Group Participants and Group Facilitator	Identifying level of engagement expected for group participants to have with each other and with the school counselor within each lesson	*Will the group be focused on the delivery of information or lots of hands-on group activities? How well will the counselor allow the students to get to know each other on a deeper level? How often will team-building activities and icebreakers take place?*

Figure 7.2   Engagement Strategy: Student Reward Board

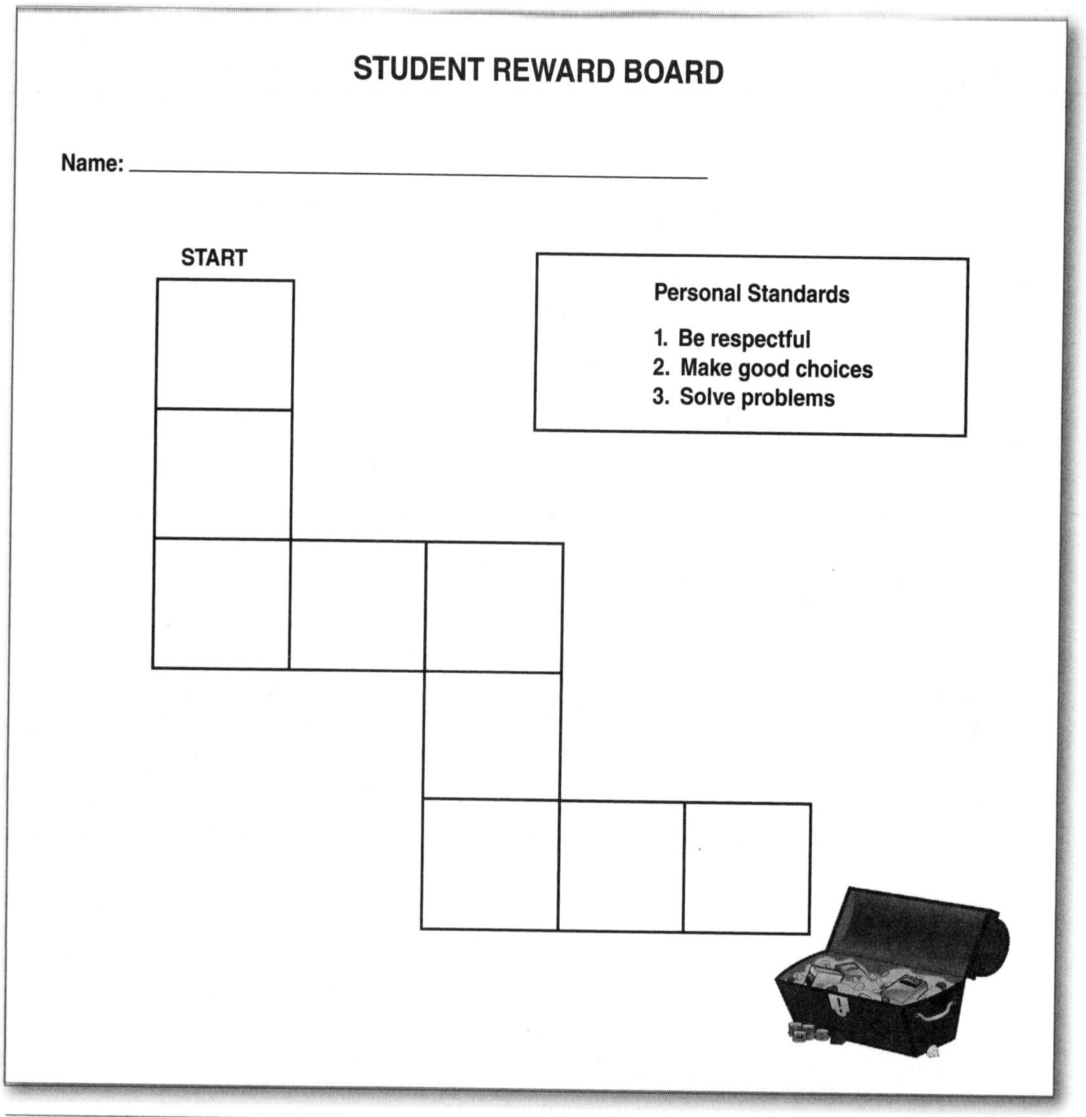

Image Source: pixabay.com/openclipart-vectors

Understanding the Purpose of Small Group

"Establishing the purpose of a lesson, often through a written objective, is a common educational practice. . . . [Educators are] encouraged to consider what their students will know and be able to do. An established purpose alerts learners to important information and garners their attention while helping teachers decide how best to use their instructional time" (Fisher & Frey, 2011). Just as teachers are encouraged to share learning objectives, so too are school counselors encouraged to identify and inform the students of the purpose of the small group. This is usually done during the initial planning and screening phase and prior to facilitation; however, revisiting the specific purpose of the group in depth again during the first lesson helps to reinforce the goal and focus of the group work. Helping students understand the *why* behind their efforts and actions allows them to stay focused, creates a sense of purpose, and offers the opportunity for valuable contributions to group efforts. Referring back to the group purpose in later lessons can also be a helpful strategy when some students require redirection or get off track and start to become distracted or disengaged. An example of having explained and to remind students of the purpose of the small group may sound like this: "Friends, let's refocus and practice respectful listening. Remember, at the beginning, we discussed that the purpose of this group and our time together is to discover new and helpful ways to help us be better learners at school."

Group Norms

Setting clear expectations for group norms and behaviors early in the facilitation process supports strong structure and sets the tone. Creating group expectations *with* the students during the first counseling lesson, allows them a voice in the process. When students work collaboratively to develop agreed-upon expectations, they are more likely to be accountable to upholding these expectations. Reminding students of the agreed-upon expectations throughout the lessons will benefit the structure of the group and improve facilitation. If students observe that group members who do not respect agreed-upon norms are immediately redirected, they will learn that expectations are enforced. Consider the agreed-upon norm, "Listen quietly to the speaker," for example. If someone were to interrupt a group lesson, the school counselor might state, "Does anyone remember the group norm we agreed was important for us all to practice when someone was speaking, so we all can hear each other? . . . Yes! 'Listen quietly to the speaker'—thank you for remembering. Let's all try again to practice that."

Creating Procedures/Routines

Creating structure by means of modeling and practicing consistent procedures and routines builds a sound foundation for effective group facilitation. Once procedures are established, expected actions are completed in a certain order or manner for how each student enters group, how each group counseling lesson unfolds, and how the students leave the group.

School counselor Henry decided he wanted to utilize a "pass procedure" for his students in group. The individual passes identified the date, time, and group counseling location for his students. He explained to the teachers that these passes would be in their mailbox at the beginning of the group counseling day to give to the students, who then were responsible to take the pass at their designated group counseling time. The students were conditioned to know that whenever they received a pass from their teacher on a particular day, they needed to pack up their school materials by a certain time for group counseling.

In comparison, Vanessa, a school counselor at a different school, worried that due to the nature of her role as a counselor, she would at times need flexibility before any calendared counseling groups. With this challenge in mind, she preferred to pick her students up herself, to ensure they would not arrive at her office without adult supervision. During the beginning of the group process, Vanessa explained to her students that, although they already knew the day and time of their group counseling lesson, they would not be attending group until she picked them up from their classroom. Vanessa's structural "pickup" procedure not only allowed her control and flexibility, but the opportunity to observe her students in class as well. The students were taught that as part of a successful pickup, as soon as they saw their school counselor holding up their name, they would neatly put away their work and materials, quietly push in their chairs, silently walk out of the classroom, and form a single-file line outside the door. Creating and teaching everyone the same pickup procedure allowed the students an efficient exit out of the classroom without distracting others from their learning.

Referring to the example in the shaded box, Henry and Vanessa each taught their students different procedural routines during the very first lesson to create structure for the time prior to the facilitation of group counseling. When structure is created and the way each counseling lesson unfolds are consistent, students know what to expect and can anticipate what is coming next. If students know what steps are expected for certain situations, they will have fewer questions and spend less time figuring out how to complete the task at hand, leaving more time for other activities or content. Procedures and routines protect time for critical components of the lesson plan to be implemented thoroughly, with more efficiency and with fidelity. For example, the school counselor creates a routine for the students for the beginning of group, which sets the expectation for the weeks to follow. If students know that every week they will begin group by having a chance to share during check-in, they will enter group prepared with the mindset that they will have an opportunity to share. If the routine is that during check-in time students will review their self-identified weekly goal, they will be conditioned to enter the group ready each week with their self-evaluation. If a routine is created for the students to be engaged in listening and learning of a topic at a specific time, they will learn to be quiet and respect the speaker during that time every week. If a routine is in place where students expect to have time at the end of the lesson to practice their knowledge and skills with a partner, they will be more likely to observe the group expectation of focusing on the content because they can count on having that practice time to engage with their peers.

Use of ASCA Lesson Plans

The ASCA National Model lesson plan is a helpful tool for listing regular procedures and routines for students to follow. As discussed in Chapter 6 ("Selecting and Developing Small Group Curriculum"), the lesson plan provides a consistent and organized outline. The school counselor becomes accustomed to the components of an effective group lesson, and the structure of the lessons become part of the school counselor's toolbox. With consistency, the students know what to expect and recognize certain times have been designated for identified activities during the group lesson, improving the likelihood they will stay on task.

ASCA lesson plans outline the content and activities in a step-by-step guide and explain how to teach the content, facilitate activities and discussions, and perform an evaluation check for comprehension. As noted in Chapter 6, there is flexibility in the order school counselors facilitate process, but a typical outline of a group counseling procedure may include

- a check-in, icebreaker, or team builder;
- a revisit of the last topic;
- an introduction to a new topic;
- instruction of knowledge and skills;
- an engaging activity reinforcing the new knowledge and skills;
- a check for comprehension; and
- closure.

Figure 7.3 is Nicash's use of the ASCA National Model small group lesson plan template, and highlights how an "Introduction to Group" lesson incorporates important components in this chapter. These include Bloom's Taxonomy (see Chapter 6, Figure 6.9, page 156) within learning objectives, the purpose of group, the structure and procedural routines, Positive Behavioral Interventions and Supports (PBIS), games, group norms, positive language, and the location of each within the lesson.

Note: School counselors looking to apply for RAMP after 2021 are required to utilize the templates provided within the 4th edition of the ASCA National Model.

Figure 7.3 Nicash's Lesson 1: Introduction to Academic Success Skills Group

Lesson Plan 1: Introduction to Academic Study Skills Group

School Counselor: Ms. Nicash Krublo

Date: 10/24/17

Topic & Title: Introduction to Academic Study Skills Group

Grade: 4th grade

Learning Objective:

1. Students will be able to:

Note the use of **Bloom's Taxonomy within the learning objectives** of the lesson plan.

- Demonstrate the retention of the names of other group members
- Explain procedural routines on how to prepare for group
- Formulate group norms and group name as a team
- Recognize the importance of confidentiality and reasons the school counselor would need to breach confidentiality

ASCA Mindsets & Behavior:

- M 3: Sense of belonging in the school environment
- M 6: Positive attitude toward work and learning
- B-SS 2: Create positive and supportive relationships with other students

Materials:

- Counseling center space (includes table and 1 chair for each student)
- Access to technology and projector
- Laptop
- School-counselor generated PowerPoint presentation
- Positive Behavior Intervention Support (PBIS) tickets
- Poster board
- Markers
- Prize box
- Comprehensive Small Group Pre-Survey copies (1 per student)

Preparation for Group:

- Remind the students and teachers of students in group that group counseling will begin soon (i.e.; email; verbal reminder)
- Ensure there are enough working computers on the day of group counseling that have the pre-survey link already up

Procedure/Lesson Outline:

1. **Introduction:**

   a. **Welcome (3 minutes):**

      School counselor introduction -

      - Welcome students to the counseling center and ask them to each pick a seat around the table.

      - Thank the students for attending group, for quietly entering the counseling center respectfully, and inform them that they will later be learning the exact procedures for entering group.

      - Re-introduce yourself and express excitement for the group.

      - Explain your role at the school, including important points of academic, social/emotional, and college/career support and advocacy for students, being there to support students become problem-solvers and to simply listen.

      - Ask the group for examples of potential topics students can turn to the school counselor for help (i.e.; help with a friend, angry or sad feelings, making better decisions, being more organized and learning to stay focused). Reinforce and clarify student suggestions and explain that the small group is another way (aside from class presentations and individual counseling) the school counselor may support students.

   2. **Lesson Purpose & Procedures (5 minutes):**

188

reinforced at school that may also earn a PBIS ticket in group. Inform students that the PBIS tickets from group may be used for a raffle to choose a prize from the prize box at the end of each group or saved for the school-wide weekly raffles. Communicate to the students that on top of the weekly group participation PBIS tickets that they can earn, if the students are able to attend the entirety of the 8 weeks of group, there will be a celebration party at the end with their favorite food.

- Tell the students that each group session has a similar structure that will unfold the same, so that they know what to expect:
  i. Practice leaving classroom entering group counseling procedure
  ii. Check in/ice breaker/team builder
  iii. Revisit/review of the last topic from week prior
  iv. Introduction of new topic
  v. Instruction of knowledge and skills
  vi. Engaging activity reinforcing the new knowledge and skills
  vii. Check for comprehension
  viii. Closure (includes wrap up, prize box, and free time, if it was earned)

3. Icebreaker 1 (5 minutes)

a. Now that they know the purpose of group and have learned some of the procedures and incentives to look forward to, inform the students that they will begin with a counseling center tour and ice breaker.

b. Walk the students around the counseling center highlighting where everything is and the resources they will have access to during free time.

c. Inform the students that they will now be playing an ice breaker called "Blow Wind Blow" to get to know each other.

d. Instruct the students to bring their chair to the center of the room, where there is more space for movement, and create a circle with their chairs. Once seated, explain that there will always be one person standing in the middle who does not have a chair and is 'it' for that round. The person in the middle must begin by saying the same phrase "My name is (insert name here). Blow wind blow" and

Note the use of a physical game as an engagement strategy within the ice breaker of the lesson plan.

Note the explicit reinforcement of the purpose of group within the introduction lesson plan.

- Ask the students if anyone remembers the reason why they are in group from the interview and after validating their answers, reinforce that the purpose of group is to have some time and a place to get to know each other, learn and practice some activities and strategies to become even better learners, so that they are even more academically successful. Describe some of the academic study skill lesson topics that will be addressed throughout group each week.

Note the time spent teaching the students the structure the procedural routine expectations for the "leaving the class and entering group" within the lesson plan.

- Explain that each group will have a specific structure or procedural routines, beginning from prior to entering the group, how the group lesson will unfold each week, as well as the same reinforcement/incentive systems for each group session.
- Explain and model the procedure for "leaving the class and entering group counseling pick up".
  - School counselor stands at the door with a sign with the group members name on it
  - Student silently clean up their current work, push in their chair, grab their backpack and walk outside the classroom to line up behind other group members
  - As school counselor walks to other potential classrooms to pick up the remainder of the students, the students stay quiet in their line outside of the new classroom
  - Students enter the group counseling center, sit down at a seat, and put their backpack on the back of their chair and show active listening in preparation for the weekly check-in
- Have students briefly work together to explain the "leaving the class and entering group counseling pick up" procedure.

Note the explanation and use of the management strategy of PBIS reinforcements within the lesson plan.

- Thank the students for their participation and give each one a Positive Behavioral Intervention Support (PBIS) ticket.
  Explain that the school-wide PBIS reinforcement ticket will be used in group as a way to reinforce positive behaviors (such as participation and attendance) that were observed. Ask and validate the students for other behaviors that are

(Continued)

189

Figure 7.3 (Continued)

190

d. *Creating Group Norms* - Take out a poster board, marker, and explain to the group that now that they understand the purpose of group, have had a chance to get to know each other a little bit, it is important to work together to come up with group norms/rules that they can write on the poster board to refer back to. State that these norms are created in order to continue to successfully work together and support each other to learn as much as they can during group counseling.
  - Share an example of the importance of attending group each week as an important norm and explain how someone's lack of attendance can affect the collective learning.
  - Illicit 5-7 group norms, ensuring each student has had a chance to contribute a norm. Ask the students if they are all in agreement and inform them that these norms will be out during each group as a visual aid reminder.
  - Verbally thank the students for their participation with creating the group norms and give them each a PBIS ticket.

b. *Group Name*
  i. Explain now that the norms are created, collectively deciding on a group name would build cohesion and be a fun way to refer to the group they belong to.
  ii. Inform the students that they will have one minute to brainstorm quietly to themselves and that the group will reconvene after the minute.
  iii. Once the group is done brainstorming individually, ask the students if they have any suggestions that you can write down on the back of the poster for the group to vote on afterwards.
  iv. Remind the students of the purpose of group and to be creative with the name, while keeping the purpose in mind.
  v. Allow time for some suggestions and take a silent and unanimous vote for the most popular group name. Share that if there are a couple of names that are close in votes, it is okay to blend the two top choices together.

Note the use of **group norms** within the lesson plan.

Note the commonly **used systems and positive language** within the lesson plan.

the rest of the group will respond after with "blow what"? Once the group has responded, the student in the center respond "blow wind blow to people who...." and will pick something they like or are interested in, which can be related to school or something more personal for them. For example, "blow wind blow to people who love to eat pizza." Tell the students that if the statement that the person in the center said applies to them, they must get out of their seat and find another seat. Inform the students that there are a few caveats to be aware of 1) Students need to be honest if the statement applies to them, so that they can genuinely get to know each other. 2) If the statement applies to the student, they must get out of their seats and switch with another student or the person in the middle. They are not allowed to stand up and sit back in the same seat. 3) Must be careful and keep their bodies to themselves and watch out for possible collisions, as this game can become competitive. If the game gets out of hand, it will need to stop and the group will move on to the next activity. 4) Fun and deeper statements (vs. surface statements) are encouraged to challenge each other to share more about themselves and give example of a surface statement (i.e.; "blow wind blow to people who like the color blue" compared to deeper statements such as "blow wind blow to people who struggle with math. Or people who may feel lonely at school." Check for student comprehension and model the first round with a statement that relates to all the students in the group "My name is Ms. Nicash. Blow wind blow to all the students who attend elementary school" to ensure they have the opportunity to get up and switch seats.

e. After a number of rounds, inform the students to sit back in their seats, ask if one student can name everyone in the group and allow a couple of students to try, and illicit things they might have learned from engaging in the ice breaker (i.e.; names, things they have in common).

f. Inform the students that each week, there will be a fun activity similar to "blow wind blow".

4. **Content (15 minutes)**

vi. Once the name is created, ask if all the students are in agreement and write the final group name on the top of the group norms side of the poster.

5. **Activity**

   a. *Pre-survey (5 minutes)*

      i. Explain to the students that the last thing on the agenda is completing the group counseling pre-survey. Inform them that they will each have five minutes to complete a quick 10 question survey on the computers to help inform the facilitators what the students already know and what the school counselor needs to focus on teaching them.

      ii. Ensure that the students know there will be no grade, there will be questions they may not know the answers to and that is okay. Inform them that the pre-survey will not affect their grades, but encourage them to try their best.

      iii. Set a five minute timer on projector, walk around the group space to check on timing and check in when the time has run out. Thank students for their effort on the pre-survey and inform them that they will be taking the exact same survey at the end of group to show us all the things they have learned.

6. **Closure** (5 minutes)

   a. Inform the students that at this time, they can sign the back of their PBIS tickets for a chance to enter the raffle for the three winners who will get the opportunity to pick from the prize box.

   b. Reinforce with the students that since they completed all the group session tasks successfully, as mentioned, they earned "free play time." Put the allotted amount of time on the projector.

   c. Give a warning minute for the students to clean up and come back to the circle. Once time is up and students are back in the circle, thank them for attending the first group and express excitement for future sessions.

   d. Ask the students to identify activities they completed during this first session and what they enjoyed the best.

   e. Remind the students that as they are dropped off to their classrooms, they need to mirror the same positive behavioral expectations they did as they left for group, as they return from group.

   f. Walk students back to class.

Plan for Evaluation:

Process Data:

Who: Two groups of six to eight 4th grade students

What: Lesson on Introduction to Academic Study Skills Group

When: 10/24/17 at 1:30pm

Perception Data: Pre/Post Survey

Outcome Data: Improvement in Work Habits section of the report card

Follow Up: School counselor will review introduction lesson during check-in

Reference:

191

Engagement Strategies

Some students may be more authentic and better behaved when working with a counselor on an individual level. When working in groups, focus must be paid to activities that promote positive behavior by students and encourage their more authentic and responsive selves. Social processes that occur within groups are complex and impact actions and outcomes (Lewin, 1948). Group dynamics occur in all groups and involve the interactions of group members and leaders over time (Gladding, 1994). Even when utilizing data to select the students and topics of a group, each group will inevitably have its own unique needs and culture. When school counselors come equipped with a game plan and a variety of engagement and management tools in their toolbox to meet the diverse group members' needs, it will help to ensure smoother and more effective facilitation of group counseling.

After creating the structure of the group, it is vital for school counselors to keep the students engaged during the group counseling lessons (Marks, 2000). Considering developmental appropriateness and an elementary student's attention span, an effective group counseling facilitator continuously embeds engagement strategies within each lesson to ensure student focus.

Group engagement strategies are techniques that can be used to

- encourage meaningful participation,
- facilitate deeper thinking and engagement with the material,
- sustain student involvement, and
- offer opportunities for enjoyable use of learning group time for the students.

Research behind Bloom's Taxonomy on the depths of knowledge suggests that comprehension and application of content are more likely to occur when students are meaningfully involved in the participation process and using critical thinking skills rather than simply absorbing the material (Bloom, Englehart, Furst, Hill, & Krathwohl, 1956). The goal for counseling students in a group setting is to help them gain the attitudes, knowledge, and ability to apply these skills in their everyday lives. Engagement strategies are helpful techniques that enable counselors to teach the content effectively so that students participate fully, comprehend the material at a deeper level, continue to grasp scaffolded instructional content in later lessons, add to their prior knowledge, and enjoy their time with their peers and counselor in group.

There are many different engagement strategies available to school counselors, which can be easily and effectively used within a variety of different settings. In Chapter 5 of *Hatching Results for Elementary School Counseling* (Hatch, Duarte, & De Gregorio, 2018), Danielle Duarte explores an assortment of Advancement Via Individual Determination (AVID) student engagement strategies. These helpful strategies can be used in the classroom as well as in small groups. A sample of these engagement strategies can be referenced in Chapter 6 (see Figure 6.10, page 158). When choosing from a variety of engagement strategies, the effective and consistent implementation of these techniques will ensure better learning and a more successful group counseling lesson.

Using Movement

Group curriculum that regularly incorporates movement and creativity for the students can be very beneficial, especially for younger students. Elementary students often naturally have more energy (Birat et al., 2018), and allowing for movement during group lessons lets students focus their energy in a productive and positive way. At this developmental age, utilizing role play, practice time, and skill building is also more helpful than solely using traditional counseling worksheets. Implementing curriculum with activities that allow for creativity also encourages students to become more involved. Motivating students to use their personal skills and interests to learn allows them to practice the content in a way that is interesting and more enjoyable for them to learn in a group environment. It can also provide them with the opportunity to use their unique strengths (making up original songs that include what they have learned on the topic, changing the lyrics to current songs to align with the topic, creating games, etc.). For example, an appropriate icebreaker or group break for an active listening lesson may be allowing each student to lead the "head, shoulders, knees, and toes" song while pointing to the body parts. Students may then be given the extra challenge of leading the song with the condition of only pointing to body parts that are predominately used for active listening.

Games and Competitions

Another small group counseling engagement strategy is diversifying mundane activities by incorporating games and competitions. Research shows that people are more engaged and learn better when they enjoy the activity or task at hand (Willis, 2007). This may be especially true for elementary students. One example of competition during group is to inform them that they need to demonstrate their newly learned skill within a certain amount of time, against other peers, or for a prize. During a group lesson on organization, students may be tasked to work in teams to create an infomercial or a game show on "how to organize your binder/backpack," which they will present to the group. The implementation of the creative demonstration of organizing backpack content through means of a game or competition and role play also allows for opportunities of collaboration, communication, leadership, and engagement, and fosters creativity.

Peer Teaching

Peer teaching is another way to innovatively engage the group. Students often appreciate and grow from the opportunity to take on leadership roles and help one another. The use of peer teaching allows the students to experience leadership opportunities while practicing what Bloom's Taxonomy refers to as the higher-level thinking skills of analyzing and application. As the students teach their peers, they must articulate or demonstrate their new knowledge or skill. Additionally, the content taught is synthesized and communicated through a student perspective and voice, which may be dually helpful to their peers. As a result, peer teaching often boosts the students' confidence in themselves, their practice of effective peer relationships, and successful implementation of the desired behavior (Coe, Aloisi, Higgins, & Major, 2014).

Olivia Rae, a school counselor, had a kindergartener with behavior issues whom she was called to support at the same time she was scheduled to facilitate a group. Being creative and inclusive, Olivia Rae decided that it might be beneficial to both the kindergarten student and the fourth-grade students in the group if the older students taught the younger student what they had just learned about active listening. Assuming the leadership role, the fourth-grade students were able to peer teach the kindergartener with confidence and ease.

Video Recording

Incorporating the recording of students during the practice or demonstration of the new group counseling content serves as another engagement strategy. Since recordings become artifacts that can be seen and revisited over and over, students may put their "best foot forward," perform with the most accurate content, and to the best of their ability. For some students, the ability to review a recording may help them become more aware of their own behaviors (positive or negative). For example, students who do not realize how disruptive or inappropriate their behavior is in a particular setting may be able to identify their actions in comparison to their peers' when viewing the video. The recording may also provide positive examples of expected behavior, modeled by their peers. In addition, recordings create an opportunity for students who respond well to or seek attention to experience a creative way to shine. Archiving recordings also provides the option for teachable moments as part of future curriculum. Prior to implementing such a recording project, however, school counselors are cautioned to be aware of the existence of any school and/or district policies regarding informed consent for the photographing or filming of students.

Peer Teaching Through Videos

Not surprisingly, students tend to enjoy video content when learning, especially if they see their peers or themselves in the videos. When teaching skills aligned with curriculum from programs such as Second Step, Boys Town, or PBIS expectations, short and simple videos (30–90 seconds) can be created to show students teaching their peers the content and demonstrating skills being taught. Students may also benefit from involvement in planning, producing, and starring in these videos, which contributes to improving successful habits in school.

Videos may be created utilizing a mobile device (e.g., iPad), some basic editing software (e.g., iMovie), and a place to land or distribute the completed video (e.g., YouTube, Google Drive, OneDrive). Many students dream of becoming "YouTubers," and peer teaching through videos offers them opportunities to build skills for success as well as model positive skills for their peers.

Over the last eight years, Felipe, an elementary school counselor, has helped his students develop hundreds of videos, allowing them to star in teachable moments such as *walking in line, getting the teacher's attention,* and *calming down.* Examples of Felipe's students' videos can be found in the online appendix.

Management Strategies

Managing group behavior is an essential skill for successful group counseling. One of the gifts and challenges of facilitating small groups is that no group will ever be the same. Students' needs, personalities, and levels of engagement will differ from group to group, impacting group dynamics. As such, no perfect recipe fits the needs of each and every small group, and thoughtful decision making regarding management strategies is in order. Preparation and planning are key. If students who struggle with acting out behaviorally are grouped together with others exhibiting similar behaviors, challenges with group management for school counselors are to be expected. Thoughtful decision making regarding which students to include in a group must balance inclusivity, ensuring equity and access to additional student supports, with thoughtful group constitution.

School counselors will benefit from proactive work, predicting management needs and developing strategies to utilize within their small group toolbox. Small group management strategies are instructional tips and techniques that assist facilitators in guiding student behaviors and supporting their readiness to learn. School counselors can learn a great deal by co-leading groups with more experienced counselors or observing master classroom teachers to develop new, effective management strategies. Successfully implementing recommended strategies can build school counselors' confidence to create and reinforce a safe and positive learning environment. Thoughtful preparation of management strategies when designing small group counseling can be the difference between an effective group counseling facilitation and an unfortunate and unproductive use of time. It is vital, therefore, for school counselors to come prepared to meet the differing needs of students, to practice flexibility, and to have their school counselor toolbox of management strategies ready.

Management strategies to consider include

- effective use of space,
- common and positive language to redirect behaviors, and
- reinforcements and incentives.

Use of Space

How big is the group space? Are students squeezed into a small table and sitting so close they touch each other even without trying? This could be a recipe for trouble. Is there a table? Will the students sit on the floor? Or at a desk? Is the space quiet and confidential? Or near other students, activities, or noise? Consider the benefits of advocating for appropriate spaces for counselor groups.

Proximity matters. When running a group, much like teaching a lesson in the classroom, position yourself in close proximity to the students. By sitting closer to students who are often off-task, the counselor will keep the focus on the teaching and instruction, while also non-verbally redirecting the students in a neutral, non-threatening way. If students are not within reach or are in a larger group, walking around the entire space from one area to another throughout the group counseling lesson will help the students track and continue to focus their attention on the school counselor as the lesson content is facilitated. As the counselor shifts position, students may not know where the school counselor might stand or sit next, which encourages the students to stay on task.

If a student is off task, using proximity and non-verbal redirection can be as simple as the school counselor's silent touch on the student's shoulder or back. This allows the counselor to continue to teach content or listen to another student's sharing while providing a kinesthetic reminder for the off-task student to focus. Thoughtful use of space and non-verbal redirection may also help build rapport between the counselor and the student, as the student recognizes the silent request from the counselor encouraging redirection without negative and public attention.

Commonly Used
Positive Language to Redirect Behaviors

Many schools have adopted PBIS strategies that promote commonly used positive language for behavioral expectations throughout the building. The goal is to build consistent, predictable understanding of expectations and to keep the school environment positive, safe, and consistent. In schools that have adopted common behavior expectations, stakeholders participate in both the creation and the uniform implementation of statements like the following:

* *Be Respectful, Be Responsible, and Be Safe*
* *Respect Yourself, Respect Others, and Respect Property*
* *Respect Relationships and Respect Responsibilities*
* *Be Kind, Be a Friend, and Be-There-Be-Ready*

In group, using consistent positive language designed for use schoolwide serves to promote consistency and reinforce expectations. For example, the school counselor saying "Thank you for being respectful" or "Thank you for keeping your hands and feet to yourself" is preferable to saying "You need to be quiet" or "Stop touching her" because it is, first, more respectful and positive and, second, more consistent with the language used by other stakeholders in the school. Using positive language to verbally thank students who demonstrate the expected group behaviors rather than focusing attention on undesirable behaviors is always preferable, if possible. The positive attention to the desired demonstrated behavior serves as an example of how the students are expected to act in group and becomes a learning opportunity for the students who are not displaying these expected behaviors. For example: "Wow, Johnny, I love how you are listening with your ears and have your eyes focused on me." Students will learn to identify the desirable and undesirable behaviors through the modeling, giving way to improved student comprehension, a safer learning environment, and an efficient use of time for the school counselor.

When redirecting a rambunctious student who was talking loudly out of turn, Alyssa, the school counselor, reminded the student of the importance of upholding the group's norms. Alyssa asked the student if he believed "talking out of turn during group" aligned with any of the posted major school expectations (Be Safe, Be Responsible, or Be Respectful). The student was able to independently identify that talking out of turn was not practicing one of the school expectations and that he needed to "Be Respectful" to his group members because interrupting others did not show respect. The student then apologized to the teacher and group and was able to wait for his turn to speak. Alyssa was thankful she was able to keep a positive tone for the group culture in that situation, as well as allow for a learning opportunity for the student.

Reinforcements and Incentives

Another common management strategy is the consistent use of reinforcements and incentives. Because "one of the main challenges of working with a group is the ebb and flow of the students' motivation levels, rewards may be used for students who show active engagement and are motivated to work on group goals" (Sink et al., 2011, p. 212). Reinforcing the student's desired behaviors with verbal or tangible incentives teaches identified students, as well as the other students in group who are observing the reinforcement, that if they perform the same desired behavior, they will receive the verbal reinforcement or incentive.

Reinforcements and incentives

- give positive feedback,
- offer visual reminders of desired behaviors,
- increase buy-in and motivation to participate, and
- improve on-task and group behavioral expectations.

A wide range of reinforcements and incentives can be implemented in a plethora of ways. Deciding which one(s) will work best for the school counselor, as well as the group's needs, is an important consideration prior to facilitation. Reinforcements and incentives can be delivered for the entire group or provided individually. They can be immediately delivered or deferred. School counselors may use a ticket or point system throughout the group counseling lesson, where students earn either group or individual incentives. Reinforcements and incentives can be part of a token system, free of cost, or purchased (reward store items). Introducing an incentive system at the beginning of the group counseling lessons will support management of the expected behaviors and student engagement. A quick internet search will yield endless ideas for different types of token systems, incentives, and reinforcements. PBISrewards.com offers numerous suggestions, such as incentives that are free (e.g., flexible seating choice, free-choice play time, principal for a day, no homework passes) and for purchase (e.g., pizza party, fidgets, school supplies).

School counselor Elena facilitated a first-grade social skills group for the first time. Despite the group being composed of only four students, Elena quickly realized after her first counseling group lesson that she would need to use a reinforcement system to better manage behaviors. Since these students were from the same class, and she was aware that they were motivated by classroom group goals in their class, Elena decided to utilize the teacher's method of assigning them points on the board whenever she observed appropriate whole group participation as well as positive behavior throughout the lesson. At the end of each group, if the collective group earned a certain number of points on the board, the students would have the opportunity to enjoy their "free time" activity after group closure. They enjoyed the reinforcement system and practiced the expected appropriate behaviors in group.

Elena was fortunate the students were from the same class—but what if they were not, and the teachers all had different systems? In this case, school counselors would need to create their own system and be consistent in implementing it. Depending on developmental levels, school counselors may want to consider creating and using an immediate reinforcement system for younger students, such as giving them tokens or a ticket after each desirable behavior or response during group. The immediate reinforcement helps teach the students the desired behavior quickly, rather than allowing time to pass, which may not be as effective for students with shorter attention spans.

As previously mentioned, some schools implement the PBIS management strategy, which promotes the use of agreed-upon incentives and reinforcements schoolwide. By using the same PBIS reinforcement system and incentives that the students are already familiar with, counselors parallel their group counseling program and management systems with schoolwide initiatives. The use of this management strategy also allows counselors more time, since an incentive/reinforcement system has already been created and understood throughout the school.

As Joseph, the school counselor, facilitated his kindergarten small group counseling lesson on anger management, anytime he observed the students behaving appropriately (e.g., quietly listening or raising their hand to participate), he would walk over to the students, thank them for the expected behavior, and hand them the schoolwide reinforcement item, a raffle ticket. At the end of each group lesson, the students were able to enter the tickets they had earned into a raffle for prizes in his treasure box, or save them to be entered in the schoolwide raffle. These students were also allotted "free-choice play time" if they earned a certain amount of tickets. By the end of group, Joseph's consistent use of the reinforcement management strategy helped the students model the desired, positive behavioral expectations on their own, with less and less reinforcement.

Each week during group check-in, Alex, the school counselor, would incorporate a review of the students' progress toward their goals. Alex made it a point to publicly reinforce a student's progress and give a small prize to each student whose teacher reported improvement that week. This allowed for a weekly reinforcement of goals. Students soon began to make the positive behavioral changes during the week to reach their goals and came prepared to group the next week with an update, desiring and knowing they would receive the same previous reinforcement as their peers.

Reinforcement management strategies can also be applied to longer-term scenarios, particularly for older students. Discussing and agreeing upon some long-term group goals allows the students to keep the focus on longer efforts and the bigger picture. For example, if attendance is voluntary due to group being held at lunch, students can be given a desirable incentive (e.g., a snack, a front-of-the-line lunch pass) to reinforce their dedication and attendance. If the students cumulatively attended a certain amount of group counseling lessons, as agreed upon in one of the first lessons, their efforts could be reinforced with a prize or an "end-of-group celebration" for their consistent attendance. This long-term reinforcement management strategy allows for student voice, elicits student suggestions for buy-in to meet the attendance goal, and teaches students to practice the desired behaviors.

FINAL CONSIDERATIONS

Once the counselor's toolbox is filled with the knowledge of group development phases, counseling skills, structure, and engagement and management strategies, the counselor is almost ready for success! Some final considerations and helpful tips for effective small group counseling include

- facilitating vs. leading,
- strategies for difficult behaviors,
- collaborating with stakeholders,
- allowing for flexibility, and
- recognizing that some students may need more.

Facilitating vs. Leading

When building effective group cohesion, school counselors are encouraged to be aware of how much time they spend as facilitators of student learning as opposed to leading student learning within the group. When facilitating a group, counselors are doing something *with* the group, empowering students to take the lead in their own and *each other's* learning. For example, when a counselor facilitates a group by proposing options and allowing the group to decide on final choices, the members may experience buy-in and take more ownership within the group. When school counselors are able to distribute leadership among group members, students may feel more empowered to become more involved in group activities. When counselors lead the group, they are more in control of the content and flow, with less facilitation of groupthink and decision making. While both are important, depending on the developmental maturity of the students and the purpose of the group, the time spent facilitating or leading may vary. Younger groups or groups designed to increase content knowledge and skills may require more leading and instructional time, while groups focused on shifting student attitudes, motivation, or feelings of empowerment may benefit from increased facilitation. Thoughtful school counselors are encouraged to consider the benefits and challenges of facilitating versus leading.

Strategies for Difficult Behaviors

Despite school counselors' best efforts implementing everything taught in this chapter, they may still be faced with difficult student behaviors at times. Strategies for working with students who exhibit challenging behaviors during small group counseling lessons include the following:

- *Private conversations.* Have a private conversation with students who are not following expectations to redirect their behaviors without potentially making them feel embarrassed in front of the group.
- *Reinforce group-created norms.* Review the norms that the students created at the beginning of group on a regular basis or when redirection is needed.
- *Provide leadership roles.* Prior to the group lesson, meet privately with individual students to ask if they can help with a leadership role.
- *Individualized incentives.* Meet individually with the students to develop an individualized incentive plan for meeting small group expectations.
- *Use individualized non-verbal strategies.* Meet with the student to develop private, agreed-upon, non-verbal cues to help indicate the need for student redirection.

Communication With Stakeholders

Communication with stakeholders is particularly valuable during the implementation phase of group. Regularly sharing goals, activities, and skills taught in group offers the opportunity for continued reinforcement at home and in the classroom. Sending a quick, weekly email to the students' parents (and teacher) that shares the lesson topic, activity, main ideas, and new vocabulary allows parents to recognize and reinforce what their student is learning. This communication could be generated from the weekly lesson plan. It would also allow teachers to reinforce or praise new behaviors observed in class, supporting an improved sense of pride and accomplishment in the student.

Allowing for Flexibility

School counselors understand that flexibility is one of the most important skills we practice daily in our profession. Flexibility is necessary in effective group counseling facilitation as well. School counselors may feel the pressure to "stay on track" with their lesson plans when a topic takes longer for the students to comprehend, or group behavior management requires more time than expected. Building in time for some flexibility in group is critical, as it allows counselors to cover material in more than a superficial way and to effectively monitor student behaviors. Group counseling usually takes 6 to 8 weeks, affording the school counselor and students time to deviate somewhat from the lesson plan if important and relevant topics arise. Conscientiousness to the outcomes, combined with flexibility, allows the counselor to facilitate a topic that may need to be addressed. So it's okay if the entire lesson is not completed each time. The advantage of small group counseling is the flexibility in following up with unfinished business the following week.

As group cohesion builds throughout the weeks, students who previously participated less may be more willing to share during check-ins, discussions, and activities. Flexibility requires balance, ensuring the knowledge and skills within the lesson are still taught and allowing space for students to express themselves. As students increase their connectedness and a sense of belonging, they may also be motivated to work harder to achieve their group's collective goals. Being flexible can allow for all these desired outcomes.

Recognizing That Some Students May Need More

Despite the implementation of an effective curriculum and a variety of group facilitation strategies, some students may lack the desired progress, and/or their behaviors may begin to impact the rest of the group. In these situations, the counselor is encouraged to stay positive and try not to personalize the lack of progress. Instead, consider whether the group setting is still in the students' best interest or if they require a different intervention, such as more individualized support. Knowing when to re-evaluate and provide a different intervention is part of the art and science of school counseling. Effective group facilitation requires school counselors to know when to intervene, staying cognizant of not only the particular students' needs but also those of other group members who may be impacted by such behaviors. Intensive Tier 3 interventions are discussed in Chapter 9 ("Tier 3 Intensive Interventions").

8

Assessments and Progress Monitoring

NICASH'S STORY CONTINUES

Nicash finally finished her first round of small groups! At the weekly meeting with her principal, she was asked how the students did. Nicash replied proudly, "They did great. I can tell they have really improved!" Nicash's principal responded, "How do you know that they've improved?" Nicash took a moment to think and realized that she did not really know that the students had made progress; she only assumed that they did, based on observations during the small group, but she had no real evidence.

Nicash then realized that while she collected data and created her small groups based on that information, she did not utilize any assessments to evaluate the effectiveness of her groups. Nicash informed her principal that she would do some research on how to create meaningful pre-/post-assessments so that she could use them for future small groups.

TYPES OF DATA

Today's school counselors are called on to measure both the impact and the effectiveness of interventions in their comprehensive school counseling programs (ASCA, 2012; Hatch, 2013). One of the four critical components of the ASCA National Model is *accountability* (the 4th edition calls this "assess" [ASCA, 2019a]). It is vital for school counselors (just like teachers) to demonstrate that they are contributing to student achievement and improvements in student outcomes (ASCA, 2012; Hatch, 2013). So important is the measuring of outcomes from small groups that the American School Counselor Association (2019c) requires school counselors to include reports of small group counseling results in their application for the Recognized ASCA Model Program (RAMP) award. The ASCA Ethical Standards (2016a) specifically discuss evaluation with regard to small group counseling, asking school counselors to "measure the outcomes of group participation (process, perception and outcome data)." Introduced in Chapter 2, these terms are defined as follows:

- *Process data* describe the details of the intervention. They answer the question of *who* received the intervention, *what* type of intervention was provided, *when* and *where* the intervention was provided, and how long the intervention was provided. Like teachers, school counselors create a "lesson plan."
- *Perception data* are most often collected by administering pre-/post-assessments prior to and after the intervention. These data answer the question of whether any *change occurred* in the *attitudes, skills, and knowledge* of students. A pre-/post-assessment is designed to measure the learning of a particular skill or topic. Like teachers, school counselors assess the effectiveness of their interventions.
- *Outcome data* report measurements of the targeted student behaviors the intervention is attempting to improve (achievement and achievement-related data).

As a reminder, the 4th edition of the ASCA National Model now calls process data "participation data" and perception data "Mindsets and Behaviors data" (see Chapter 2, p. 25, for more information).

This chapter provides a detailed description of the use of perception data pre-/post-assessments and progress monitoring as a means of evaluating student growth and the impact of group counseling or another Tier 2 intervention. Specifically, we walk readers through the process of creating a meaningful pre-/post-assessment with effective attitude, skill, and knowledge questions, as well as how and when to conduct progress monitoring assessments. Whether you are using the 3rd or 4th edition of the ASCA National Model, what follows in this chapter will assist you in creating meaningful assessments.

CONCEPTUAL DIAGRAM REVISITED

In Chapter 2, we introduced and described in detail the Hatching Results Conceptual Diagram: Elementary (see Figure 2.2, page 26). As a review of the intentional component, when providing Tier 2 interventions, the Conceptual Diagram (reproduced in Figure 8.1) reads from right to left. School counselors begin looking at outcome data (achievement and achievement-related data) as a means of identifying students in need of assistance because they meet the minimum data element previously identified.

In Figure 8.2, follow along with the arrow to the left, and note school counselors screen students (*attitudes, skills, and knowledge*) to assess their specific needs and determine which type of intervention—direct or indirect (see Chapter 3)—fits best. Finally, the intervention is developed and implemented to meet the students' identified need. Once the intervention is assigned, the forward arrow guides the counselor back through the process of describing the intervention (*process data*) and perception data (*attitudes, skills, and knowledge*), leading to the identified expected behavior change in outcomes (*achievement and/or achievement related*).

Figure 8.1 Hatching Results Conceptual Diagram: Elementary Interventions

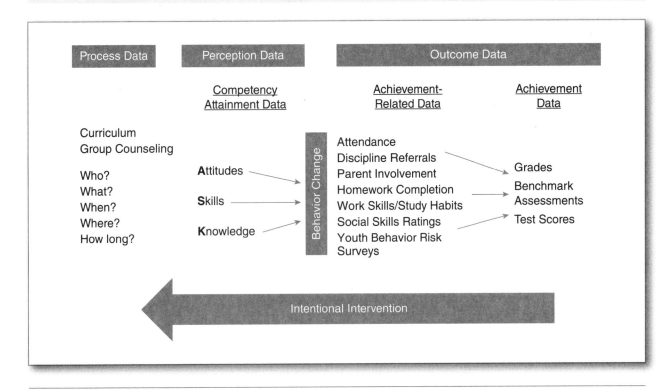

Source: Hatch, T. (2006).

The Conceptual Diagram for determining the intentional intervention (see Figure 8.3) details the *process data* of fourth-grade students receiving six to eight weeks of group counseling on study skills during trimesters 2 and 3 in the school counseling office. The outcome data indicate both the *achievement-related data* and the *achievement data*. The figure includes examples of the types of data that align with the student behaviors the school counselor is planning to measure prior to, throughout, and after the six to eight weeks of group counseling provided. The expectation is that when school counselors support improvements in student perception data (attitudes, skills, and knowledge), student behaviors will begin to improve as well (see Figure 8.4). In order to assess what students believe, know, and demonstrate, school counselors create pre-/post-assessments that align with the content of the group counseling curriculum.

Figure 8.2 Hatching Results Conceptual Diagram: Determining Intervention

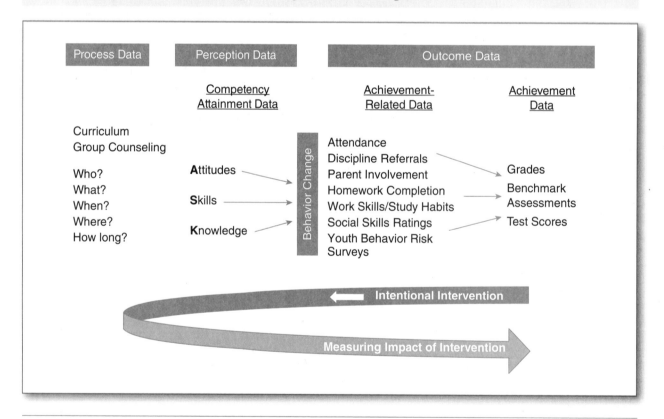

Source: Hatch, T. (2006–2018).

Figure 8.3   Hatching Results Conceptual Diagram: Determining Intervention (Ns on Report Card Example)

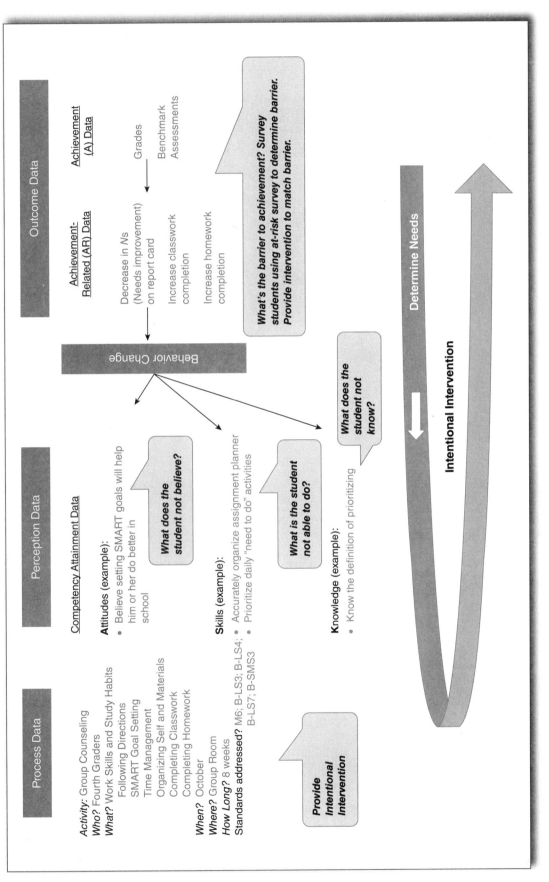

Source: Hatch, T. (2018).

Figure 8.4   Hatching Results Conceptual Diagram: Intentional Interventions

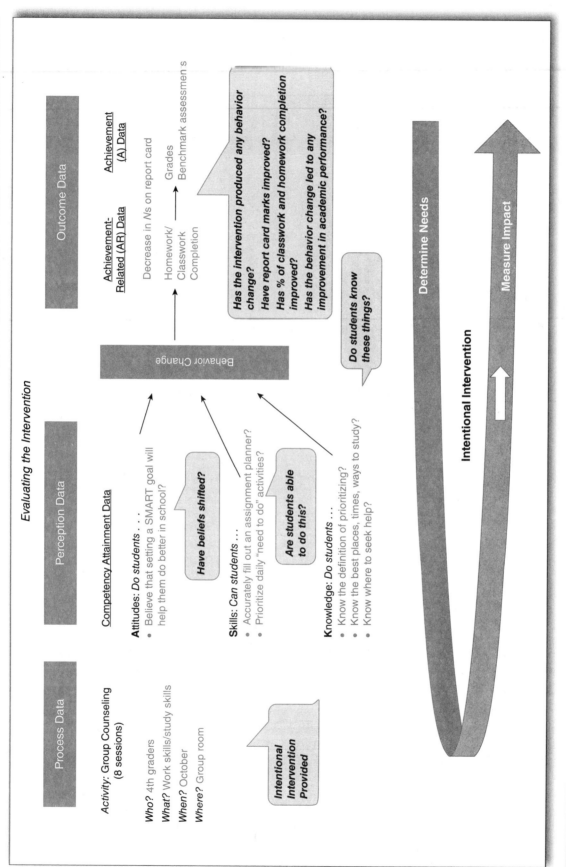

Evaluating the Intervention

Process Data

Activity: Group Counseling (8 sessions)

Who? 4th graders
What? Work skills/study skills
When? October
Where? Group room

Intentional Intervention Provided

Perception Data

Competency Attainment Data

Attitudes: *Do students . . .*
• Believe that setting a SMART goal will help them do better in school?

Have beliefs shifted?

Skills: *Can students . . .*
• Accurately fill out an assignment planner?
• Prioritize daily "need to do" activities?

Are students able to do this?

Knowledge: *Do students . . .*
• Know the definition of prioritizing?
• Know the best places, times, ways to study?
• Know where to seek help?

Behavior Change

Do students know these things?

Outcome Data

Achievement-Related (AR) Data

Decrease in *N*s on report card

Homework/
Classwork
Completion

Achievement (A) Data

Grades
Benchmark assessmen s

Has the intervention produced any behavior change?
Have report card marks improved?
Has % of classwork and homework completion improved?
Has the behavior change led to any improvement in academic performance?

Determine Needs

Intentional Intervention

Measure Impact

Source: Hatch, T. (2018).

Perception Data

When seeking behavior change, school counselors work to ensure those receiving interventions have the appropriate *attitude* (belief that the behavior change is important), *skill* (ability to demonstrate the desired behavior), and *knowledge* (of the steps needed to create a behavior change). For example, if a student *believes* it is important to control his emotions and *knows* the three steps to calm down but cannot *demonstrate* the calming-down steps when he is upset, the likelihood of the student changing his behavior is low. Similarly, if a student *knows* what time management is and can *demonstrate* ways to effectively manage her time but does not *believe* that managing her time will help her to be successful, the behavior is unlikely to occur. Therefore, group counseling interventions are most effective when all three types of perception data (attitudes, skills, and knowledge) are regularly addressed in the lessons and evaluated throughout the process.

You may recall from Chapter 2 that combining the first letter of the words *attitudes, skills,* and *knowledge* create the acronym ASK, which reminds counselors to measure what students gained or learned as a result of an intervention. In order to determine the effectiveness of an intervention, school counselors can "ASK" students what they believe, what they can do, and what they know *before* the intervention and again after the intervention. Perception data, therefore, measure whether (a) students' attitudes or beliefs changed or shifted as a result of an activity or intervention, (b) students learned the skill taught (attained the competency), or (c) students' knowledge increased. Throughout the text, readers may find this order varies (see, e.g., the Helpful Tip box on page 212), but don't fret—remembering there are three is what matters most.

Attitudes and Beliefs

An attitude or belief statement measures what students *think* or *feel*. The most common way school counselors measure attitudes or beliefs is by administering pre-/post-assessments. The following are a few examples of what an attitude/belief question on a pre-/post-assessment might measure with students or parents/guardians:

- Before receiving the study skills small group intervention, 52% of fourth- and fifth-grade students *believed* using their planner could help them get better grades. After the intervention, 79% *believed* using their planner could help them get better grades.
- Before participating in the attendance intervention workshop designed for parents of habitually truant K–2 students, 41% *believed* attendance in early grades was a predictor of high school graduation. After the workshop, there was an increase to 89%.
- Before participating in the Check In Check Out (CICO) program, 26% of fourth-grade students believed that there was an adult on campus who cared about them. After the program, 91% of students believed there was an adult on campus who cared about them.

Skills

A skill describes what students can actually *demonstrate*. School counselors collect data to indicate a student has achieved the competency desired. Skills may be assessed through observing a successful role play or by having students complete an activity, document, assessment, pre-/post-assessment, or other task. The following are a few examples of skill measurement:

- 100% of students participating in the small group intervention can accurately write a SMART (specific, measurable, achievable, relevant, and time-bound) goal.
- 79% of students participating in the small group intervention can accurately demonstrate the Second Step problem-solving process (as observed through role play).
- 92% of students who participated in the small group intervention can demonstrate the ability to accurately organize a binder (as demonstrated through an activity).

Knowledge

Pre-/post-items addressing knowledge indicate whether students learned the content presented in the lesson. The following are a few examples of what a knowledge question on a pre-/post-assessment might measure:

- Prior to the small group intervention, 32% of students knew and could identify the four problem-solving steps as outlined in the Second Step curriculum; after the lesson, 92% of students successfully identified the four problem-solving steps.
- Before a series of anger management group counseling lessons, 56% of fifth-grade males *knew* and could identify three ways to divert anger in a healthy way; after the lessons, this increased to 92%.
- Prior to participating in a small group, 22% of students knew and could identify the definition of *prioritizing*, and after the intervention, 89% of students accurately identified the definition.

Putting It All Together: Attitudes, Skills, and Knowledge

Attitudes, skills, and knowledge work together to influence behavior change. When school counselors design activities and lessons that both address and measure all three of these data areas, behavior change is more likely to follow (Hatch, 2013)—and it is this behavior change that supports improvement in student outcomes (see Figure 8.2). If the school counselor measures the students' attitudes, skills, and knowledge and identifies progress in all three areas, typically, behavior change will follow; however, if a behavior change does not occur despite the positive growth in ASK, the school counselor may want to consider an alternative or more intensive intervention (see Chapter 9, "Tier 3 Intensive Interventions").

Many elementary school counselors can tell a story about students who seem to know that hitting others in frustration is against school rules and has consequences, and can identify appropriate, alternative ways to express themselves. Despite this, however, some students continue to receive referrals for hitting others at school. To address this need, school counselors might review perception data.

In this situation, the *perception data* may indicate that these students *know* the calming-down steps and can *demonstrate* alternative ways of expressing their anger. But do they *believe* that fighting is wrong? If the data reveal no change in the students' behaviors, what might be the missing ingredient? Perhaps it is the students' *attitudes*. If students do not *believe* hitting another student is wrong, they are less likely to stop hitting other students in frustration or anger. As a result, overall incidences of hitting may not decrease, and the content moving forward may need to include conversations about attitudes, either in group or (perhaps) individually if needed.

Stakeholders want to know that school counseling activities and interventions make a real difference (e.g., referrals and suspensions decrease in number). If the data do not show improvement, the lessons may have only been partially effective. By assessing the ASKs, school counselors can determine where additional belief change, skill development, or education is needed.

CREATING PRE-/POST-ASSESSMENTS

Pre-/post-assessments help school counselors to answer the following questions:

- *Was the intervention or activity a good use of instructional learning time?*
- *Was this intervention a valuable use of the school counselor's time?*
- *Did the students learn what was taught?*
- *Do the students possess an attitude that will help them to succeed in the identified area?*
- *In which areas can the students apply what they have learned?*
- *Is more instruction needed in certain areas?*

To create an effective pre-/post-assessment tool, it is essential that the questions be strongly aligned to standards, objectives, and lesson content. When lesson planning, teachers are encouraged to use the Understanding by Design framework (Wiggins & McTighe, 2005), commonly called backward design. This approach involves the instructor "beginning with the end in mind" by developing first learning objectives, then an assessment, and finally the "how" or method of teaching the content (see Figure 8.5).

Figure 8.5 Backward Design

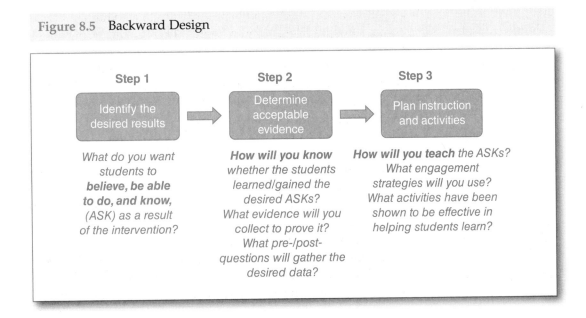

Step 1	Step 2	Step 3
Identify the desired results	Determine acceptable evidence	Plan instruction and activities
*What do you want students to **believe, be able to do, and know,** (ASK) as a result of the intervention?*	***How will you know** whether the students learned/gained the desired ASKs? What evidence will you collect to prove it? What pre-/post- questions will gather the desired data?*	***How will you teach** the ASKs? What engagement strategies will you use? What activities have been shown to be effective in helping students learn?*

The authors of this text recommend that school counselors also follow this approach to ensure that the pre-/post-test strongly aligns to what is taught. It also helps school counselors to think purposefully about the outcomes of the intervention and which activities are most likely to promote the desired student learning. "Teachers are coaches of understanding, not mere purveyors of content knowledge, skill, or activity. They focus on ensuring that learning happens, not just teaching" (Wiggins & McTighe, 2011, p. 1). This fundamental concept is often not taught in school counselor preparation programs and therefore may be overlooked when teaching lessons. We don't teach to merely give information; we teach to help students learn. Therein lies the beauty of backward design. It helps school counselors to facilitate student learning by intentionally thinking about the desired results *before* designing the lesson. For more information on backward design, see McTighe and Wiggins (2012).

Just as pre-packaged small group counseling curricula are available, pre-developed pre-/post-assessments may also accompany the curriculum that you are using. School counselors should analyze pre-made assessments before administering them to ensure that the assessment utilizes questions directly from the curriculum and accurately assesses students' attitudes, skills, and knowledge. Creating pre-/post-assessments skillfully takes practice. This section provides a step-by-step guide on how to develop an effective pre-/post-assessment.

Helpful Tip

ASK

The acronym ASK is simply a reminder that when school counselors finish teaching a lesson, they should ASK the students what they learned. ASK stands for *attitudes, skills,* and *knowledge*. While the acronym reminds school counselors to measure all three areas when constructing the actual pre-/post-assessment, arranging questions in the order of *attitudes, knowledge,* and *skills* is suggested. When school counselors teach students with the goal of changing a behavior, it is most logical to first shift their beliefs, then inform their knowledge. The ultimate goal is that, with a change in beliefs and with more knowledge, students will be able to demonstrate the desired skills, which will lead to behavior change.

Before creating the pre-/post-assessment, consider the following questions:

- What do you want students to *believe* after they receive the intervention? (*attitudes*)
- What do you want students to *know* after they receive the intervention? (*knowledge*)
- What do you want students to be able to *demonstrate* after they receive the intervention? (*skills*)

Creating an Attitude Question

In order to assess students' opinions or beliefs, creating questions using a Likert scale is helpful (Likert, 1932). The Likert (pronounced "LICK-ert") scale, the most widely used scale for assessment research, asks respondents to indicate their level of agreement with a particular statement. Usually, the responses are written in a bipolar scaling manner (measuring responses to the item from positive to negative). For example:

a. Strongly agree

b. Agree

c. Disagree

d. Strongly disagree

Some school counselors include a middle value representing a neutral position, such as *neutral* or *neither agree nor disagree*, or an *unsure* value. Sometimes using a forced-choice scale by removing the neutral response gives a clearer picture of the students' real opinion, as respondents are forced to decide whether to lean more toward *agree* or *disagree*. If the content is new, however, and it's possible the student does not have an opinion, then *unsure* is an appropriate answer option. For example, "I believe fighting is wrong" does not need a neutral response, as students do have an opinion on this. However, students may be unsure how to respond to a statement such as "I believe using restorative circles will reduce conflict" if they do not yet know what restorative circles are.

Table 8.1 provides some examples of an attitude question.

Table 8.1   Attitude Question Examples

Attitude Question				
I believe doing homework matters	Strongly Disagree (a)	Disagree (b)	Agree (c)	Strongly Agree (d)
I believe using study strategies will help me do better in school	Strongly Disagree (a)	Disagree (b)	Agree (c)	Strongly Agree (d)
I believe staying organized will help me get better grades	Strongly Disagree (a)	Disagree (b)	Agree (c)	Strongly Agree (d)

While (a) *strongly disagree*, (b) *disagree*, (c) *agree*, and (d) *strongly agree* are terms often used (especially at the elementary level) when asking questions on a Likert scale, several other variations can be used. The University of Connecticut has created a chart with the most common Likert statements in areas of agreement, frequency, importance, quality, and likelihood (Siegle, 2010). Readers are encouraged to review it when creating pre-/post-assessments to determine if another type of response is more appropriate (https://researchbasics.education.uconn.edu/likert_scales/#).

It is crucial that students understand what is being asked of them. Therefore, school counselors can take several steps to ensure that the data obtained are accurate and measuring students' attitudes, knowledge, and skills, rather than testing to see if students understand the questions or have "correct" responses.

PRE/POST EXAMPLE

Prior to administering a pre-/post-assessment to his small group, school counselor Rajam spends approximately five minutes explaining the differences between the potential responses: *strongly agree, agree, disagree,* and *strongly disagree.* He does this by using an example that his students can relate to. For instance, he may explain the responses in terms of how much the students like Flamin' Hot Cheetos, the most popular snack for students at his school. Rajam may explain that choosing *strongly agree* means that you *love* Hot Cheetos and would like to eat them every single day; *agree* means that you like Hot Cheetos and you like to eat them pretty often; *disagree* means that you do not really like Hot Cheetos; and *strongly disagree* means that you *hate* Hot Cheetos and would never, ever eat one! An example like this provides students with the ability to understand what each term means on the scale. For younger students, Rajam always provides pictures to go along with each option for quicker comprehension. He also reads the questions to the students. Other examples, including a sample of using pictures to go along with options, are shown in Table 8.2.

Table 8.2   Likert Scale

	Strongly Agree	Agree	Disagree	Strongly Disagree
Hot Cheetos	I **love** Hot Cheetos! They are my favorite, and I could eat them every day!	I **like** Hot Cheetos! They taste good, but I wouldn't eat them every day!	I **do not like** Hot Cheetos! They do not taste good, and I try to avoid eating them!	I **hate** Hot Cheetos! I think they taste horrible, and I will do everything in my power to never eat one!

	Strongly Agree	Agree	Disagree	Strongly Disagree
Math	I **love** math. It is my very favorite subject.	I **like** math, but I prefer other subjects.	I **do not like** math. It is one of my least favorite subjects.	I **hate** math. I do absolutely everything I can to avoid math, and I wish I didn't have to learn it.

Icon Source: iStock.com/MonikaBeitlova

Creating a Knowledge Question

Knowledge questions assist school counselors in assessing what content the student learned as a result of the intervention. To begin developing a knowledge question, school counselors can ask themselves, "What would I like students to know to help them achieve that they may not already know?" or "Which information is most important for students to *know* in order to be more successful?" If school counselors conclude that students already know the information (either by observation or from previous experience with the students), they should not include that content in the intervention.

Pre-/post-assessments can also help school counselors determine what students know and do not know before the intervention, which may, in turn, prompt the school counselor to alter the curriculum to address the missing areas of content.

Consider a school counselor who is running a "Closing the Gap" small group for English language learners who scored "near standard" on the state benchmark exam in the previous year. The three goals of this group are for the students to *believe* that scoring well on the benchmark exam is important, to *know* the minimum score they need to be considered "proficient," and to *demonstrate* at least one test-taking strategy.

If school counselors would like students to *know* the minimum score they must receive on a benchmark in order to be considered "proficient," they will need to include that content in the lessons. Knowledge questions are different from attitude questions in that they focus on facts. Conversely, attitude questions assess students' beliefs or opinions—there are no right or wrong answers with an attitude question.

Mateo, a school counselor, selected six fifth-grade students who were English language learners performing at "near standard" on their benchmark tests. One important piece of knowledge Mateo taught the students in the small group was that they would need a score of 1,000 in order to be considered "proficient" for the fifth-grade benchmark test. Since Mateo personally taught his students this piece of information during the group, it was appropriate to create a question directly related to this content. Additionally, it was helpful for him to use the exact same language taught in the group lesson to ensure a quicker connection. An example of a pre-/post-test question he included is as follows:

What score do you need to earn in order to be considered "proficient" on the fifth-grade benchmark test?

a. 600

b. 700

c. 900

d. 1,000

Notice the response choices for this question do not utilize a scale. It would not be appropriate to use a scaled response (used to determine the level of agreement) because this question is not one of opinion—rather, there is only one correct answer.

ACTIVITY 8.1

Imagine planning to teach elementary school students the four steps to problem solving (using the Second Step curriculum): (1) say the problem, (2) think of solutions, (3) explore consequences, and (4) pick the best solution.

How might you improve the following question?
The "second step" in the Second Step problem-solving process is to "think of solutions."

a. Strongly agree

b. Agree

c. Disagree

d. Strongly disagree

Did you note the disconnect in Activity 8.1 between a knowledge question and an attitude (belief) response? If so, you are correct! It is a *fact* that "think of solutions" is the second step in the problem-solving process taught. Therefore, the scaled attitude response doesn't make sense for or fit the statement because the question has a clear, correct answer. The answer is either *true* or *false*.

However, the use of true/false questions may not assess the student's learning as accurately as multiple-choice questions. True/false questions provide students with a 50% chance of guessing the correct answer, while multiple-choice questions increase the likelihood that students' answers indicate the level of learning that took place during the intervention. The more options given for possible answers, the less likely the student will get the correct answer by simply guessing (see Table 8.3). A multiple-choice question that assesses knowledge of the "second step" could be written instead as follows:

The "second step" in the Second Step problem-solving process is to:

a. Pick the best solution

b. Explore consequences

c. Think of solutions

d. Say the problem

Table 8.3 illustrates the reasoning behind the recommendation to use multiple-choice questions instead of true/false questions.

Table 8.3   The Probability of Guessing the Correct Answer on a Pre-/Post-Assessment

Type of Question	Guessing Factor	Pre-Test Sample Correct %	Post-Test Sample Correct %	% Increase
True/False	50%	50%	80%	60%
3-Item Multiple Choice	33%	33%	80%	142%
4-Item Multiple Choice	25%	25%	80%	220%
5-Item Multiple Choice	20%	20%	80%	300%

One way to determine how many options to provide is to consider the developmental level of the students being assessed. For example, fifth-grade students are less likely than second graders to be overwhelmed by a question with five possible choices. In addition, it is recommended that school counselors use "all of the above" and "none of the above" only for older students (fourth grade and above), as these options can be confusing to younger students. Questions with options such as "both a and b" or "neither c nor d" are also not recommended, as this concept may be too developmentally advanced for elementary students.

Furthermore, we suggest that elementary school counselors keep the questions and possible answers as straightforward as possible. Double-negative questions may confuse students, and school counselors may lose the ability to accurately assess the knowledge of a student because the student does not understand what is being asked. Imagine the following belief statement:

It is not okay to push people out of line if they cut in front of you.

a. Strongly agree

b. Agree

c. Disagree

d. Strongly disagree

Students may choose *strongly disagree* because they believe it is wrong to push someone who cuts in line, but this answer is considered undesirable. Double negatives are confusing even for adults. Therefore, this question may be written to eliminate the use of a double negative:

It is okay to push people out of line if they cut in front of you.

a. Strongly agree

b. Agree

c. Disagree

d. Strongly disagree

School counselors should take the following questions into consideration when creating pre-/post-assessment questions:

- *Did I explicitly and clearly cover the content during the lesson?*
- *Do I have the appropriate amount of questions for my students' developmental level?*
- *Did I minimize answers that may be confusing, such as "all of the above" or "both a and b"?*
- *Did I use any double negatives?*
- *Did I use multiple-choice questions instead of true/false, fill-in-the-blank, and essay questions?*

Creating a Skill Question

The third area of assessment determines whether the student has learned the skill(s) the lesson intended to teach. Creating a *skill* question can be a bit more challenging and complex than creating a knowledge question, because it assumes the student has the knowledge and the ability to apply the content to a particular situation/scenario (Bloom, Englehart, Furst, Hill, & Krathwohl, 1956). Students have to think about what they learned, identify the knowledge necessary to answer the questions, and then apply the knowledge to a new situation or scenario (Dimmitt, Carey, & Hatch, 2007). Skills are most often assessed through role play, demonstration of the skill, or answering a scenario-based question on a pre-/post-test. (See Table 8.4 for some dos and don'ts for creating a pre-/post-test.)

Table 8.4 Dos and Don'ts for Pre-/Post-Tests

DO	DON'T
Assess student learning through a pre-/post-test in order to measure the impact of your intervention on student attitudes, skills, and knowledge (ASKs).	Assume students learn what you teach. How do you know if you don't measure?
Determine learning objectives (ASKs) *before* creating pre-/post-test questions.	Create the lesson plan before determining learning objectives or pre-/post-test questions.
Determine how many questions are developmentally appropriate for the age group.	Use too many questions.
Use multiple-choice questions primarily.	Use essay or fill-in-the-blank questions.
Use true/false and yes/no questions sparingly.	Ask questions that make it easy to guess the correct answer.
Consider content validity when designing questions so that you are teaching what is being assessed.	Include questions on content you didn't explicitly teach during the lesson/intervention.
Ask questions that provide evidence that students know something or know how to do something (e.g., "If you see someone being bullied, which of the following is something you should do?").	Ask students whether they know something or know how to do something (i.e., "Do you know what to do if someone is being bullied?").
Use questions that will demonstrate change over the course of the lesson.	Include survey questions on a pre-/post-test (e.g., "How often do you do your homework?").
Word questions in a way that makes them easy to understand.	Use double negatives in questions (e.g., "I <u>don't</u> think it's <u>not</u> okay to push people if they push me first."
Ask only one question at a time.	Use compound questions (e.g., "I believe it's important to do my homework, study for tests, and go to sleep early on school nights").
Use words/emojis that are developmentally and culturally appropriate.	Use words that students will have a difficult time understanding.
Use the appropriate question format for attitude, knowledge, and skill questions.	Use a Likert scale for knowledge questions.
Teach students how to take a pre-/post-test before giving it to them.	Assume students know how to take a pre-/post-test.
Use technology to give a pre-/post-test when possible and appropriate.	Burden yourself with hand-tallying results when easier options are available (Google Forms, Plickers, etc.).
Use the pre-/post-test examples in the online appendix and tweak them as needed to align with your goals, objectives, and curriculum. online resources	Reinvent the wheel.

NICASH'S STORY CONTINUES

As discussed in Chapter 5, Nicash decided to hold an Academic Success Skills small group. Table 8.5 shows the outline for the eight-week lesson.

Table 8.5   Small Group Counseling: Academic Success Skills Outline

Week	Date	Topic
1	10/24	Introduction to Group
2	10/31	Following Directions
3	11/7	SMART Goal Setting
4	11/14	Time Management and Prioritizing
5	11/21	Organizing Self and Materials
6	12/5	Completing Classwork
7	12/12	Completing Homework
8	12/19	Closure

During Lesson 3, students were explicitly taught and had the opportunity to practice writing a SMART goal. Lesson 4 focused on teaching students the skill of properly using a planner to manage their time, and students learned how to organize their binder and their backpacks during Lesson 5. Since students were taught four specific skills, it was appropriate for the school counselor to assess these skills prior to the lessons and after the lessons to determine if the instruction was effective. More specifically, Nicash could assess these skills by asking students to

- *accurately write a SMART goal,*
- *organize their binder,*
- *organize their backpack, and*
- *locate missing parts of an assignment planner.*

We do not advise that school counselors assess skills by asking students whether they know how to do something (e.g., "Do you know how to write a SMART goal?"). Such questions may result in students responding in the affirmative even if they really cannot accurately write a SMART goal. Strong skills questions ask students to demonstrate this knowledge—in this case, either by asking them to actually write their own SMART goal or through a question similar to the following:

Which of the following is a SMART goal?

- a. *I will improve my reading grade.*
- b. *I want to get in trouble less.*
- c. *By the end of the grading period, I will earn a higher grade in math.*
- d. *By the end of the grading period, I will improve my science grade from a D to a C.*

This question results in a more accurate assessment of student learning.

Assessing skill acquisition through role play or demonstration before and after a classroom lesson can be time-consuming; however, it is much easier to accomplish when evaluating a small group Tier 2 intervention due to the smaller number of students (e.g., small groups typically involve four to eight students). With group counseling, it is much more feasible to assess whether students have learned a skill by observing them individually in role play or having them "act out" how they would react in a given situation. An option for school counselors that may help with time efficiency is to allow peers to assess other students' responses as an activity.

Post-Only Assessment of Skills

With skill assessment, a pre-test may not always be needed. Sometimes, post-only assessments can be very beneficial. As previously mentioned, Nicash wanted the students in her academic success skills group to learn the skill of accurately filling out a planner. What if the students had never even seen a planner? Would the school counselor ask the students to fill a planner out incorrectly to gather pre-test data? In a case where the school counselor is confident that the students do not currently possess the skill that will be taught, it may be helpful to wait until after teaching the skill to assess whether the students can accurately apply it.

For example, the school counselor may want to consider having all the students fill out a planning sheet as part of the lesson and then report that X number of students performed this task accurately. If done during a lesson, it is possible for 100% of students to be successful. Alternatively, the school counselor could provide a sample of an assignment planner sheet with errors on it. In the assignment space, the school counselor might write, "Math due Tuesday." The goal would be for the students to identify what is missing or inaccurate in the planner. For instance, missing or inaccurate items might include the math book page number, the number of problems to complete, whether students are to complete odd or even problems, and so on. Again, the results could be that X% of the students accurately identified errors in an assignment planner.

Aligning Pre-/Post-Assessment Questions to Content

Do the questions on the pre-/post-test measure what they are intended to measure? For example, if a school counselor is teaching students about *study skills* and includes questions on the pre-/post-assessment about *calming down when angry* (assuming this was not taught), the results of the assessment will be impacted, as the school counselor is not assessing what was actually taught. A reminder for creating a pre-/post-assessment: *If you do not teach it, you do not test it. If you teach it, you test it.*

To begin creating your own questions, look closely at the curriculum you plan to teach. What core knowledge does the curriculum want the students to know? What core belief do the students need to create a behavior change? What skills are taught within the lesson? It is important to remember that no matter how good a question is, students must also know what is expected of them. To ensure students fully comprehend what you are asking them in a pre-/post-assessment, always include clear instructions.

NICASH'S STORY CONTINUES

Now that Nicash has reviewed her academic success skills curriculum and aligned portions with potential attitude, knowledge, and skill questions, she can begin developing the pre-/post-assessment questions. Nicash is designing her pre-/post-assessment for Lesson 5: Time Management and Prioritizing. She begins by reviewing the PowerPoint slides she has created based off of the lesson plan. The PowerPoint slides in Figures 8.6 through 8.9 are provided to assist the reader in understanding how pre-/post-assessments are created directly from curriculum.

In Figure 8.6, Nicash creates two attitude questions from one slide. The content of this slide is aimed at changing students' attitudes by teaching them specific ways that time management can benefit them. The pre-/post-questions she designed ("I believe it is important to manage my time" and "I believe time management can help me reduce stress") assess to what degree students' attitudes about time management shifted as a result of the lesson.

Figure 8.6   Attitude Question Sample

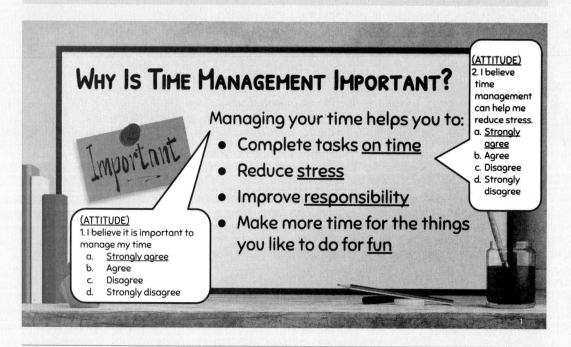

Source: Template by Seyton, retrieved from https://www.slidescarnival.com/

Image source: pixabay.com/clker-free-vector-images

Figure 8.7 incorporates the knowledge being taught about the definition of the word priority. *Readers can see in the slide that the exact definition of the word* prioritizing *is used in the question to ensure that students have been tested on what they have been taught.*

Figure 8.7   Knowledge Question Sample 1

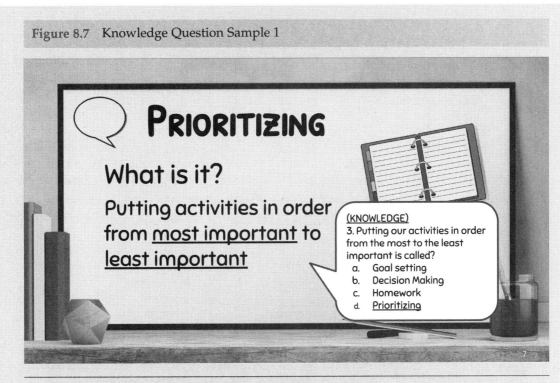

Source: Template by Seyton, retrieved from https://www.slidescarnival.com/.

Image sources: pixabay.com/clker-freevectorimages, and pixabay.com/openclipartvectors

In Figure 8.8, Nicash asks another knowledge question, based on the video shown as part of the lesson (Academic Success Skills Curriculum, Lesson 4). Rather than expecting students to remember everything in the video, Nicash includes a summary slide consisting of the information that will be tested.

Figure 8.8   Knowledge Question Sample 2

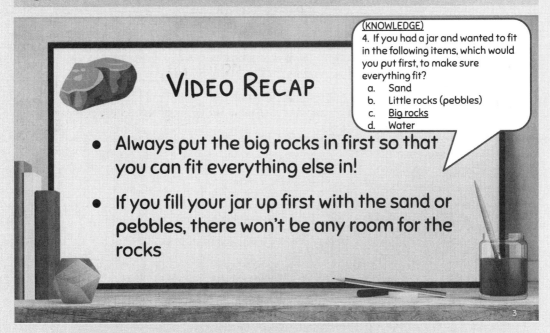

Source: Template by Seyton, retrieved from https://www.slidescarnival.com/

Image source: pixabay.com/clker-freevector-images

(Continued)

(Continued)

Finally, in Figure 8.9, Nicash asks a knowledge and skill question to assess the students' learning through the guided worksheet. Notice that students must use the information they learned in the guided worksheet to complete the skill question in Figure 8.9.

Figure 8.9   Knowledge and Skill Question Sample

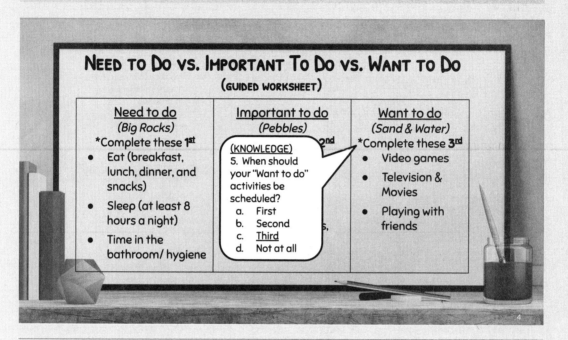

Source: Template by Seyton, retrieved from https://www.slidescarnival.com/.

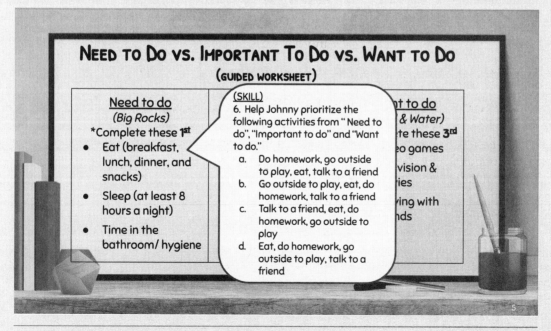

Source: Template by Seyton, retrieved from https://www.slidescarnival.com/.

Creating Pre-/Post-Assessment Questions From Pre-Packaged Curriculum

As discussed in Chapter 6, school counselors sometimes use pre-packaged and/ or self-generated curriculum. Some of the pre-packaged curriculum may include surveys for students, teachers, or parents to assess the perception of whether or not students have shown improvement; however, the surveys provided do not always assess whether or not the students learned what was directly taught to them in the lesson. As critical consumers of curriculum and assessments, school counselors review and *tweak/improve* what they receive to determine if students gained attitudes, knowledge, and skills as a result of the curriculum provided.

The following is an example of a pre-/post-assessment survey in a counselor-generated curriculum obtained from Teachers Pay Teachers. The first question states, "I know how to make a new friend." The response options are *strongly agree, agree, disagree,* and *strongly disagree.* There are a few problems with this: First, scaling responses are only used for *attitude* questions, such as "I believe listening is an important quality in a friend." Attitude questions ask the student for an opinion. Second, using the example above, if a student circles *strongly agree,* at first glance, the school counselor may think the student learned what was taught in the lesson (how to make a new friend). However, how does the school counselor *know* the student truly knows how to make a new friend and doesn't just *believe* it? If students do not show that they *know* a concept or *demonstrate* a particular skill, the school counselor is unable to determine if they actually learned what was taught.

One way to rewrite this question to make it a knowledge question:

Which of the following is *not* a way to make a new friend?

a. Introducing yourself to someone new

b. Telling other students they can join your basketball game

c. Asking other students questions about their interests

d. Showing care and concern for another student who may need your help

This can also be a *skill* question, where students in a small group are asked to role play ways to make a new friend. By demonstrating this action, students prove that they have learned how to make a friend.

ACTIVITY 8.2: Fix this Pre/Post

How would you *rewrite* the following statements to better assess students' knowledge, attitudes, and skills? As a reminder, *believing they know* does not mean they know.

Pre-/Post-Assessment (*Needs Improvement*) for Friendship Small Group

1. I know how to make a new friend.
   a. Strongly agree
   b. Agree
   c. Disagree
   d. Strongly disagree

2. I know how to show someone I am a good listener.
   a. Strongly agree
   b. Agree
   c. Disagree
   d. Strongly disagree

3. I can resolve a problem with my friend.
   a. Strongly agree
   b. Agree
   c. Disagree
   d. Strongly disagree

4. I know how to use "I" messages.
   a. Strongly agree
   b. Agree
   c. Disagree
   d. Strongly disagree

5. I know how to identify how my friend is feeling.
   a. Strongly agree
   b. Agree
   c. Disagree
   d. Strongly disagree

6. I can show empathy to my friend.
   a. Strongly agree
   b. Agree
   c. Disagree
   d. Strongly disagree

Benefits of a Pre-Test

There are many benefits to utilizing a pre-test. Pre-tests provide baseline data of what students already believe, know, and can do. It also allows the school counselor to evaluate whether the attitudes, knowledge, or skills taught have changed as a result of the intervention. A pre-test can also guide school counselors to ensure the curriculum being used is meaningful and necessary. For example, if a pre-test is administered prior to the academic success skills lesson and it is determined that 95% of the students in the small group can already write an accurate SMART goal, it will not be an effective use of time for the school counselor to spend a full lesson teaching the students this skill. Conversely, the students may indicate on the pre-test that they do not think SMART goals are helpful for them. This information would allow the school counselor to shift the focus of the lesson to address *why* SMART goals are important for academic success. Once the pre-test provides the baseline data, the lessons can be finalized, and school counselors can be confident that the content they include will be meaningful for the students' needs. School counselors then provide engaging lessons with the goal of seeing improvement on the post-test assessment.

When Should the Post-Test Be Administered?

Some school counselors may think it is important to give students a post-test after each lesson. One benefit of measuring the post-test immediately after the conclusion of each lesson is that the school counselor can ensure the content taught was learned and that it is appropriate to move on to the next level of material or a different topic. As with teachers, school counselors do not need to measure everything they do. Many teachers determine the most important content they would like students to learn and assess how well the students have learned that particular content at regular intervals, as appropriate. This is important to remember, as assessing each group lesson is time-consuming and school counselors may have limited time for each lesson.

Many school counselors administer the pre-test prior to the beginning of the small group counseling lesson or during the first lesson. Similarly, it is common for school counselors to deliver the post-test during the last small group lesson or shortly thereafter. Measuring the students' attitudes, knowledge, and skills at the very end of the group, once all counseling lessons have been completed, allows the school counselor to assess whether students learned and actually retained what was intended throughout the 6 to 8 weeks of small counseling group lessons.

To equal degrees, the post-test measures the growth in the students' attitudes, knowledge, and skills and the school counselor's ability to deliver an effective lesson. Should the data indicate that the students did not show competencies in the intended areas, it is essential for the school counselor to revise instructional strategies and/or content to meet the students' needs and ensure competency attainment.

HOW TO COLLECT PRE-/POST-ASSESSMENT DATA

Many school counselors collect pre-/post-assessment data by providing students with paper assessments. While collecting data using the paper-and-pencil method is perfectly acceptable, it can be time-consuming for larger or multiple groups. Fortunately, several free data collection programs can be utilized to increase the efficiency of collecting pre-/post-assessment data. While school counselors could collect pre-/post-assessment data in countless ways, this section provides a few examples of technology tools that can support their ability to efficiently collect and analyze students' attitudes, knowledge, and skills.

Google Forms

Google Forms, a free, online tool, is user-friendly for anyone with a Google account. Google Forms allows school counselors to create questionnaires and assessments for multiple purposes (staff assessments, student assessments, parent feedback, etc.). Using Google Forms to create a pre-/post-assessment will allow school counselors to easily measure and organize students' attitudes, knowledge, and skills, and this tool can be used before and/or after an intervention is implemented. School counselors have the option to ask questions in multiple formats, including scaling (attitude questions), multiple choice (knowledge questions), checked boxes (knowledge questions), and short answer (skill questions). Students can access the assessment online using a tablet, cell phone, computer, or laptop by following a link that is generated once the Google Form has been created.

After students complete the assessment, their responses are automatically recorded into an Excel spreadsheet, which can then be stored and used by the school counselor to analyze student responses. School counselors can view individual students' raw data, which allows them to identify which students may need more support and in which specific area. In addition, Google Forms allow for viewing the data in a graph format. These graphs allow school counselors to view student responses as a whole, which makes it easier to identify positive patterns as well as areas for improvement. For example, the school counselor may see a graph that shows that before the intervention, 23% of students could identify the score necessary to be "proficient" on the benchmark test, and afterwards, 83% of students were able to identify the score. Although not every student possessed this knowledge at the time of the post-test, the school counselor can conclude that a positive shift occurred in students' knowledge in this area. All of this information can be easily shared with other stakeholders for improved collaboration and advocacy. For more information about Google Forms, visit https://gsuite.google.com/learning-center/products/forms/get-started/.

Plickers

Unlike Google Forms, Plickers is a technology tool that does not require students to have access to an electronic device. School counselors can purchase Plickers cards on Amazon.com at $20 for a set of 40 laminated cards. Plickers cards are also available for free (for up to five questions, or more questions for a small fee) at https://get.plickers.com/ and can be printed. If school counselors print out the cards, it is recommended that they laminate the cards for extended use.

School counselors can use the online platform to create the pre-/post-assessment questions. After creating and inputting all of the questions, school counselors can download the Plickers app on their smartphone or tablet (a camera must be accessible on the device). Each Plickers card has a unique visual code that can be read by the smartphone or tablet's camera using the Plickers app. The visual code on the card has four sides, labeled *A*, *B*, *C*, and *D*, in small letters. The pre-/post-assessment questions can be projected on a screen, and students are asked to hold up their card with their response (*A*, *B*, *C*, or *D*) at the top of the card. The school counselors can then use their smartphone or tablet to slowly scan the visual codes on each of the cards around the room using the camera on their device. The responses will be recorded on the device so that the school counselors can see which students have not yet answered. School counselors can also modify the settings on the app so that the responses project onto the screen. This allows students to be more engaged and provides them the ability to see how many responses were correct/incorrect (anonymously). Once all students have responded, school counselors can continue on to the next question.

All results are saved automatically to the online platform and can be accessed at any time. Similar to Google Forms, both individual and overall responses can be viewed.

Kahoot!

Kahoot! is another online technology tool than can be used to collect pre-/post-assessment data in a fun and engaging manner. School counselors can sign up for a free account and set up the assessment. When they are ready to facilitate the assessment, a unique code will be generated, and students will use a laptop, cell phone, tablet, or desktop computer to begin the assessment. Kahoot! is set up like a game, where students have a certain amount of time to answer each question (determined and inputted by the school counselor). Students can play the game as individuals or on different teams. As with Google Forms and Plickers, they can access the results at any time and view the responses either individually or as a whole. For more information, visit https://kahoot.it.

ONGOING ASSESSMENTS: PROGRESS MONITORING FOR SMALL GROUPS

Teachers monitor students' academic progress as a means of assessing the effectiveness of the instruction provided. "Student progress monitoring is a practice that helps teachers use student performance data to continually evaluate the effectiveness of their teaching and make more informed instructional decisions" (Safer & Fleischman, 2005, p. 81). School counselors also have a responsibility to ensure that the interventions provided are beneficial and effective for student growth. One way to accomplish this is by progress monitoring students during small group counseling.

Ensuring students benefit from the Tier 2 intervention they receive requires collecting data *before*, *during*, and *after* the small group or other intervention. While progress monitoring can be implemented with activities other than group counseling (large group workshops, mentoring, tutoring, etc.), the following is an example of a progress monitoring form for small group interventions. Progress monitoring is an effective way to improve outcomes by obtaining intermittent feedback from the teacher during the intervention. In this way, the school counselor can assess teacher-reported improvements or challenges regarding student behaviors. In addition, the delivery and/or instructional strategies can be adjusted if necessary. Garnering support for this activity is more successful when school counselors provide a quick and simple tool for teachers to use to gather progress monitoring data.

Baseline Data Before Small Group

As discussed in Chapter 5, school counselors can utilize the Work Habits/Social Skills sections of the report card (see Figure 8.10) and office discipline referrals as a means of gathering baseline data before beginning small groups. These data allow school counselors to narrow down their areas of focus to meet the specific needs of each student.

While report card data are useful and provide strong baseline data, the school counselor may want to gather more detailed information for students selected to participate in a particular small group. Consider a student who receives an *N* (*Needs Improvement*) in the "organizes self and materials for learning" section on

Figure 8.10 Work Habits and Social Skills Report Card

Work Habits and Social Skills				
Growth Mindset	**Q1**	**Q2**	**Q3**	**Q4**
Demonstrates effort				
Has a positive attitude toward learning				
Perseveres through challenges				
Be Respectful	**Q1**	**Q2**	**Q3**	**Q4**
Cooperates with others				
Respects others' rights, feelings, and property				
Solves problems appropriately				
Shows concern for others				
Fosters peer relationships				
Be Responsible	**Q1**	**Q2**	**Q3**	**Q4**
Organizes self and materials for learning	N	N	N	N
Listens and follows directions	N	N	N	N
Completes classwork consistently	N	N	N	N
Completes homework consistently	N	N	N	N
Be Safe	**Q1**	**Q2**	**Q3**	**Q4**
Keeps all hands, feet, and other objects to self				
Follows school and classroom rules				
Uses materials appropriately				

the report card. There may be a range in which the student's *N* mark falls. Providing teachers with a progress monitoring tool that asks them to rate "to which degree" the student performs the skill will allow school counselors to determine whether students show any progress throughout the small group. It is important that school counselors use the same progress monitoring tool before, during, and after group to ensure consistency in reporting. Figures 8.11, 8.12, and 8.13 are examples of tools provided to the teachers of students who participated in Nicash's academic success skills group.

In the *before* example, Mrs. Morgan, Lillian's teacher, reports that at this time, Lillian *almost never* demonstrates the skills of organizing herself and her materials and listening and following directions, and *rarely* completes classwork and homework. This suggests that Nicash has quite a bit of work to do supporting Lillian in learning the tools necessary to demonstrate these skills.

Figure 8.11 Progress Monitoring: Baseline (Before) Data for Lillian

Progress Monitoring: Baseline Data (Before Group)		
Student Name: Lillian Johnson	Your Name: Mrs. Morgan	Date: 10/23/17
"Needs Improvement" Area	**Scaled Rating** (Two samples—continuum and numbered)	
Organizes self and materials for learning	How often does your student demonstrate this skill? 1---**X**---------------------- 2 ----------------------- 3 ----------------------- 4 ----------------------- 5 Almost Rarely Sometimes Usually Almost Never Always	
Listens and follows directions	How often does your student demonstrate this skill? 1---**X**---------------------- 2 ----------------------- 3 ----------------------- 4 ----------------------- 5 Almost Rarely Sometimes Usually Almost Never Always	
Completes homework	How often does your student demonstrate this skill? 1 **(2)** 3 4 5 Almost Rarely Sometimes Usually Almost Never Always	
Completes classwork	How often does your student demonstrate this skill? 1 **(2)** 3 4 5 Almost Rarely Sometimes Usually Almost Never Always	

Note: As this example shows, the response can be either on a continuum or a whole number. The continuum allows the participating teacher to place a mark between numbers, which may provide the school counselor with more detailed information regarding progress. Whole numbers allow for easier evaluation and comparison on pre-/post-assessments; either is acceptable, and this might be counselor preference.

Data During Small Group

The students in Nicash's small group will learn various skills for how to be a better listener, follow directions, and stay more organized. Systems will also be put in place to assist the students in improving the completion rate of both classwork and homework. Rather than waiting until the 6- to 8-week intervention ends, it may be helpful for Nicash to assess how the students in the small group are progressing throughout the intervention period.

If students are not showing progress during this time, the school counselor may want to evaluate the current curriculum or instructional strategies being used, to determine if a change in the intervention or the manner of instruction will be beneficial. If students are showing progress (regardless of how small), the information can be shared with students as a way of encouraging them to continue working hard toward their goals, and the intervention can continue as planned.

According to Mrs. Morgan's progress monitoring report (see Figure 8.12), completed during the four-week mark of the small group, Lillian has shown some improvements. While *rarely* demonstrating a behavior is not necessarily what would bring Lillian from "Needs Improvement" to "Approaching Expectations" on her report card, it is important data. Note that using a continuum provides room for incremental shifts in behavior, which can be encouraging and more realistic since behavior often does not change dramatically overnight. Nicash knows that Lillian is

Figure 8.12   Progress Monitoring: Intermittent (During) Data for Lillian

Progress Monitoring: Intermittent Data (During Group)		
Student Name: Lillian Johnson	Your Name: Mrs. Morgan	Date: 11/24/17
"Needs Improvement" Area	Scaled Rating: Continuum	
Organizes self and materials for learning	How often has your student demonstrated this skill in the past **4 weeks**? 1------------------------ 2 -**X**------------------------ 3 ------------------------ 4 ---------------------- 5 Almost Rarely Sometimes Usually Almost Never Always		
Listens and follows directions	How often has your student demonstrated this skill in the past **4 weeks**? 1------------------------ 2 ----**X**---------------------- 3 ------------------------ 4 ---------------------- 5 Almost Rarely Sometimes Usually Almost Never Always		
Completes homework	How often has your student demonstrated this skill in the past **4 weeks**? 1------------------------ 2 ------------------------**X**-- 3 ------------------------ 4 ---------------------- 5 Almost Rarely Sometimes Usually Almost Never Always		
Completes classwork	How often has your student demonstrated this skill in the past **4 weeks**? 1------------------------ 2 -------------------------- 3 --**X**-------------------- 4 ---------------------- 5 Almost Rarely Sometimes Usually Almost Never Always		

benefiting from the small group to some degree, since she is progressing. In addition, these data can be shared with Lillian so that she knows the teacher is noticing her progress and her hard work is helping her to be more academically successful.

Data After Small Group

The goal of running a small group is for students to gain the attitudes, knowledge, and skills needed to change their behavior, resulting in improvement in data that first identified them as "in need of an intervention" (in this case, their report card marks). However, a student's progress is not always completely reflected on the report card. Therefore, school counselors are encouraged to use a progress monitoring tool during the intervention, as well as assess report card data at the end of the next marking period when determining the effectiveness of an intervention. By using the progress monitoring tool, the school counselor can compare the baseline and "end of group" data to determine the extent to which progress was made. Even if a student did not move from "Needs Improvement" to "Approaching Expectations," the student could move from "Almost Never Demonstrates This Skill" to "Sometimes Demonstrates This Skill" on the progress monitoring tool, which would indicate that the intervention was impactful to a degree and that this particular student may need more time to fully integrate the skills learned. Figure 8.13 is a copy of Lillian's final progress monitoring report from Mrs. Morgan.

Figure 8.13   Progress Monitoring: End of Group Data for Lillian

Progress Monitoring: <u>End</u> of Group Data		
Student Name: Lillian Johnson	Your Name: Mrs. Morgan	Date: 12/22/17
"Needs Improvement" Area	Scaled Rating	
Organizes self and materials for learning	How often has your student demonstrated this skill in the past **8 weeks**? 1------------------------- 2 ---**X**------------------------ 3 ---------------------- 4 ---------------------- 5 Almost Rarely Sometimes Usually Almost Never Always	
Listens and follows directions	How often has your student demonstrated this skill in the past **8 weeks**? 1------------------------- 2 ------------------------- 3 ---**X**------------------ 4 ---------------------- 5 Almost Rarely Sometimes Usually Almost Never Always	
Completes homework	How often has your student demonstrated this skill in the past **8 weeks**? 1------------------------- 2 ------------------------- 3 ----------------------- 4 -**X**------------------- 5 Almost Rarely Sometimes Usually Almost Never Always	
Completes classwork	How often has your student demonstrated this skill in the past **8 weeks**? 1------------------------- 2 ------------------------- 3 ------------------**X**--- 4 ---------------------- 5 Almost Rarely Sometimes Usually Almost Never Always	

Mrs. Morgan has reported progress in all identified areas for Lillian. For the areas in which Lillian demonstrates the skill *rarely*, a "Needs Improvement" mark may still be given on the next report card. This does not mean that the intervention was unsuccessful, because Lillian was able to move from *almost never* demonstrating the skill to *rarely* or, in some cases, *sometimes* demonstrating the skill. This is progress!

Figure 8.14 is another sample progress monitoring tool that can be used for students individually or in a small group, or for any other Tier 2 intervention.

In addition, it may be helpful to continue monitoring the students in your small groups long after the groups have ended, by having teachers continue to assess students' progress throughout the year. This will provide school counselors with valuable information regarding the depth of the behavior change: Did the student revert to old behaviors two months after the group ended? Or did the student continue to utilize the attitudes, knowledge, and skills learned during the small group counseling intervention?

As a reminder, while the examples provided focus on progress monitoring for small groups, these same tools can be utilized with other types of Tier 2 interventions to determine if progress is being made or if different or additional interventions are required. The progress monitoring example (Figure 8.14) can be used for any intervention.

Figure 8.14 Weekly Progress Monitoring Sample

Weekly Progress Monitoring

Student Name: _____ Date: _____

Teacher Name: _____ Teacher's Signature: _____

% of classwork completion prior to small group: _____

% of classwork completion **this** week: _____

% of homework completion prior to small group: _____

% of homework completion **this** week: _____

Effort in class **this** week:	1	2	3	4	5
	No Effort				Full Effort

Focus in class **this** week:	1	2	3	4	5
	Poor Focus				Exceptional Focus

In an era of increased accountability for school counselors, it is crucial that data are collected before and after an intervention to assess whether the intervention contributed positively to student improvement. As noted in the Conceptual Diagram (Figure 8.1), in order for behavior change to occur (outcome data), attitudes, skills, and knowledge must first be changed/improved. Pre-/post-assessments are useful for gathering and analyzing whether the intervention contributed to a change in students' attitudes, skills, and knowledge. School counselors are encouraged to create pre-/post-assessment questions that align with the content of the lesson curriculum, to ensure that students are being asked questions based on what was directly taught to them through the lesson. Progress monitoring before, during, and after an intervention allows school counselors to track student behavior and provides important information as to whether the intervention is benefiting the student. Data collected throughout the intervention can also motivate students (e.g., "Look how much you have improved in this area"), encourage students (e.g., "It looks like there wasn't much progress this week. What can we do to make sure there is more progress next week?"), and lead to altering the curriculum if necessary (if none of the students are showing progress on a regular basis, the school counselor may want to consider adjusting the small group curriculum or methods of facilitation).

NICASH'S STORY CONTINUES

Nicash has gathered many tools that have helped her create pre-/post-assessments for her future small groups and for any other Tier 2 intervention she provides. Nicash feels confident in her ability to create questions that assess changes in students' attitudes, skills, and knowledge to determine if the students truly learned what was taught throughout the intervention. Nicash also recognizes the importance of gathering perception data not only from the students, but also from the teacher, to see if the things the students have learned in group or any changes in the students' beliefs have shifted behavior demonstrated in the classroom.

9

Tier 3 Intensive Interventions

NICASH'S STORY CONTINUES

After the second grading period, Nicash queried the report card data to determine which of her elementary students again showed a need for Tier 2 small group counseling support. Jordan was one of these students. Clearly, after a few weeks of group, even though Nicash was utilizing several proactive engagement and management strategies, Jordan continued to struggle with displaying appropriate behaviors. Not only did this impact Jordan, but the other students in the group, and their learning, were affected as well. Once the eight-week group counseling lesson ended, the new report card data revealed Jordan was still facing challenges at school. Nicash decided to shift Jordan into a Tier 3 intervention and work with him on the same necessary curriculum topics in a more individual counseling setting. What began as a few individual meetings, however, eventually became a weekly or multi-weekly intervention. Soon Nicash noticed she had to drop everything to support Jordan's misbehavior. After a couple of weeks of this, she started to feel the effects of compassion fatigue and realized that Jordan needed more than she alone could offer. She referred Jordan and his family to additional resources inside and outside of school to better support him.

TIER 3

Introduction

The previous chapters in this text outlined data-driven Tier 2 interventions. School counselors provide different types of direct and indirect interventions for students in need at the Tier 2 level. While most interventions produce positive student outcomes, some students may continue to struggle and need additional, Tier 3 intensive supports. In some cases, students are referred directly to the school counselor at the Tier 3 level. These students may be experiencing a crisis or transferring into the school with data that position them as having a high need for Tier 3. This chapter discusses referring students for more intensive Tier 3 interventions, and the different types of direct and indirect Tier 3 interventions, inside and outside of the school.

Tier 2 vs. Tier 3

Tier 2 is the second level of support for students (approximately 20%) who need more targeted data-driven interventions (e.g., small group counseling, consultation) over a monitored, short-term period of time. Conversely, Tier 3 is the highest level of support for more individualized and intensive interventions, designed for even fewer students (approximately 5–10%). Students referred to Tier 3 supports exhibit continued barriers to learning or may be experiencing a crisis situation that is affecting their academics or behavior. While direct and indirect interventions are also still short term, the level of collaboration, the intensity of interventions, and referrals to other professionals are increased. This continued collaboration takes place between the school counselor and stakeholders both within and outside of the school and becomes more in-depth and more frequent for Tier 3 interventions. Supporting students receiving Tier 3 interventions requires school counselors to thoroughly understand their roles and responsibilities within the Multi-Tiered, Multi-Domain System of Supports (MTMDSS) model and to utilize the collaborative team approach and support of other experts.

Identifying Students in Need of Tier 3 Interventions

Generally, students are identified to receive more intensive Tier 3 supports in one of three ways. Students receive Tier 3 supports when they

- continue to lack progress and exhibit barriers to learning after receiving Tier 2 interventions,
- experience a crisis, or
- transfer to the school with data that position them as having a high need for Tier 3.

Lack of Progress

When a student receiving Tier 2 interventions lacks progress over time, supports to receiving more intensive Tier 3 interventions shift. Sometimes, despite best efforts to serve students in small group counseling or other Tier 2 interventions, behaviors escalate, requiring more intensive time and attention. Students who meet the criteria to receive more intensive supports do not necessarily need to continue to stay at that same level of support (e.g., receiving more intensive Tier 2 interventions). The idea is that the process of receiving supports and interventions is fluid depending on the need.

Referring to the previous example, Jordan's shift from Tier 2 to Tier 3 interventions was transitional because he continued to struggle. Evidently, he needed more intensive support, and the next step to support Jordan was a team meeting to discuss more individualized interventions.

Helpful Tip

Figure 9.1 MTMDSS Video Resource

HOME   TRAINING   BOOKS   ONLINE LEARNING   GRANTS   EVENTS   NEWS & RESOURCES   ABOUT

HATCHING RESULTS BLOG
SHORT VIDEO DEMONSTRATING MULTI-TIERED, MULTI-DOMAIN SYSTEM OF SUPPORTS
November 02, 2017 / Danielle Duarte

The silent video below is an example how the Multi-Tiered, Multi-Domain System of Supports (MTMDSS) works within the school setting, and the description below can be used to talk through the MTMDSS framework within a comprehensive school counseling program.

Figure 9.1 shows part of a blog post about a helpful video resource that explains the fluidity of students receiving Tier 2 and 3 interventions within the MTMDSS model. Visit https://www.hatchingresults.com/blog/2017/11/short-video-demonstrating-multi-tiered-multi-domain-system-of-supports to view the video in full.

NICASH'S STORY CONTINUES

After small group counseling ended, Jordan continued to act out in class. He refused to work, was aggressive toward his teacher and peers, and ran out of the classroom. Jordan's teacher and assistant principal were confident they could count on Nicash to help him de-escalate. Once Jordan's teacher followed the protocol and connected him with Nicash, everyone was able to return to their responsibilities for the day—everyone except Nicash. After a period of little to no academic or behavioral progress from Jordan, Nicash knew it was time for another team meeting to discuss additional supports and next steps.

Crisis Response

Students often come to school affected by a myriad of issues outside of their own control, which may negatively impact their education. These issues vary, ranging from minor situations, such as an argument with a sibling, to more serious situations, such as a lack of basic needs (e.g., homelessness), transition inside the home (e.g., divorce), or loss of a loved one. Students' behavioral responses to the variety of crises differ from student to student. Some students may be referred to the school counselor due to a dramatic change in their social/emotional behavior. Students who experience a crisis may disengage from their class and peers, while others may exhibit the opposite behavior and inappropriately engage excessively. Students may interact with others in a negative way, such as calling out more than usual or acting aggressively toward others. Regardless of the type of crisis, school counselors support *all* students, including those who are experiencing a temporary response to a serious crisis.

Crisis examples include each of the following:

- Death of an immediate family member
- Suicidal ideation
- Threat to harm self or others
- Child abuse/neglect
- Witnessing a violent or aggressive incident
- Displacement of a parent/guardian (e.g., incarceration, deportation)
- Recent family transition (e.g., divorce, new stepfamily)
- Medical issues

> One day after school, as school counselor Abbey was documenting notes from group, she received a visit from one of the first-grade teachers. Mrs. Penelope Jane disclosed that during her class's journal time, one of her students, Andre, typically a quiet and hardworking student who meets grade-level standards, drew a photo of someone lying on the ground bleeding. Mrs. Penelope Jane asked Andre to describe the photo, and he shared that his older cousin, who lives at home with him, had been shot in the neighborhood park and passed away the night before. Mrs. Penelope Jane shared that she noticed that Andre was more aggressive with his peers and resistant to work that day, and now she understood why. Abbey helped Mrs. Penelope Jane process her feelings about the situation, informed her administrative team, set an appointment to meet with Andre the following day, and reached out to Andre's family that afternoon.

The immediate and increased communication between Mrs. Penelope Jane, the administration, and Andre's family is one of the more intensive Tier 3 school counseling interventions. This example reinforces the importance of Abbey's staff and their understanding of her role, ways to access her, and how imperative it is for stakeholders to collaborate to support the student as a team.

New Transfer With a Tier 3 Data Need

In some cases, students may receive more intensive Tier 3 interventions when they transfer to the school with data that position them as having a high need for Tier 3 supports. The front office staff are pivotal in helping identify newly transferred students with high needs. Their initial interactions with registered families, as well as their primary access to important cumulative file data, is beneficial for school counselors to identify students in need of Tier 3 interventions. School counselors are then able to proactively contact these students and their families and quickly build rapport for any additional support needed. Checking in preventively with new students and their families may shed light on whether or not that student will need more immediate interventions in place to ensure a smooth transition. In some cases, students benefit from monitoring alone and may not need the intensive Tier 3 intervention, but the initial and immediate contact is important to inform the student of the available counseling supports and to determine the need for any other additional services.

Examples of a Tier 3 data need include the following:

- Lengthy discipline history
- Lengthy social/emotional history
- Lengthy legal agency contact history
- Educational gap
- Attendance issues
- Medical issues
- Custody issues
- Receiving a number of outside services
- Displaced/foster youth
- Family trauma, death, etc.

Noah, a school counselor, received an email from Maxine, the front office attendance clerk, who requested to meet in person to communicate some confidential information about a student starting school the next day. Maxine shared that she experienced a strange encounter with the new first-grade student, Cody, and his grandmother, who was also his guardian. Maxine explained how she noticed Cody's behavior in the front office, which led Noah to investigate in his cumulative file where he found Cody's extensive discipline and custody history. Upon reaching out to Cody's grandmother, Noah learned that Cody was born into a family with a history of substance abuse and domestic violence and had a growing discipline file. His grandmother also reported the difficult time she was experiencing while raising Cody and requested community parenting resources. Cody's grandmother was pleased with the plan for Cody to meet Noah before school and to connect with a trusted adult on his new campus, who he could also visit during his recess and lunch that day.

Referring to the previous example, Noah's proactive connection and positive transition plan for Cody and his grandmother would not have been possible without the prompt collaboration of the office staff. When school counselors work as a team with the front office to support new transfer students in need of immediate intensive interventions, the new students are more likely to be set up for success with additional supports for a positive transition to the school.

Figure 9.2 offers the Hatching Results Tier 2 and 3 flow chart as a visual resource to help clarify the intervention process.

Efficient Use of Time for Tier 3 Interventions

Tier 3 interventions are designed for approximately 5–10% of the students. These intensive Tier 3 supports are meant to be short term and fluid. The more conscientious school counselors are with their use of time supporting Tier 3 interventions, the more preventative their comprehensive school counseling program is, and the more accessible the school counselors and their services are for all students.

Figure 9.2   Hatching Results Tier 2 and 3 Flow Chart

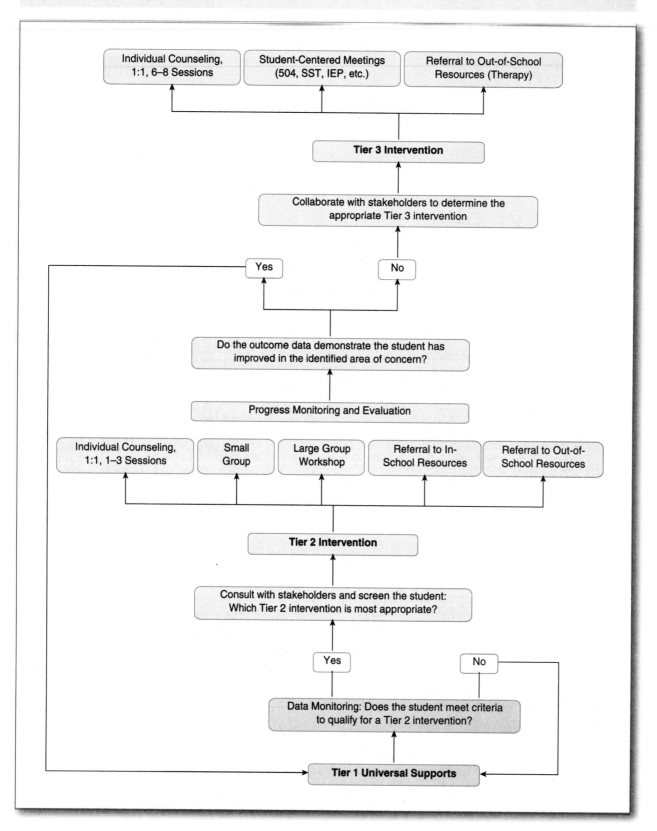

Short-Term Support

Tier 3 interventions provided by the school counselor are short term (6 to 8 weeks) and help the student to learn the attitudes, skills, and knowledge to overcome current barriers to learning. Ideally, after this short, monitored period of time, the students return to school feeling better adjusted and showing improvement. If a student continues to lack progress and requires additional Tier 3 supports, the student and family members are referred to outside resources. This can help ensure the effective balance of time for all schoolwide services.

Fluid Access to Tiered Interventions

It is important to note that access to different tiered interventions is not always prescriptive, but more fluid and transient. This fluidity, in turn, helps with the goal of the interventions remaining in place for only a short term. It is not necessary for students to receive Tier 2 interventions prior to accessing Tier 3 interventions. Students receiving Tier 2 interventions also may not need to continue receiving Tier 2 interventions for the remainder of the school year, or to receive more intensive Tier 3 interventions. In the earlier example with Andre, Mrs. Penelope Jane described him as a "quiet and hardworking student who meets grade-level standards" who was likely not receiving any additional Tier 3 supports until news of the crisis concerning his cousin's recent death. The fluidity of access helps students receive the supports they need quickly, as well as offers a return to normalcy when the interventions are effective.

Helpful Tip

Appropriate Use of Time for Tier 3 Interventions

The American School Counselor Association recommends that school counselors spend 80% of their time delivering direct and indirect services to students (see Figure 9.3). The goal of a comprehensive school counseling program is to be preventative in nature, proactively delivering content for the attitudes, skills, and knowledge necessary to achieve academic success, college and career readiness, and social/emotional development. Although Tier 3 crisis response is a necessary direct service, school counselors spend the majority of their time preventatively, within Tier 1 services. When school counselors provide Tier 3 interventions, it is especially important to monitor their role and balance their time. Due to their training in crisis management, school counselors are often the "go to" people when a crisis occurs. While school counselors are important members of the school intervention team, it is important to remember that school counselors are not the only ones responsible for students' success; they are one of the players on the team.

The following questions may help school counselors reflect on their appropriate use of time for Tier 3 interventions.

- Am I spending the ASCA-recommended 80% of my time for direct and indirect services?

- Am I using my time effectively to ensure *all* students are served?

(Continued)

(Continued)

- Does my time supporting each tier generally align with the recommended time in Figure 9.3?

  - Tier 1: Most of your time
  - Tier 2: Some of your time

- Am I am spending more time in Tier 2 or 3 instead of Tier 1, causing my MTMDSS pyramid to be upside down?
- When is the counseling beyond my scope as a school counselor?
- Is my counseling with the student short term and solution focused, or does this student need more therapeutic support, which is out of my scope?
- Does my documentation show that I am seeing this student on a regular basis?
- Am I collaborating with other stakeholders, but the students still need continuous support?
- Is it time for me to ask for more help with specific students?
- Are my tasks and responsibilities worthy of a master's degree?

Figure 9.3   ASCA National Model Suggested Use of Time

	Delivery System Component	Elementary School % of Time	Middle School % of Time	High School % of Time	ASCA Recommendation
Direct Services	Core Curriculum (Tier 1)	35%	30%	20%	
	Individual Student Planning (Can be Tier 1/2/3)	5%	15%	25%	80% or more
	Responsive Services (Can be Tier 1/2/3)	25%	20%	20%	
Indirect Services	Referrals, Consultation, Collaboration (Can be Tier 1/2/3)	20%	20%	20%	
	System Support (Can support Tiers 1/2/3)	15%	15%	15%	20% or less

Source: Adapted by Whitney Triplett from Gysbers & Henderson (2000) and American School Counselor Association (ASCA). (2012). *ASCA National Model: A framework for school counseling programs* (3rd ed.). Alexandria, VA: Author.

School counselors are able to reach *all* students by ensuring that access to the different tiers of support is *fluid* and *short term*. Keeping this in mind will help school counselors use their time more efficiently to support *all* the students with the appropriate amount of support needed in the different tiers. It is important for school counselors to remember that Tier 3 interventions are the most intensive supports offered, require intense collaboration, and are meant for only a small number of the student population.

TYPES OF TIER 3 INTERVENTIONS

Direct vs. Indirect

School counselors implement different types of Tier 3 interventions, considered either direct or indirect services to students. Direct services are facilitated directly *with* or *to* the student, while indirect services are facilitated indirectly *for* the student (ASCA, 2013, 2019a). Direct Tier 3 interventions are provided by working directly with the students and include individual counseling and crisis response (e.g., risk and threat assessments). Indirect Tier 3 services are interventions that school counselors engage in with other stakeholders to indirectly support the student. Indirect services may include student-centered meetings and increased collaboration with stakeholders within and outside of the school. Despite the differences among the variety of Tier 3 interventions, the unwavering common components of each intervention are short-term implementation and intensive support for the few students who need it most.

TYPES OF <u>DIRECT</u> TIER 3 INTERVENTIONS

Direct Tier 3 services are intensive student interventions designed to address emergency and crisis-response events. These interventions are facilitated directly *with* the student and tend to be more individualized. The most common direct Tier 3 interventions are individual counseling and crisis response. For a summary of these services, see Table 9.1.

Table 9.1   Direct Tier 3 Interventions

Direct Tier 3 Intervention	Description
Individual Counseling	Short-term (6–8 weeks), solution-focused counseling provided to students as appropriate to address the severe lack of progress, crisis situations, or other Tier 3 needs
Crisis Response: Self-Harm Assessment	Evaluation of the potential risks of a student harming *themselves*
Crisis Response: Threat Assessment	Evaluation of the potential risks of a student harming *others*
Crisis Response: CPS Report	Agency contact for suspected child abuse or neglect
Intensive Post-Suspension/ Alternative School Re-Engagement Counseling	Student meeting to discuss the student's transition back to school from a suspension or alternative school setting
Referral to and Collaboration With Internal/External Supports	Referral of the student (and family, if appropriate) to additional Tier 3 supports, both within or outside of the school (i.e., mental health counseling, food depositories, shelters)

Individual Counseling (Tier 3 Level)

As discussed in Chapter 3, school counselors connect with students who meet the pre-determined criteria and may be a potential fit to receive Tier 2 interventions. While meeting with them to gather more information regarding their needs, the school counselor decides whether students would benefit from a targeted Tier 2 intervention (e.g., small counseling group) or need a more intensive Tier 3 intervention. The school counselor may decide that their needs would not be met in a small counseling group (e.g., for students with intense behavioral challenges) and that they would be better served working with the school counselor on pro-social/behavioral skills individually for a short period of time. When a few sessions produce desired results and the student is exited from individual counseling, counselors are encouraged to support the home–school connection by sending a co-constructed closure note home where the student reflects on what was learned in counseling (see Figure 9.4, "Individual Counseling Closure Letter"). If a student continues to lack progress after 6 to 8 weeks of individual counseling, it is recommended that the counselor refer the student for another intervention (referral to more intensive support inside or outside the school building) and discussion of next steps required at a student-centered team meeting, addressed later in this chapter.

Figure 9.4   Individual Counseling Closure Letter

Date: _____

Dear _____,

Today was my last day of individual counseling with Ms. Duarte at school. We met together for _____ sessions. During those sessions we talked about my feelings, read books, created art, played games, and did role play activities.

Even though today is my last day, I know that I can still come and talk to Ms. Duarte if I'm having really big feelings or if I need help solving a problem. Here are some things I learned that I want to share:

_____

_____

_____

_____

_____

_____

_____

Sincerely,

_____

I read this letter with my son/daughter.

_____
(parent/guardian signature)

*Adapted from letter created by Sarah Terry, school counselor at Stevensville Elementary School

Helpful Tip

What's the Difference Between Tier 2 and Tier 3 Individual Counseling?

The distinction between Tier 2 and Tier 3 individual counseling is the *nature of* or *reason for the referral* combined with the *level of urgency*. In Tier 2, individual counseling is often used as a *screening device* for determining the appropriate intervention (group counseling, tutoring, referral to outside resources, etc.) when a student is referred due to data-driven elements. Tier 2 individual counseling can also *serve as the actual intervention*. In many cases, a few meetings using solution-focused counseling skills or re-teaching an important academic, behavior, or conflict resolution skill will support students enough that they either no longer need a Tier 2 intervention or are ready to participate in another type of Tier 2 activity such as group counseling, mentoring, or tutoring.

In contrast, Tier 3 individual counseling is provided when urgent needs arise or when Tier 2 services are not effective and the student requires more intensive or specialized assistance. Tier 3 individual counseling is provided on a short-term basis until the student either re-enters Tier 2 or 1 or, when necessary, can be provided with additional intensive Tier 3 supports. Typical Tier 3 individual counseling responds to situations such as

- a family crisis (death, moving, divorce, etc.),

- a social/emotional traumatic event (e.g., the student is a victim of bullying or child abuse),

- short-term 1:1 as part of Individualized Education Program (Designated Instructional Services) counseling,

- a newly arriving student (foster, homeless, English language learner), or

- academic re-assignment of classroom or retention.

Distinguishing between the two levels of support serves as a reminder that students do not need individual counseling all year; rather, individual counseling can serve to quickly support a resolution of the problem, or referral to the appropriate short- or long-term intervention.

Evidence-Based Tier 3 Curriculum and Programs

When school counselors are called on to provide (or to support another student services professional in school to provide) individual sessions or group counseling at the Tier 3 level, consideration should be given to evidence-based approaches and curriculums that have been proven to impact student outcomes. Although school counselors do not provide therapeutic counseling on campuses, it is still important to be aware of the types of programs, practices, curriculums, and interventions others might provide in order to serve as an advocate for evidence-based models and approaches. Similar to Chapter 6 (see Table 6.1b, page 140), Table 9.2, compiled by Dr. Carey Dimmitt, provides recommendations from the Ronald H. Fredrickson Center for School Counseling Outcome and Research Evaluation (CSCORE). Some of these have been previously mentioned.

Table 9.2 Evidence-Based Tier 3 Interventions

Title	Description
Case Management	Coordination of services with family, community service providers, tutors, school psychologist, nurse, special education, truancy officers, school social worker, etc.
Check and Connect http://checkand connect.umn.edu	Dropout prevention intervention • Monitoring of school performance • Case management • Individualized attention and connection in school • Community and family supports
Check In Check Out	Focuses on improving classroom behaviors • The teacher provides clear behavioral expectations and incentives • The teacher checks in with the student to set behavioral goals at the start of the period, then checks out with the student at the close of the period to rate that student's conduct and award points or other incentives earned for attaining behavioral goal(s)
Cognitive Behavioral Therapy	Has consistent, considerable evidence of effectiveness for social skills, anxiety disorders, phobias, depression, academic failures, behavior disorders, post-traumatic stress disorder (PTSD), and other mental health, physical health, and relational difficulties
Cognitive Behavioral Intervention for Trauma in Schools https://cbits program.org/	• Designed to reduce post-traumatic stress disorder (PTSD), depression, and anxiety among children with symptoms of PTSD • 10-session school-based intervention • Teaches cognitive behavioral skills in a group format, 6–8 students per group • Mix of didactic presentation, examples, and games to solidify concepts • Components of the program include relaxation training, combating negative thoughts, reducing avoidance, developing a trauma narrative, and building social problem solving skills • Includes 1–3 individual child sessions, 2 optional parent sessions, and a teacher in-service session

Title	Description

Coping Cat
 	
Amazon.com
	• Meets SAMHSA's standards for evidence-based practice (SAMHSA, 2005)
	• Designed for students with generalized anxiety disorder, social phobia, and/or separation anxiety disorder
	• Manualized Cognitive-Behavioral Treatment (CBT) and related workbook with client tasks
	• Ages 6–12 with parent companion materials
	• 16 sessions for youth with 8 skills training sessions on
	   ○ Physiological components of anxiety
	   ○ Recognition of anxious self-talk
	   ○ Modifying problematic self-talk
	   ○ Developing stress management, distraction, and coping strategies
	   ○ Self-evaluation
	   ○ Success attribution
	   ○ Self-reward for successful management

Incredible Years
 	
www.incredibleyears.com/
	• Linked programs for parents, teachers, and children aged 0–13
	• EBP with children aged 2–8
	• Teach parents and teachers to
	   ○ Promote children's social, emotional and academic competence
	   ○ Prevent, reduce, and treat aggression and emotional problems
	• Strengthens adult competencies
	• Fosters parent-school communication

Solution-Focused Counseling	Much of what school counselors do is solution-focused.
	• Time limited (1–5 sessions)
	• Interventions introduced quickly
	• Very focused session, with high level of counselor activity
	• Counseling is as unobtrusive, relevant, accessible, and quick as possible
	• Increasing evidence of effectiveness for
	   ○ Relationship issues
	   ○ Anxiety disorders
	   ○ Academic difficulties
	   ○ Behavior disorders
	• More for internalizing than externalizing behaviors, more for girls than boys

Source: Compiled by Carey Dimmitt (Ronald H. Fredrickson Center for School Counseling Outcome and Research Evaluation (CSCORE).

Crisis Response

One of the most common social/emotional interventions for students who receive Tier 3 interventions is immediate crisis response. These students may have had a death or transition in the family, or witnessed a violent or aggressive act. Some serious situations require school counselors to respond and work immediately with a student utilizing approved protocols. These can include

- self harm assessments,
- threat assessments,
- Child Protective Services reports, and
- intensive post-suspension/alternative school re-entry counseling.

Some considerations school counselors need to make after initially managing the crisis response include whether or not the student will continue to need additional supports and, if so, what this will look like. After a serious crisis, follow-up check-ins provide transitional support. They also allow school counselors to assess whether the student will need follow-up counseling, and whether that should entail short-term, school-based counseling or referral to an outside counseling agency for more long-term support. Including the student's parent/guardian in this conversation may also better inform the decision-making process for the follow-up plan of support services when dealing with a student who recently experienced a crisis.

MODEL DISTRICT POLICY ON SUICIDE PREVENTION

The American School Counselor Association (ASCA) has partnered with the Trevor Project, the National Association of School Psychologists (NASP), and the American Foundation for Suicide Prevention (AFSP) to produce a Model School District Policy on Suicide Prevention. This comprehensive document details model policies and best practices for school districts to follow when protecting the safety and health of students. It includes language for

- defining terminologies (suicide behaviors, contagion, ideation, etc.),
- risk and protective factors,
- prevention,
- assessments and referrals,
- strategies for managing in-school suicide attempts,
- bullying and suicide,
- re-entry procedures,
- parent notification,
- postvention, and
- a list of guidebooks and tool kits and resources.

Readers are strongly encouraged to download this comprehensive guide and to review it with their school counseling team. It is available from www.schoolcounselor.org/asca/media/asca/home/ModelPolicySuicidePrevention.pdf.

Self Harm Assessments

A self harm assessment is an "evaluation of a student who may be at risk for suicide, conducted by the appropriate school staff (e.g., school psychologist, school counselor, or school social worker). This assessment is designed to elicit information regarding the student's intent to die by suicide, previous history of suicide attempts, presence of a suicide plan and its level of lethality and availability, presence of support systems, and level of hopelessness and helplessness, mental status, and other relevant risk factors" (AFSP, ASCA, NASP, & The Trevor Project, n.d., p. 2).

A self-harm assessment, one type of intensive social/emotional intervention that requires the school counselor's immediate response, occurs when a student has reportedly made a comment, drawn a picture, or evidenced another behavior that in some way eludes to having tried or wanting to hurt or kill him- or herself. These alleged comments, drawings, or behaviors may take place on social media or otherwise incorporate technology and may also include reports of self-harming behaviors (e.g., cutting).

Self-harm is "behavior that is self-directed and deliberately results in injury or the potential for injury to oneself. Can be categorized as either nonsuicidal or suicidal. Although self-harm often lacks suicidal intent, youth who engage in self-harm are more likely to attempt suicide" (AFSP et al., n.d., p. 2).

These types of serious assessments call for the school counselor's collaborating with staff and students—whether the student who reportedly made the comment, or the staff and/or students who reported it—to assess the seriousness of the self-harming report. During an initial assessment, the school counselor ensures the student feels supported and has the opportunity to process choices, potential consequences, and alternative coping strategies and that the parents and other appropriate stakeholders are notified. Regardless of what may result from the determined level of seriousness of the assessment, parents/guardians are notified, and outside referrals are made for suicide assessments, longer-term interventions, or therapy, when needed. School counselors are responsible for adhering to ethical standards (e.g., responsibility "to inform students and the family when a student poses a danger to self or others" [ASCA, 2018a]), using the ASCA Position Statement on the School Counselor and Confidentiality to further inform their actions.

Not all school counselors are trained in the appropriate way to do a self-harm or suicide assessment. Further, schools and districts differ with regard to school counselor expected behaviors and actions when faced with students in need of a self-harm or threat assessment. Counselors are strongly encouraged to read Dr. Stone's recommendations, found in the shaded box that follows, regarding suicide assessments and to discuss them with district administrators.

> Dr. Carolyn Stone, a national expert on ethical and legal issues in school counseling, shared her perspectives of extreme caution on the use of suicide assessments:
>
> > Suicide assessments are inaccurate at best and dangerous at worst. Assessing the possibility of suicide is using discretion and creating programs on a number of levels, not the least of which is the consequence of being wrong. School counselors who rely on suicide assessments for definitive answers are risking danger for
>
> *(Continued)*

(Continued)

themselves and their students. Using a suicide assessment to negate the possibility of a suicide attack is a faulty practice. If used at all, a suicide assessment should be a tool to underscore to parents/guardians the urgency of the need to monitor their child and get the child professional help. (Stone, 2018, pp. 7–8)

The standard of care for school counselors when informally assessing students who are identified as a potential suicide risk is to employ these assessments with extreme caution, with a follow-up assessment completed by a mental health professional who has been trained to assess the risk. School counselors who rely on an in-school suicide assessment for definitive answers are not only negligent, but wanton and reckless in their evaluation. (Stone, 2019)

When informing parents/guardians of potential danger, school counselors follow site and district policies. Some districts require parents/guardians to sign and document that they were informed of the concern on a specific, standard district form. Checking with the appropriate supervisors ahead of time regarding these potential processes and documents is essential. Furthermore, when students are referred out to additional resources—such as behavioral-crisis centers—with proper parent/guardian consent, additional communication with the outside resource is necessary. School counselors collaborate with the outside resource professionals to discuss the student's assessment, therapy, or coping strategies, so a re-entry plan can be developed. This may include the student's potential health and medical history or status, as well as a support action plan that outlines additional resources for the student, which the school counselor may reinforce. It is also advantageous for school counselors to obtain the support action plan, if available, with the outside resource or parents/guardians. If other classmates were affected by the incident, a follow-up with those students and/or their parents may be required as well.

School counselors ensure parents are provided appropriate written notification and referrals to outside resources for their child. The Riverside Unified School District (2017) *Suicide Prevention, Intervention, and Postvention Handbook* contains 46 pages of samples, protocols, and procedures for educators, counselors, and schools to follow. Readers are encouraged to locate these district procedures and, if none exist, to utilize documents like this to advocate for the creation of such protocols.

Figure 9.5 is an example of a Parent Notification of Suicide Risk form.

When students return to school after a referral for a medical/psychiatric evaluation or in-patient service, they require re-entry counseling. It is imperative for school counselors to meet with these students immediately upon return to support their transition back to school. This immediate check-in upon return allows for the opportunity to discuss the support action plan and reinforces school-based resources, should the concern arise again in the future. After the initial check-in, the student's progress should be monitored for any changes in behavior or difficulty transitioning back to school. Figure 9.6 is an example of one district's safety transition plan that may be helpful to go over with the student, parent, and other stakeholders immediately after the student's return to school.

Figure 9.5   Example Self Harm Assessment Parent Notification

Example Unified School District
00000 Washington Avenue, San Diego, CA 00000
Parent Notification of Suicide Risk

This is to verify that I have spoken with XYZ staff member

_____

on_____. This conversation was to inform me that my child,

_____, has verbalized suicidal ideation and/or been deemed to be at risk
of possible suicide. It is strongly recommended that I seek an immediate mental health
assessment for my child. I have received referrals for community agencies to support this
action, including agencies that provide assessments at no charge.

Student's words and/or actions of concern: _____

_____

_____

X_____

Parent/Guardian's Signature/Date

X_____

School District Representative's Signature/Title/School Site/Date

X_____

Law Enforcement Witness' Signature/Date (*if applicable*)

MENTAL HEALTH ASSESSMENT FROM OUTSIDE AGENCY

Name of Professional Who Evaluated Your Child

Agency Name/Address/Phone Number (*Please include direct extension*)

X_____
Professional's Signature/Title/Date

Any Recommendations: _____

_____

_____

PLEASE PRESENT THIS FORM TO SITE PRINCIPAL OR DESIGNEE PRIOR TO STUDENT'S RETURN TO SCHOOL

White – School   Green – Outside Agency   Pink - Return to School   Yellow – Parent

Figure 9.6   Example Student to School Transition Plan

Example Unified School District
00000 Washington Avenue, San Diego, CA 00000
Student to School Transition Checklist

Student: _____   Counselor: _____

Absence Start Date:_____   Return to Site Date:_____

☐ No Hospitalization   ☐ Hospitalization

Date	Initials	
		Parent Meeting with Administrator, School Psychologist, and Counselor In Attendance:
		Discharge instructions received by school:
		Health Technician notified of return and transition instructions: HT Initials_____
		Doctor/Therapist Name: **Contact Number:**
		Release of Information form signed:
		Parents agree to the following staff being notified for the safety and well-being of their student:
		Transportation plan:
		Additional site services:
		Identified staff as agreed upon, notified of student's return:
		Counselor will check in with student on the following dates:
		Counselor will check in with parent on the following dates:
		Counselor notates transition meeting in conference notes:

Parent: _____   Administrator: _____

Counselor:_____   Psychologist: _____

Threat Assessments

Similar to self harm assessments, threat assessments are intensive social/emotional crisis response interventions that require immediate response to student safety. Threat assessments occur following a report of a student or students intending to harm another. When completing a threat assessment, students and/or staff are interviewed to assess the seriousness of the threat. Some of the students who may be assessed would be

- on the receiving end of the threat,
- those who reportedly made the threat, or
- other students involved who may have been affected.

The threat assessment ensures that the students feel safe, process choices and consequences, explore healthier solutions, and reinforce available resources. A vital step in the process is informing any stakeholders, particularly the receivers of the threat and their parents/guardians, of the situation and offering any resources available to them. Ensuring the student and family on the receiving end are made aware of the threat is a requirement school counselors are bound to by their ethical and legal responsibilities. Based on the Tarasoff law of 1976 (*Tarasoff v. Regents of the University of California*), most states have laws that require mental health professionals to disclose to potential victims information that a patient may become violent. With regard to breaking confidentiality to ensure student safety, the ASCA Code of Ethics (Section A.2) aligns with the Tarasoff law and requires school counselors to inform parents/guardians and/or appropriate authorities when a student poses a serious and foreseeable risk of harm to self or others (ASCA, 2016a).

Additionally, similar to risk assessments, collaborative communication, follow-up counseling, and progress monitoring of the assessed threat situation and the students involved are crucial to support continued student safety. Restorative mediations (as discussed in Chapter 3) may also be offered as another intervention, if appropriate and if both sides agree.

It is important to note that although school counselors are strongly encouraged to be educated in threat assessment procedures, they should *not* be completing them in a silo. School counselors are vital members of the larger threat assessment team. Additionally, threat assessments completed by school staff should be considered "informal" or "unofficial" until a follow-up mental health professional is able to complete a more formal assessment.

Collaborating With Administration on Discipline

Risk and threat assessments often require more intensive collaboration with administration for follow-up on any safety concerns or disciplinary consequences (e.g., the possession of a dangerous object). Depending on district policies or site agreements between administration and staff, risk and threat assessments may be done by the school counselor, who later relays vital information to the administrators or facilitates the assessment in conjunction with the administrators present. It is important to discuss this process early on with district leads and/or principals to ensure appropriate protocols are followed. It is also imperative to

(Continued)

(Continued)

be conscientious of the lines that may be blurred for students and staff between counseling and discipline when collaborating with administration.

As ASCA (2013) outlines in its school counselor and discipline position statement, school counselors have "specialized training in promoting appropriate student behaviors and preventing disruptive student behavior"; however, "school counselors are not disciplinarians, but should be a resource for school personnel as they develop individual and schoolwide discipline procedures . . . to establish policies encouraging appropriate behavior and maintaining safe schools." Becoming involved in the disciplinary component of a threat assessment may jeopardize the relationship between the school counselor and the student, but an agreed-upon degree of collaboration with administration is critical.

Child Protective Services (CPS) Report

Students often build a close and trusting relationship with school counselors. In some cases, students become so trusting in this relationship that they report extremely sensitive information regarding their safety or potential abuse at home. Within the Child Protective Services (CPS) crisis response, the school counselor validates the student's concerns and ensures the student's safety, coping strategies, resiliency, and available resources. When faced with a child abuse referral, as "mandated reporters," school counselors must adhere to the law and report all known or suspected cases of child abuse or neglect to the appropriate law enforcement or child welfare agencies. Depending on the outcome of the CPS or law enforcement process, the school counselor may collaborate with CPS regarding student displacement or return, if possible. Whether the student is removed from the home for a period of time or referred to outside resources, an immediate follow-up upon the student's return is crucial. Similar to the risk and threat assessments, checking in with any affected staff or students is important as well. CPS reports can be an extremely sensitive crisis response intervention for all involved. Upholding appropriate confidentiality for these crises is critical and can become a legal matter (Zarenda, 2019).

For more information on the school counselor's role in abuse/neglect reports, please see the following article:

- Stone, C. (2011). Child abuse: Who must report? *School Counselor*. Retrieved from https://www.schoolcounselor.org/magazine/blogs/november-december-2011/child-abuse-who-must-report

Intensive Post-Suspension/Alternative School Re-Engagement Counseling

Another direct service that school counselors provide is intensive post-suspension/ alternative school re-entry or re-engagement counseling. We discussed a less intensive variation of this post-suspension counseling as a Tier 2 intervention in Chapter 3; however, the level of seriousness or intensiveness for a Tier 3 post-suspension or re-entry counseling intervention is increased. This type of intervention occurs to help ensure the student has a smooth return after a major disciplinary situation that may or may not have resulted in a change of school placement for a period of time. The goal is to help guarantee that the more serious situation (e.g., a physical fight or possession of a dangerous or illegal object) that led to the suspension or temporary change of school placement does not occur again. Intensive post-suspension re-engagement counseling may occur during the administrative incident investigation, but typically occurs after the student returns and is transitioning back to school (see Figure 9.7). Due to the seriousness of the situation, parents/guardians are often invited for the intensive post-suspension/re-entry counseling.

Topics typically addressed in intensive post-suspension/school re-engagement counseling are

- processing the situation,
- lessons learned,
- coping strategies for the future, and
- available resources.

Figure 9.7   Post-Suspension Behavior Reflection for Re-Engagement Meeting

Post Student Suspension Reflection Sheet

Name: _____   Date:_____

Teacher: _____   Grade: _____

I did not follow the following school rule. (Please check one.)

☐ Being Respectful   ☐ Being Responsible   ☐ Being Ready to Learn

I understand that I was suspended from Example Elementary for _____ days.

1. I was suspended from school because . . .
(Please describe why you were suspended.)

_____
_____
_____
_____

2. What was wrong with what I/we did?

_____
_____
_____

3. I/we made the decision to make the wrong choice because . . .

_____
_____

The school counselor processes the situation that mandated disciplinary action, addresses strategies and resources in place, and allows the student's voice to be heard. This may include a reflection, a contract, or an action plan, and also includes strategies for possible settings or situations that might trigger a similar response. Intensive post-suspension/alternative school re-engagement counseling can also include restorative mediations with staff or peers to alleviate potential tension that may have occurred or may occur.

TYPES OF <u>INDIRECT</u> TIER 3 INTERVENTIONS

Indirect services are the second type of intensive interventions provided in Tier 3. Rather than supports directly facilitated *with* the student, these interventions are indirectly provided to help the student and are usually in conjunction with the team of stakeholders. Indirect Tier 3 services include student-centered meetings, assessments, and tools to more deeply analyze the student's challenges. For a summary of these services, see Table 9.3.

Table 9.3   Indirect Tier 3 Interventions

Indirect Tier 3 Intervention	Description
Student-Centered Meetings: Parent/Guardian Meeting	Meeting with parent/guardian to discuss concerns and intervention next steps
Student Study Team (SST)	Meeting with key stakeholders to discuss concerns and determine intervention next steps
504 Plan/Individualized Education Plan (IEP) Meeting	Meeting with key stakeholders to discuss disabilities impacting learning and 504 Plan/IEP supports
Response to Intervention (RTI)/ Multi-Tiered Systems of Support (MTSS) Meeting	Meeting with key stakeholders to discuss concerns about groups of students, systems issues, and next steps
Student Meeting Assessments and Tools	Assessments and tools that student-centered teams may use to support students' Tier 3 needs

Student-Centered Meetings

After continued Tier 2 interventions prove ineffective, a structured, student-centered meeting is scheduled with a variety of relevant stakeholders to focus on the concerns of the student and next steps for support. Transparent, solution-focused discussions allow the team to consider diverse perspectives, experiences, and expertise to collectively determine the best set of options for supporting the student. Common types of student-centered meetings include parent/guardian conferences, Student Study Team (SST) meetings, 504 Plan meetings, Individualized Education Program (IEP) meetings, and Response to Intervention (RTI)/MTSS meetings. It is important to note that student-centered meetings should include structured agendas, norms, and protocols, so the meeting remains positive and focused on solutions.

Parent/Guardian Meetings

School counselors promote parent/guardian engagement throughout the intervention process. Research shows that "[p]arental engagement with children has been linked to a number of adaptive characteristics in preschool children, and relationships between families and professionals are an important contributor to school readiness . . . Specifically, we conceptualize school readiness to include the capabilities of children, families, and practicing professionals that promote positive and adaptive student outcomes in formal and informal educational settings" (Sheridan, Knoche, Edwards, Bovaird, & Kupzyk, 2010). Engaging families is crucial to supporting the student's readiness for and success at school.

Families contribute rich, contextual information about a student's background, experiences, needs, interests, and strengths. They can also play an important role in identifying next steps of support for their child. Collaboration with parents/ guardians opens the lines of communication, creates more cohesive school-family partnerships, and ultimately, better systems of support for students.

Student Study Team (SST) Meetings

Another specific type of student-centered meeting is the Student Study Team (SST). Sometimes referred to by other names (e.g., Student Success Team, Child Study Team, Student Success Supports, etc.), the focus and process is typically similar, with the following agenda:

1. Opening: introduction to stakeholders and discussion of purpose of meeting

2. Student strengths/interests

3. Student concerns

4. Attempted past interventions

5. Current progress of student

6. New interventions action plan

7. Closure

Based on the amount of time devoted by different stakeholders to individualized problem solving for a specific student, the SST meeting may be viewed as an actual intervention in itself, as it produces additional ideas and action plans for supporting the student. These action plans can include both academic and social/ emotional/behavioral interventions to be monitored over an agreed-upon time-frame (i.e., 4 to 6 weeks). Allowing enough time to implement the intervention with fidelity is important, to ensure a fair opportunity for positive change and results. Schools may often also facilitate a follow-up SST meeting to monitor and discuss progress from the previous meeting and a plan of action for the agreed-upon interventions.

Effective Intervention Time

Research suggests 4 to 10 weeks to fairly verify whether an intervention is working. "A review of school counselor-led small group interventions reveals that interventions are typically implemented on a weekly basis for thirty minutes to an hour at a time and are implemented anywhere between four and ten weeks" (Olsen, 2019, p. 150). While this represents a range of time rather than an exact length of intervention—similar to the suggestion in the RTI Action Network article, "Myths About Response to Intervention (RTI) Implementation," by Bill East (2006), executive director of the National Association of State Directors of Special Education—the concern must be significantly impacted for 4 to 6 weeks.

Regardless of how many weeks it takes to implement the intervention, school counselors are required to both balance and support the suggested intervention time with immediate needs and concerns, such as the negative impact of the student's behaviors on the rest of the class's learning, or overall student safety. It is important to recognize that positive change may take time, especially with young elementary students who are still developing. A quick, reactive response may not allow enough time for change. Likewise, deeming an intervention as ineffective too soon is detrimental to the integrity of the intervention process, counterproductive to the student, and may defeat the team's efforts to support the student. Such actions may also disproportionately impact special populations, such as students of color and foster youth. As student advocates, it is essential that school counselors reflect upon and remind others of the need for sufficient intervention implementation time.

---

504 Plan/Individualized Education Program (IEP) Meetings

School counselors support *all* students, including those with disabilities, in specific ways as outlined in the ASCA (2016b) position statement on the school counselor and students with disabilities. Because research has shown that "students with disabilities have not always received adequate educational services and supports" (Rock & Leff, 2007, p. 314), Section 504 of the Rehabilitation Act of 1973 was created to protect students with disabilities and allows eligibility for special education, accommodations, and related services in schools. "Students with disabilities" are defined as "persons with a physical or mental impairment that substantially limits one or more major life activities."

Students with a disability needing more intensive interventions, such as classroom or work modifications and accommodations, may be eligible for referral to the formal legal document guaranteeing them these accommodations, called a 504 Plan. A type of indirect Tier 3 service, the 504 Plan "provides individually designed services and accommodations to address the impact of the disability on the school program or activity. It addresses the participation needs of the student in order to allow him or her to access these opportunities, to a similar degree as students without disabilities do" (Skalski & Stanek, 2010).

If it has come to the attention of the school staff that a student has a disability, the team may discuss the student's eligibility for a 504 Plan and facilitate a 504 meeting.

Another type of indirect Tier 3 service is an Individualized Education Program (IEP). The IEP is a Tier 3 intervention that thoroughly assesses students' learning styles, abilities, and other possible barriers to their academic and/or behavioral progress. This formal, legal, collaborative, and documented plan is related to the student's identified disability. The IEP assessment allows for special education team members to determine if the student's disability is negatively impacting his or her academic progress. Once the student has been evaluated, the stakeholders, including the school psychologist, case manager, parents/guardians, teacher(s), school counselor (in some instances), and other members of the special education team, come together to develop a plan to support the student's individualized needs. The plan includes the student's current academic progress, needs-based measurable goals, and the specific outline for instruction and accommodations that, by law, are required to be implemented. Some accommodations can greatly support the student, including a different classroom setting or additional personnel to support the student's particular needs. The school counselor may also be included in a student's Designated Instructional Services (DIS) as providing short-term support (e.g., 6 to 8 sessions) until more long-term, outside services can be found. The IEP team meets annually to discuss the student's progress and modify goals and interventions, as necessary. While the school counselor may be initially involved in supporting the steps toward the IEP process, typically the special education team members lead and facilitate this process (Klose, 2010; National Association of School Psychologists, 2019).

To be clear, it is inappropriate for school counselors to coordinate, supervise, facilitate, or write IEPs or 504 Plans (ASCA, 2016b). Rather, they operate within their scope, training, and ethics to support students with disabilities, as outlined in the ASCA position statement:

AMERICAN
SCHOOL
COUNSELOR
ASSOCIATION

The School Counselor and Students with Disabilities
(Adopted 1999; Revised 2004, 2010, 2013, 2016)

American School Counselor Association (ASCA) Position
School counselors encourage and support the academic, career and social/emotional development of all students through comprehensive school counseling programs. School counselors are committed to helping all students realize their potential and meet or exceed academic standards with consideration for both the strengths and challenges resulting from disabilities and other special needs.

Rationale
The Individuals with Disabilities Education Act (IDEA) requires public schools to provide a free, appropriate public education in the least restrictive environment for all students. However, research suggests "students with disabilities have not always received adequate educational services and supports" (Rock & Leff, 2007, p. 314). In addition, Section 504 of the Rehabilitation Act of 1973 protects qualified individuals with disabilities defined as persons with a physical or mental impairment that substantially limits one or more major life activities. (For a complete list of major life activities refer to ADA Amendments Act of 2008.) School counselors strive to assist all students in achieving their full potential, including students with disabilities, within the scope of the comprehensive school counseling program.

School counselors recognize their strengths and limitations in working with students with disabilities. School counselors also are aware of current research and seek to implement best practices in working with students presenting with any disability category and who, by reason thereof, need special education and related services. IDEA defined disabilities include:
- autism
- deaf-blind
- developmental delay
- emotional disturbance
- hearing impairments (including deafness)
- intellectual disability (formerly mental retardation)
- multiple disabilities
- orthopedic impairments
- other health impairments
- specific learning disabilities
- speech or language impairments
- traumatic brain injury
- visual impairments (including blindness)

The School Counselor's Role
School counselors provide direct and indirect services to students in the least restrictive environment (as determined by each student's individualized education plan [IEP]) and in inclusive settings when possible (Tarver-Behring, Spagna & Sullivan, 1998). School counselor responsibilities may include, but are not limited to:
- providing school counseling curriculum lessons, individual and/or group counseling to students with special needs within the scope of the comprehensive school counseling program
- providing short-term, goal-focused counseling in instances where it is appropriate to include these strategies as a part of the IEP or 504 plan
- encouraging family involvement in the educational process
- consulting and collaborating with staff and families to understand the special needs of a student and understanding the adaptations and modifications needed to assist the student
- advocating for students with special needs in the school and in the community

- contributing to the school's multidisciplinary team within the scope and practice of the comprehensive school counseling program to identify students who may need to be assessed to determine special education or 504 plan eligibility
- collaborating with other related student support professionals (e.g., school psychologists, physical therapists, occupational therapists, special education staff, speech and language pathologists) in the delivery of services
- providing assistance with developing academic, transition and postsecondary plans for students with IEP's and 504 plans as appropriate

Inappropriate administrative or supervisory responsibilities for the school counselor include but are not limited to:
- making singular decisions regarding placement or retention
- serving in any supervisory capacity related to the implementation of the IDEA
- serving as the school district representative for the team writing the IEP
- coordinating, writing or supervising a specific plan under Section 504 of Public Law 93-112
- coordinating, writing or supervising the implementation of the IEP
- providing long-term therapy

Summary

The school counselor takes an active role in student achievement and postsecondary planning by providing a comprehensive school counseling program for all students. As a part of this program, school counselors advocate for students with special needs, encourage family involvement in their child's education and collaborate with other educational professionals to promote academic achievement, social/emotional wellness and college/career readiness for all.

References

ADA Amendments Act of 2008, Pub. L. No. 110-325, 122 Stat. 3553 (2008). Retrieved from https://www.congress.gov/110/plaws/publ325/PLAW-110publ325.pdf.

Individuals with Disabilities Education Act. Public Law 108-446 108th Congress http://www.gpo.gov/fdsys/pkg/PLAW-108publ446/html/PLAW-108publ446.htm.

Rock, E., & Leff, E. (2007). The professional school counselor and students with disabilities. In B. T. Erford, *Transforming the School Counseling Profession* (2nd ed.), 314-341.

Tarver-Behring, S., Spagna, M. E., & Sullivan, J. (1998). School counselors and full inclusion for children with special needs. *Professional School Counseling, 1*(3), 51-56.

Resources

Oesterreich, H. A., & Knight, M. G. (2008). Facilitating transitions to college for students with disabilities from culturally and linguistically diverse backgrounds. *Intervention in School and Clinic, 43*, 300-304.

Redmond, S. M., & Hosp, J. L. (2008). Absentee rates in students receiving services for CDs, LDs, and EDs: A macroscopic view of the consequences of disability. *Language, Speech, and Hearing in the Schools, 39*, 97-103.

ONE DISTRICT'S JOURNEY TO REMOVE IEP/504 CASE MANAGEMENT FROM THE SCHOOL COUNSELOR'S ROLE

In my work with school counselors across the country, one of the biggest challenges I often hear relates to "other duties as assigned." Non-counseling duties, defined as any duty, task, or activity that falls outside of the ASCA National Model, severely impede the ability of school counselors to implement a comprehensive school counseling program. When school counselors engage in non-counseling duties, not only do they have less time to engage in activities worthy of a master's degree that impact the achievement of students, but it also impacts school counselors' overall self-efficacy, results in role diffusion, and diminishes the perceived importance of the school counseling program among key stakeholders.

In Chicago, one of the most challenging and pervasive non-counseling duties among elementary (K–8) school counselors has been IEP/504 case management. For over three decades, this well-established system that typically consists of the only school counselor in each K–8 building also serving as the case manager has plagued Chicago's students and schools, robbing them of the comprehensive school counseling program that they deserve. Case management in this district has typically included overseeing every aspect of the IEP/504 Plan process, including such tasks as

- coordinating, writing, supervising, and finalizing all IEPs/504 Plans;
- scheduling, rescheduling, and facilitating all meetings in order to maintain 100% compliance in accordance with federal law;
- coordinating calendars with all teachers and related service providers (speech therapists, psychologists, social workers, nurses, etc.);
- sending communications about upcoming annuals and triennials, including sending two-week notices to parents;
- serving as the school district representative for the team writing the IEP;
- attending monthly case manager meetings; and
- being accountable for legal ramifications if timelines and other requirements are not met.

At one point, approximately 80–90% of the 450+ elementary school counselors, with average student-to-counselor ratios well over 1:500 and sometimes even higher than 1:1,200, were serving as case managers, which often accounted for over 90% of their contracted time. This left over 200,000 students each year without access to a comprehensive school counseling program until high school where the school counselors did not serve as case managers and were free to implement comprehensive programs.

Through steady, consistent, intentional advocacy, education, evidence-based tools, and the collection and sharing of the results, Chicago Public Schools has seen a dramatic decline in the percentage of K–8 school counselors serving as case managers in recent years—a 61.8% reduction, in fact, at the time of publication (see Figure 9.8)! To learn about the successful strategies used to effect systemic change in Chicago Public Schools and ensure that *all* students throughout the district have access to a comprehensive school counseling program, please check out the links that follow.

- Hatch, T. (2017, January 13). Case management and advocacy in Chicago Public Schools. *The Hatching Results Podcast*, Episode 3. Retrieved from https://www .hatchingresults.com/podcasts/2017/3/episode-3-case-management-and-advocacy-in-chicago-public-schools
- Triplett, W. (2019). *Advocating for the removal of non-counseling duties: Closing an opportunity gap.* Retrieved from bit.ly/CPSCaseManagement2019 and bit.ly/CPSCaseManagementPres

Perhaps *you* can adapt some of these strategies to advocate for the removal of any non-counseling duties that prevent your students from having access to a comprehensive school counseling program! #closingtheopportunitygap #advocacyworks

Figure 9.8 Decline in CPS K–8 School Counselors Performing the Non-Counseling Duty of IEP/504 Case Management

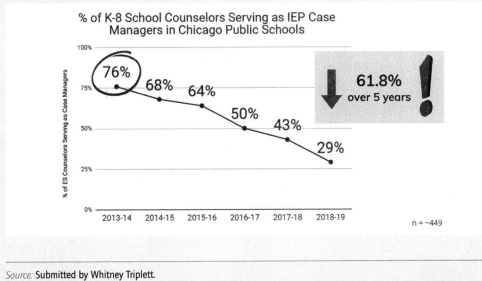

Source: Submitted by Whitney Triplett.

Response to Intervention (RTI)/Multi-Tiered System of Supports (MTSS) Meetings

Another type of student-centered meeting is the Response to Intervention (RTI) or Multi-Tiered System of Supports (MTSS) meeting. These meetings are fundamentally different from other types of student-centered meetings, because they do not focus on just one student; but on groups of students, often to uncover and address systemic barriers to student success.

At RTI/MTSS meetings, stakeholders review both aggregate and disaggregate attendance, behavior, and achievement data, to analyze trends and patterns in the data, as well as to identify students eligible for Tier 2 and 3 supports. Participants follow protocols for looking at data, discuss the root causes of student challenges, and identify potential solutions, interventions, and next steps. The following are some considerations when discussing Tier 2 and Tier 3 protocols for students who continue to experience barriers to learning:

- Type(s)/number of interventions the student has received with no/little progress
- Length of time the student has been receiving services
- Frequency/intensity of the behaviors
- The gap or lack of progress

Compared to meetings that focus on particular students, RTI/MTSS meetings can be incredibly powerful when used to focus on equity, access, disproportionality, institutional racism, and ineffective systems. When student groups are struggling at disproportionate rates to their peers, RTI/MTSS groups center conversations on changing the system to better and more equitably support students. These conversations can also revolve around the school's menu of services and protocols for how and when students access the different supports. Critical dialogues regarding systems issues help strengthen processes ahead of time and allow students to more efficiently and equitably access the variety of supports available to them.

NICASH'S STORY CONTINUES

Nicash's school had a Response to Intervention (RTI) team in place. Nicash and her administrators, social worker, school psychologist, behavioral specialist, and intervention teacher met weekly to discuss students of concern and follow up on progress monitoring. May, the school's social worker, facilitated the meeting, while the others gave valuable input. They discussed students receiving Tier 2 supports, shared updates, and came up with other intervention ideas. The intervention teacher, Nancy, analyzed academic data to identify the students for the small group reading intervention. At one of the RTI meetings, Nancy and Nicash realized they could work more closely together by cross-referencing the small group counseling list and reading intervention elective class list. They continued to cross-reference their information on a regular basis to help ensure students did not fall through the cracks and that they received as many resources as the school could offer them.

As the school year continued, Nicash and her RTI team became more comfortable with each other at their RTI meeting and began to challenge each other for the benefit of the students. Nicash pointed out how the more vocal teachers would only ask for help for their more rambunctious disciplinary students, which left less attention and support for the quieter or compliant, underperforming students of concern. Recognizing that the natural situation occurring was "the squeaky wheel (teacher and student) gets the grease," as well as the teacher's general failure to use the existing referral process due to lack of time, Nicash's RTI team decided to restructure the old RTI referral paper process (see Figure 9.9). The team spent time compiling research, surveying teachers, upgrading the referral process to include a newly created electronic collaborative document and progress monitoring systems, and educating the school staff on ways to address inequities and to ensure that students did not fall through the cracks.

Figure 9.9   MMS Team Intervention Worksheet (District Sample)

Student last name, first initial 1

MMS Team Intervention Worksheet (TIW)

This worksheet is a step-by-step process to help organize a student's progress within the intervention process.

Instructions:

Step 1 - Make a copy of this original TIW & share with your team & CSAT Team Leader (file-->make a copy-->rename ie:gradelevel_lastname_firstinitial_teamname)

      a. Please e-mail the copied form to:
- CSAT Team Leader

Step 2- Teacher(s) brings student concerns to the TEAM during team meeting to collaborate on possible interventions or instructional research-based strategies that may help the student. Implement research-based interventions for 4-6 weeks and monitor.

Step 3- Team Meeting minutes need to indicate when TIWs are completed with 4-6 week interventions and progress. Attach updated link of TIW on Team Meeting minutes

Step 4- CSAT team reports next steps and team continues to monitor and share progress.

Student Name	Referring Teacher(s)

Team Name	Grade	G.P.A

Student Strengths and/or Interests

Primary Concern with Student: Academic, Emotional, or Behavioral Concern?

Please 'X' any current concerns with student:

__ Classwork Completion	__ Bullying
__ Homework Completion	__ Physical Aggression
__ Reading Comprehension	__ Anxiety
__ Reading Skills	__ Self-injury
__ Outbursts/Disruption	__ Alcohol/Drug use
__ Math Computation	__ Theft of Property
__ Math Reasoning	__ Threats to Harm
__ Written Expression	__ Irritability
__ Receptive Language	__ Suicidal Ideation

(Continued)

(Continued)

Figure 9.9 (Continued)

Student last name, first initial 2

__ Hyperactivity	__ Divorce
__ Expressive Language	__ Gang Interest
__ Listening Skills	__ Defiance
__ Understanding	__ Depression
__ Retention of Information	__ Social Withdrawal
__ Inattention	__ Grief/Loss
	__ Other:

Previous Intervention Form Link

Behavior Support Plan

Previous year	Current year

Counselor cumulative record review date	Summary of findings

Current NWEA Data

Reading	Language	Math

Current CELDT Data

Overall	Speaking	Listening	Reading	Writing

Health Concerns

Discipline Record

Team S.M.A.R.T. Goal

Student last name, first initial 3

Specific: Exactly what is it you want to achieve with student.
Measurable: You must be able to track progress and measure the result of your goal.
Attainable: Your goal must be relevant to your student and agree with them.
Realistic: Your goal should be realistic and relevant to student.
Time-Specific Goal: Goals must have a deadline, when will student achieve his/her goal?

Ie: By Oct. 14th, Ariana will be able to stay in her seat 80% of time in each class.
By (date,) (student) will
Academic:
Behavior:

CLASSROOM Management Plan (proactive)	Intervention Comments	Date	Comments/ Results (After 4-6 weeks)
Give choices			
Check in beginning of the period			
Token economy			
Self reflection			
Peer Buddy			
Breaks during class			
Positive Praise			
Use different learning approaches (visual, auditory, kinesthetic)			
CLASSROOM Management Plan (reactive)	Intervention Comments	Date	Comments/ Results (After 4-6 weeks)
Seat change/ preferential seating			
Buddy room			
Differentiation			

(Continued)

(Continued)

Figure 9.9   (Continued)

Student last name, first initial 4

Note to parent			
Parent contact (phone, text, e-mail, note)			
After School Academic Intervention (ASAI)			
Behavior reflection			
Infraction			
Implemented Pre-Referral Intervention Manual (PRIM) strategies			
Implemented PBIS World strategies			
Universal Design for Learning			
Behavior card			

Step 2- Teacher(s) brings student concerns to the TEAM during team meeting to collaborate on possible interventions or instructional research-based strategies that may help the student. Implement research-based interventions for 6-8 weeks and monitor

Team Interventions *(Resources- teacher expertise, counselors, social workers, admin, PRIM, menu of services, etc)*	**Intervention** (Description of intervention & name of person responsible for facilitating/monitoring)	**Start & End Date of Intervention**	**Step 2- Comments/ Results** (After 4-6 weeks Was it effective? How was effectiveness measured?)
Team meeting to discuss strategies/interventions			
After School Academic Intervention, (ASAI)			
1:1 Teacher/student meeting			
Team meeting with student & parent			
Consulted counselor/social worker			
Consulted assistant principal			
Consulted with literacy coach			

Student last name, first initial 5

Consulted with math coach			
Weekly goal setting			
Use different learning approaches (visual, auditory, kinesthetic)			
Research-based instructional strategies			
Parent signature in agenda			
Parent conference			
Behavior contract			
Modified work			
Reading intervention class			
Wildcat Academy			
Connected to clubs/positive activities			
Universal Design for Learning			

Step 3 - Team Meeting minutes need to be indicated when TIWs are completed with 6-8 week interventions and progress. Attach updated link to TIW on Team Meeting minutes

Step 4- CSAT team reports next steps and team continues to monitor and share progress

CSAT	Date:	Update:
Teacher consults with CSAT CORE Team Member		
Teacher updates information on this Team Intervention Worksheet and only shares document with CSAT Team Leaders and specific grade level team: • RTI Team Leader		
CSAT CORE team reviews referral		
CSAT CORE team informs teacher / team of outcome of referral		
Referral to Assistance Team (SST, 504, SART/SARB) Work samples to bring to meetings:		

(Continued)

(Continued)

Figure 9.9 (Continued)

	Student last name, first initial 6	
• pre-assessments • formative assessments • Engage New York samples • mentor texts • writing samples (informational, argument or narrative) • journals • benchmarks • MAP scores • CELDT scores		
Behavior contract		
Student success plan		
Behavior summary form		
Outside referrals		
Before/after-school intervention support		
Home visit		
Schedule change (ie: ALC period placement)		

Step 5- SST Meeting

Step 6- Follow-Up SST Meeting

As a result of this collaboration, a simple RTI meeting sparked an improved system for all students. Nicash's RTI team is just one of the many examples of leadership and systems change that can occur when stakeholders hold student-centered meetings to collaborate on more intensive interventions, and have an evaluation of intervention systems. Their diverse perspectives, commitment to collaborate, and teamwork helped create a better system to monitor and advocate for all students receiving Tier 2 and 3 supports.

Student Meeting Assessments and Tools

Student-centered teams often utilize various assessments (e.g., Functional Behavior Assessments) and tools (e.g., Behavior Intervention Plans) when collaborating to meet student needs and to develop potential accommodations and modifications. These Tier 3 interventions look at the student's behaviors more individually and allow for plans to replace or accommodate the problematic behaviors. Functional Behavior Assessments (FBA) allow for a deeper analysis of students' behaviors, through an intensive process of information gathering from various stakeholders such as teachers and support personnel. Information such as direct observations and interviews are analyzed to determine the function of the behavior. Different stakeholders, such as the student's teachers, may participate in the gathering of information; however, the support personnel, which may include the school counselor, the school psychologist, school social worker or other behavioral specialists, typically compile the information into an FBA to summarize the behavioral findings and recommendations for the team. The process of completing an FBA may take some time, but eventually, it results in a detailed report of potential functions of the challenging behaviors and offers intervention strategies to replace the inappropriate behavior with more desirable behaviors that serve the same function. The strategies are implemented, monitored, and adjusted over time for progress.

Behavior Intervention Plans (BIPs) or Behavior Support Plans (BSPs) are intensive Tier 3 intervention tools that engage stakeholders to gather data regarding any undesirable student behaviors and to outline behavioral strategies with the goal to change the behaviors. While an FBA can assist in better informing an effective BIP/BSP, in some schools, stakeholders may choose to only create a BIP/BSP. Different stakeholders, including school counselors, may be asked to assist with compiling the behavioral data and developing the BIP/BSP; however, the development of a BIP/BSP is a collaborative process utilizing the expertise of other stakeholders on the team and, similar to the special education functions, such as the previously mentioned IEPs, is inappropriate for school counselors to coordinate. The suggested strategies are also implemented and monitored for a certain amount of time. Similar to the FBA, the school counselor may collaborate, support the process, and add valuable information to the BIP/BSP, but other support personnel, such as the school psychologist, are usually trained and will complete the BIP/BSP (Lambros, Culver, Angulo, & Hosmer, 2007; Neitzel & Bogin, 2008).

Accommodations. Similar to situations involving students receiving Tier 2 supports, accommodations for students who receive Tier 3 services are often provided in even smaller groups. This type of small group accommodation increases the amount of attention and individualized learning. Modifications are usually made to the learning to help students reach academic success, such as additional time to review foundational concepts more intensively. Amount and level of work expected may be modified or lessened for the students, and more accommodations, such as time to complete assignments, use of additional technological resources, seating arrangement, or academic breaks, may be provided to better support students' needs.

Some students receiving Tier 3 supports continue to struggle even with or without 504 Plans and IEPs. In these cases, a collaborative team meeting—to include parents, teachers, support staff, administration, special education team, case manager, and school psychologist—should be held to discuss concerns, appropriateness of placement, and additional supports. Discussions are then held regarding additional accommodations, such as a change of placement to a more restrictive environment or modified school schedule.

Collaboration

As discussed in Chapter 3 ("Determining the Appropriate Tier 2 Intervention"), collaboration is a key component to the success of intervention implementation. The interventions for students receiving Tier 3 supports require even more collaboration by all stakeholders, within and outside of the school. Due to the communal and ultimate goal of student success, holistic, team-based decision making is crucial for Tier 3 interventions. Whether the interventions are academic and/or social/ emotional/behavioral, oftentimes, all stakeholders have a role in and responsibility for some part of the Tier 3 intervention.

The ASCA National Model highlights collaboration as an important theme for the work that school counselors do. It is essential for the many different stakeholders in a student's life to work together for student success. Stakeholders in the school may include the student's administrator, teachers, intervention specialists, special education personnel, and other support staff such as school psychologists, social workers, and may even include classified staff. Other stakeholders outside of school in the life of a student receiving Tier 3 interventions may include the student's family, community members such as coaches, and any outside resources the student may be receiving. "All hands on deck" is a beneficial goal to keep in mind for everyone working together, as "it takes a village to raise a child."

When a diverse variety of stakeholders are involved, each one brings a unique perspective and set of expert skills in a particular field. Each person may see a different side of the student and understand issues and solutions through a different lens, adding to the dialogue and viewing perspectives from different angles. These differing perspectives also allow the variety of stakeholders to utilize their specialized skills and add ideas to the possible solutions for individual students. The stakeholders may offer additional interventions that others may not think of or know the student could have access to. For example, a social worker might speak to the case management he or she has been doing with the student's outside therapist. A school psychologist can speak about students with similar behaviors and offer new strategies, such as an FBA. The addition of perspectives and possible interventions can be helpful when other interventions have not been effective.

Collaboration is one of the major themes among all the components of the ASCA National Model (2003, 2005, 2013, 2019a). Without collaborating with stakeholders, the effectiveness of Tier 2 or 3 interventions is likely to be compromised, as the students need support from multiple people and in multiple settings.

Collaboration Within the School

Being open and working with the many staff on campus not only benefits the school counselors' balanced use of time, but most importantly, it allows more supports for the students in need. School counselors who work in silos may miss out on opportunities for students. Collaboration allows counselors to use their time more efficiently by taking advantage of all the time, talents, and resources within the school. Lacking this, the school counselor may become spread too thin with too many responsibilities and students and not enough time. The ASCA Ethical Standards (2016a, Section B.2q) support school counselors to "[c]ollaborate as needed to provide optimum services with other professionals such as special educators, school nurses, school social workers, school psychologists, college counselors/admissions officers, physical therapists, occupational therapists, speech pathologists, [and] administrators." The collaboration may manifest in different ways, from a simple referral phone call to an increased amount of contact with and continued progress monitoring with an outside resource.

Nicash, Ariana, and Gabby's close collaboration resulted in the development of an effective triaging system of Tier 2 and 3 supports. Staff collaboration is not always as seamless as this, however, due to different factors, such as varied days on campus, lack of knowledge, or proximity. But with commitment, it is possible. Ongoing collaboration among experts increases awareness of services available, provides creative problem-solving opportunities, and may offer a better match between the student concerns and the appropriate intervention. It is especially helpful when the staff take ownership of their roles so the lines between professionals are more efficient and clear. This ensures that staff are effective and students are not doubling up on similar services but receiving the exact support they need.

NICASH'S STORY CONTINUES

Nicash loved sharing an office with Ariana, the social worker, and Gabby, the school psychologist. They often collaborated very closely and clearly understood the similarities and specialties of their individual roles and expertise. When staff or parents would drop in looking for additional supports, Nicash, Ariana, and Gabby were all able to speak with them, determine the concern, and make a referral to the appropriate support staff personnel among them. For example, although they were all trained in behavioral crisis intervention, because that was a larger part of the school social worker's role, Ariana was the first line of defense. If she was not available, the other two would be able to lend support. They were also able to improve their small group counseling systems. Nicash and Ariana would analyze the "Needs Improvement" (N) or "Unsatisfactory" (U) markings in the Work Habits and Social Skills area on the report card data. Based on the area in which students received the majority of their markings (e.g., Work Habits or Social Skills), Nicash and Ariana would determine which students would receive a study skills group with the school counselor or a social skills group with the social worker. Many students struggled in both Work Habits and Social Skills. A needs assessment was given to the students to better inform which group was the best fit. Gabby offered group counseling support for the report card–identified students with IEPs and monitored the students in groups who lacked progress and would possibly be referred for a special education evaluation later. If at the next grading period the students who participated in group still had Ns in both areas (Work Habits and Social Skills), they were offered another small group they had not yet participated in. This ensured that they continued receiving supports, while feeling engaged with different curriculum.

Collaboration Outside of the School

Similar to the collaboration with stakeholders within the school system, collaboration with stakeholders *outside* of school may also vary in intensity and frequency, but benefit everyone involved. Collaborating with stakeholders outside of the school may provide valuable insights into the following:

- Student's current status
- Known stressors
- Medical diagnosis
- Psychiatric conditions
- Past/current medications
- Topics discussed
- Knowledge taught
- Skills/strategies practiced
- Intervention plans
- Available resources for the family

Collaborating with extended family, religious mentors, extracurricular coaches, medical specialists, or outside counseling services, strengthens the work that school counselors do. Thus, attending to the interconnectedness of the child's world through collaboration between the student's advocates and stakeholders both inside and outside of the school setting can support student success.

COLLABORATION WITH COMMUNITY PARTNERS

When I worked as a school counselor at Lawndale Elementary Community Academy in Chicago, many of my students experienced trauma, which affected both their psychological well-being and their academic focus. Through collaboration with community partners, I was able to provide students and parents with access to important services both inside and outside of the school setting. Students and parents had access to everything from individual therapy, to community mentors, and career professionals to support their overall health and individual needs. Collaborating with community partners allowed me to expand my reach and my impact. For so many students and families, the school counselor can be that missing link to opportunity and supports located in the community that can have a lasting impact on their lives.

Source: Contributed by Kirsten Perry, 2018 ASCA National School Counselor of the Year.

Collaboration With Families

Families are crucial contributors in students' success, especially at the elementary level. Parents/guardians have had experiences with the student from a young age and have observed them in multiple settings and in different circumstances and environments. This historic perspective adds to the richness of the current information about the student and contributes to a more culturally sensitive and holistic picture. Parents/guardians have experience with the students' strengths and challenges, and what interventions have and have not been effective in settings outside of schools. Family members contribute to the team's understanding of students' values, expectations, responsibilities, and effective discipline or redirection systems. Parents and guardians are also instrumental in the sharing of information that guides the work of the school counselor in the following ways:

- Confirming whether basic needs are or are not being met
- Sharing past experiences that may have affected the student's development
- Medical concerns and medications
- Strengths/interests that can be supported
- Trends and patterns of areas of concerns
- Expectations and responsibilities at home
- Discipline and systems reinforcements/consequences that are and are not effective
- Effective and non-effective reinforcements
- Student's social circle and its impact on the student's behavior
- Extracurriculars and level of involvement
- Role models/relatives/extended family in the student's life outside of school
- Religious and/or community mentors
- Other community resources or agency involvement

Collaboration With External Mentors

External mentors can make the difference in a child's motivational commitment to staying in school. Mentors often provide culturally relevant guidance and wisdom. Connecting children with mentors who look like them and who have had similar life experiences can contribute to improving a child's attitude, where other interventions may not.

Role models and mentors, often found through involvement with extracurricular activities, religious affiliations, or community activities in students' lives, can also become highly influential people in a child's life. Inviting individuals who have a favorable influence on the student can offer a different voice and perspective regarding the strengths and interests of the students. Mentors who partner with counselors to assist in motivating students to change behaviors can have conversations with the student, weaving in the knowledge and skills being taught by the school counselor. For some students, hearing it from another person they trust, aside from the school counselor or parents/guardians, can make a big impact.

Collaboration and Referrals to Community Resources and Agencies

The ASCA (2015b) position statement on the school counselor and student mental health outlines that "[s]chool counselors are prepared to address barriers and to assess ways to maximize students' success in schools, communities and their family structure by offering education, prevention and crisis and short-term intervention until the student is connected with available community resources." Sometimes, when students who have received Tier 2 or Tier 3 supports continue to struggle, they need additional or longer-term supports. As discussed in Chapter 3, because long-term support is out of the scope of the school counselor's role, outside referrals are made. Outside resources may include therapy or basic needs resources for families who are coping with a situation. Some examples of outside referrals to professionals, paraprofessionals, and community resource agencies include the following:

- Individual therapy
- Family therapy
- Parent education
- Therapeutic groups
- Behavioral crisis centers
- Social workers or case managers
- Public safety
- Homelessness referral
- Financial support
- Legal professionals
- Immigration services
- Medical referrals

Collaboration is an essential role for school counselors who may oversee and/or take the lead to coordinate with other school supports. When they do, it is helpful to include all collaborators in documents such as the one shown in Figure 9.10, which was created to support an elementary grant delineating services for students at grant schools.

For more information on successful ways to collaborate with other student service providers, refer to pages 97–99 on the importance of role classification.

Figure 9.10   XYZ Unified School District Elementary Programs and Collaborative Services

XYZ Unified Elementary and Secondary School Counseling Grant
2012-2013 Programs and Services Coordinated and Provided by School Counselor's
at: ABC, DEF, GHI, and JKL Elementary Schools

	ABC	DEF	GHI	JKL
Elementary School Counseling Grant Specific				
• Classroom Guidance Lessons (>1,020)	X	X	X	X
• External Community Support Referrals (>50 serious outside referrals)	X	X	X	X
• Group Counseling (>185; 720 Students for Study Skills, Behavior, Attendance)	X	X	X	X
• Individual Counseling (Crisis, Academic, Behavior, Attendance)	X	X	X	X
• Parent and Staff Consultations	X	X	X	X
• Parent Education Trainings/ Seminars (>70)	X	X	X	X
• Parent Specific Referrals (housing, medical, food, career, legal etc.)	X	X	X	X
• Peace Patrol Conflict Mediation Program (>500 Trained)	X	X	X	X
• RTI/Student Support Team	X	X	X	X
• Second Step Violence Prevention Guidance Curriculum (>1,020)	X	X	X	X
SDSU School Counseling Practicum Students (*5 Students at each site all year*)				
• Classroom Guidance Lessons	X	X		
• Classroom Support	X	X		
• Group Counseling	X	X		
• Individual Counseling	X	X		
• Peace Patrol	X	X		
SDSU Building Capacity Military Grant (*3 Students at each site all year*)				
• Classroom Support			X	X
• Individual Counseling			X	X
• Military Counseling Groups			X	X
• Military Family Night			X	X
• Second Step Violence Prevention Guidance Curriculum			X	X
• Veteran's Day & Memorial Day Activities			X	X
USC Building Capacity Military Grant (*1 Student at each site*)				
• Attendance Monitoring	X	X		
• Classroom Support	X	X		
• Group Counseling	X	X		
• Individual Mentoring	X	X		
• Military Family Day	X	X		
Additional Responsibilities with BEST Grant				
School-Wide Positive Behavior Support Program				
• Co-Facilitate regular noon-duty trainings	X	X	X	X
• Collaborate in regular meetings w/Palomar Family Counseling liaisons	X	X	X	X
• Coordinate and order positive reinforcements/materials	X	X	X	X
• Coordinate school-wide expectations lessons	X	X	X	X
• Creation and reinforcement of 3 school rules	X	X	X	X
• Data Analysis	X			
• Organize reward systems	X	X	X	X
• Positive reinforcement weekly support	X	X	X	X
School-Age Services				
• Coordinate with teachers to ensure successful implementation of Incredible Years curriculum lessons	X	X	X	X
• Coordinate, collaborate and oversee process and implementation of parent consent forms for social skills groups by outside service provider	X	X	X	X
Parent Family Connection Support				
• Coordinate effective implementation of Parent Coordinator in charge of 2-3 parent volunteer leaders	X	X	X	X
Coordinate with or Oversee Other School Supports				
• Afterschool Activities (Study Skills, Art, Mad Science)		X	X	
• College and Career Day Chair	X			
• Elizabeth Hospice (Grief) On-Site Counseling	X			
• EPSDT On-Site Counseling	X	X	X	X
• Family Forces Counseling	X			
• Got Your Back Weekend Nutrition Program (Meals)	X			
• OTA Site Rep.	X			
• Playground Activities	X	X	X	X
• Positive School Culture Activities/Assemblies	X	X	X	X
• Project School Bell	X	X	X	X
• School Site Council Secretary	X			
• School-Wide Prevention (Red Ribbon Week, Anti-Bullying, Random Acts Kindness)	X	X	X	X
• Shop With a Cop Collaboration	X	X	X	X

This document highlights the collaborative and consistent nature of activities by four different elementary school counselors. Most were similar, but some were different as the schools' community resources were grant based and/or included neighboring universities that offered additional supports and community resources.

Memorandum of Understanding (MOU) and Release of Information (ROI)

As discussed in Chapter 3 ("Determining Appropriate Tier 2 Interventions"), how a school counselor collaborates with outside resources to support students can vary. It can differ in length and frequency, from a one-time situation to more long-term collaboration, and in intensity, from simply sharing contact information or current information, to disclosing more sensitive information. However the collaboration takes place, the information benefits the work to support the students on an individual or systemic level. The collaboration can range from a quick consultation phone call to a more intensive partnership, utilizing a release of information (ROI). For the more intensive Tier 3 cases where more consistent collaboration may need to take place, creating a memorandum of understanding (MOU) between the partnering organizations (e.g., outside agency, school, and parent/guardian) can be advantageous.

> Emery came into school counselor Norie's office with some news that she had been going to the doctor for what initially was chest pain. Emery shared that her doctor visit the following day would be different, as she would be tested for cancerous cells on a lump doctors found on her spine. Norie counseled her through the rest of the conversation and attempted to keep Emery's spirits positive. After Emery left her office, Norie immediately called Emery's mother, who confirmed her daughter's disclosure. A couple of weeks later, the family found out that it was indeed cancer. As Norie stayed in communication with the family, she was able to connect them with outside resources during this difficult time. Emery's mother also requested that Norie speak to Emery's class regarding her current condition and her future absences due to her chemotherapy. Learning from Emery's mother that Emery was receiving therapy from a social worker at the hospital, Norie asked for Emery's family's permission to have an ROI signed by the social worker to collaborate and discuss Emery's progress. This ensured that Norie could help the mother put more intensive supports in place for her daughter's absence from school, such as home health. Emery's mother was happy to have all parties sign the ROI to ensure her daughter received as much support as possible during this tough time.

As discussed in this chapter, when students continue to experience barriers to learning, whether due to a crisis situation, continued lack of academic progress, or a student transfer with high needs, Tier 2 interventions may not be enough. In these cases, the students require more intensive Tier 3 interventions. The delivery of these different academic and social/emotional interventions varies, but a team-based approach is consistent and pivotal to the success of any Tier 3 supports.

10

Other Tier 2 and 3 Evaluations and Sharing Results

COLLECTING OUTCOME DATA

NICASH'S STORY CONTINUES

As Nicash's academic school year came to an end, she felt proud of the 20 small, data-driven counseling groups that she had completed. She collaborated with teachers and coordinated logistics. Nicash and her district school counseling team worked together to self-create and align their group lessons with the report card data criteria used to identify the students. She felt accomplished after facilitating her lessons with new engagement and management strategies. She led small groups twice a day, each day of the week! When calculating the process data, she calculated supporting approximately 90 students in group each trimester, with a grand total of 270 students! Nicash took the right steps to lead her team in evaluating the effectiveness of the lessons by means of the pre-/post-assessments that they created. Nicash learned valuable lessons from both the successes and the challenges, made deeper connections with the students, and built stronger partnerships with her teachers and parents. She felt proud and believed herself to be an effective school counselor who was excited to share the positive impact of her work, but did the students' behaviors actually change? How would she measure the impact of her intervention on student behavior and academic achievement?

Nicash had some pretty impressive process data (e.g., number of students served, number of small groups) and collected perception data to demonstrate the impact of her Tier 2 interventions on students' attitudes, skills, and knowledge. However, what *difference* did she actually make? Effective data-driven school counselors take intervention evaluation a few steps further, analyzing outcome data and sharing their program results with stakeholders. Outcome data analysis is the most critical component of the evaluation process. Not only does it help school counselors determine which interventions worked and which didn't, but it also enables them to demonstrate the intervention's impact on student achievement. Rather than *feeling* like the small groups made a difference, school counselors can *measure* outcome data to determine whether positive changes actually occurred in student behavior and academic achievement as a result of the school counseling intervention.

Once Tier 2 or 3 interventions have been successfully completed, the next step is to gather and analyze the different types of data available (e.g., progress monitoring, perception data; see Chapter 8) and report any impact on student outcome data. Taking time to evaluate outcome data can assist the school counselor in determining the impact of the intervention. Central to the process of delivering interventions is to regularly evaluate and reflect *during* (progress monitoring) and *after* their implementation. Critically analyzing the students' perception data and outcome data is crucial for program improvement and planning for any upgrades or additional actions the next time the intervention is implemented. In reference to Nicash's example, the school counselor may learn that some lessons appear to have been more impactful than others. This evaluation helps inform the school counselor as to the program effectiveness as a whole. After evaluating the intervention, it is time to share results with stakeholders. Evaluating and sharing outcomes highlights the continuous improvement cycle, informing future improved practices in the counseling program. This is demonstrated visually in the ASCA National Model (2019a) *deliver* and *manage* components, which point into the assess component that consists of program assessment, reporting results, and reflection for improvement (see Figure 10.1). Although two arrows point into the *assess* component, one arrow also points toward the *define* component, where the cycle begins again. The *assess* section in the ASCA National Model is a crucial step in the process.

This chapter reviews and outlines the steps for evaluating Tier 2 and 3 school counseling interventions:

- Collecting outcome data
- Analyzing the data for impact
- Evaluating the intervention
- Sharing results with stakeholders

Outcome Data

When measuring the impact of students' behavior, two types of data are considered: *achievement data* and *achievement-related* data. While the American School Counselor Association no longer separates these two types of data, we use this approach to remind school counselors that when data show improvement in attendance and behavior, for example, research supports the long-term impact on students' achievement (ASCA, 2012).

Achievement-Related vs. Achievement Data

Historically, achievement data were identified as aligning specifically with student academic achievement. Prior to the Every Student Succeeds Act (ESSA), academic achievement data were seemingly all that districts cared about. It was challenging for elementary school counselors to show the difference made when so much of their role involved supporting the achievement-related data elements that in turn support academic achievement. As a reference, *achievement data* at the *secondary level* are most commonly measured by grade point averages (GPAs), graduation rates, SAT/ACT scores, Advanced Placement (AP) test scores, and college attendance and persistence rates. For elementary school counselors, some examples of achievement data are grades, benchmark assessments, promotion rates, and standardized test scores.

Figure 10.1   ASCA National Model, 4th Edition (2019)

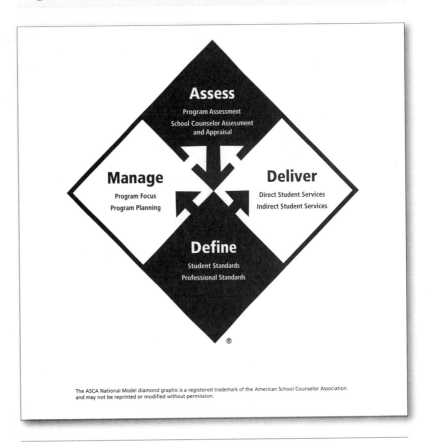

Source: Reprinted with permission from the American School Counselor Association.

Achievement data elements include the following:

- *Benchmark scores* for third- and fourth-grade students participating in small group interventions improved by 31% from trimester 1 to trimester 2.
- Fourth-grade students identified as "at risk" showed an increase in their *state testing scores* from third grade to fourth grade after attending "test-taking workshops."
- 70% of fifth-grade students who participated in the "Academic Success Skills" small group intervention saw improvement in *grades* (reduction of *D*s and *F*s) in English language arts from trimester 1 to trimester 2.
- *Promotion rates* for sixth- or eighth-grade students in a K–6 or K–8 school increased from 95% to 98% from the previous year to the current year.

- *DIBELS scores* increased for kindergarten students with attendance issues whose parents participated in a series of parent education events addressing attendance and student success skills.

More recently, schools, districts, and states are focusing on the data elements that research tells us *support* student academic achievement. ESSA (U.S. Department of Education, 2018) now requires that state and district report cards include the most recent school environment information about in-school suspensions, out-of-school suspensions, expulsions, school-related arrests, referrals to law enforcement, chronic absenteeism, and incidents of violence (including bullying and harassment).

Office discipline referrals (behavior) are an important data element, as research supports that students who behave better in school are more likely to achieve (Van Horn, 2003). In other words, achievement-related data (e.g., an improvement in decreased suspension rates) support improved student achievement data (e.g., improved test scores on end-of-the-year summative assessments). Similarly, research shows that better attendance (achievement-related data) improves academic achievement (achievement data) (Easton & Englehard, 1982). If students attend school regularly, they are more likely to perform well on benchmark and other achievement tests. Elementary school counselors most commonly measure these types of data elements, called *achievement-related data*, including attendance, discipline referrals, marks in the Work Habits/Social Skills section of the report card, homework completion, and classwork completion.

Achievement-related data elements include the following:

- Fourth and fifth graders who participated in the "Academic Success Skills" group improved their *attendance rate* by 115%.
- The number of *discipline referrals* for defiance in the classroom decreased by 51% from the first semester to the second semester for students participating in the "Making Better Choices" small group intervention.
- From trimester 2 to trimester 3, students participating in small group interventions decreased the number of "Needs Improvement" marks by 62% in the *Work Habits/Social Skills* section of the report card.

In summary, collecting the different types of data is necessary when evaluating school counseling intervention effectiveness.

- When school counselors collect *process data* for the interventions they conduct within the school counseling program, important questions about *how many* and *which* students were involved, as well as *what* the students received, are answered.
- When school counselors measure the *perception data* of *attitudes, skills, and knowledge* attained as a result of intervention, they confirm that students acquired a particular *mindset* or *behavioral standard* or *competency*.

- When school counselors measure *behavior change*, which they can then measure by *achievement-related* and *achievement data*, they demonstrate the intervention's effectiveness in improving the behaviors that support the ultimate goal of student achievement.

Applying the Conceptual Diagram (reproduced in Figure 10.2) to Nicash's story, the school counselor taught the small group curriculum (academic success skills), and students reported learning on the pre-/post-assessment and progress monitoring (strategies to stay organized and complete homework), but did the students actually *apply* the attitudes, skills, and knowledge (consistently stay organized and complete their homework) and ultimately perform better on their tests and in school?

Measuring Impact of Intervention Conceptual Diagram

Figure 10.2 Hatching Results Conceptual Diagram: Elementary (Measuring Impact of Interventions)

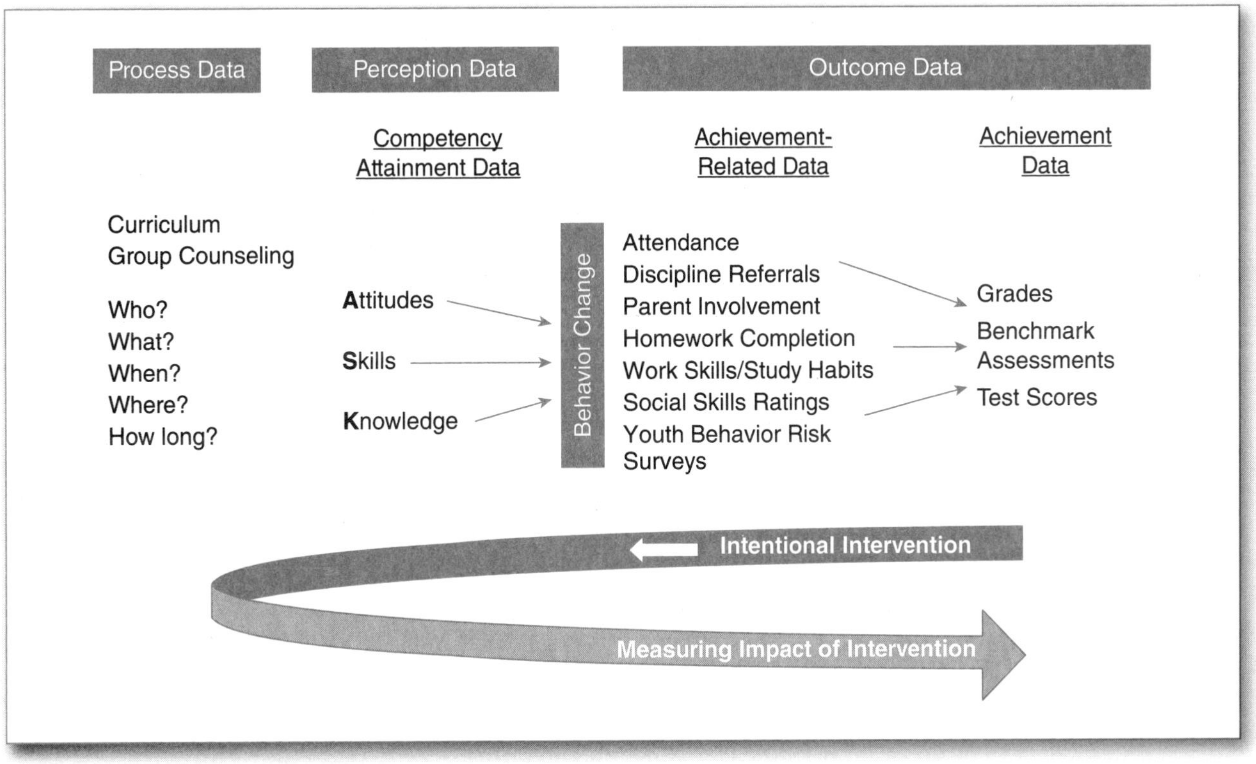

Source: Hatch, T. (2006).

WHY REPORT RESULTS?

Elementary school counselors are central members of the school leadership team, collaborating with all stakeholders to improve student success. As they create, implement, and evaluate their Tier 2 and 3 interventions, school counselors are called on to share the impact of their activities with parents, students, teachers, and the educational community. Historically, school counselors only reported process data (how many groups were held?) when held accountable. Today's school counselor knows, like every other educator in the building, that implementing an intervention comes with an expectation for accountability that shows results.

Increasingly, schools and districts are required to publicly share data via the internet on discipline, attendance, suspensions, and other measures. These data are then compared from school to school, district to district, and state to state (see Figure 10.3). Local control of funding sources in many states has led to wider flexibility for districts when employing more mental health and other student service professionals than in previous years. In California, for example, the number of school counselors hired between 2011 and 2017 increased by 35% (an improvement ratio of 1,018:1 to 663:1). As additional funds are invested into hiring more student service professionals (school counselors, social workers, psychologists, or other personnel), accountability measures are required through the very public reporting of the Local Control and Accountability Plan (LCAP).

As mentioned in Chapter 1, designing a Multi-Tiered, *Multi-Domain* System of Supports (MTMDSS) is an outgrowth of MTSS and a new way of thinking about how school counselors structure, identify, design, deliver, and evaluate their delivery of services to students. To ensure school counseling program funding continues or is expanded as needed, school counselors must collect and share results with stakeholders who are wisely charged to ask:

- Was the intervention a good use of school counselor and/or student time?
- Did the additional expense of hiring an elementary counselor make a difference?
- What changes or improvements were seen in attendance, behavior, and achievement?
- Should funds continue to be expended in this way?

Essentially, policymakers want to know:

- Was the value added worth the cost of the person or program?

When it comes to conceptualizing these answers, it means sharing not only the "what" but more importantly the "so what" of the program. In order to do this, data must be analyzed for effectiveness.

Figure 10.3 Improvement in Student to School Counselor Ratio

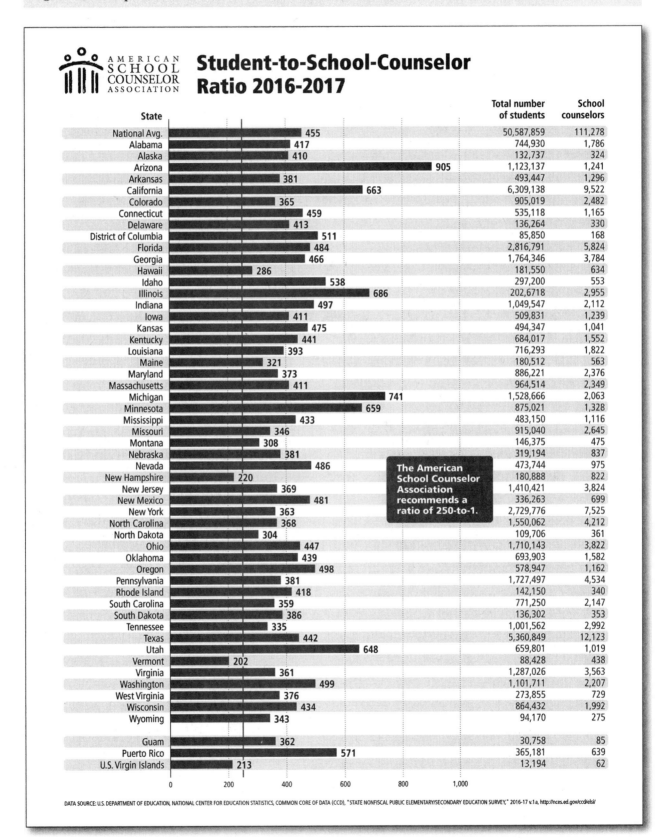

Student-to-School-Counselor Ratio 2016-2017

The American School Counselor Association recommends a ratio of 250-to-1.

State	Ratio	Total number of students	School counselors
National Avg.	455	50,587,859	111,278
Alabama	417	744,930	1,786
Alaska	410	132,737	324
Arizona	905	1,123,137	1,241
Arkansas	381	493,447	1,296
California	663	6,309,138	9,522
Colorado	365	905,019	2,482
Connecticut	459	535,118	1,165
Delaware	413	136,264	330
District of Columbia	511	85,850	168
Florida	484	2,816,791	5,824
Georgia	466	1,764,346	3,784
Hawaii	286	181,550	634
Idaho	538	297,200	553
Illinois	686	202,6718	2,955
Indiana	497	1,049,547	2,112
Iowa	411	509,831	1,239
Kansas	475	494,347	1,041
Kentucky	441	684,017	1,552
Louisiana	393	716,293	1,822
Maine	321	180,512	563
Maryland	373	886,221	2,376
Massachusetts	411	964,514	2,349
Michigan	741	1,528,666	2,063
Minnesota	659	875,021	1,328
Mississippi	433	483,150	1,116
Missouri	346	915,040	2,645
Montana	308	146,375	475
Nebraska	381	319,194	837
Nevada	486	473,744	975
New Hampshire	220	180,888	822
New Jersey	369	1,410,421	3,824
New Mexico	481	336,263	699
New York	363	2,729,776	7,525
North Carolina	368	1,550,062	4,212
North Dakota	304	109,706	361
Ohio	447	1,710,143	3,822
Oklahoma	439	693,903	1,582
Oregon	498	578,947	1,162
Pennsylvania	381	1,727,497	4,534
Rhode Island	418	142,150	340
South Carolina	359	771,250	2,147
South Dakota	386	136,302	353
Tennessee	335	1,001,562	2,992
Texas	442	5,360,849	12,123
Utah	648	659,801	1,019
Vermont	202	88,428	438
Virginia	361	1,287,026	3,563
Washington	499	1,101,711	2,207
West Virginia	376	273,855	729
Wisconsin	434	864,432	1,992
Wyoming	343	94,170	275
Guam	362	30,758	85
Puerto Rico	571	365,181	639
U.S. Virgin Islands	213	13,194	62

DATA SOURCE: U.S. DEPARTMENT OF EDUCATION, NATIONAL CENTER FOR EDUCATION STATISTICS, COMMON CORE OF DATA (CCD), "STATE NONFISCAL PUBLIC ELEMENTARY/SECONDARY EDUCATION SURVEY," 2016-17 v.1a, http://nces.ed.gov/ccd/elsi/

Source: Reprinted with permission from the American School Counselor Association.

ANALYZING DATA FOR EFFECTIVENESS

Nolan, a recently graduated school counselor, was excited to start his work at Libby Elementary, where there had previously never been a school counselor. Being the pioneer counselor at this site was right up his alley, as he believed he was well prepared in the use of data to build his counseling program. When Nolan began his baseline data collection at the beginning of the year and asked for access to report cards, he found that the only way to access the report cards of the school's 700 students was by looking through their individual cumulative files. As daunting as the task seemed, Nolan knew the value of having baseline data, so he made time. While sifting through the report cards, he discovered that the previous records clerk had not finished organizing the report cards into the cumulative files, leaving Nolan with an incomplete baseline data collection. Trying not to become discouraged, Nolan pushed through and ensured he was able to collect the upcoming report card data. He expressed the concern for a more organized and consistent report card collection system to his principal, who was unaware of the issue and, in order to solve the problem, switched over to a computer-based program, making querying of the reports accessible. Nolan also made certain to create pre-/post-tests for his small group lessons and work with teachers to monitor the students' progress on a weekly basis. Although Nolan was still disappointed not to have well-founded baseline data, he was able to utilize what he had available at the time until better systems were developed.

School counselors may understand and believe that analyzing data is important (*attitude*), know which data to collect (*knowledge*), and even be able to analyze and collect data (*skills*), but they may be unaware of *how* to analyze it for effectiveness. When in the beginning stages of this counseling intervention work, similar to the new school counselor Nolan in the example, it is also important to keep in mind that as well intentioned and motivated as some counselors may be to improve their practices, they may not always have immediate access to all the necessary types of data. It can be helpful to start with the more available short-term process, perception, and progress monitoring data as a foundation. As the steps in collecting and analyzing more short-term or immediate data become a systematic process, the evaluation and accountability components of continuing to build upon, obtain, and analyze longer-term types of data, such as outcome data, may become easier and allow for evaluation over time.

Compare Baseline Data With Post-Intervention Data

There are a number of ways to analyze the impact of Tier 2 and 3 interventions. The first is to *collect baseline data* and compare student-to-student or group-to-group post-intervention data. Baseline data indicate a student's starting point and, when compared to post-intervention data, suggest how the student is different as a result of the intervention. In order to calculate quality data and compare it pre- and post-intervention, we encourage elementary counselors to use their school's

Student Information System (SIS). Some of today's student database systems are sophisticated enough to identify dates and times of interventions and to calculate, through queries, the number of interventions, as well as any impact data assigned to the intervention. Many school counselors may not have access to electronic grading, assessment, or discipline data systems that can query "before" and "after" intervention data. In schools with a database system, we encourage counselors to become well-trained users of the software. In the case of schools that don't have these systems in place yet, counselors are asked to take the lead in advocating for state-of-the-art student database systems.

Control vs. Experimental Groups

When considering baseline data, analyzing the impact of the intervention group versus a control group can be very powerful. The control group can consist of students who met the criteria for additional supports but for whatever reason (e.g., lack of parent consent, lack of attendance) did not participate in the intervention. Outcome data for participating students are compared with data for non-participants. While it is never advisable to deny any student access to additional available supports, the ability to access and evaluate data for students who could be viewed as a control group compared to an experimental group (students who participated in the intervention) can be beneficial in encouraging other students to participate next time, as well as garner additional support for the intervention from faculty and stakeholders.

Telling a Story With Slides: Data Over Time

Creating data slides provides a visual comparison of data from trimester to trimester, quarter to quarter, beginning to end of year, year to year, or cohort to cohort. The more data there are showing that the participating students continue to find success long after receiving the intentional intervention, the more credibility and effectiveness the program will have. These data, paired with the comparison of baseline and outcome data results, tell a powerful story of the positive impact on students because of the intervention. Once the baseline data for these students are collected, the impact can be reported out in many ways as data are monitored over time. See Figures 10.4, 10.5, 10.6, 10.7, and 10.8 for examples.

Figure 10.4   Report Card *N*s Over Time: Class Cohort, Year to Year

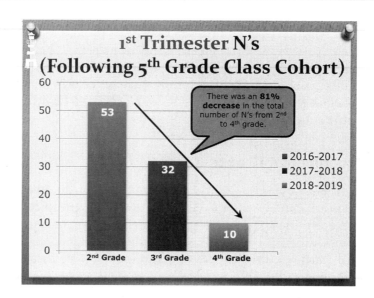

Figure 10.4 indicates the number of students in trimester 1 over a three-year period who received an *N* (Needs Improvement) on their citizenship report card. As school counselors provided prevention (core curriculum) and intervention (small groups), the number of *N*s decreased over time. While 53 students in second grade qualified for interventions, only 10 students required interventions once this "cohort" of students arrived in fourth grade.

Figure 10.5   Report Card *N*s: Trimester to Trimester

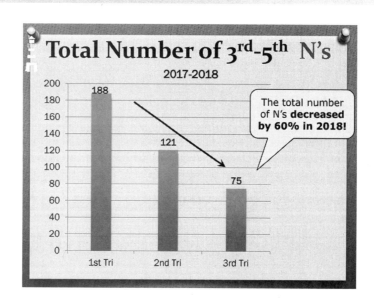

Figure 10.5 indicates the number of students with *N*s in trimester 1 (188) decreased greatly in trimester 3, from 188 to 75 (60%), as a result of interventions in grades 3–5.

Figure 10.6   Report Card *N*s: Trimester to Trimester

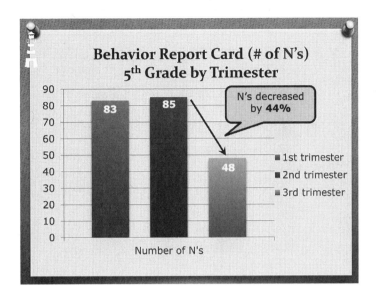

Figure 10.6 indicates the number of students with *N*s in trimester 1 (83) and trimester 2 (85) decreased greatly in trimester 3 (48), by 44%, as a result of interventions.

Figure 10.7   Suspensions: Year to Year

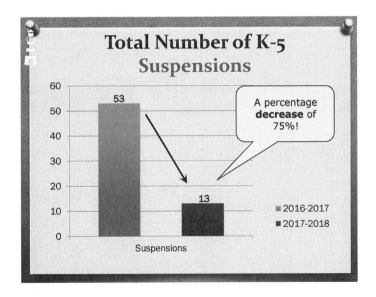

Figure 10.7 indicates the number of students suspended (53) decreased greatly (75%) to 13 (in trimester 3) as a result of intensive classroom and small group interventions in grades K–5 with students who were suspended.

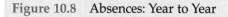

Figure 10.8   Absences: Year to Year

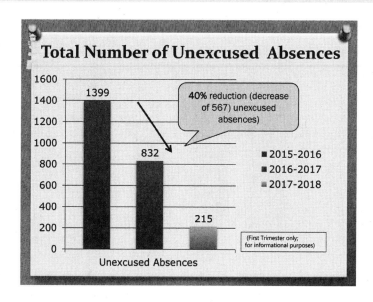

Figure 10.8 indicates the number of unexcused absences (1,399) in 2015–2016 decreased greatly (40%) to 832 in 2016–2017, and to 215 in trimester 1 of 2017–2018. This slide helps to show the impact early in the third year and lets the counselor know the school is "on target" to reduce the number of unexcused absences this year.

NICASH'S STORY CONTINUES

After eight weeks, Nicash completed two of her academic success skills groups. She had the perception data collected from both the student and teacher pre-/post-assessments and began to collect student outcome data, starting with the Work Habits/Social Skills marks on the report card. She was certain that the students would show improvement, as their responses on the pre-/post-assessments indicated that they had already started to improve their attitudes, skills, and knowledge in the area of academic success. However, when Nicash analyzed the data, she was surprised and disappointed. Only half of the students in her small group reported reduced "Needs Improvement" or "Unsatisfactory" marks in Work Habits/ Social Skills. The other students still had three or more N or U marks in the areas in which Nicash had worked with them. Nicash was in disbelief! How could the report card data reveal that the students had not made progress?

EVALUATING THE INTERVENTION

Analyzing different types of data in multiple ways allows school counselors to evaluate the impact of both schoolwide and Tier 2 or 3 interventions. When thoughtfully reviewing and comparing the data, counselors may be able to see trends in the data, indicating what worked and what did not, certain areas of strength as well as areas of growth, and implications for future upgrades. As a result of this evaluation, counselors are better equipped to see the whole picture and make informed decisions, not only on the improvement of the intervention but on the comprehensive counseling program as a whole.

Helpful questions to ask when looking at analyzed data include the following:

- *Did the intervention improve students' outcomes?*
- *Do the data indicate that the amount of time spent for both students and the school counselor was a good use of time?*
- *Did the timing of the intervention (e.g., time of the school year, breaks, time of the day/week that the intervention occurred) work well?*
- *Did I need more support (e.g., someone available to co-facilitate)?*
- *Were the group lessons truly aligned to the data?*
- *Were the group lessons effective (e.g., comprehension, retention, level of engagement)?*
- *Did I meet the needs of all students' levels of engagement and learning styles?*
- *Was I able to collect enough of the correct data to show effectiveness?*
- *Were there any changes in the attitudes, skills, and knowledge taught and desired?*
- *Where there any limitations that impacted the success of the group?*
- *Are there any factors within my control that would have helped?*
- *Are there any factors that were out of my control that affected the data?*

Many of these questions are highlighted in the Tier 2 Results Report (see Figure 10.9a), a key tool in designing an evaluation of the intervention. Once completed, it can be shared as is, or used in creating a PowerPoint presentation of results and future references for program improvement.

Tier 2 Results Reports for Tier 2 Interventions

This text provides Tier 2 Results Report templates (see Figures 10.9a and 10.9b), which mirror the Tier 2 Action Plan for Small Groups (discussed in Chapter 5, "Planning for Small Groups") with a few differences for a more in-depth look at the data-driven results of the intervention as well as possible implications. It is recommended that school counselors utilize this tool for

- accountability to ensure the Tier 2 Action Plan for Small Groups was implemented,
- program evaluation and impact of small groups or other Tier 2 intervention, and
- marketing and advocacy to share process, perception, and outcome data.

The Tier 2 Results Report is much more than an accountability tool. As readers will notice, Figure 10.9a serves as an instructional document for completing the results report. Figure 10.9b provides the detailed results report of Nicash's small group intervention. The primary purpose of the results report is for program evaluation, following up on

- fidelity of facilitation plans,
- appropriateness of lesson topics' alignment with need,
- appropriateness of ASCA Mindsets & Behaviors for need,
- timing of projected start/end date,
- process data,
- perception data,
- outcome data, and
- any implications for improvement (plan improvements to inform future programs and practices).

The completion of the Results Report for Tier 2 intervention ensures systematic reflection to evaluate the intervention and determine whether the intervention was appropriate to meet the students' needs for the desired achievement.

Questions to consider upon reflection of the results report include the following:

- *Was the Action Plan realistic?*
- *Were the selected lesson topics relevant to the students' needs?*
- *Were the selected lesson topics able to teach the attitudes, skills, and knowledge?*
- *Was the projected timing of small groups appropriate?*
- *How many and which students were impacted?*
- *Was there an impact on the students' attitudes, skills, and knowledge (perception data)?*
- *Was the impact on the students' attitudes, skills, and knowledge (perception data) aligned with the desired behavior change?*
- *Was there an impact on achievement data, achievement-related data, or outcome data?*
- *What implications came up, and how can they be preventatively avoided in the future?*

Figure 10.9a   Tier 2 Results Report

SCHOOL COUNSELING TIER 2 RESULTS REPORT - COMPLETION GUIDE

School Name: _____   School Year: _____

Target Group: *What target group did you select for this Tier 2 intervention? What specific data criteria did you use to select this group?*

SMART Goal: *If applicable, which SMART goal does this intervention address?*

Title/Type of Tier 2 Activity & Content	Process Data			Perception Data		Outcome Data	Implications, Limitations, and Recommendations
	Materials and Resources Needed	When and for How Long?	Number of Students	ASCA Mindsets & Behaviors *(or other standards)*	Attitudes (A), Knowledge (K), & Skills (S) Measured	Achievement-Related Data (AR) Achievement Data (A)	
What type of Tier 2 intervention did you implement (e.g., small group, large group workshop)? What was the title of the intervention? What were the big buckets of content that you delivered during the intervention (use bullet points)?	Which curriculum did you use, or was it self-generated? What materials, supplies, and staffing were used?	What were the start and end dates? If applicable, how long were the sessions and how many sessions were delivered?	How many students qualified to receive the intervention? How many students actually received it?	Which student standards were met?	What were the results of the pre-test vs. post-test (perhaps choose a few samples and attach the full results)? <u>ATTITUDES:</u> ***Prior to*** the intervention, ___% believed XYZ. ***After*** the intervention, ___% believe XYZ. <u>KNOWLEDGE:</u> ***Prior to*** the intervention, ___% knew XYZ. ***After*** the intervention, ___% knew XYZ. <u>SKILLS:</u> ***Prior to*** the intervention, ___% demonstrated XYZ. ***After*** the intervention, ___% demonstrated XYZ.	<u>ACHIEVEMENT-RELATED DATA:</u> Which achievement-related data did you collect or are monitoring for improvement (e.g., discipline, attendance, homework completion, parental involvement)? <u>ACHIEVEMENT DATA:</u> Which achievement data did you collect or are monitoring for improvement (e.g., benchmark scores, grades, standardized tests)?	What worked? What didn't? What recommendations do you have for next time?

School Counselor: _____   Administrator: _____   Date: _____

Source: Hatching Results (2019).

Figure 10.9b Nicash's Tier 2 Results Report

SCHOOL COUNSELING TIER 2 RESULTS REPORT

School Name: Nicash's Elementary School

Target Group: *4th graders with 2 or more Ns (Needs Improvement) in the Work Skills/Study Habits of their report card, who were pre-screened and identified as appropriate for a small group intervention*

SMART Goal: *The number of 4th graders with 2 or more Ns on their report card will decrease by 10% from trimester 1 to trimester 3.*

School Year: 2019–2020

Process Data				Perception Data		Outcome Data	Implications, Limitations, and Recommendations
Title/Type of Tier 2 Activity & Content	Materials and Resources Needed	When and for How Long?	Number of Students	ASCA Mindsets & Behaviors *(or other standards)*	Attitudes (A), Knowledge (K), & Skills (S) Measured	Achievement-Related Data (AR) Achievement Data (A)	
Small Group on Academic Skills (work skills and study habits) • Following directions • SMART goal setting • Time management • Organizing self and materials • Completing classwork • Completing homework	• School counselor-generated 8-week curriculum • Group space • Writing tools • Projector • Computer • Internet access • Audio speakers • Incentives • Pre/post assessment	Oct. 22, 2019– Dec. 10, 2019 8 sessions	16 students (2 groups of 8 students)	B-LS 3. Use time-management, organizational, and study skills B-LS 4. Apply self motivation and self direction to learning B-LS 7. Identify long- and short-term academic, career and social/emotional goals	Below are the results from the pre/post-test . . . Attitudes: • **100% increase** in # of students who believe setting short- and long-term SMART goals will help them improve in school (from 5 to 10) Knowledge: • **Significant increase** in # of students who are able to identify the definition of "prioritizing." (from 2 to 12!) Skills: • **88%** (vs. 19% pre-test) of students are now able to organize their student planner given a set of tasks. • **100%** (vs. 6% pre-test) of students are able to prioritize daily "need to do" activities.	Below is the outcome data that I monitored for improvement . . . Achievement-Related Data: • 52% decrease in Ns on report cards of targeted groups • 75% increase in classwork completion • 60% increase in homework completion Achievement Data: • 11% increase in benchmark assessments in English and Language Arts	What Worked: • Strategic alignment of T2 group intervention topics with the previously delivered T1 lessons & the report card work habits and study skills • Engaging kinesthetic group lessons • Weekly teacher/ parent communications What Didn't Work: • Timing of the group (before recess) was challenging some days, with their focus on going to recess with friends Limitations/What I will do differently next time: • Consider extended number of weeks for small group interventions • Consider holding group after recess • Preventative academic success skills groups for lower grades

School Counselor: _____ Administrator: _____ Date: _____

Source: Hatching Results (2019)

ASCA Closing the Gap Results Report

In Chapter 3, we discussed equity issues and introduced a Closing the Gap Action Plan as a tool for use in two different instances:

1. Students are identified based on an overrepresentation or underrepresentation of a particular subgroup in a targeted area (attendance, achievement, or behavior).

2. Systems issues are identified based on an overrepresentation or underrepresentation of a subgroup (based on ethnicity, gender, etc.) as a result of a discrepancy in policies and procedures.

The ASCA Closing the Gap Results Report (ASCA, 2017) heavily mirrors the components of the Tier 2 Results Report, but focuses on how intervention or activity changes the outcome for the identified equity discrepancies.

SHARING RESULTS

Marketing, Advocacy, and Systemic Change

School counselors so often go above and beyond what's required, pouring their time and dedication into supporting their students. However, when it comes to sharing all the positive work that they do, counselors may spend less time and have less experience. School counselors who promote their program's effectiveness and student success are practicing the important ASCA National Model theme of "advocacy." When school counselors consistently analyze data and share their results, they not only help others understand the value in the work they do; they also help support the comprehensive counseling program and the profession.

Sharing program results can either speak to the students' improvement and the positive impact of their participation in small group counseling or demonstrate continued need for more intervention. Whether or not the intervention yields the desired results in academic achievement (as measured by outcome data), school counselors can use the results to advocate for improved programs, for changes in current policies and practices, and even for the need to increase student supports. Additionally, they can utilize these results to advocate for the value in collaboration of instruction time for small group interventions to support student skill building to better access academic curriculum.

Sharing program results falls within the "assess" component of the ASCA National Model and may reinforce the themes of "systemic change" and "advocacy." Sharing with stakeholders reinforces the role of a school counselor, highlights the many services accessible to students, reinforces how counselors most effectively use their time, and communicates the impact of small group counseling programs. When counselors fail to share their results, it is a missed opportunity and can be a disservice to the students.

Just as there are numerous ways to evaluate the effectiveness of small group interventions, there are just as many ways to report results and share the impact of Tier 2 or 3 interventions. It is imperative that school counselors step up as advocates for their students, the program, and the profession as a whole by sharing program results and how counseling efforts affect student achievement. By sharing the successes of school counseling programs and small group counseling services, school counselors build capacity, credibility, support, and sustainability for continued school counseling services for students who need it most.

Sharing Results Reports

The Report is one type of accountability resource that may also be used as a marketing tool. The results report, while not as "pretty" as a presentation, can be edited into a one-page document to share as a quick accountability resource, an informative reference, or even an outline to guide the creation of other marketing tools or presentations.

When to Share Results

Fortunately, with the pervasiveness of the internet and social media access, it has become more of a norm and much easier to access and share information. Rather than simply waiting for a dedicated time to share results, counselors can be creative, as ample times during the school year make for a logical and complementary opportunity to share with all stakeholders.

- *Beginning of the school year.* This allows for collaboration when other "beginning of the year" program updates are shared, and informs and updates new staff and community members on the counseling program services and processes. It is also a good time to announce the curriculum interventions (Tier 1 and Tier 2 activities) counselors plan to provide.
- *After grading periods.* This is a good time to update the staff on the data garnered through queries at the marking period and to announce any interventions as they begin. Counselors can share process data, action plans, and achievement-related expected results.
- *After small group or other intervention ends.* This announces to staff the completion of group. Counselors can share perception data while waiting until the next marking period to compare pre-/post-outcome data and results.
- *End of the school year.* This allows school counselors to wrap up results and present next steps for the upcoming school year.
- *National School Counseling Week (NSCW).* This usually occurs midway through the academic school year in February, allowing time to raise awareness about the school counseling program.

Using National School Counseling Week and Other Opportunities to Share Small Group Counseling Program Results

ASCA (2019b) sponsors an annual National School Counseling Week (NSCW) during the first week in February. NSCW allows time to focus attention on the unique contributions of the school counseling profession within

U.S. public and private school systems and highlights the integral impact of school counselors on achieving academic success and preparing students for a successful future. NSCW provides an opportunity for school counselors to share about their own programs and highlight how the work they do positively affects students. It is an opportune time for student and staff outreach—to remind the students of the services available, and to thank the staff for their valuable collaboration.

NICASH'S STORY CONTINUES

Nicash is now an experienced and proactive school counselor. She regularly utilizes NSCW as a time of the year to analyze data, evaluate her program, and update and share school counseling program results with staff and stakeholders. Every year, the months approaching February serve as a reminder to make time to follow up on the current data collection and evaluation—in particular, highlighting any recent and exciting small group counseling program results. She aligns her local theme with the annual ASCA NSCW theme and plans a different activity for staff, students, and parents each day of the week to raise awareness.

On the first day of NSCW, Nicash emails the staff and has some of her group students speak on the school's public announcement system, informing the school of NSCW and the week's upcoming activities. Throughout the week, she continually makes different announcements related to the school counseling profession or program at her school (e.g., college/career readiness statistics, programs and resources available). Nicash also facilitates different student lunch activities, such as scavenger hunts and "What I Want to Be When I Grow Up" photo booth opportunities. Also during the week, she presents her Tier 2 Flashlight Results Presentation at a staff meeting and a parent meeting, which also includes a brief summary of her other programs. On the last day of school that week, as a closing celebration and thank-you for staff collaboration, Nicash prints the Tier 2 Flashlight Results Presentation and leaves it as part of the decoration for the NSCW celebration, with sweet treats in the staff lounge. For example, she leaves mint candies and other flavored treats next to a graph highlighting the improvement in report card citizenship marks from her group counseling students with a sign thanking the staff for their com"MINT"ment to and collaboration in the group counseling program. Nicash's staff end that week with a better understanding of the current school counseling program and its impact.

Figure 10.10 is a sample PowerPoint slide from a NSCW staff presentation on the Tier 2 large group workshop (refer to Chapter 3, "Determining the Appropriate Tier 2 Intervention"). It conveys process data (number of students who participated and number of students whose GPA increased) to the staff in a quick and easy-to-understand visual.

Figure 10.10   Sharing Large Group Workshop Process Data: Tracker Project

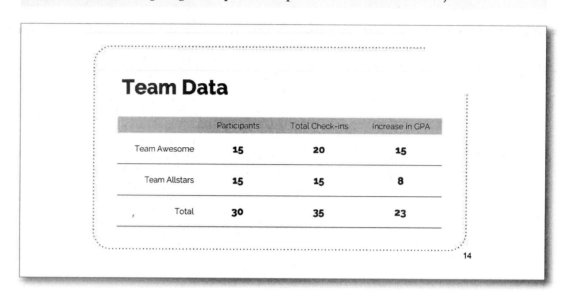

Ways to Share Results

In addition to the numerous *times of year* to choose from to share program results, there are a variety of *ways to share* the accumulated data, starting with easier and smaller-scale methods such as simple conversations, email updates, and bulletin boards and moving to a larger scale, with more in-depth Tier 2 Results Reports and Flashlight Results Presentations to families, staff, board members, or professional organizations. Fortunately, there is an option and starting place for everyone. Regardless of how school counselors choose to deliver the results, the fact that they are sharing these results is a very important responsibility.

Sharing Results

Sharing results can be as easy as communicating the process or results of the group with colleagues, parents, or other stakeholders, even in passing conversations. This sharing of results may also take the form of sharing the group's process or perception data via email, social media accounts, school newsletters, or the school counseling web page or school website.

While sharing Tier 2 intervention results in any form is commended and recommended, the more in-depth the information shared about the program's effectiveness or the more targeted the audience is, the more it benefits the program, profession, and students. Initial conversations about the intervention's effectiveness can take place at staff meetings or school counseling advisory meetings, where stakeholders are updated on the school counseling program and its impact on student achievement. Other pre-existing templates or more formal ways to share results may come in the form of a

- flashlight "one pager,"
- Tier 2 Flashlight Results Presentation,

- school board meetings presentation,
- professional conference presentation, or
- application for the Recognized ASCA Model Program (RAMP).

Presenting at Professional Venues (Board Meetings and Professional Conferences)

Sharing results at professional venues, such as school district board meetings and conferences, brings focus to the importance of school counselors and highlights their impact. Sharing data results can benefit those who would like to re-create the success of the intervention and others who want to learn about the curriculum and helpful tips to implement with their students. Not only are counselor advocates sharing the positive effects of their program, but they are also benefiting colleagues in the profession, which will affect more systemic change within the field. A number of opportunities are available to share results and to present at local county conferences and professional state organizations, as well as the national ASCA Annual Conference.

Figure 10.11 is a sample of the description of the Tier 2 process and data shared at the California Association of School Counselors (CASC) professional conference in October 2017.

Figure 10.12 is a photo of Nicole and Ashley presenting on their small group counseling curriculum at the CASC annual conference.

Figure 10.13 is an example of a progress report board presentation shared by four Oceanside Unified School District (OUSD) elementary school counselors.

Figure 10.11   Professional Presentation: CASC

Figure 10.12   Professional Presentation: CASC Nicash

Recognized ASCA Model Program (RAMP)

Sharing program results through the American School Counselor Association's RAMP recognition not only highlights the school counseling program's effectiveness, but also contributes to the legitimacy of the profession. The RAMP designation formally recognizes the successful implementation of comprehensive, data-driven school counseling programs across the nation. Awarded to school counseling programs (not individuals) that align with a set of established criteria, RAMP demonstrates to stakeholders the school counselor's commitment to delivering a comprehensive, developmental, data-driven school counseling program that contributes to student success.

Figure 10.13   Progress Report Board Presentation: OUSD

Elementary School Counseling Grant

Progress Update

Kathie Huisenfeldt – School Counselor (San Luis Rey)
Lauren Aponte – School Counselor (Palmquist)
Monica Loyce – School Counselor (Del Rio)
Nicole Pablo – School Counselor (Libby)

Randi Gibson – Grant Director, OUSD Director of Student Services
Trish Hatch, PhD – External Evaluator, SDSU Director of School Counseling

Grant Program Description

- **Federal Elementary & Secondary School Counseling Grant**
  - $349,618 yearly
  - $1,048,854 million over 3 years
- **Grant funding for:**
  - Four school counselors
  - School counseling materials
  - Second Step curriculum
  - Program evaluation
  - Professional development

Elementary Grant Delivery of Services

(**Few** Students)
Individual/Referral

(**Some** Students)
Intentional Group
Interventions

(**All** Students)
Core Curriculum

Grant Program Description

- **Goal 1:** Implement a comprehensive elementary school counseling program that is data-driven

- **Objectives:**
  - Hire four highly qualified school counselors
  - Provide extensive training and support for school counselors and school staff
  - Systematically screen, assess, and provide appropriate prevention and intervention services

Prevention Goal

Goal 2: Ensure **all students** develop the *knowledge, attitudes,* and *skills* that will lead to behaviors that support academic achievement

Objectives:
- 10% *decrease* in overall *discipline* referrals
- 10% *decrease* in N's and U's in *learner responsibilities*
- 10% *increase* in *feelings of safety* on California Healthy Kids Survey (CHKS)
- 10% *increase* in proficient & above on Math/ELA

School-Wide Curriculum: Activities Addressing Goal 2

- **School Culture and Connectedness:**
  - **465 Classroom Core Curriculum Lessons**
    - Bully prevention, Second Step, test preparation
  - **254 Trained in Conflict Resolution (Peace Patrol)**
    - Playground conflict mediators, problem solvers, positive decision makers
  - **51 Parent Education Trainings**
    - Drug and bully prevention, positive parenting, managing behavior, attendance
  - **50 Community Partnership/Referrals**
    - North County Lifeline, Family Forces, Rady Children's Hospital

Results of Bully Guidance Curriculum Lesson Pre-Post

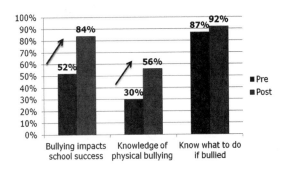

Intervention Goal:
"Some Kids Need More"

- **Goal 3:** Identify data-driven **systematic interventions** for students experiencing barriers to academic success

- **Objectives:**
  - 10% *decrease N's and U's* on *Learner Responsibilities*
  - 10% *decrease discipline* referrals & suspensions
  - 10% *decrease in unexcused absences*

Collecting Data by Need

Image Source: © 2009 Phillip Martin. All Rights Reserved.

School-Wide Activities Addressing Goals 2 and 3

- **Small Group Counseling Interventions**
  - **128** Total Groups
    - 257 Students serviced through *Social Skills* Groups
    - 225 Students serviced through *Study Skills* Groups
- **Positive Discipline and Individual Support**
  - Individual counseling and monitoring
  - Collaboration with staff in PLC/SST/IEP meetings
  - Behavior support plans/positive reinforcement
  - Post-discipline reflections
  - Parent contact

Trimester Report Card Data

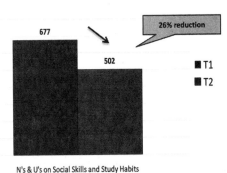

N's & U's on Social Skills and Study Habits

Attendance: Truancy Reduced
(Y1- Y2*)

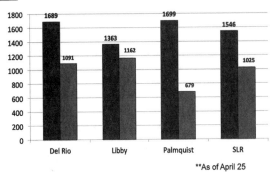

**As of April 25

(Continued)

Figure 10.13 (Continued)

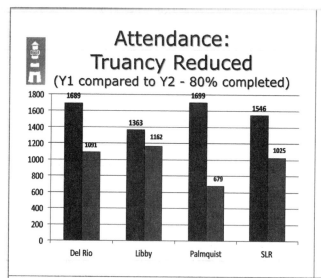

Attendance: Truancy Reduced
(Y1 compared to Y2 - 80% completed)

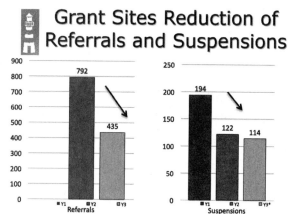

Grant Sites Reduction of Referrals and Suspensions

*Y3 is 80% of the year – as of April 25

Moving Forward...

- Address other data not yet presented in presentation

- Evaluate and assess school practices and culture

- Improve the implementation of the elementary school counseling grant program at all four schools

- Fine tune the structures and best practices to develop systemic sustainability of a comprehensive school-wide counseling program

Testimonials

Principal
"Our school is <u>fortunate</u> to have an elementary counselor who provides <u>outstanding</u> interventions, counseling, and support programs for all students and families. She ensures that all students are in a <u>safe</u> and comfortable environment. She has earned the respect of the staff, students, and families. We are <u>thankful</u> to have her on our staff, serving the kids and their families."

Teacher
"I can't imagine <u>not having her at our school</u>. She <u>understands</u> that <u>when kids are not happy, they struggle with learning</u>."

Student
"In <u>social skills group</u>, I learned how to <u>control my anger</u> so that I <u>don't get into fights anymore</u>."

Closing

Through the school counseling program, each school counselor strives to guide all students to achieve their full potential in order to contribute to their academic success.

Thank you to the OUSD School Board, District Office, and to our administrators, teachers, school staff, and parents for supporting the school counseling program!

The application takes at least one full school year to complete, from start to finish. ASCA recommends that school counselors apply for RAMP once they have a comprehensive school counseling program in place, which is being implemented fully and with fidelity. If interested, visit ASCA's website (https://www.school counselor.org/school-counselors/recognized-asca-model-program-(ramp)) for requirements, templates, samples, webinars, and tips.

Tier 2 Intervention Flashlight Results Presentations

A Tier 2 Flashlight Results Presentation is a short, quick, and effective way to share the Tier 2 Results Report for visual learners. Much like an actual flashlight, the Tier 2 Flashlight Results Presentation "shines a light" on the small group counseling process and its impact. We encourage school counselors to share Tier 2 Flashlight Results Presentations regularly with stakeholders.

The Flashlight PowerPoint Template

Utilizing pre-developed templates is an easy way to begin to set a system in place. Fortunately for school counselors, a Tier 2 Flashlight Results Presentation PowerPoint template is available for use in this text to make creating and sharing small group outcomes even easier. One of the benefits of having a template is that once school counselors have completed the first one, it is far easier to complete the next one, as many of the slides can be easily tweaked and reused.

Figure 10.14 serves as the Tier 2 Flashlight Results Presentation PowerPoint template. The example outlines essential elements to include in the presentation in an order that builds upon the prior information and tells the story of the small group counseling process. Note that many components of the flashlight PowerPoint mirror the components detailed in the Results Report. School counselors can modify and adjust the template to enter information about their own school, interventions, and data. They may also edit, add, and delete slides as needed. For example, if school counselors are unable to collect a certain component of data at one time, they can omit the slide for the current presentation and plan to collect those data for the next presentation. Recognizing there is a flexible template to work from may alleviate some of the pressures and time required for the tasks of collecting information, deciding which information to share, and then sharing these results with stakeholders. The template also has helpful slide notes with guiding tips on what to highlight during a presentation. The full downloadable template is available in the online appendix.

Figure 10.14 Tier 2 Flashlight Results Presentation PowerPoint Templates

Flashlight Presentation Template

The Tier 2 Flashlight Results Presentation template may be used to share intervention results.

Nicash and Tier 2 Flashlight Presentation Example

The Tier 2 Flashlight Results Presentation template slides are side-by-side with Nicash's Small Group Flashlight Results Presentation to offer a sample presentation alongside the template.

[Title of School Counseling Programs Tier 2 Intervention Flashlight Presentation]

[School Name's] School Counseling Department

[Insert school counselor names]

[Insert School Photo/ Mascot Image/ Counseling Program Photo]

From *The Use of Data in School Counseling: Hatching Results for Students, Programs, and the Profession* by Trish Hatch, PhD   Hatching Results®, LLC

Challenger Elementary School Counseling Program Tier 2 Intervention Flashlight Presentation

Ms. Nicash Krublo
Elementary School Counselor
Challenger Elementary School Counseling Department

From *The Use of Data in School Counseling: Hatching Results for Students, Programs, and the Profession* by Trish Hatch, PhD   Hatching Results®, LLC

School Counseling Program Goal

[Write the relevant Tier 2 Intervention S.M.A.R.T. goal statement here]

School Name – School Counseling Department   1

School Counseling Program SMART Goal

The number of 4th graders with 2 or more N's on their report card will decrease by 10% from trimester 1 to trimester 3 (from 40 students to 36 students)

Challenger Elementary – School Counseling Department

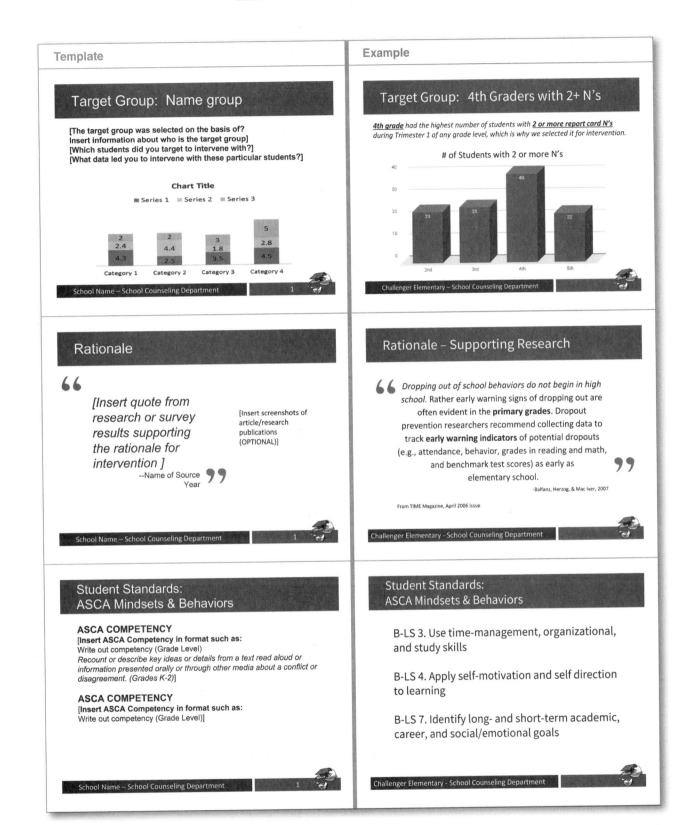

(Continued)

Figure 10.14 (Continued)

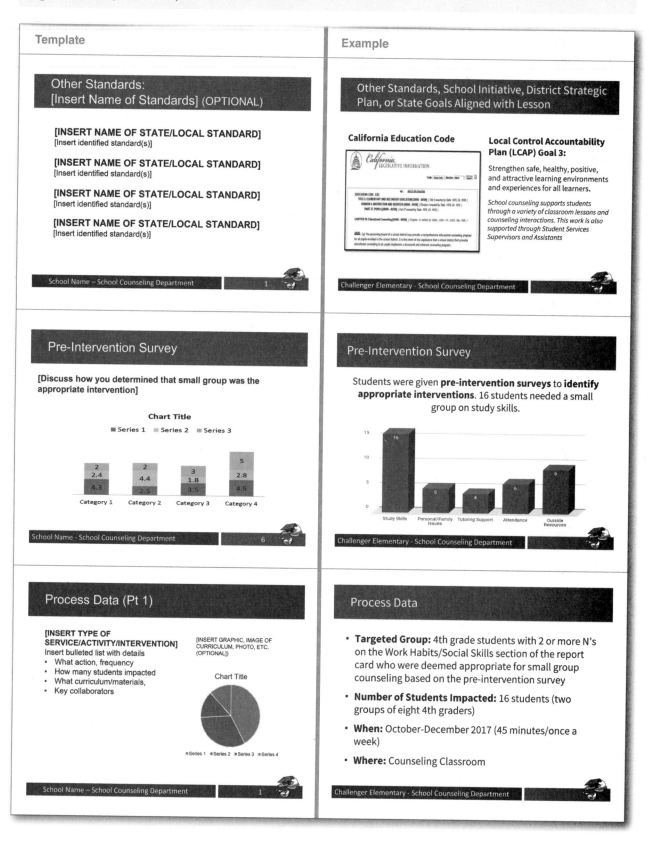

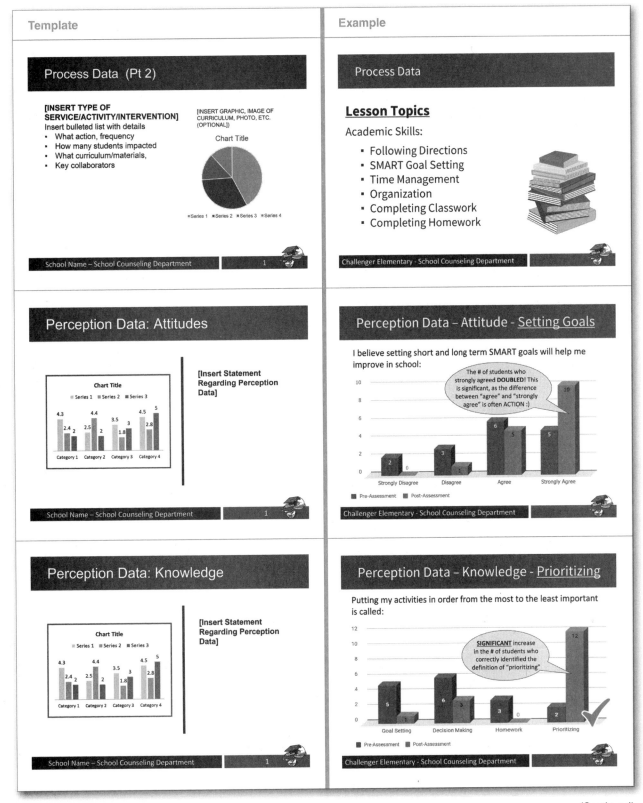

(Continued)

Image source: Pixabay.com/clker-freevector-images

Figure 10.14 (Continued)

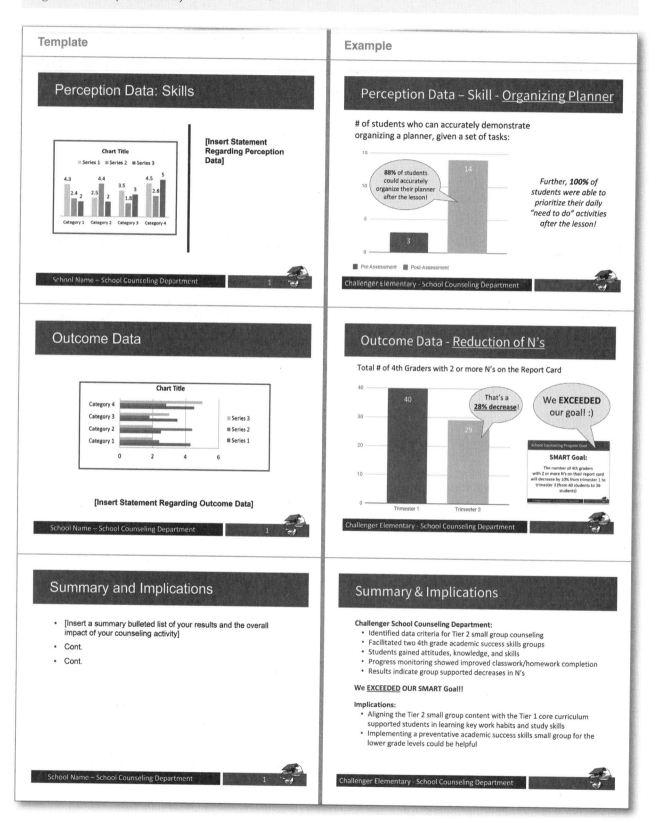

Template

Example

Limitations (OPTIONAL)

- [Insert bulleted list of challenges encountered]
- Cont.
- Cont.

School Name – School Counseling Department   1

Limitations/Lessons Learned

- Thanksgiving break and school-wide testing schedule affected consistency of small groups
- More time needed for strategic grouping of students
- Students responded well to engagement strategies & reinforcements - increase use next group counseling cycle

Challenger Elementary - School Counseling Department

Lessons Learned and Next Steps

- [Bulleted list of the next steps in your school counseling program]
- Cont.
- Cont.

School Name – School Counseling Department   1

Next Steps

- Utilize data to evaluate core curriculum activities related to work habits and social skills
- Continue to share results with community stakeholders
- Collaborate with lower grade levels to implement developmentally appropriate groups

Challenger Elementary - School Counseling Department

THANK YOU!

Many thanks to administration, staff, and parents for your contributions to these efforts and your support of the school counseling program!

School Name – School Counseling Department   14

THANK YOU!!

We appreciate the administration, staff, and parents for their contributions to the success of this intervention, as well as their support of the school counseling program!

Challenger Elementary - School Counseling Department

Figure 10.15 Flashlight One-Pager Template

[INSERT FLASHLIGHT PRESENTATION TITLE]
[INSERT SCHOOL NAME] SCHOOL COUNSELING PROGRAM

20XX-20XX

Abstract/Summary

Lorem ipsum dolor sit amet, consectetur adipiscing elit. Nam faucibus urna vitae pellentesque porta. Etiam tristique dapibus viverra. Maecenas rutrum nec eros eu varius. Suspendisse sit amet est justo. Vivamus sed facilisis purus. Donec laoreet nulla dui, ac sagittis mauris hendrerit vel.

Lorem ipsum dolor sit amet, consectetur adipiscing elit. Nam faucibus urna vitae pellentesque porta. Etiam tristique dapibus viverra. Maecenas rutrum nec eros eu varius. Suspendisse sit amet est justo. Vivamus sed facilisis purus. Donec laoreet nulla dui, ac sagittis mauris hendrerit vel. Lorem ipsum dolor sit amet, consectetur adipiscing elit. Nam faucibus urna vitae pellentesque porta.

School Counseling Program Activities

- [Insert text]
- [Insert text]
- [Insert text]

[Insert photo of counseling program at work or other image]

Rationale and Need

- [Insert text]
- [Insert text]
- [Insert text]
- [Insert text]
- [Insert text]

Mindsets & Behaviors/Standards

- **[Standard bullet point]**
  [Description/details]
- **[Standard bullet point]**
  [Description/details]
- **[Standard bullet point]**
  [Description/details]
- **[Standard bullet point]**
  [Description/details]

Competencies

- **[Competency bullet point]**
  [Description/details]
- **[Competency bullet point]**
  [Description/details]
- **[Competency bullet point]**
  [Description/details]
- **[Competency bullet point]**
  [Description/details]

Source: From *Hatching Results for Elementary School Counseling: Implementing Core Curriculum and Other Tier One Activities* (Hatch, T., Duarte, D., & De Gregorio, L. K., 2018).

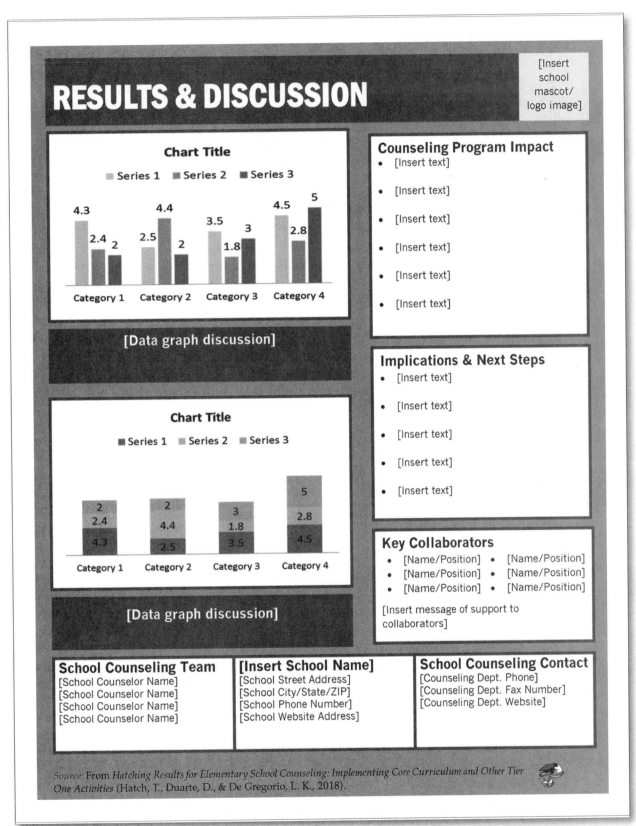

RESULTS & DISCUSSION

[Insert school mascot/logo image]

Chart Title

■ Series 1   ■ Series 2   ■ Series 3

Category 1: 4.3, 2.4, 2
Category 2: 2.5, 4.4, 2
Category 3: 3.5, 1.8, 3
Category 4: 4.5, 2.8, 5

[Data graph discussion]

Chart Title

■ Series 1   ■ Series 2   ■ Series 3

Category 1: 2, 2.4, 4.3
Category 2: 2, 4.4, 2.5
Category 3: 3, 1.8, 3.5
Category 4: 5, 2.8, 4.5

[Data graph discussion]

Counseling Program Impact
- [Insert text]
- [Insert text]
- [Insert text]
- [Insert text]
- [Insert text]
- [Insert text]

Implications & Next Steps
- [Insert text]
- [Insert text]
- [Insert text]
- [Insert text]
- [Insert text]

Key Collaborators
- [Name/Position]   • [Name/Position]
- [Name/Position]   • [Name/Position]
- [Name/Position]   • [Name/Position]

[Insert message of support to collaborators]

School Counseling Team
[School Counselor Name]
[School Counselor Name]
[School Counselor Name]
[School Counselor Name]

[Insert School Name]
[School Street Address]
[School City/State/ZIP]
[School Phone Number]
[School Website Address]

School Counseling Contact
[Counseling Dept. Phone]
[Counseling Dept. Fax Number]
[Counseling Dept. Website]

Source: From *Hatching Results for Elementary School Counseling: Implementing Core Curriculum and Other Tier One Activities* (Hatch, T., Duarte, D., & De Gregorio, L. K., 2018).

Flashlight Presentation "One Pager"

Another benefit of the Tier 2 Flashlight Results Presentation is the ability to pull information from the presentation to briefly highlight some of the results. A "one pager" is a one-page tool that can be compiled from the flashlight to create a visual summary of key components, slides, or data for a quick reference (see Figure 10.15). School counselors can also use it during the full Tier 2 Flashlight Results Presentation to reference or take notes on. In addition, it can easily be shared with stakeholders or serve as a stand-alone document. The one pager can also be help-ful for people who are unable to hear the presentation, but can receive and under-stand a brief summary of the key points, whether shared by email, placed in mailboxes, uploaded to websites, posted on bulletin boards, shared with parents and community members, or placed on a poster to be exhibited at a district meet-ing or conference workshop.

Measuring and sharing results is a vital and necessary activity for today's school counselors. When counselors take responsibility for program evaluation and program improvement, they are better able to serve as student and program advocates, as well as systemic change agents. As school counselors improve their practice and see improvements in student outcomes, it will be tempting to cele-brate, but we encourage counselors to remember that many factors contribute to students' shifts in perception and outcome data. Changes in administration, teachers, policies, and practices can all contribute to improvements (or setbacks, for that matter). It is recommended that counselors take caution before assuming sole credit (or responsibility) for improvements or lack thereof. Thoughtful analysis of improvements or obstacles should be taken into consideration in the limitations portion of any program or activities evaluation. Careful attention should also be given to remembering that others in the school are working on these things, too, and refraining from assuming causality. Rather, the terminology of "contributing in a meaningful way" or "seems to be contributing to student improvements" is a more professionally responsible claim. Drawing the concep-tual link between activities and outcomes is important in the reporting process; taking all the credit (or blame) is not. We encourage counselors to share credit and challenges with other student services professionals and faculty in the schools, recognizing that everyone makes forward progress when improvements are seen in students' outcomes.)

NICASH'S STORY CONTINUES

As the school year came to an end, Nicash's program evaluation and results reflected her hard work and focus on collaborating and creating an intentional, equitable, data-driven, comprehensive ASCA National Model program that was student focused. She began at her school with the vision of using data to drive Tier 2 and 3 interventions. She worked closely with stakeholders from the beginning and along the way, by identifying the qualifying data criteria they would use to ensure no students fell through the cracks and all students who needed the additional supports were connected with the appropriate interventions. Nicash partnered with her district counseling team to standardize the data used for the counseling group interventions across the different elementary schools. She continuously collected and monitored the progress data from students, teachers, and parents, and thoughtfully planned her small groups. Nicash and her district counseling team also collaborated to select and create the most appropriate Academic Success Skills small group curriculum. Nicash successfully utilized her basic counseling skills and engagement and management strategies to effectively facilitate the small groups. Nicash and her team even created their own progress monitoring and assessment tools, which directly aligned with the content chosen, and evaluated their curriculum to ensure the interventions were achieving the desired results. They then circled back to find more intensive Tier 3 supports for those students who proved to need more. After all her work successfully planning and facilitating her small groups throughout the year, she collected and analyzed the data and the effectiveness of her program and shared her results through a Tier 2 Flashlight Results Presentation with her staff, which later led to the sharing of their counseling results with the district school board, community, and professional state association conference.

Nicash's Story Doesn't End There

As Nicash continued to share the powerful results of her data-driven work, opportunities continued to find her, expanding her program and shining a light on her advocacy, leadership, and districtwide collaboration to support students. Not only did stakeholders become aware of the effectiveness of her comprehensive school counseling program, but they wanted to duplicate her results and turned to her to lead the charge. As a result, she advocated and ensured an elementary school counselor was hired at all the sites, and she was asked to take on a Counselor on Special Assignment role to oversee and coordinate the district counseling teams. Her collaboration with the local university led to an adjunct lecturer position, teaching a data-driven group counseling course as a graduate program educator. Nicash continues to support students, staff, communities, and the school counseling field in a more systemic way, but she knows that as long as students are not achieving their highest potential and reaching their academic, social/emotional, and college/career goals, there is still more work to do.

Appendix A

Practitioner-Focused Research

Successful Implementation of a Federally Funded Violence Prevention Elementary School Counseling Program: Results Bring Sustainability

Danielle Duarte is head school counselor at Fallbrook Union Elementary School District in Fallbrook, CA. Email drduarte@gmail.com. **Trish Hatch, PhD,** is an associate professor at San Diego State University in San Diego, CA.

Sixty-four federal Elementary and Secondary School Counseling (ESSC) program grants were awarded in 2009. One awarded school district implemented a comprehensive school counseling program based on the ASCA National Model at three high-needs elementary schools. This case study describes a district initiative that provided prevention education for all students and interventions for students with identified needs. Based on improvements in attendance, behavior, and achievement, the district funded and expanded the program after federal funds ended.

This Appendix is a reprint of an earlier publication Trish Hatch wrote with colleague Danielle Duarte.

Source: **Duarte, D., & Hatch, T. (2014).** *Successful Implementation of a Federally Funded Violence Prevention Elementary School Counseling Program: Results Bring Sustainability.* Professional School Counseling. Volume:18, issue: 1. https:// doi.org/10.1177/2156759X0001800106

Thirteen school districts in California were among the 64 national Elementary and Secondary School Counseling (ESSC) program grants awarded by the U.S. Department of Education in 2009. The purpose of the ESSC grant (84.215E) is to fund the establishment or expansion of school counseling programs with the goal of expanding the quality of school counseling services (U.S. Department of Education, 2009). One awarded school district in southern California designed and implemented a comprehensive school counseling program based on the ASCA National Model (American School Counselor Association [ASCA], 2005) and evidence-based practices (Dimmitt, Carey, & Hatch, 2007). The requirements of the grant were written to include providing developmental prevention education curricula for all students and targeted interventions for students with identified needs. The grant proposal included three main goals: (a) implement an assessment-based, results-driven, comprehensive school counseling program that will serve as a catalyst and model for expansion throughout the district; (b) increase the social and emotional competencies and academic achievement of all students; and (c) minimize the barriers and increase resilience for students who are at higher risk of school failure. Through designing and implementing a comprehensive program with school counselors and a school social worker, prevention education would be provided to all students, and social and academic interventions would be created for students in need of more support. The purpose of this article is to share the successes and challenges of designing, implementing, and evaluating a comprehensive elementary school counseling program, for use as other schools begin or refine their own counseling programs. This case study's emphasis on sustaining and expanding school counseling programs also provides practitioners with suggestions about how to gain school, district, and community buy-in, with the goal of continuing school counseling programs despite budget changes.

LITERATURE REVIEW

Comprehensive, Data-Driven School Counseling Programs

Data-driven practices have become increasingly necessary in the profession of school counseling (ASCA, 2012; Carey, Dimmitt, Hatch, Lapan, & Whiston, 2008; Hatch & Chen-Hayes, 2008). ASCA's professional competencies, position statements, ethical guidelines, and the ASCA National Model call for school counseling programs to use data to systematically identify and address the needs of students for purposes of accountability and program improvement (ASCA, 2008, 2010a, 2010b, 2012). School counselors are urged to implement research-based interventions and accurately measure the impact of their activities on the students they serve (Carey et al., 2008; Johnson, 2002; Poynton & Carey, 2006). Wilkerson, Pérusse, and Hughes (2013) compared school-wide Adequate Yearly Progress (AYP) results in Indiana K–12 schools between Recognized ASCA Model Program (RAMP) schools and non-RAMP schools. Results indicated that professional school counselors are willing to collect data in order to create comprehensive school counseling programs. Furthermore, the implementation of data-driven school counseling programs continues to yield positive results on student achievement. In addition to collecting and analyzing data, sharing positive results with school administrators, school district officials, and other school stakeholders is essential to garnering support for school counseling programs (Hatch, 2014; Sink, 2009). To ensure the needs of the student population are being met, it is important for professional school counselors to identify evidence-based curriculum and interventions using a data-driven decision-making process.

Second Step Violence Prevention Program

"Second Step" (Committee for Children, 2010) is a violence prevention curriculum used to teach social skills and reduce social/emotional problem behavior. Classroom lessons are focused around three unit topics: empathy training, impulse control, and anger management. The National Panel for School Counseling Evidence-Based Practice (Carey et al., 2008), which independently analyzes outcome research of school counseling interventions, described Second Step as an "exceptionally well-researched intervention" (p. 203). Results include findings of improvement in elementary school participants' prosocial beliefs and behaviors, such as caring, cooperation, and positive coping mechanisms (Cooke et al., 2007). Other research found decreases in aggressive behaviors and less adult intervention in minor conflicts for students who received Second Step lessons, in contrast to students who did not (Frey, Nolen, Edstrom, & Hirschstein, 2005). Results such as these prompted the school district in this case study to select and implement Second Step to address the social/emotional competencies of all students.

> The primary measures for the ESSC grant program are the reduction of student-to-school-counselor ratios and the reduction of incidences of violence.

ELEMENTARY AND SECONDARY SCHOOL COUNSELING (ESSC) PROGRAM GRANT

Federal Elementary and Secondary School Counseling (ESSC) program grants fund the establishment or expansion of school counseling programs with the goal of improving the quality of counseling services available (U.S. Department of Education, 2009). The primary measures for the ESSC grant program are the reduction of student-to-school-counselor (or mental health provider) ratios and the reduction of incidences of violence as measured by the number of student discipline referrals. Grantees are required to report these data along with other project-specific goals and objectives they identify, such as improving student attendance, academic performance, social skills development, parent involvement, and professional development (U.S. Department of Education, 2009). Grantees are also expected to share their projects as potential models of effective practice to assist schools and communities across the nation to improve their programs (U.S. Department of Education, 2009).

The award-winning grant that led to this case study was written to address both the needs of the students and the needs of the district. Within this rapidly growing southern California school district, student performance measures were steadily decreasing as behavior problems and social/emotional needs increased. District demographic trends revealed an ever-growing, ethnically diverse, high-needs student population (Stowers & Hatch, 2008). In the early 1990s, the district had an elementary school counseling program that provided comprehensive services for all students. Over the next decade, the fiscal crisis in California resulted in the elimination of district-funded elementary school counseling positions, leaving only two school counselors serving 8,600 students in 10 schools. The grant award provided funds for additional staffing and a new approach to designing, implementing, evaluating, improving, and sustaining school counseling services in three of the district's most needy elementary schools.

METHOD

This case study focused on the implementation and impact of one particular federally funded ESSC grant that was written with a focus on three main goals: (a) implement an assessment-based, results-driven, comprehensive school counseling program that will serve as a catalyst and model for expansion throughout the district; (b) increase the social and emotional competencies and academic achievement of all students; and (c) minimize the barriers and increase resilience for students who are at higher risk of school failure.

The first goal of the grant was to address the creation and execution of school counseling services at each school. This goal was accomplished by hiring four grant staff consisting of one full-time credentialed school counselor at each of three school sites (one of whom also served as the project director for the grant), and a school social worker who provided services for high-needs students and families at all three schools. The external evaluator (also the co-author of this article) provided extensive training to the grant staff; she also provided consultation, support, and training on the ASCA National Model (ASCA, 2005) and evidence-based practices. The grant team members attended a series of additional trainings and conferences on topics including Second Step implementation, Positive Behavioral Interventions and Supports (PBIS), and effective teaching pedagogy.

The second goal addressed the school-wide culture and climate: increase social and emotional competencies and academic achievement of all students. This was accomplished through the delivery of Second Step (Committee for Children, 2010), a research-based violence prevention program that includes a series of classroom lessons and school-wide prevention activities like Stand Up to Bullying Month, Red Ribbon Week, and College and Career Day. Ancillary programs such as Peace Patrol, student council, coordinated recess activities, and parent education also contributed to overall learning. Dropout prevention researchers recommend collecting data to track early warning indicators of potential dropouts (e.g., attendance, behavior, grades in reading and math, and benchmark test scores) as early as elementary school (Balfanz, Herzog, & Mac Iver, 2007). Targets for goal two aligned with these early warning indicators and were determined collaboratively by the grant writing team. Measures of success for the school-wide grant goal reflected proposed increases over a 3-year period and were identified as follows:

- 10 percent increase in Satisfactory (S) and Excellent (E) marks on teacher-reported Life Skills and Work Habits section on student report cards;
- 10 percent increase in students reporting high levels of empathy/problem solving skills, as reported on the California Healthy Kids Survey (CHKS); and
- nine percent increase in students scoring proficient and above on California Standards Test (CSTs).

The third goal focused on providing interventions for at-risk students: minimize barriers and increase resilience in students who are at higher risk of school failure. The intervention goal was written to identify students who were off-track and in need of more intensive interventions and support (Balfanz et al., 2007). These students were provided small group counseling, individual counseling services (i.e., short-term individual counseling, parent and teacher contact and collaboration, behavior support plans), and attendance interventions (i.e., parent contact, student incentives). Measures of success for the third goal, intervention for at-risk students, reflected increases over a 3-year period, and were identified as:

- 10 percent decrease in Needs Improvement (N) or Unsatisfactory (U) on teacher-reported Life Skills and Work Habits section on student report cards,
- 10 percent decrease in school-wide discipline referrals and suspension rate, and
- 10 percent decrease in school-wide unexcused absences and truancy rates.

Baseline data prior to the grant implementation indicated that the number of combined N's and U's at each school ranged from 6.7% to 12.6% of students. The three schools reported 808 discipline referrals during the year prior to services (287 at School A, 275 at School B, and 246 at School C). At all schools, 2,140 unexcused absences were recorded before the program began.

> Student performance measures were steadily decreasing as behavior problems and social/emotional needs increased.

Participants

The participants in this research comprised students in kindergarten through fifth grade who attended one of the three schools within the same district in southern California receiving federal funds to implement a comprehensive ESSC program. During program implementation, school sizes ranged from 609 to 936 students, with average enrollment of approximately 775 students; that figure varied slightly each year. The three school communities were fairly homogeneous: approximately 70% Latino, 20% Caucasian, and 10% varying ethnicities, with a high percentage of English Language Learners. During the first year of grant implementation (beginning in 2009), 64.7% of the students attending the three identified schools received free and reduced meals (FARMs), compared to 43.2% of the elementary schools districtwide (see Table 1). In this first year, School A enrolled 649 students: 86.6% Latino and 9.7% White with 81.2% FARMs. School B was in its second year with 777 students: 72.2% Latino and 16.9% White with 73.7% FARMs. School C was the largest with 907 students: 38.8% Latino, 35% White, and 39.9% FARMs. In the second year of the grant, School A's free and reduced percentage increased to 91%, indicating the extreme financial challenges for families during this time period (Ed-Data, 2014). This same school had a truancy rate of 45.8%, in comparison to average truancy rates of 22.6% for the non-grant funded schools (in 2007). The sheriff's department also reported that a high percentage of the city's gang population lived in this area, and the department received a disproportionate number of police calls, criminal activity, incidents of domestic violence, and arrests in this region (Stowers & Hatch, 2008).

> Teachers openly shared their appreciation of the support of students' social and emotional needs, which allowed them more time to focus on teaching.

ASCA National Model Implementation

The ESSC grant reported in this case study was created to systematically design, implement, and evaluate a comprehensive school counseling program based on the ASCA National Model (ASCA, 2005). The ASCA National Model provided a framework for the development and implementation of a comprehensive school counseling program, through which the schoolwide (goal 2) and intervention (goal 3) goals were met. The program's foundation was established at the beginning of the first year when the school counseling team created a mission statement and developed a common philosophy aligning with the program focus. Utilizing the management system, the grant team analyzed school-wide and individual student baseline data to guide the selection and assessment of prevention and intervention services. The school counseling program was organized through the establishment of yearly calendars, weekly classroom curriculum lesson schedules, and action plans for addressing schoolwide and small group intervention activities. Within the delivery system, "Second Step: A Violence Prevention Curriculum" (Committee for Children, 2010) was selected and implemented regularly, along with other preventative programs such as Peace Patrol, a peer mediation program. A menu of counseling services was created to appropriately address the varying needs of students. Finally, the accountability component was met through the grant review team's collection, monitoring, and review of process, perception, and impact data quarterly, yearly, and prior to and at the end of interventions. The team created results reports and used them to monitor changes in the beliefs and behaviors of students as a whole, and based on intervention groups. Review of data resulted in modification of services and counseling practices as needed.

Schoolwide Activities

All three schools focused on the same goals, and grant team members collaborated at monthly meetings to design, implement, and assess the school counseling programs. Although the needs of each school were similar, different school cultures, varying numbers of students, dynamics of administration, and school demographics called for slightly different ways of implementation. For example, all schools utilized Second Step classroom lessons. The curriculum was taught in every classroom at least two times per month, and many classes received weekly lessons. At some schools, the counselors led the lessons, and at others, the teachers taught the curriculum. Sometimes school counseling trainees and/or other counseling staff taught the lessons. Despite slight differences in program curriculum implementation, all three schools demonstrated positive results achieved for the grant goals.

The California Healthy Kids Survey (CHKS) is a statewide measure assessing risk and protective factors related to health, violence, and drug abuse prevention. The grant team reviewed CHKS data to compare student reported perceptions and behaviors to state averages and to determine the focus of schoolwide activities, classroom curriculum, and intervention needs specific to each school. For example, School A had an increasing number of students reporting they were spreading rumors and/or other students were spreading rumors about them. At this site, the school counselor addressed this challenge through classroom lessons around rumors. At School B, 16% of the 100 fifth-graders who took the CHKS reported they "saw another kid bring a weapon to school." This led to a school-wide lesson addressing what students should do if they see a weapon at school. Each school counselor identified and appropriately addressed their own site-specific, data-driven concerns based on the California Healthy Kids Survey data.

Group Counseling Interventions

At each school site, counselors identified students in second through fifth grade for participation in small counseling groups based on receiving five or more Needs Improvement (N) or Unsatisfactory (U) ratings (out of 13) on the Life Skills and Work Habits section of report cards. Examples of report card items include: "works without disturbing others," "observes classroom rules," and "works cooperatively with others." School discipline referrals were also used to help select students for group counseling interventions. The raw number of discipline referrals for the baseline year (2008–2009) was 287 for School A, 275 for School B, and 246 for School C, for a total of 808 discipline referrals. Students were screened to determine if they might benefit best by participating in the counseling group or in another type of intervention. In some cases, students were already participating in group counseling because their report card behavior marks reflected a previous referral. Once students were selected, school counselors sought parental or guardian consent for each identified child to participate in an 8-week group led by the school counselor or school counseling trainees/staff, with sessions lasting for approximately 35 minutes. During the 2010–2011 school year, 167 students participated in counseling groups (see Table 2). School A served 82 group participants, School B provided groups for 35 students, and School C had 50 students who participated in groups. Each group counseling intervention was created by the school counselor and was based on student needs as identified during screening processes. Topics included goal setting, self-control, problem solving, and academic skill building. Participating students were monitored over time to evaluate the impact of interventions and to provide additional and/or different services if improvement was not made.

Table 1 Positive Life Skills and Work Habits Report Card Marks: 2009–2010

Report Card 2009–2010	E's T1	Target (+10%)	E's T2	E's T3	% Change	Goal Met?
School A (*n* = 619)	29.5%	32.5%	35.2%	42.6%	+44.0%	YES
School B (*n* = 787)	62.1%	68.3%	63.8%	65.3%	+5.1%	NO
School C (*n* = 931)	54.9%	60.4%	60.8%	65.3%	+18.9%	YES
Average (*N* = 2288)	45.5%	50.0%	53.3%	57.7%	+22.6%	YES

Note: T1 = trimester 1, T2 = trimester 2, T3 = trimester 3

Table 2   Positive Life Skills and Work Habits Report Card Marks: 2010–2011

Report Card 2010–2011	E's T1	Target (+10%)	E's T2	E's T3	% Change	Goal Met?
School A (*n* = 609)	30.4%	33.8%	39.2%	46.9%	+54.2%	YES
School B (*n* = 817)	45.6%	50.2%	52.6%	59.0%	+29.3%	YES
School C (*n* = 901)	57.3%	63.0%	61.9%	67.7%	+18.1%	YES
Average (*N* = 2327)	44.4%	49.0%	51.2%	57.8%	+33.8%	YES

Note: T1 = trimester 1, T2 = trimester 2, T3 = trimester 3

Description of Data Collection Methods

Data collection was accomplished utilizing (a) an online report card grading system for Life Skills and Work Habits data, (b) California Healthy Kids Survey (CHKS) data, (c) California Standards Test (CST) scores, (d) individual school site records for discipline referrals, and (e) student information systems for attendance and truancy rates. For purposes of measuring the positive marks on Life Skills and Work Habits, school counselors researched the number of E's (for Excellent) and S's (for Satisfactory) on the first trimester report cards. However, since enrollment shifted slightly year to year, the percentage (rather than the number) of students who received positive marks was reported. The California Healthy Kids Survey was administered to fifth-grade students every other year, and school counselors assessed specific reports on empathy, problem solving, and feelings related to school environment. Grant team members analyzed data quarterly, yearly, and prior to and after completing interventions for students receiving individual services.

> By seeing the positive changes in student behaviors through second step lessons, teachers welcomed the school counselors into their classrooms.

Evaluation of Grant Goals

The ESSC program was evaluated in each of the three school years the grant was funded, beginning in fall 2009 and ending in spring 2012. Particular emphasis was placed on year 2 data collection, analysis, and dissemination. The rationale for highlighting second-year data was to garner early support from stakeholders for the allocation of district funds necessary to sustain school counseling services at the end of the third and final year of federal grant funding. Presenting the results of year 2 implementation in the fall of the third year of the grant allowed time for key stakeholders to advocate for the district and school board members to approve new funding to sustain the positions when the grant ended.

SCHOOLWIDE RESULTS

Results for this case study presented below report the impact of the grant program on schoolwide data. Schoolwide data include report card ratings by teachers on Life Skills and Work Habits, student self-reported perception data on the CHKS, state standardized test scores in Math and Language Arts, discipline referrals, unexcused absences, and truancy rates. The authors also share results from one school's group interventions.

Life Skills and Work Habits

The first schoolwide measurement of achieving grant goals was through positive citizenship and work habits marks on report cards, attaining Satisfactory (S) and Excellent (E) marks. School counselors set a goal of achieving a 10% increase from Trimester 1 to Trimester 3. In the second year of implementation, all three schools had a 33.8% increase in scores of Excellent comparing the first trimester to the last trimester, with School A improving from 30.4% E's to 46.9%. See Tables 1 and 2 for school-specific gains of E's received by students at all three schools for years 2009–2010 and 2010–2011. The average of the three schools indicates that the school-wide grant goal was met. Targeted interventions also supported this schoolwide increase; students receiving five or more Needs Improvement (N) and/or Unsatisfactory (U) marks on their report cards were identified for interventions (see Targeted Group Intervention Results).

California Healthy Kids Survey

The second schoolwide data collected was the fifth-grade assessment on the California Healthy Kids Survey (CHKS). In 2009, 37.3% of the students who self-reported were categorized as "high" in the empathy/problem solving and positive school environmental factors on the CHKS. No baseline data existed for one of the three schools (School B) during the baseline year of 2008–2009 because it was a new school that was not open during that school year. CHKS data for 2011 (see Table 3) indicate that 43.8% of the students surveyed reporting "high," a 41% increase that surpassed the grant goal of a 10% increase.

Table 3   Levels of Empathy and Problem Solving as Reported in California Healthy Kids Survey

California Healthy Kids Survey (CHKS) Total Average	High 2008–2009	Medium 2008–2009	Low 2008–2009	Target (Increase % High by 10%)	High 2010–2011	Goal Met?
Empathy/Problem Solving: Positive School Environment	37.3%	55.2%	7.3%	41.0%	43.8%	YES

Standardized Test Scores

The third schoolwide measurement was the number of students who scored proficient and above on the California Standards Tests (CST). The objective was to increase the number of students who scored proficient and above on the CST by 9%. Data analysis (see Tables 4 and 5) required disaggregation to separate Math scores from English Language Arts (ELA) scores. Both categories were disaggregated by grade level, by category, and by school. Although all three schools reported an increase in CST scores, only School C met their goal of increasing by 9% in the first year (2010). In 2011, all schools met their CST ELA goals and two of the three schools met their CST Math goals. In averaging results from all three schools, the overall grant goals of improvement greater than 9% in both Math and ELA were met.

Discipline Referrals

A 10% decrease over a 3-year period in discipline referrals was proposed for the grant schools. The raw number of discipline referrals for the baseline year (2008–2009) was 287 for School A, 275 for School B, and 246 for School C, for a total of 808 discipline referrals. The goal was to reduce the incidences of discipline by 10% over the three years of grant funding. The target for 2012 (–10%) was 728. In 2009–2010, the total number of discipline referrals decreased by 43%, from 808 in 2009 to 464 in 2010. All three schools on the grant reduced their number of discipline referrals (ranging from 21% to 64%). In 2010–2011, the total number of discipline referrals decreased by 64%, from 808 in 2009 to 289 in 2011. Every school on the grant reduced their number of discipline referrals (ranging from 64% to 65%). The goal was met (see Table 6).

> Garnering administrative support early on was extremely crucial for the ongoing success of the ESSC program.

Unexcused Absences and Truancy Rates

The final schoolwide data element collected was unexcused absences at all three schools. The grant proposed a 10% decrease in this category over a 3-year period.

Table 4   English Language Arts (ELA) Proficiency Levels on California Standards Test (CST)

CST (grades 2–5) Proficient and above	ELA 2008–2009	GOAL (+9%)	ELA 2009–2010	Goal Met?	ELA 2010–2011	Goal Met?
School A	46.0% ($n = 603$)	50.1%	48.3% ($n = 619$)	NO	52.0% ($n = 609$)	YES
School B	54.3% ($n = 754$)	59.1%	55.3% ($n = 787$)	NO	72.8% ($n = 817$)	YES
School C	69.9% ($n = 951$)	76.1%	76.8% ($n = 931$)	YES	81.0% ($n = 901$)	YES
Total (Average)	56.7% ($N = 2308$)	61.8%	60.1% ($N = 2288$)	NO	68.6% ($N = 2327$)	YES

APPENDIX A **327**

Table 5 Math Proficiency Levels on California Standards Test (CST)

CST (grades 2–5) Proficient and above	Math 2008–2009	GOAL (+9%)	Math 2009–2010	Goal Met?	Math 2010–2011	Goal Met?
School A	66.0% (n = 603)	71.9%	67.0% (n = 619)	NO	65.3% (n = 609)	NO
School B	69.5% (n = 754)	75.8%	71.3% (n = 787)	NO	81.0% (n = 817)	YES
School C	77.3% (n = 951)	84.3%	84.5% (n = 931)	YES	88.0% (n = 901)	YES
Total (Average)	70.9% (N = 2308)	77.3%	74.5% (N = 2288)	NO	78.1% (N = 2327)	YES

Table 6 Number of Discipline Referrals

Referrals	2008–2009	GOAL (−10%)	2009–2010	Goal Met?	2010–2011	Goal Met?
School A	287 (n = 603)	258	104 (n = 619)	YES (−64%)	100 (n = 609)	YES (−65%)
School B	275 (n = 754)	248	216 (n = 787)	YES (−21%)	100 (n = 817)	YES (−64%)
School C	246 (n = 951)	221	144 (n = 931)	YES (−41%)	89 (n = 901)	YES (−64%)
Total	808 (N = 2308)	728	464 (N = 2288)	YES (−43%)	289 (N = 2327)	YES (−64%)

The raw number of unexcused absences for the 2008–2009 year was 732 for School A, 666 for School B, and 742 for School C, for a total of 2,140 unexcused absences. The goal was to reduce the number of unexcused absences by 10% and the target for 2010 was 1,926 total unexcused absences. In 2009–2010, the total number of unexcused absences increased for all three schools. The largest increase was at School C (+16.8%). However, in 2010–2011, the total number of unexcused absences for all three schools showed a significant overall decrease of 39.8%: School A decreased by 64.2%, School B by 37.8%, and School C by 17.5% (see Table 7). The overall goal for the data element was met. Based on the school district's average daily attendance rates of $40 per day per student, more than $40,000 was earned/saved for the school district. Related to this attendance improvement, the number of students classified as truant—receiving three or more unexcused absences in one school year—decreased by more than half, as 339 students were classified as truant in 2010, and only 137 in 2011.

The counselors and social worker further promoted the services provided by presenting program goals and results to their entire school staff during staff meetings.

Table 7   Truancy Rates

Truancy	2008–2009	GOAL (–10%)	2009–2010	Goal Met?	2010–2011	Goal Met?
School A	732 ($n = 603$)	659	742 ($n = 619$)	NO (+1.3%)	262 ($n = 609$)	YES (–64.2%)
School B	666 ($n = 754$)	599	684 ($n = 787$)	NO (+2.7%)	414 ($n = 817$)	YES (–37.8%)
School C	742 ($n = 951$)	668	866 ($n = 931$)	NO (+16.8%)	612 ($n = 901$)	YES (–17.5%)
Total	2140 ($N = 2308$)	1926	2292 ($N = 2288$)	NO (+6.6%)	1288 ($N = 2327$)	YES (–39.8%)

Targeted Group Intervention Results

Although small group intervention impact data was not required as a part of this grant, each school implemented and evaluated the impact of small group interventions. For example, School B's small group intervention had a total of 54 students participate (35 in 2010 and 19 in 2011). Prior to group, the identified students received a total of 305 Needs Improvement (N) and Unsatisfactory (U) marks on their first trimester report card. After intervention, their third trimester report card data revealed only 212 N's and U's—a reduction of 30%. These students also demonstrated improvement in "effort" marks on their report card for showing more discipline and dedication to their math and language arts work (also rated on the E, S, N, U scale). In addition, more than half (63%) of the fourth- and fifth-grade students who received group interventions showed improvement on their Language Arts portion of the CST when compared to the previous year. In 2010, the average score for students receiving interventions was 329; scores improved to 356 in 2011—an average gain of more than 25 points.

> With the threat of losing school counseling services the following year, administrators helped advocate for funding school counseling programs.

DISCUSSION

During their 3 years as grant-funded school counselors, each school counselor became integrated into the schools as they supported improved school climate and were referred to as esteemed colleagues on the team. They participated on school site team meetings including the parent teacher organization, school site council, and leadership teams, and were also integrated into schoolwide activities. Teachers openly shared their appreciation of the support of students' social and emotional needs, which allowed them more time to focus on teaching.

Administrators were particularly impressed that the school counselors and social worker both collected and shared data on improved attendance and the reduction of behavior referrals and suspensions. They believed this information was an eye-opener for teachers and staff about the positive effects of prevention and intervention programs. Successes were celebrated schoolwide, and these behavior improvements were viewed as contributing factors of the academic increases of students.

Although class time and instructional minutes are highly coveted in the educational setting, by seeing the positive changes in student behaviors through Second Step lessons, teachers welcomed the school counselors into their classrooms. School counselors also provided teachers with behavioral interventions to be implemented in the class setting, which was a huge support to the staff. As school counselors became influential adults on campus, students self-referred when they had a problem or challenge such as family changes, arguments with friends, or bullying. Parents also became more receptive to working with the school counselors and social worker to support their children and actively pursued the support. During 2010–2011 (year 2), 413 parent/guardian attendees participated in the variety of parent workshops coordinated by the school counselors and school social worker, a reportedly large increase from previous years (although no specific data had been collected previously), demonstrating improvement in the home-school connection. Overall, the services provided by the school counselors and social worker helped develop and refine a three-tiered model for behavioral and social/emotional interventions, while positively contributing to the schoolwide climate and culture.

The ESSC grant team in this selected southern California school district purposefully and meaningfully shared the successes of the school counseling program with key school stakeholders, with the specific intention of continuing the school counseling program services at the conclusion of federal funding. Garnering administrative support early on was extremely crucial for the ongoing success of the ESSC program. At the beginning of the grant, each school counselor met with his or her site's principal and assistant principal, along with the project director and external evaluator, to discuss the program's missions and goals and gain buy-in. School counselors communicated with site administrators regularly to update them on the program activities and share results. The counselors and social worker further promoted the services provided by presenting program goals and results to their entire school staff during staff meetings. The ESSC program team received positive feedback from administrators, teachers, and families on the services provided and ongoing progress.

The positive results collected and the support of school administration helped to fully realize the goal of implementing an assessment-based, results-driven, comprehensive school counseling program that would serve as a catalyst and model for expansion throughout the district. At the start of the third year, with the threat of losing school counseling services the following year, administrators helped advocate for funding school counseling programs. The grant team attended a meeting with the district superintendent of instructional services, the director of curriculum and instruction, the director of student services, and all three site principals. At this hour-long meeting, the school counselors, school social worker, and program evaluator presented a comprehensive PowerPoint presentation that included straightforward charts and graphs. The team showed process, perception, and outcome data to explain the progress toward program goals, how they were being addressed, and the positive results achieved from the first two years. Decreases in truancy rates were emphasized, highlighting the growth in Average Daily Attendance (ADA). Improvements in student attendance since the start of the ESSC program earned/saved nearly $40,000 for the district. During this meeting, the grant team also explained the potential impact of discontinuing the program when the federal funding ceased at the close of the school

Improvements in student attendance since the start of the ESSC program earned/saved nearly $40,000 for the district.

year and suggested alternative funding scenarios for program continuation. Based on site administrator support and the positive data presented, the school district agreed to not only fund but also expand the elementary school counseling program to service the feeder middle school after grant funds ended.

IMPLICATIONS FOR SCHOOL COUNSELORS

California has the highest ratio of students to school counselors in the nation, at 1,016 students per counselor (ASCA, 2011). Yet, despite the California budget crisis, which has contributed to the decrease and even elimination of school counselors in districts throughout the state (Murphy, 2011), the school district in this case study chose to continue their school counseling programs at all three schools and expand services to a middle school after federal funding diminished. The success of the programs presented in this study is attributed to the design, development, implementation, and evaluation of a school counseling program aligned with the ASCA National Model (ASCA, 2005; 2012) and the strategic decision to present positive program results early in the process to key central office administration.

The success of garnering sustainability is also attributed to effective marketing of the ESSC program. The school counselors created websites for each of their schools, which shared the program mission and services, introduced the staff, provided resources and promoted program results (as they became available). Bilingual brochures with this same information were created and readily available for families and staff. A Support Personnel Accountability Report Card (SPARC)—"a continuous improvement document sponsored by the California Department of Education and the Los Angeles County Office of Education" (California Department of Education, 2014)—was created for each school, publicizing the school program by highlighting services and results. This document was disseminated to school staff, families, school board members, and community partners. School counselors also periodically and informally shared program successes with school communities, school board members, and key district staff. For example, one school counselor spoke during open session at a school board meeting about the successful College and Career Day, including improvements in students' knowledge of two or more careers. During National School Counseling Week, another school counselor displayed declines in students' behavior referrals after participating in a group, thanking school staff for supporting the school counseling program and providing cookies.

The school counselors created websites for each of their schools, which shared the program mission and services, introduced the staff, provided resources and promoted program results.

The team also wrote an article about their program implementation, which was featured in *The California School Counselor* magazine, and contacted the local newspaper to feature several school programs that were implemented by the school counselors. The counselors and social worker were also selected to present their programs and results at the California Association of School Counselors' annual conference. Each of these marketing activities was intended to promote understanding of and gain buy-in to the ESSC program by school staff, families, school board members, district personnel, and community members. Through this publicity, school counseling services were well defined and understood and, therefore, recognized as important and essential to promoting well-rounded student development.

Regular and purposeful ESSC team meetings were another essential part of the effectiveness of the grant implementation, evaluation, and sustainability. During the first year, meetings took place every other week to address program implementation, create action plans, review data, and consult about ethical situations. The grant team created a mission statement and designed school-specific core curriculum action plans addressing academic, career, and personal/social student development domains. Once referral, attendance, and report card data were available and analyzed, the grant team identified specific needs and designed Tier 2 action plans to address these needs via group counseling and other supports. School counselors also made yearly calendars for each school site, incorporating events throughout the year such as Red Ribbon Week, Stand Up to Bullying Month, and College and Career Day. The bimonthly planning meetings allowed the grant team to continually review each school's action plans and yearly calendars, while also analyzing data.

The school district's technology department set up a system for the school counselors to easily access academic and behavior (Life Skills and Work Habits) grades of all their students, which was extremely valuable in accessing data, and therefore analyzing it. The skill level in accessing and analyzing data varied between members of the ESSC team, and regular meetings allowed school counselors to support one another. By regularly examining the data, the grant team monitored program success in order to continue implementing components that showed positive results. This also helped them recognize areas for improvement as the program progressed, helping ensure that goals were met. During the second and third year of the grant, meetings took place monthly, but continuing meetings every other week might have supported further consistency of implementation and school counselor and social worker role definition, which is noted as a concern below.

LIMITATIONS

One of the important clarifications necessary in this study is the varying ways in which each ESSC team member responded to the specific needs of the student populations served by the grant. Each school counselor delivered the curriculum and held group counseling sessions a bit differently to accommodate differing school cultures and administrator requests. For example, at some grade levels at grant schools the counselors led all of the Second Step classroom lessons, while at other sites, the teachers, school counseling trainees, and/or other counseling staff taught the lessons. Some schools and grades received weekly lessons, while others received lessons every other week. The curriculum implementation differences may have impacted the outcome results, but to what degree is not known. The role of the school social worker also varied slightly at each school based on site administration expectations, which at times impacted the social worker's ability to focus primarily on student attendance and other high-need situations. At School A, where the social worker's responsibilities were most clearly aligned with the grant, the largest reduction in unexcused absences (64%) was seen. The authors recommend greater consistency in program implementation by grant team members to determine if this provides more reliable results and supports greater student improvements.

The results shared herein were designed for use in program evaluation only, not research (Weiss, 1998). The outcome data were collected and shared through a systematic assessment that aligns with the fundamental elements of program evaluation, and the data are not intended to imply or attribute outcomes to causation (Weiss, 1998). Continual evaluation will be needed to assess the impact of the school counseling programs in these schools over time. Evaluating the expansion of the program to the middle school will be important to determine the relationship between the school counseling services and any improvements in attendance, behavior, and achievement. Finally, research is recommended to determine whether shifts in data at these three schools differs greatly when compared with data at other schools in the district that did not have elementary school counseling programs.

CONCLUSION

This case study presents one example of program implementation and evaluation conducted by practicing school counselors in consultation with their program evaluator. It tells the story of how a comprehensive, evidence-based school counseling program that aligns with the ASCA National Model (ASCA, 2005; 2012) can be developed, analyzed, marketed, and sustained. This study also demonstrates and validates the importance of collecting data and sharing results with appropriate stakeholders to create awareness of services and to highlight obtained results. The authors encourage practicing school counselors to recognize the importance of analyzing and presenting results data to strengthen and promote the sustainability of their school counseling programs.

REFERENCES

American School Counselor Association. (2005). *The ASCA National Model: A framework for school counseling programs* (2nd ed.). Alexandria, VA: Author.

American School Counselor Association. (2008). *ASCA school counselor competencies.* Alexandria, VA: Author.

American School Counselor Association. (2010a). *ASCA position statements.* Alexandria, VA: Author.

American School Counselor Association. (2010b). *Ethical standards for school counselors.* Alexandria, VA: Author. Retrieved from http://www.schoolcounselor.org/files/Ethical Standards2010.pdf

American School Counselor Association. (2011). *Student-to-school-counselor ratio 2010–2011.* Alexandria, VA: Author. Retrieved from http://www.schoolcounselor.org/asca/media/asca/home/ratios10-11.pdf

American School Counselor Association. (2012). *The ASCA National Model: A framework for school counseling programs* (3rd ed.). Alexandria, VA: Author.

Balfanz, R., Herzog, L., & Mac Iver, D. J. (2007). Preventing student disengagement and keeping students on the graduation path in urban middle-grades schools: Early identification and effective interventions. *Educational Psychologist, 42*(4), 223–235.

California Department of Education. (2014). *Support personnel accountability report card.* Retrieved from http://www.cde.ca.gov/ls/cg/re/sparc.asp

Carey, J. C., Dimmitt, C., Hatch, T. A., Lapan, R. T., & Whiston, S. C. (2008). Report of the National Panel for Evidence-Based School Counseling: Outcome research coding protocol and evaluation of Student Success Skills and Second Step. *Professional School Counseling, 11,* 197–206.

Committee for Children. (2010). *Second step violence prevention curriculum.* Retrieved from http://www.cfchildren.org/second-step.aspx

Cooke, M. B., Ford, J., Levine, J., Bourke, C., Newell, L., & Lapidus, G. (2007). The effects of city-wide implementation of "Second Step" on elementary school students' prosocial and aggressive behaviors. *The Journal of Primary Prevention, 28*(2), 93–115.

Dimmitt, C., Carey, J. C., & Hatch, T. (2007). *Evidence-based school counseling: Making a difference with data-driven practices.* Thousand Oaks, CA: Corwin Press.

Ed-Data: fiscal, demographic, and performance data on California's K-12 schools. (2014). School profile. Retrieved from https://www.ed-data.k12.ca.us

Frey, K. S., Nolen, S. B., Edstrom, L. V., & Hirschstein, M. K. (2005). Effects of a school-based social-emotional competence program: Linking children's goals, attributions, and behavior. *Journal of Applied Developmental Psychology, 26,* 171–200.

Hatch, T. (2014). *The use of data in school counseling: Hatching Results for students, programs and the professions.* Thousand Oaks, CA: Corwin.

Hatch, T., & Chen-Hayes, S. F. (2008). School counselor beliefs about ASCA model school counseling program components using the SCPSC Scale. *Professional School Counseling, 12,* 34–42.

Johnson, R. (2002). *Using data to close the achievement gap: How to measure equity in our schools.* Thousand Oaks, CA: Corwin.

Murphy, K. (2011, July 15). The end of the school counselor. *The Oakland Tribune,* CA. Retrieved from http://www.dailytitan.com/2011/07/the-end-of-the-school-counselor/

Poynton, T., & Carey, J. C. (2006). An integrative model and data-based decision making for school counseling. *Professional School Counseling, 10,* 121–130.

Sink, C. A. (2009). School counselors as accountability leaders: Another call for action. *Professional School Counseling, 13,* 68–74.

Stowers, S., & Hatch, T. (2008). *The Federal Elementary and Secondary School Counseling Demonstration Act Grant.* Department of Education, Office of Elementary and Secondary Education.

U.S. Department of Education. (2009). *Elementary and secondary school counseling programs.* Retrieved from http://www2.ed.gov/programs/elseccounseling/fy2009awards.html

Weiss, C. (1998). *Evaluation: Methods for studying programs and practices.* Englewood Cliffs, NJ: Prentice Hall.

Wilkerson, K., Pérusse, R., & Hughes, A. (2013). Comprehensive school counseling programs and student achievement outcomes: A comparative analysis of RAMP versus non-RAMP schools. *Professional School Counseling, 16,* 172–184.

Appendix B

Online Appendix

Readers looking for additional samples or examples will find them in the Hatching Results Online Appendix.

Visit the online appendix at http://www.hatchingresults.com/elementary-t2-t3-online-appendix for additional resources.

References

Agnew, N. C., Slate, J. R., Jones, C. H., & Agnew, D. M. (1993). Academic behaviors as a function of academic achievement, locus of control & motivational orientation. *NACTA Journal, 4,* 24–27. Retrieved from https://www.nactateachers.org/attachments/article/802/Agnew_NACTA_Journal_June_1993-4.pdf

American Foundation for Suicide Prevention (AFSP), American School Counselor Association (ASCA), National Association of School Psychologists (NASP), & The Trevor Project. (n.d.). *Model School District Policy on Suicide Prevention: Model language, commentary, and resources.* Retrieved from https://www.schoolcounselor.org/asca/media/asca/home/ModelPolicySuicidePrevention.pdf

American School Counselor Association (ASCA). (2003). *ASCA National Model: A framework for school counseling programs.* Alexandria, VA: Author.

American School Counselor Association (ASCA). (2005). *ASCA National Model: A framework for school counseling programs* (2nd ed.). Alexandria, VA: Author.

American School Counselor Association (ASCA). (2012). *ASCA National Model: A framework for school counseling programs* (3rd ed.). Alexandria, VA: Author.

American School Counselor Association (ASCA). (2013). *The school counselor and discipline* [Position statement]. Retrieved from https://www.schoolcounselor.org/asca/media/asca/PositionStatements/PS_Discipline.pdf

American School Counselor Association (ASCA). (2014). *ASCA Mindsets & Behaviors for student success: K–12 college- and career-readiness standards for every student.* Alexandria, VA: Author. Retrieved from https://www.schoolcounselor.org/asca/media/asca/home/MindsetsBehaviors.pdf

American School Counselor Association (ASCA). (2015a). *The school counselor and cultural diversity* [Position statement]. Retrieved from https://www.schoolcounselor.org/asca/media/asca/PositionStatements/PS_CulturalDiversity.pdf

American School Counselor Association (ASCA). (2015b). *The school counselor and student mental health* [Position statement]. Retrieved from https://www.schoolcounselor.org/asca/media/asca/PositionStatements/PS_StudentMentalHealth.pdf

American School Counselor Association (ASCA). (2016a). *ASCA ethical standards for school counselors.* Retrieved from https://www.schoolcounselor.org/asca/media/asca/Ethics/EthicalStandards2016.pdf

American School Counselor Association (ASCA). (2016b). *The school counselor and students with disabilities* [Position statement]. Retrieved from https://www.schoolcounselor.org/asca/media/asca/PositionStatements/PS_Disabilities.pdf

American School Counselor Association (ASCA). (2017). *RAMP component webinar: Section 11—Closing the gap results reports* [Video]. Retrieved from https://www.youtube.com/watch?v=WJFdcnRJBbo

American School Counselor Association (ASCA). (2018a). *The school counselor and confidentiality* [Position statement]. Retrieved from https://www.schoolcounselor.org/asca/media/asca/PositionStatements/PS_Confidentiality.pdf

American School Counselor Association (ASCA). (2018b). *The school counselor and multitiered system of supports* [Position statement]. Retrieved from https://www.schoolcounselor .org/asca/media/asca/PositionStatements/PS_MultitieredSupportSystem.pdf

American School Counselor Association (ASCA). (2019a). *The ASCA National Model: A framework for school counseling programs, fourth edition*. Alexandria, VA: Author.

American School Counselor Association (ASCA). (2019b). *National School Counseling Week*. Retrieved from https://www.schoolcounselor.org/school-counselors-members/about-asca-(1)/national-school-counseling-week

American School Counselor Association (ASCA). (2019c). *Recognized ASCA Model Program (RAMP)*. Retrieved from https://www.schoolcounselor.org/school-counselors/ recognized-asca-model-program-(ramp)

American School Counselor Association (ASCA). (n.d.). Executive summary. *ASCA National Model: A framework for school counseling programs*. Alexandria, VA: Author. Retrieved from https://schoolcounselor.org/ascanationalmodel/media/anm-templates/anmexecsumm .pdf

Anderson, C. M., & Borgmeier, C. (2010). Tier II interventions within the framework of school-wide positive behavior support: Essential features for design, implementation, and maintenance. *Behavior Analysis in Practice, 3*(1), 33–45. doi:10.1007/BF03391756

Balfanz, R., Bridgeland, J. M., Moore, L. A., & Fox, J. H. (2010). Building a grad nation: Progress and challenge in ending the high school dropout epidemic. Civic Enterprises Report. Retrieved from https://www.edweek.org/media/14grad1.pdf

Balfanz, R., Herzog, L., & Mac Iver, D. J. (2007). Preventing student disengagement and keeping students on the graduation path in urban middle-grades schools: Early identification and effective interventions. *Educational Psychologist, 42*(4), 223–235. Retrieved from http://web.jhu.edu/CSOS/images/TDMG/PreventingStudentDisengagement.pdf

Barbetta, P. M., Norona, K. L., & Bicard, D. F. (2005). Classroom behavior management: A dozen common mistakes and what to do instead. *Preventing School Failure, 49*(3), 11–19.

Birat, A., Bourdier, P., Piponnier, E., Blazevich, A. J., Maciejewski, H., Duche, P., & Ratel, S. (2018). Metabolic and fatigue profiles are comparable between prepubertal children and well-trained adult endurance athletes. *Frontiers in Physiology, 9*, 387. Retrieved from https://doi.org/10.3389/fphys.2018.00387

Bloom, B., Englehart, M., Furst, E., Hill, W., & Krathwohl, D. (1956). *Taxonomy of educational objectives: The classification of educational goals. Handbook I: Cognitive domain*. New York and Toronto: Longmans, Green.

Bore, S. K., Hendricks, L., & Womack, A. (2013). Psycho-educational groups in schools: The intervention of choice. *National Forum Journal of Counseling and Addiction, 2*(1), 1–9.

Boyko, T. (2016). *AVID culturally relevant teaching: A schoolwide approach*. San Diego, CA: AVID Press.

Bridgeland, J. M., Dilulio, J. J., Morison, K. B. (2006). *The silent epidemic: Perspectives of high school dropouts*. Washington, D.C.: Civic Enterprises.

Brigman, G., & Goodman, B. E. (2008). *Group counseling for school counselors: A practical guide* (3rd ed.). Portland, ME: Walch Education.

Brophy, J. E. (2017). Fostering student learning and motivation in the elementary school classroom. In S. G. Paris, G. M. Olson, H. W. Stevenson (Eds.), *Learning and motivation in the classroom* (pp. 283–306). London: Routledge.

Campbell, A., & Anderson, C. M. (2011). Check-in/check-out: A systematic evaluation and component analysis. *Journal of Applied Behavior Analysis, 44*(2), 315–326. doi:10.1901/ jaba.2011.44-315

Cassidy, S. (2004). Learning styles: An overview of theories, models, and measures. *Educational Psychology, 24*(4), 419–444. Retrieved from https://doi.org/10.1080/0144341042000228834

Center for Substance Abuse Treatment. (2005). 6: Group leadership, concepts, and techniques. In *Substance abuse treatment: Group therapy* [Treatment Improvement Protocol Series, no. 41]. Retrieved from https://www.ncbi.nlm.nih.gov/books/NBK64211/

Coe, R., Aloisi, C., Higgins, S., & Major, L. E. (2014). *What makes great teaching? Review of the underpinning research*. Centre for Evaluation & Monitoring, Durham University, and The Sutton Trust. Retrieved from https://bit.ly/2x0NoR6

Coleman, J. S. (1966). *Equality of educational opportunity*. Washington, DC: National Center for Education Statistics. Retrieved from https://eric.ed.gov/?id=ED012275

Collaborative for Academic, Social, and Emotional Learning (CASEL). (2013). *CASEL guide: Effective social and emotional learning programs—preschool and elementary school edition*. Retrieved from https://casel.org/preschool-and-elementary-edition-casel-guide/

Collaborative for Academic, Social, and Emotional Learning (CASEL). (2015). *CASEL guide: Effective social and emotional learning programs—middle and high school edition*. Retrieved from https://casel.org/middle-and-high-school-edition-casel-guide/

Committee for Children. (2019). *Second Step social-emotional learning*. Retrieved from https://www.cfchildren.org/programs/social-emotional-learning/

Cowan, K. C., Vaillancourt, K., Rossen, E., & Pollitt, K. (2013). *A framework for safe and successful schools* [Brief]. Bethesda, MD: National Association of School Psychologists.

Cristóvão, A. M., Candeias, A. A., & Verdasca, J. (2017). Social and emotional learning and academic achievement in Portuguese schools: A bibliometric study. *Frontiers in Psychology, 8,* 1913. Retrieved from https://doi.org/10.3389/fpsyg.2017.01913

Crone, D. A., Hawken, L. S. & Horner, R. H. (2010). *Responding to problem behavior in schools* (2nd ed.). The Behavior Education Program. NY: Guilford Press.

Dimmitt, C. (2017). *Tier 1 school-based programs* [PowerPoint presentation]. Ronald H. Frederickson Center for School Counseling Outcome and Research & Evaluation (SCORE). Retrieved from http://www.umass.edu/schoolcounseling/

Dimmitt, C., Carey, J. C., & Hatch, T. (2007). *Evidence-based school counseling: Making a difference with data-driven practices*. Thousand Oaks, CA: Corwin.

DiPerna, J. C., & Elliott, S. (2002). Promoting academic enablers to improve student achievement: An introduction to the mini-series. *School Psychology Review, 31*(3), 293–297.

Duarte, D., & Hatch, T. (2014). Successful implementation of a federally funded violence prevention elementary school counseling program: Results bring sustainability. *Professional School Counseling, 18*(1). Retrieved from https://bit.ly/2W0Jja0

Dweck, C. S., Walton, G. M., & Cohen, G. L. (2014). *Academic tenacity: Mindsets and skills that promote long-term learning*. Seattle, WA: Bill & Melinda Gates Foundation. Retrieved from https://ed.stanford.edu/sites/default/files/manual/dweck-walton-cohen-2014.pdf

East, B. (2006). *Myths about Response to Intervention (RTI) implementation*. NY: RTI Action Network. Retrieved from http://www.rtinetwork.org/learn/what/mythsaboutrti

Easton, J. Q., & Engelhard, G., Jr. (1982). A longitudinal record of elementary school absence and its relationship to reading achievement. *The Journal of Educational Research, 75*(5), 269–274. Retrieved from https://doi.org/10.1080/00220671.1982.10885393

Elliott, T. R., Godshall, F., Shrout, J. R., & Witty, T. E. (1990). Problem-solving appraisal, self-reported study habits, and performance of academically at-risk college students. *Journal of Counseling Psychology, 37*(2), 203–207.

Equality. (2019). In *Merriam-Webster* [Online]. Retrieved from http://www.merriam-webster.com/dictionary/equality

Erford, B. T. (2014). *Transforming the school counseling profession* (2nd ed.). London: Pearson.

Everett, S., Sugai, G., Fallon, L., Simonsen, B., & O'Keeffe, B. (2010). *Schoolwide Tier II interventions: Check-in check-out getting started workbook*. Center for Behavioral Education and Research, University of Connecticut. Retrieved from http://www.pent.ca.gov/mt/schoolwidetier2.pdf

Every Student Succeeds Act of 2015 (ESSA), Pub. L. No. 114-95 § 114 Stat. 1177 (2015–2016).

Farrington, C. A., Roderick, M., Allensworth, E., Nagaoka, J., Keyes, T. S., Johnson, D. W., & Beechum, N. O. (2012). *Teaching adolescents to become learners: The role of noncognitive factors in shaping school performance* [Literature review]. Chicago: University of

Chicago Consortium on Chicago School Research. Retrieved from https://consortium .uchicago.edu/publications/teaching-adolescents-become-learners-role-noncognitive-factors-shaping-school

Finn, J. D. (1993). *School engagement and students at risk* (NCES 93-470), U.S. Department of Education, National Center for Educational Statistics. Washington, D.C.: U.S. Government Printing Office.

Finn, J. D. (2006). *The adult lives of at-risk students: The roles of attainment and engagement in high school. Statistical analysis report.* U.S. Department of Education, National Center for Educational Statistics. Washington, D.C.: U.S. Government Printing Office.

Fisher, D., & Frey, N. (2011). Establishing purpose for yourself and your students. In *The purposeful classroom* (Chapter 1). Alexandria, VA: ASCD. Retrieved from http://www .ascd.org/publications/books/112007/chapters/Establishing-Purpose-for-Yourself-and-Your-Students.aspx

Fleming, W. C. (2006). Myths and stereotypes about Native Americans. *Phi Delta Kappan, 88*(3), 213–217. Retrieved from https://doi.org/10.1177/003172170608800319

Frerer, K., Sosenko, L. D., & Henke, R. R. (2013, March). *At greater risk: California foster youth and the path from high school to college.* San Francisco: Stuart Foundation.

Frey, K. S., Nolen, S. B., Edstrom, L., & Hirschstein, M. K. (2005). Effects of a school-based social-emotional competence program: Linking children's goals, attributes and behavior. *Journal of Applied Developmental Psychology, 26*(2), 171–200.

Fuchs, D., & Fuchs, L. S. (2006). Introduction to response to intervention: What, why, and how valid is it? *Reading Research Quarterly, 41*(1), 93–99.

Gay, G. (2010). *Culturally responsive teaching: Theory, research, and practice.* New York, NY: Teachers College Press.

Gersten, R., & Dimino, J. A. (2006). RTI (Response to Intervention): Rethinking special education for students with reading difficulties (yet again). *Reading Research Quarterly, 41*(1), 99–108.

Gladding, S. T. (1994). *Effective group counseling.* Greensboro, NC: ERIC Clearinghouse on Counseling and Student Services. Retrieved from https://files.eric.ed.gov/fulltext/ ED366856.pdf

González, T. (2012). Keeping kids in schools: Restorative justice, punitive discipline, and the school to prison pipeline. *Journal of Law and Education, 41,* 281.

Goodman-Scott, E., Betters-Bubon, J., & Donohue, P. (Eds.). (2019). *A school counselor's guide to Multi-Tiered Systems of Support.* New York: Routledge.

Goodman-Scott, E., Doyle, B., & Brott, P. (2014). An action research project to determine the utility of bully prevention in positive behavior support for elementary school bullying prevention. *Professional School Counseling, 17,* 120–129.

Gregory, A., Clawson, K., Davis, A., & Gerewitz, J. (2016). The promise of restorative practices to transform teacher-student relationships and achieve equity in school discipline. *Journal of Educational and Psychological Consultation, 26*(4), 325–353.

Hatch, T. (2013). *The use of data in school counseling: Hatching results for students, programs, and the profession.* Thousand Oaks, CA: Corwin.

Hatch, T. (2017, March 8). Multi-tiered, multi-domain system of supports. *Hatching Results* [Blog]. Retrieved from https://www.hatchingresults.com/blog/2017/3/multi-tiered-multi-domain-system-of-supports-by-trish-hatch-phd

Hatch, T. (2018, December 3). Multi-tiered, multi-domain system of supports (MTMDSS). *Hatching Results* [Video]. Retrieved from https://www.hatchingresults.com/videos/

Hatch, T., Duarte, D., & De Gregorio, L. K. (2018). *Hatching results for elementary school counseling: Implementing core curriculum and other Tier One activities.* Thousand Oaks, CA: Corwin.

Hatch, T., Triplett, W., Duarte, D., & Gomez, V. (2019). *Hatching results for secondary school counseling: Implementing core curriculum, individual student planning, and other Tier One activities.* Thousand Oaks, CA: Corwin.

Hawken, L. S., Vincent, C. G., & Schumann, J. (2008). Response to Intervention for social behavior: Challenges and opportunities. *Journal of Emotional and Behavioral Disorders, 16*(4), 213–225. Retrieved from https://doi.org/10.1177/1063426608316018

Illinois State Board of Education. (2010). *Understanding RTI/MTSS: Multi-tiered system.* Retrieved from https://illinoisrti.org/i-rti-network/for-educators/understanding-rti-mtss

Institute of Education Sciences (IES). (2011, October). *Coping power.* Retrieved from https://ies.ed.gov/ncee/wwc/Intervention/767

Jacobs, E. E., Shimmel, C. J., Masson, R. L. L., & Harvill, R. L. (2015). *Group counseling: Strategies and skills* (8th ed.). Boston: Cengage Learning.

Jones, C. H., Green, A. E., Mahan, K. D., & Slate, J. R. (1993). College students' learning styles, academic achievement, and study behaviors. *Louisiana Education Research Journal, 19,* 40–48.

Jones, C. H., Slate, J. R., & Marini, I. (1995). Locus of control, social interdependence, academic preparation, age, study time, and the study skills of college students. *Research in the Schools, 2*(1), 55–62.

Kennelly, L., & Monrad, M. (2007). *Approaches to dropout prevention: Heeding early warning signs with appropriate interventions.* Washington, DC: National High School Center, American Institutes for Research. Retrieved from https://files.eric.ed.gov/fulltext/ED499009.pdf

Klose, L. M. (2010). Special education: A special guide for parents. In *Helping children at home and school III.* Bethesda, MD: National Association of School Psychologists. Retrieved from https://www.nasponline.org/.../Special_Education_a_Basic_Guide_for_Parents.pdf

Lambros, K. M., Culver, S. K., Angulo, A., & Hosmer, P. (2007). Mental health intervention teams: A collaborative model to promote positive behavioral support for youth with emotional or behavioral disorders. *The California School Psychologist, 12*(1), 59–71. Retrieved from https://link.springer.com/article/10.1007/BF03340932

Lehr, C. A., Johnson, D. R., Bremer, C. D., Cosio, A., & Thompson, M. (2004). *Essential tools: Increasing rates of school completion: Moving from policy and research to practice.* Minneapolis: University of Minnesota, Institute on Community Integration, National Center on Secondary Education and Transition.

Lemov, D. (2010). *Teach like a champion: 49 techniques that put students on the path to college* (2nd ed.). San Francisco: Jossey-Bass.

Lewin, K. (1948). Resolving social conflicts. In G. W. Lewin (Ed.), *Selected papers on group dynamics.* New York: Harper & Brothers.

Likert, R. (1932). A technique for the measurement of attitudes. *Archives of Psychology, 22*(140), 1–55.

Low, S., Cook, C. R., Smolkowski, K., & Buntain-Ricklefs, J. (2015). Promoting social-emotional competence: An evaluation of the elementary version of Second Step. *Journal of School Psychology, 53*(6), 463–477.

Marks, H. M. (2000). Student engagement in instructional activity: Patterns in the elementary, middle, and high school years. *American Educational Research Journal, 37*(1), 153–184.

McTighe, J., & Wiggins, G. (2012). *Understanding by Design framework.* Alexandria, VA: ASCD. Retrieved from https://www.ascd.org/ASCD/pdf/siteASCD/publications/UbD_WhitePaper0312.pdf

Murphey, D. (2014). The academic achievement of English language learners: Data for the U.S. and each of the states [Research brief]. *Child Trends, 62.* Retrieved from https://www.childtrends.org/wp-content/uploads/2015/07/2014-62AcademicAchievementEnglish.pdf

Musu-Gillette, L., de Brey, C., McFarland, J., Hussar, W., Sonnenberg, W., & Wilkinson-Flicker, S. (2017). *Status and trends in the education of racial and ethnic groups.* Washington, DC: National Center for Education Statistics, U.S. Department of Education. Retrieved from: https://nces.ed.gov/pubs2017/2017051.pdf

National Association of School Psychologists. (2019). *Individuals with Disabilities Education Improvement Act (IDEA).* Retrieved from https://www.nasponline.org/research-and-policy/current-law-and-policy-priorities/current-law/individuals-with-disabilities-education-improvement-act-(idea)

National Education Goals Panel. (1997). *Special early childhood report: Get a good start in school.* Washington, DC: U.S. Government Printing Office.

Neitzel, J., & Bogin, J. (2008). *Steps for implementation: Functional behavior assessment*. Chapel Hill: National Professional Development Center on Autism Spectrum Disorders, University of North Carolina.

Nelsen, J., Lott, L., & Glenn, H. S. (2013). *Positive discipline in the classroom: Developing mutual respect, cooperation, and responsibility in your classroom* (4th ed.). New York: Three Rivers Press.

Ockerman, M. S., Mason, E. C. M., & Feiker-Hollenbeck, A. (2012). Integrating RTI with school counseling programs: Being a proactive professional school counselor. *Journal of School Counseling, 10*(15). Retrieved from http://rtinetwork.org/?gclid=CNati4-J2ZM-CFQEQGgodmTvPaA

Olsen, J. (2019). *Tier 2: Providing supports for students with elevated needs*. In E. Goodman-Scott, J. Betters-Bubon, & P. Donohue (Eds.), *The school counselor's guide to Multi-Tiered Systems of Support*. pp. 133-162. New York: Routledge.

Positive Behavioral Interventions & Supports (PBIS). (2019). *MTSS*. Retrieved from https://www.pbis.org/school/mtss

Riverside Unified School District. (2017). *Suicide prevention, intervention, and postvention handbook*. Retrieved from http://www.riversideunified.org/UserFiles/Servers/Server_580721/File/Departments/Specia l%20Education/Psychological%20Services/SUICIDE%20PREVENTION%20INTERVENTION%20HANDBOOK.pdf

Rock, E., & Leff, E. (2007). The professional school counselor and students with disabilities. In B. T. Erford (Ed.), *Transforming the school counseling profession* (2nd ed., pp. 314–341). London: Pearson.

Rouse, M. (2018). *Definition: Memorandum of understanding (MOU or MoU)*. Retrieved from https://whatis.techtarget.com/definition/memorandum-of-understanding-MOU-or-MoU

RTI Action Network. (n.d.). *What is RTI?* Retrieved from http://rtinetwork.org/learn/what/whatisrti

Ryan, T., Kaffenberger, C. J., & Carroll, A. G. (2011). Response to Intervention: An opportunity for school counselor leadership. *Professional School Counseling, 14*, 211–221.

Sabella, R. (2017). *Develop a closing-the-gap report* [ASCA Webinar series]. Retrieved from https://www.schoolcounselor.org/asca/media/PDFs/WebinarPowerPoints/WEB120717_Sabella.pdf

Sackett, D. L., Straus, S. E., Richardson, W. S., Rosenberg, W., & Haynes, R. B. (2000). *Evidence-based medicine: How to practice and teach EBM* (2nd ed.). London: Churchill Livingstone.

Safer, N., & Fleischman, S. (2005). Research matters: How student progress monitoring improves instruction. *Educational Leadership, 62*(5), 81–83.

Shapiro, E. S. (n.d.). *Tiered instruction and intervention in a response-to-intervention model*. New York: RTI Action Network. Retrieved from http://www.rtinetwork.org/essential/tieredinstruction/

Shepard, J. M., Shahidullah, J. D., & Carlson, J. S. (2013). *Counseling students in levels 2 and 3: A PBIS/RTI guide*. Thousand Oaks, CA: Corwin.

Sheridan, S. M., Knoche, L. L., Edwards, C. P., Bovaird, J. A., & Kupzyk, K. A. (2010). Parent engagement and school readiness: Effects of the getting ready intervention on pre-school children's social–emotional competencies. *Early Education and Development, 21*(1), 125–156. Retrieved from https://doi.org/10.1080/10409280902783517

Siegle, D. (2010). *Likert scales*. Storrs: Neag School of Education, University of Connecticut. Retrieved from https://researchbasics.education.uconn.edu/likert_scales/#

Sink, C. A. (2016). Incorporating a multi-tiered system of supports into school counselor preparation. *The Professional Counselor Journal, 6*(3), 203–219. Retrieved from http://tpcjournal.nbcc.org/wp-content/uploads/2016/09/Pages203-219-Sink.pdf

Sink, C. A., Edwards, C., & Eppler, C. (2011). *School based group counseling*. Boston: Cengage Learning.

Skalski, A. K., & Stanek, J. (2010). *Section 504: A guide for parents and educators*. National Association of School Psychologists. Retrieved from https://www.nasponline.org/Documents/.../35-1_S8-35_section_504.pdf

Snow, K. L. (2006). Measuring school readiness: Conceptual and practical considerations. *Early Education and Development, 17*(1), 7–41. Retrieved from https://doi.org/10.1207/s15566935eed1701_2

Snow, K. L. (2007). Integrative views of the domains of child function: Unifying school readiness. In R. C. Pianta, M. J. Cox, & K. L. Snow (Eds.), *School readiness and the transition to kindergarten in the era of accountability* (pp. 197–216). Baltimore, MD: Brookes.

Sporleder, J., & Forbes, H. T. (2016). *The trauma-informed school: A step-by-step implementation guide for administrators and school personnel.* Boulder, CO: Beyond Consequences Institute.

Springer, S. I., Moss, L. J., Cinotti, D., & Land, C. W. (2018). Examining pre-service school counselors' site supervisory experiences specific to group work. *The Journal for Specialists in Group Work, 43*(3), 250–273.

Stone, C. (2018). Suicide and child abuse reporting. *ASCA School Counselor, 55*(6), 7–8.

Stone, C. (2019). *Legal and ethical FAQs.* Alexandria, VA: American School Counselor Association. Retrieved from https://www.schoolcounselor.org/school-counselors-members/legal-ethical/legal-ethical-faq

Stone, C. B., & Dahir, C. A. (2015). *The transformed school counselor* (3rd ed.). Boston: Houghton Mifflin.

Stormont, M., Reinke, W. M., & Herman, K. C. (2010). Introduction to the special issue: Using prevention science to address mental health issues in schools. *Psychology in the Schools, 47*(1), 1–4.

Substance Abuse and Mental Health Services Administration (SAMHSA). (2005). *Substance abuse treatment: Group therapy* [Treatment Improvement Protocol Series, no. 41]. Retrieved from https://store.samhsa.gov/system/files/sma15-3991.pdf

Tincani, M. (2011). *Preventing challenging behavior in your classroom: Positive behavior support and effective classroom management.* Waco, TX: Prufrock Press.

Triplett, W. (2017). *Utilizing a multi-tiered system to implement your school counseling program* [PowerPoint slides]. Created for Chicago Public Schools.

U.S. Department of Education. (2002). *No Child Left Behind: Elementary and Secondary Education Act (ESSA).* Retrieved from https://www2.ed.gov/nclb/landing.jhtml

U.S. Department of Education. (2018). *A parent guide to state and local report cards.* Retrieved from https://www2.ed.gov/policy/elsec/leg/essa/parent-guide-state-local-report-cards.pdf

Van Horn, M. L. (2003). Assessing the unit of measurement for school climate through psychometric and outcome analyses of the school climate. *Educational and Psychological Measurement, 63*(6), 1002–1019.

Vavrus, M. (2008). Culturally responsive teaching. In T. L. Good (Ed.), *21st century education: A reference handbook* (Vol. 2, pp. 49–57). Thousand Oaks, CA: Sage.

Wiggins, G. P., & McTighe, J. (2005). *Understanding by design.* Alexandria, VA: ASCD.

Wiggins, G. P., & McTighe, J. (2011). *The understanding by design guide to creating high-quality units.* Alexandria, VA: ASCD.

Willis, J. (2007). The neuroscience of joyful education. *Educational Leadership, 64*(6), 1–6. Retrieved from http://www.ascd.org/publications/educational-leadership/summer07/vol64/num09/The-Neuroscience-of-Joyful-Education.aspx

Zarenda, N. (2019). *Child abuse prevention & reporting guidelines.* California Department of Education. Retrieved from https://www.cde.ca.gov/ls/ss/ap/childabusereportingguide.asp

Ziomek-Daigle, J., Goodman-Scott, E., Cavin, J., & Donohue, P. (2016). *Integrating a Multi-Tiered System of Supports with comprehensive school counseling programs.* Retrieved from http://tpcjournal.nbcc.org/integrating-a-multi-tiered-system-of-supports-with-comprehensive-school-counseling-programs/

Index

Figures and tables are indicated by f or t following the page number.

CORWIN
A SAGE Publishing Company

Helping educators make the greatest impact

CORWIN HAS ONE MISSION: to enhance education through intentional professional learning.

We build long-term relationships with our authors, educators, clients, and associations who partner with us to develop and continuously improve the best evidence-based practices that establish and support lifelong learning.